THE
URBAN NATION
1920-1980

THE
URBAN NATION
1920-1980

Revised edition
George E. Mowry and Blaine A. Brownell

The Making of America

GENERAL EDITOR: DAVID HERBERT DONALD

American Century Series
HILL and WANG : NEW YORK
A division of Farrar, Straus and Giroux

099833

TO MARDI
AND THE MEMORY OF
LA VERNE

The authors gratefully acknowledge the
assistance of Waltraud E. Bastia
and Jeanne Holloway

Library of Congress Cataloging in Publication Data
Mowry, George Edwin.   The Urban Nation, 1920-1980.
(The Making of America) (American Century Series)
Edition of 1965 published under title:
The Urban Nation,1920–1960.
Bibliography: p.   Includes index.
1. United States—History—20th century. 2. Urbanization—United States.
I. Brownell, Blaine A., joint author.   II. Title.
E741.M7 1981   973.9   80-27929
ISBN 0–8090–9541–6   ISBN 0–8090–0148–9 (pbk.)

Contents

Foreword

DURING the last sixty years, the United States has experienced more change, and more rapid change, than during any other comparable span of time in its history. Anyone who writes of these years is tempted to offer a chronicle of dramatic events, a catalogue of crises—the boom of the 1920's, the Great Depression, the New Deal, World War II, the cold war, the Vietnam conflict, the student rebellions of the 1960's, Watergate, the energy shortage. Such an account can be colorful and controversial, but it lacks consequence; it fails to reveal much more than could be learned by skimming the daily newspapers of the period.

Wisely, the authors of *The Urban Nation* have eschewed the "you are there" approach in favor of a thoughtful analysis of the long-term trends of the period. For this task they are admirably qualified by training and by temperament. George E. Mowry, of the University of North Carolina at Chapel Hill, who wrote the original edition of this book published in 1965, is one of the most distinguished senior historians in the United States. In books such as *Theodore Roosevelt and the Progressive Movement, The California Progressives,* and *The Era of Theodore Roosevelt* he has demonstrated his broad mastery of the political and social history of recent America. Dean Blaine A. Brownell, of the University of Alabama in Birmingham, is one of the ablest of the younger generation of American historians. Author of *The Urban Ethos in the South* and co-editor of *The City in Southern History,* he has brought to the revising and updating of this book his special understanding of Southern and urban developments.

The main theme of *The Urban Nation* is the transformation of American life during the past sixty years through the rapid growth of cities and the accompanying emergence of a mass-production, mass-consumption economy. Professors Mowry and Brownell show how these forces have produced a threefold revolution in the United States, shifting the center of social, economic, and political power from the country to the city, strengthening national authority at the expense of state and local governments, and converting the hesitant world power of the 1914–18 war into the dominant superpower of the 1980's.

To trace these broad social, economic, and political trends is no small achievement, but Professors Mowry and Brownell have done more: they have shown how these changes affected the minds of Americans, who during the past sixty years have abandoned the "old virtues and values" of "mystical religion, hard work, thrift, sobriety, optimism, progress," to accept the "mostly secular, hedonistic, spendthrift, sensual, and perhaps even pessimistic" attitudes that prevailed by the late 1970's. Equally perceptive in discussing the role of American intellectuals and in evaluating the impact of mass-communication media on the popular mind, they have made their book an important contribution to American intellectual history.

For all these reasons, *The Urban Nation* admirably fulfills the purposes of the Making of America series, a six-volume series designed not only to make the best of historical scholarship available to the general reader but to suggest new and basic reinterpretations of the American past.

DAVID HERBERT DONALD
HARVARD UNIVERSITY

THE
URBAN NATION
1920-1980

1

Rise of the Urban Mass Mind

THE census of 1920 showed, for the first time, that most Americans lived in cities and towns. Between 1915 and 1920 the old rural majority living on the producing land, or close to it in small towns and villages, had become a minority. The census also showed that the cities in which many Americans now lived were very large. A dozen had more than 600,000 inhabitants; three had more than one million; and New York City, with a population of over 5,620,000, was a world metropolis. The changes that resulted from this transformation of a rural to an urban nation were momentous.

The white rural classes, which dominated the nation's society and politics prior to the massive urbanization and immigration from abroad in the late nineteenth century, had been remarkably of one kind, and also of one mind on many of the broader questions of social import, no matter what section of the country they lived in. By origin, the greater majority of them were from Northern Europe; by occupation, they were farmers or small businessmen; by religion, they were mostly Protestants of either Calvinist or Evangelical persuasion. Although parochial and racially conscious, they were on the whole inclined toward an egalitarianism among their own kind. In social and economical matters they believed in self-help, hard work, thrift, and personal sobriety. They disliked bigness, diversity, the exotic, leisure, elegance, and personal indulgence. Restraint and moderation marked most aspects of their lives. And if individually they often violated various aspects of their credo, as a group they lived by it to a remarkable degree and were even more intense in their conviction that other people should also conform to it.

Life in the commercial city, even in colonial times, had offered

3

significant variations in this provincial pattern, and rural complaints against the city as the home of the irreligious, the amoral, and the unproductive were standard. This rural criticism grew steadily in the nineteenth century as the population centers were increasingly industrialized and became increasingly the home of the new immigrant groups from Southern and Eastern Europe. The sharp class stratification of the cities with conspicuous luxury on the one hand and slums, unemployment, and bread lines on the other, the growth of unions and industrial warfare, the increasingly Jewish and Roman Catholic character of the urban centers, and the rise in crime and political corruption all strengthened the hand of the rural critic. By the end of the nineteenth century the agrarian assumption that the countryside in some mysterious way bred character and patriotism while the city fostered opposing vices was entrenched in American social lore, politics, and literature, though it was increasingly challenged by new assumptions arising in the city.

Although the 1920 census merely recorded a historical fact, its publication sharpened the alertness of Americans to the increasing urban tilt of the country. Simultaneously, another complex revolutionary development was rapidly assaulting many of the cherished values of the rural-minded both in the city and on the farm. The rapid evolution during the twenties of the mass-production-consumption society tied together big business and the masses in a symbiotic relationship so close that the health of one was the health of the other. Essential to this new social order was an expanded transportation system, dominated increasingly in the twenties by the automobile, which linked the towns and the countryside to the metropolitan centers. By developing new techniques and institutions necessary to bind the consuming crowd to the corporate boardroom, this new type of economic society also sapped and destroyed in daily practice much of the content of the rural creed, though verbal and emotional commitment to the old values continued to be celebrated in many social rites. The stage was thus set for a clash between rural beliefs and the actualities of the new urban pursuits, a clash which many individuals could not even logically resolve for themselves. On a more general level, the conflict was between the urban and the rural mentality, between the countryside and the city; still more generally, between the Middle West and the South as proponents of the old views, and the East and eventually the Pacific Coast as patrons of the cosmopolitan outlook.

The rise of the new mass-production-consumption economy was a logical, but not inevitable, evolution of the historic industrial combination movement. The concentration of heavy and extractive industries into a relatively few large nationwide firms was already an old story by 1920. But prior to World War I the average man, except for purchasing a few products, rarely stood in a face-to-face relationship with the agents of big business. It was during the twenties that the combination movement vigorously breached the service and retail fields. By 1930 ten holding companies controlled over 70 percent of the nation's supply of electric power, branch banking had been so extended that 1 percent of the nation's banks controlled 46 percent of its banking resources, and chain stores were doing 37 percent of the country's retail drug business, while similar figures in notions and groceries were even higher.

Of all the industrial developments contributing to the growing interdependence of the large corporations and the masses, those in the new field of mass entertainment and in household appliances and automobiles were the most important. Without the film and radio industries, it is doubtful that the mass-production-consumption culture could have fastened itself on the country as rapidly as it did. By 1922, 40 million cinema tickets were being sold weekly, and radio was carrying news and advertising into 3 million homes. By the end of the twenties, the weekly movie audience had more than doubled, and few people in the country were long out of earshot of a radio receiver. In 1929, $852 million worth of receiving sets were sold, the profits from which, when added to the millions the broadcasting industry received in advertising revenues, bulked significantly in the total corporate income of the country. In the same year, multimillion-dollar returns from a single film were not exceptional. Profits of such an order generated within the two industries the same consolidating forces that were at work in traditional business fields. By 1930, most of the nation's films were made by five or six large companies producing in Hollywood and New York. In the following decade, over seven hundred of the nation's nine hundred radio stations had been organized into four privately owned networks, two of which were preeminent.

Although the national radio-broadcasting industry subsisted entirely on revenue from advertisers, more politely called sponsors, while movies had to be sold directly to the consumer, the two industries had this in common: they were both hawking a strictly nonuseful product, entertainment for leisure time, the popularity of which rested on the relatively free choice of the public uninfluenced by utilitarian or other social considerations. In each industry, internal forces led to an assiduous search for the largest possible audience. Since advertisers wanted to know exactly what they were buying on a national broadcast, the radio networks developed a telephone polling system, which indicated to the sponsor what share of the national audience was listening to the production through which his appeals for consumer patronage were liberally sprinkled. It is true that not all advertisers adjusted their programs to conform to the taste of the greatest number, but overwhelmingly the radio listings were governed as strictly as possible by a dollars-and-cents-per-listening-head standard.

The film industry became even more obsessed by the desire to cultivate the greatest number of customers. The ever rising salaries paid to writers, directors, and actors, and especially the enormous sums paid to the leading actors after the development of the "star system," forced the budgets of films constantly upward. In 1920, the cost of an exceptionally expensive Hollywood production amounted to perhaps a few hundred thousand dollars; by 1929, the comparable figure was in the millions. Such rocketing costs constrained the producing companies to reach for the widest possible audience and therefore to tailor the product as closely as possible to the taste of the masses.

Aside from purely cultural considerations, the radio-broadcasting and film industries played a significant part in forming the mass-consumer society, contributing immeasurably to the so-called revolution in the expectations of the common man. Because the majority of the movie audience had no desire to be reminded of their shabby homes and their dreary, monotonous work, most pictures dealt with carefree individuals engaged in exciting adventures and surrounded by frivolous luxuries. The typical heroine wore expensive clothes, furs, and elegant jewels, and either lived in a mansion or flitted between the deluxe hotels of the world; the hero, usually without visible means of support, was as splendidly accoutred, drove the fanciest automobile, and pursued the most attractive young women. Since the movies set the constantly changing standards in manners, hairdos, and fashions for village maiden and city working girl alike, there is reason to assume that they changed the nation's attitudes toward more important and permanent values as well. Hollywood, with "its great bargain sale of five and ten cent lusts and dreams," John Dos Passos commented, had become the goal-inspiring source of the masses. The movie credo was one of sustained consumption, not production. And continually reiterating this theme, the industry became midwife to the birth of the leisure-seeking, pleasure-demanding, materialistic consumer society of modern America.

Lacking visual impact, radio broadcasting probably had much less effect on mass aspirations and habits than the films. But significantly the cost of the entire industry was carried by advertising, the first such development in the evolution of modern business. The advertising industry was well established by 1920, but its expansion in the next decade was enormous. Although records are uncertain, it has been estimated that the sums spent on advertising during the twenties more than doubled and probably tripled, a result to which the broadcasting industry significantly contributed. Before the advent of radio, the advertising industry was silent; it now assaulted the ears of the nation day and night, and the air was charged with the strident plea to consume.

No matter how tempted the average American was to follow the Hollywood example or to heed the pitchmen of radio and indulge himself in an orgy of purchasing, formidable obstacles to action existed at the start of the decade. Among the relatively few citizens with substantial savings, old habits of thrift had to be broken down, and for many others the basic wherewithal had to be found. Real wages and salaries had been relatively constant from 1900 to 1915, and much of the wartime increase had been wiped away by the price inflation of 1919–20 and the depression of 1921. Either wages had to be raised or some other means found to increase mass-consuming power. One of the answers was consumer credit, a device not unknown before the war, but one which had been used individually, informally, and with rather rigid discrimination based on the purpose of the loan. With the advent of the twenties the industry was rapidly organized by so-called finance companies, and retail-credit associations sprang up in practically every sizable town and city.

A forcible impetus was given to the expansion of credit by the automobile industry. Soon home appliances, radio sets, furniture, and even such luxuries as jewelry were being sold on the installment plan. By 1929, when apparently over 75 percent of the automobiles and probably more than half of all major household appliances were sold on time payments, total consumer credit, it has been estimated, had reached a peak of about $7 billion. A large fraction of consumers had learned to live on the philosophy of "a dollar down and a dollar forever," as the lighthearted phrase of the day described installment buying. With the erosion of the old American tradition which considered personal debt sinful, it was perhaps reasonable to expect the public to view public debt with something of the same complacency. Possibly, private industry's consumer-credit operations during the twenties conditioned the American people to accept the New Deal's deficit financing a decade later.

The sum of the economic results flowing from the bewildering technological advances, the rapidly rising expectations of the masses, and the widespread application of consumer credit still does not explain the replacement of the old business system by a new one based on mass production and consumption. One vital factor was still missing: the will on the part of corporate managers greatly to expand facilities and production while encouraging higher consumption by stabilizing or lowering prices and raising wages. A safer course would have been the one generally pursued by European industrialists, who, in effect, established a policy of maintaining low wage rates and high product prices, while limiting facilities, credit, and production to the size of the existing market. Why American corporate managers took the other course is not explained entirely either by the complex economic forces of the moment or by the hope for profit in the future. Such long-time social forces as the tradition of competition, the American veneration of bigness and growth, the dislike of immobility, the willingness to take risks, and the potential size of the national market in the United States all played a part in their decision.

So did an important factor not too much discussed by historians heretofore: a remarkable change in the socioeconomic outlook of the industrial leadership. During the prewar period, the standard business answers to charges that the country's productive institutions were unmindful of the common good were often couched in the old brutal language of classical economics. If prewar reformers pointed out that unbridled competition meant the destruction of thousands of small employers and the growth of monopolies, if they decried huge fortunes for the few and poverty for the many, if they assailed the conditions under which food and drugs were prepared, if they criticized high prices and low wages and proposed that political solutions be found for such social blights as unemployment and industrial accidents, the standard business answer was that that was the way the industrial machine operated most efficiently and any attempt to interfere with it by restrictive legislation would intensify the social calamities the reformers were trying to obliterate. The inference was plain: the economic machinery was necessarily impervious to finer human feelings and lay outside the moral claims of the state. Occasionally during those prewar years the economic institutions were described not only as existing of necessity but also as deserving to exist, and even as having been blessed with divine sanction.

Compared to those prewar expressions, many business statements of the twenties contained almost revolutionary phrases. True, the old "root hog or die" spirit still cropped up. But it is surprising how much social and ethical content there was in the postwar business jargon. Instead of presenting themselves as strictly private, large corporations now often described themselves as "public institutions" in which, according to one of the managers of the United States Rubber Company, "the rights of all must be accorded proper recognition." Even such an individualist as Henry Ford was, as presented by his public-relations experts, at least, ready to qualify his sense of ownership. "A machine," he wrote, "belongs neither to the man who purchased it nor to the worker who operated it, but to the public. . . . It advantages the worker and the proprietor only as they use it to the advantage of the public." Although organized business was probably more devoted to the open shop than it had been before the war, nevertheless significant changes occurred in the vocabulary, and to a perhaps lesser degree in the actualities, of labor relations. In the rhetoric accompanying the campaign to organize company unions, the "harmony of interest" doctrine frequently appeared, and not all the activities of such captive organizations were debits to labor's interests. During the early years of the twenties, strikebreaking agencies such as the one owned by Pearl Berghoff prospered, and the use of labor spies and company police was common. But so was the employment of industrial-relations experts and the institution of profit-sharing plans and shop medical schemes. Such welfare measures were often described in the business press as an indication not of the benevolence of the managers but of their hard business sense, since "the loyalties of the working men" were an unseen but very real capital asset.

Significant verbal changes occurred in the prevailing attitudes toward wages and prices. After World War I, business publications were much more likely than before to editorialize on behalf of high wages as a means of insuring peaceful labor relations and sustaining high rates of production. If one is to judge by business rhetoric alone, relations between the seller and the consumer were also substantially modified. The old rule of the marketplace—let the buyer beware—was no longer a proper or desirable principle, according to the magazine *System:* "Boiled down, *caveat emptor* was merely an attempt to get something for nothing." A like-minded magazine argued that henceforth the buyer must have equal rights with the seller. The president of one large New York merchandising house went even further. He assured the public that his firm considered itself an agent of the consumers, bound not only by the legalities but also by the "ethics of the law of agency." The traditional concepts of price and profit were undergoing redefinition by some business theoreticians. Increasingly, the classic definition of price was being modified by the significant words "legitimate" and "fair." Since industry had no other excuse for being, the president of the General Electric Corporation wrote, profit should be "the acknowledged payment for service to society."

Accompanying these departures from the doctrines of laissez-faire capitalism and the unquestioned virtues of competition in the marketplace were some dramatic changes in the nature of the corporation itself. As A. A. Berle, Jr., and Gardiner Means pointed out in the thirties in their book *The Modern Corporation and Private Property* (1932), the gigantic size of modern business enterprise had forced changes both in its organic nature and in the character of its control. The one-man corporation dominated by a capitalist owner had practically disappeared, to be replaced by a managerial group. Because of profits generated internally and changes in the nation's banking structure, the old finance control of Wall Street, while still evident, was being weakened. Ownership through stockholding was so diluted because of the gigantic size of corporate business that any consistent owner control was almost impossible. Sheltered from Wall Street direction, insulated from the demands of stockholders, and almost totally free from significant governmental regulation, the ruling corporate oligarchy, even in the twenties showing signs of being self-perpetuating, had much more room for maneuver of corporation policy.

While many corporate managers during the twenties used their newfound freedom to enrich themselves by grossly despoiling the public, the total record of increasing production and a stable price level also indicates that the great bulk of American industry was dedicated to a program of mass production and consumption. Perhaps as important as any other reason for this continued devotion to the "gospel of production" was the startling fact that by the end of the twenties big industry and the big crowd had formed a face-to-face relationship from which they neither could nor cared to withdraw. In 1920, only one among the twenty largest corporations made products for direct consumer use. By 1929, there were nine, headed by the automobile industry, whose retail dealers were franchised directly by the parent producing corporations. Small wonder then that in the late years of the decade the public was inundated with repeated surveys of consumer tastes and desires. As Henry Ford never tired of pointing out, the consumer had become the real "dictator" of success or failure.

The career of Henry Ford is almost indistinguishable from the evolution of the automotive industry. Both the man and the industry constituted major forces in the great changes that the large-scale mass-consumer industries were making in American society. Ford was something of an anachronism in the twenties, and perhaps he really belonged to the nineteenth-century era of industrial tycoons. He was a briary sort of person, a dictator who demanded agreement from his employees, even from his supervising executives. He hated unions, which he fought with labor spies and company police, and he was intensely opposed to government regulation. As late as the 1940's, he threatened to close down his factories rather than accept national-defense orders from the government. At one time in his career he was an outspoken anti-Semite and he distinctly disliked intellectuals. Books "messed up" his mind, and he preferred Napoleon to Christ, because the former was a "hustler." Though he changed the face of America as possibly no other man in his period, he had a deep-seated nostalgia for the past. Outspoken in praise of what he fancied were the institutions and virtues of the past, he collected old furniture, implements, and vehicles for his "pioneer museum." He characterized reform as "trouble-making," and warned that the destruction of old institutions was "a tricky business." Yet as much as any man of his day Henry Ford helped to destroy the social values of nineteenth-century America.

After experimenting with many shapes and types of motorcars, for most of which the basic engineering had already been developed in Europe, Ford settled on his basic Model T in 1909 and continued to make it until 1927, with only minor modifications. Its function and design were in spirit a utilitarian creation of rural America. It was black, sober-looking, innocent of sophistication or adornment, and without much provision for the comfort of its passengers. Its purpose was transportation. It was cheap, and its not too numerous parts were susceptible of simplification and standardization. In 1913, Ford introduced into his factory the moving production line along which the parts of his automobile were assembled by stationary workmen whose function, more and more, was to perform a single repetitious task. Within a few years

Ford could boast that 90 percent of his workmen could learn their allotted tasks within a few hours.

Despite the revolutionary nature of the production line, Ford's most significant social contributions were perhaps in his wage, price, and selling policies. His avowed aim was to sell an automobile to every family in the country, an objective only possible, he insisted, if wages were high and the selling price low. He lowered the price of his automobile from $950 in 1909 to $290 in 1924, at the same time raising the wages of his workers well above and reducing the working time below the standards for the industry. Though he did not succeed in placing a car with every family, he sold an enormous number. By 1927, the automobile industry had manufactured a total of 20 million cars, of which the Model T accounted for one half.

Ford's mania for cutting costs—in the early days he spent hours walking through his factory eliminating an unnecessary operation here, consolidating another there—was spurred as much perhaps by his competitors as by his social doctrines. By 1927, the competitive process in the automotive industry had reduced the number of significant producers in the field from at least twenty before the war to three: Ford, General Motors, and Chrysler. As the competitive race tightened, prices were cut and the necessity to maintain profit by mass volume was even more imperious. Consequently, increasing attention had to be paid to sales techniques and to consumer preferences, an evolution which ended in the sales and design organizations becoming as important as those devoted to engineering, production, and costs. The nation was divided into sales regions, regions into districts, and districts were allocated to franchised retail distributors. A yearly quota of automobiles was assigned to each dealer, which he had to dispose of or risk losing his franchise. When the system developed, as much pressure was put on the local distributors and their individual salesmen as was put on the workmen on the production line. Abetting this sales organization was a nationwide campaign of advertising to persuade the consumer to buy. Even with such an elaborate organization, the industry found itself in periodic difficulties. It was attempting to sell what for many people was still a high-priced luxury, the initial cost of which could not possibly be met from the average man's current income. The obvious answer was installment buying, the terms of which became increasingly lax as hard-pressed dealers sought to fulfill their factory quotas. By 1929, when some dealers were offering an automobile on the initial payment of 10 percent of the value, 75 percent of the vehicles were sold on credit. Total sales for that year amounted to over $2 billion, on which consumers paid interest charges running up to 15 percent.

The urge to sell en masse, which a visiting minister remarked had become "the new religion of Detroit," led to other radical changes in the industry. By 1927, the ownership of a late luxury-model automobile had become for many Americans a status symbol to display before envious neighbors. In deference to consumer taste and preference, the Ford Company, much against its owner's will, had to abandon its cheap, Spartan type of vehicle. Replacing the Model T, Ford brought out the Model A, incorporating a few of the luxuries but more of the engineering advances of competing vehicles. This was but the first step in the ardent wooing of the consumer by means other than price. Before Ford's death in 1947, his company had added to its line six- and eight-cylinder cars, resplendent in a rainbow of colors and equipped with many of the gadgets of the year. The company also joined the rest of the industry in bringing out a new model every year, not so much to incorporate engineering advances as to hasten obsolescence. In 1932, the Ford Company cooperated with its competitors in buying old cars for purposes of demolition in order to add to the diminishing market for new ones. Well before the Depression, Ford had had to relinquish many of his original ideas, which came straight from old America. With the demise of the Model T, a part of the tradition of thrift, the pioneer sense of utility, and the nineteenth-century air of sobriety were buried.

The automotive industry brought about so many economic, political, and social changes that a thick volume would be required to discuss them comprehensively. Automobile registrations soared from fewer than 469,000 in 1910 to more than 8 million in 1920. By 1929, there was one motorcar for every four and a half persons in the country; the car had become commonplace. Motor-vehicle production created massive new demands for raw materials—from steel to wood, glass, and rubber—and hundreds of plants and factories sprang up across the country to supply these needs. Whole new businesses appeared, including auto campgrounds, motels, roadside restaurants, and eventually drive-in movies, banks, and even funeral parlors. This new vehicle was the perfect mode of transportation for the mass-entertainment media of the time, whisking young people and whole families off to the movies or jazz spots and watering holes in the cities.

Suburbs were not created by the automobile: movement toward the edges of cities was typical throughout most of American history, and the first massive impetus in this direction was provided by the electric streetcar in the years after 1890. But the motorcar was not restricted to rails, and as roads were carved along hillsides and plunged into remote valleys, whole new areas were opened up for urban settlement. New cities in the South and West were often literally shaped by the automobile, and larger, more established communities in the Northeast and Midwest were strangled by the vehicular congestion in their narrow streets. Along with the elevator and the telephone, the automobile permitted the development of cities that were dense in economic activity at the core and expanding toward a more and more distant periphery.

In his novel *Main Street,* Sinclair Lewis observed that his hero, Will Kennicott, had four loves: his wife, his automobile, his medical practice, and hunting. Adding that he would not have known how to rate these in order of preference, Lewis gave vivid testimony to the joyful and hungry mass appetite for the automobile. Fed by a national demand, the industry waxed until it became the key factor in the American economy. In the twenties, General Motors passed the once-awesome United States Steel Corporation in earning power, and the total industry, including subsidiary manufacturers of rubber, petroleum, glass, and highway-construction items, employed more men and utilized more raw and semifinished materials than any other industrial cluster in the nation. Of all the major alterations that the industry made, possibly none was more important than its part in ushering in and acting as a talisman for the mass-production-consumption economy by which an increasing portion of the major industries was directly tied to the desires, fads and fancies, and purchasing ability of the masses. The tale told by the gross industrial statistics for the twenties is an amazing one. Efficiency per factory man-hour rose by over 70 percent. Total industrial production went up perhaps 60 percent, an increase that far outstripped gains in population. Simultaneously, real industrial wages, monthly salaries, profits, and dividends rose appreciably. All this was accomplished with little or no increase in factory employment and with a reduction of the number of men working in the mines and forests.

Because of the lack of precise statistics, most attempts to break down these national figures into ones indicating the relative welfare of various social groups have probably reflected more ideology than accuracy. But this much is clear. The industrial worker enjoyed a perceptible gain in real income of perhaps 15 to 25 percent while his hours of labor decreased moderately and working conditions improved rapidly. The six-day, 60-hour week was normal in 1920; by 1929, the standard was a five-and-a-half-day, 48–54-hour week, and such benefits as shop medical plans, recreational facilities, and paid vacations were not exceptional. The industrial worker also shared in the rapidly proliferating state and civic services.

The real gains secured by the white-collar classes were even more impressive, although exact supporting figures are impossible to produce. The increases in monthly and yearly salaries apparently were far sharper than those for the weekly worker. And the rapid expansion of new executive positions in corporate, service, and governmental functions provided opportunities for the middle classes that have seldom been equaled in the history of the country. As for the fortunes of the owning classes, again the gross national figures are eloquent, if not exact. Total dividends, interest, and rent payments went up during the decade by almost 30 percent, and income-tax records indicate that the rate of increase rose sharply as one went up the scale toward annual incomes of more than a million dollars. Thus, while the poor were slowly increasing their meager competence and the middle classes were making substantial gains, the rich were growing richer at a more than moderate rate.

Though the national economic climate was under the influence of a steadily rising barometer, neither all industry nor the entire population was prosperous. As the source of power and the patterns of production and consumption changed with bewildering speed during the decade, whole industries were in deep trouble. The coal and textile industries, as well as agriculture, were in general distress during most of the period. Producers of such anachronisms as bicycles and wagons were forced to the wall. With the assault of the automobile, the national network of electric interurban lines collapsed just a few years after it had been built, leaving a trail of rusted rails and ruined investors. As revealed later by the Temporary National Economic Committee's investigations, the struggle of the independent grocer and pharmacist against the rising chain stores was often a tale of defeated hopes and lost capital. Rapid industrial and commercial changes also meant unemployment for both white-collar and factory workers, as did the introduction of labor-saving and skill-destroying automatic machinery. A Philadelphia survey of April 1929 showed that 10 percent of the city's wage earners were unemployed, and one authority estimated that national unemployment ran from 5 to 13 percent of the total labor force. At the close of the extremely prosperous year of 1927, economist Irving Fisher of Yale University, estimating that four-fifths of the American people were earning a little more than their living expenses, declared that the country was "not as yet prosperous in any absolute sense."

Agriculture suffered economic distress throughout the decade, despite the increasingly widespread introduction of mechanization. Prices for the basic cash crops fluctuated wildly, but never seemed to return sufficient income to the farmers, who were often overextended to banks and vulnerable to bankruptcy and foreclosure. Farmers were at the mercy of the market, unable to accumulate capital, regulate production, or readily secure credit. The problem was especially serious in the South, where bumper crops of cotton periodically glutted the market and sent prices down.

Yet, for all the weak spots and imbalances in the economy, the average American, measured by his past or the past of any other industrial nation, was a man to be envied. He was better fed and better clothed than any other average man in history. Free schooling was thrust on his children. Whether through his earning power or through the workings of the credit system, he usually possessed an automobile and a radio. For the first time in world history, mass man became the master of a complicated piece of power machinery by which he could annihilate distance. The radio gave another dimension to his rapidly increasing mobility, making it possible for him to flood his house with the world's news of the instant, with music and amusement. If more varied circuses were wanted, the movie house was usually just around the corner and easily within his means. Taken together, the automobile, the movie, and the radio obliterated the village and the farm as islands of isolation from the mass luxury economy, for the entire world of fancy goods had been moved as close to the onetime provincial as the nearest movie screen or loudspeaker.

As the new mass-production-consumption business system made vast changes in the economic structure, it also had extremely important effects on American culture. In the early days of the films and radio, their potential value in leading the masses of the people toward a new and much higher cultural level was widely heralded. When both became almost purely instruments of entertainment, purveyors of modern fairy tales, the lamentations of critics became loud and unceasing. But under the spur of rising costs and competition, the key to profits was the widest possible market among viewers and listeners. Box-office receipts and Hooper's radio ratings were sensitive indices to public taste as well as grim dictators of monetary success or failure. Given the structure of the two industries and their dependence on the mass market, quality and artistic perfection had to be confined to such matters as techniques. The filmmakers concentrated on what their box-office receipts indicated the national and world audience wanted. That, in brief, was sex, sin, and sensation, set in a whipped-cream world of luxury and leisure. As flashing electric bulbs in practically every American town and city advertised movies with the promise of "jazz babies," "red hot mamas," "passionate petting parties," "champagne baths," "fast young men," and "faster automobiles," sex had undoubtedly become, as Eugene O'Neill phrased it in *Strange Interlude*, the "philosopher's stone." But in the hands of the movie alchemists the legendary stone ordinarily turned potentially rare metals into the base or the trivial.

Older cultural institutions also felt the weight of the new mass market. Both the daily and the periodical press eagerly sought new readers, more for the purpose of capturing the burgeoning national advertising than to increase the area of their influence. In 1919 the first tabloid newspaper, the New York *Daily News,* was published, creating a new journalistic style that was soon copied in New York by Macfadden's *Evening Graphic* and Hearst's *Daily Mirror* and in Chicago by the *Daily Illustrated Times.* The *Daily News,* eventually to have the largest circulation of any American paper, was scarcely a newspaper in the conventional sense. As its style matured, it carried more pictures than reading material and more advertising than either, more gossip than news, more entertainment than information, and, as one critic declared, "more sex than sense." It and the other tabloids were long on crime and divorce stories, major disasters, sports, and comic strips, and on personal columns giving advice to its readers on how to meet sex and marriage problems; short on political, economic, and social news of a serious nature; and almost entirely innocent of critical comment on literature, art, music, and the drama.

The tabloids that sponsored the first well-advertised bathing-beauty contests also ushered in the practice of "keyhole" journalism replete with alleged intimate details of the great, the notorious, the criminal, and of the gaudy, night-blooming sporting and café crowd. So popular did these intimate reporters become that the most expert among them made their names and writings widely known through nationally syndicated columns. Masters of suggestion and innuendo, this new breed walked a dangerous path between the libidinous and the libelous. Much of their information was almost astrological as they attempted to titillate their readers with predictions of major sensations and scandals to come. Of such reporters, Walter Winchell became perhaps the most skilled. Born on the Lower East Side of New York, his education having ended with the sixth grade, Winchell was contemptuous of the learned and the cultured. He defined an economic expert as "a bore running for, or holding office" and a philosopher as "somebody who knows all the platitudes and copies things that are clever out of books." When asked once whether he had ever read a book, he replied that he had, but at the moment he could not think of the name of a single one. Possibly because of his cultural limitations, Winchell was an avatar of the new mass journalism, which sought to be neither conscience nor instructor for its readers. Instead, the tabloid was a merchandiser of advertising and a conveyor of mass entertainment.

At the start of the century, William Dean Howells remarked that much of the better American writing appeared in the popular magazines rather than in books. But by 1930 Edward J. O'Brien's yearly collection of the best short stories was dependent for most of its material on the so-called little magazines and not on the mass-circulation journals. Predictably, the little magazines had to be subsidized by individual or institutional patrons, while the popular publications waxed under the stimulation of mass subscriptions and skyrocketing advertising receipts. Authors profited also: one with four successful novels to his credit reported that he had been paid more by a weekly magazine for a hastily written four-part serial than he had made from all his previous work of twenty-five years. By 1922, ten magazines were each claiming a paid circulation of over 2,500,000, and another dozen claimed a circulation of over a million. More than half of this total belonged to the "pulps," magazines printed on cheap wood-pulp paper and devoted mostly to detective, Western, or movie stories. Among the top leaders in circulation were the newly conceived confession-story magazines, full of alleged first-person accounts of moral wrongdoings and inevitable repentance. But perhaps the most significant change had come about in the material which the better and more traditional magazines chose to print. According to a study comparing the nature of magazine material in the twenties with that of twenty years before, the mass-circulation magazines of the decade carried far fewer serious factual articles and many more devoted to sports, fads, and leisure-time pursuits. The great majority of the biographical articles of twenty years before had been devoted to politicians, businessmen, and professional people. By the late twenties and the thirties, precedence had shifted to studies of movie stars, sports heroes, and radio personalities. The significant trend, the author concluded, was away from the heroes of production and culture toward the idols of consumption and leisure.

Even the staid book trade felt the impact of the new mass market. Both the Literary Guild and the Book-of-the-Month Club were organized in the decade, with the announced intention of selecting the best books, giving them a national market, and thus retailing them at a cheaper price—exactly the ends of Henry Ford with his Model T. There were prestigious literary names on the boards of editors; nevertheless, as club memberships grew, the temptation to choose books that would please the greatest number of patrons was obvious. At the end of the decade, a national survey of the book trade indicated that many publishers had in fact adopted many of the new business techniques. Instead of publishing a few quality titles, some admitted to producing many more dubious ones, in the hopes of publishing a "best seller" that could be sold en masse and the profits from which would alone insure a successful business year. The best seller, a term given currency in the decade and redolent of its newer values, was often a work of serious literature. But just as often, one critic pointed out, it was a volume seemingly written "to justify a reasonable amount of adultery in the eyes of suburban matrons."

The contents of both fiction and nonfiction changed significantly during the twenties. One of the marked developments was the rise of a new school of popular biography which so stressed the intimate details of the lives of national heroes, their more questionable activities, and their shortcomings that it was given the name "debunking." After George Washington and Benjamin Franklin had been so debunked, James Truslow Adams complained that the tendency of the age was to see "no difference between the operations of the bowels and those of the brain." When the reading public seemed to tire of such sport with the nation's venerables, some biographers turned their attention to a study of the more sensational characters of the past, a process characterized by one sour critic as a change from "pulling down idols" to "setting up criminals for inspection."

Fiction, too, was busy pulling down idols as well as venerated ways and ideals of the past. At the start of the century, Theodore Dreiser's *Sister Carrie* was withdrawn from public circulation for a decade because its heroine became the mistress of two men. But beginning with the publication of Edgar Lee Masters's *Spoon River*

Anthology (1915) and Sherwood Anderson's *Winesburg, Ohio* (1919), both inquisitorial studies of small Midwestern communities, the attack upon the village and its respected morals and ethics was heavy and continuous. During the twenties, Ellen Glasgow, whose prewar novels had dealt with the moral decay of the old Southern aristocracy, published four novels, in which two of her heroines had illegitimate children, a third left her husband for another man, and the fourth scandalized her Virginia intimates with her "gutter" ways and talk. Sinclair Lewis, F. Scott Fitzgerald, Thomas Wolfe, Ernest Hemingway, and John Dos Passos were even more explicit, and by the end of the decade what had once been immorality had now become, in the words of one of Hemingway's characters, "only the things that made you disgusted afterwards." As for writers of less ability, one can measure the distance they had departed from the old conventions by the advertising blurbs describing their works. "As intimate as a boudoir, as amusing as a peephole and as suggestive as a bill of fare," one such read.

Whether the new moral and ethical climate of the twenties was brought about more by the ideas disseminated by towering thinkers like Freud, Bergson, and Einstein, and by those of the lesser essayists and the creative writers, scholars, and artists, or more by such mundane and objective factors as urbanization, the rapid change in technology, and the complex forces let loose by the creation of the mass-production-consumption society is a historical argument without apparent end. But in the twenties it seems that in the destruction of old ways and morals the objective factors of urbanization, technology, and the new business system had as much effect as, if not more than, the so-called seminal ideas. How else is one to explain the fact that the morals of the movies, the tabloids, and the confession magazines, all presumably dictated by the crowd, were almost identical with those conveyed by the more literate novelists and essayists? There was, of course, the difference that sin and evil rarely triumphed in the end on the screen or in the pulps, whereas Hemingway could write that the good and bad perished alike before implacable natural and social forces. But in a way the movie or confession-story heroine who departed from existing conventions only to be absolved ultimately by true love and marriage made the way to transgression easier for palpitating viewers and readers. For the popular heroine had the best of both worlds; she had tasted sin and had her moral cake and security, too.

Whatever the origins of the more important forces in the assault on traditional institutions, morality, and folkways, there is little question that the twenties marked a battleground between the defenders of the old ways and the innovators. During the decade, a cultural conflict raged in which almost every existing social institution was questioned and many were modified radically. In Sinclair Lewis' *Main Street,* published in 1920, the heroine and her classmates discuss what business positions they will seek after graduation from college. Twenty years before, few girls had even attended college, and among this favored few, business was scarcely in the range of their ambition. But by the twenties the feminine-employment revolution had reached flood tide. By 1928, the number of women working was five times that of ten years before, women students at Columbia University outnumbered men for the first time, and women had been elected governors of states and had been appointed to the federal bench.

Perhaps even more startling than woman's changing occupations were her changing manners and morals. The "flapper," or the new woman of the twenties, imitated men as closely as possible. She cut both her hair and her dresses exceedingly short, deemphasized the feminine form by throwing away her corsets and by dieting, and participated with gusto in what had hitherto been masculine amusements and sports. Whereas, before 1918, she had rarely been seen in a saloon, by 1925 she was a familiar sight in the illegal speakeasy and cocktail bar. She had also become such a consumer of cigarettes that a tobacco company dared to show a woman smoking in an advertisement. One of the favorite subjects of magazines and Sunday supplements was women's changing moral standards. There was much discussion of what "necking" and "petting"—terms used with much vagueness to describe the degree of sexual activity by unmarried couples—meant for the institution of marriage. Fanny Hurst, a popular novelist, created a public scandal in 1923 when she gave an interview describing her "experiment in marriage" since she and her husband had agreed in their marriage contract to live in separate establishments so as better to pursue their individual artistic careers. A storm of opposition met Judge Ben Lindsey's proposal for companionate, or trial, marriage. But few critics dealt with his argument that since the sexual part of marriage was generally practiced before the ceremony anyway, society might as well legalize and institutionalize it. Prompted by the almost doubled divorce rate in the decade, five volumes appeared in 1929 on the so-called marriage crisis. At the same time, a scholarly survey of urban marriages showed that 50 percent of the husbands and wives interviewed were "unhappy" with their institutional state, and 15 percent felt that adultery should not be denounced, since it was a normal occurrence in modern marriages. On the basis of such evidence, it is not too much to say that modern feminine morality and attitudes toward the institution of marriage date from the twenties.

The movement toward feminine equality had of course started before the Civil War. And before the First World War the bohemian life in New York's Greenwich Village foreshadowed the breakdown of the Victorian moral code, with its emphasis on feminine purity. The war itself had much to do with upsetting old standards, and the passage of the Nineteenth Amendment probably inspired the feminine sex to seek greater conquests. The influence of Sigmund Freud and the new psychology, the movement of technology (in particular the development of the automobile), and especially the large-scale movement of women into the business and industrial world all played their part in the emancipation of the sex. But it is doubtful if the movement could have been as rapid or as marked in any other society as it was in the hedonistic, mass-producing-consuming society of the twenties.

Indeed, the developing consumer society and the feminine revolution were closely related. As new careers were offered to women in business and the rising service trades, and as the supply of household servants radically decreased, a revolution occurred in the kitchen and the home. The modern power-appliance industry throve in the twenties, with sales of refrigerators, power washers, toasters, mixers, and sweepers describing an ever mounting curve. By the end of the decade, the American kitchen was well on its way to becoming one of the most highly mechanized institutions in the world, and the most highly styled. As women increasingly became the ultimate consumers, style became as important a factor in the choice of articles as function and mechanical efficiency. Since it was easier to change exterior design and color than the basic mechanism of the equipment, built-in obsolescence was the watchword for the manufacturer. Shortly after a General Motors executive confessed that his corporation was taking as much care with the design and appearance of its automobiles as with the engineering, the practice of introducing a new model every year became standard in the industry. Most household-appliance manufacturers followed suit.

Since women had had such a large role in passing the Eighteenth Amendment and the Volstead Act, one might logically presume that their political and social enfranchisement would have brought added support to the cause of Prohibition. Instead, it might be argued that the rising influence of the sex had an opposite effect, at least in some portions of the nation. It is true that during the first month of Prohibition, when violation of the Act was already widespread, the lawbreakers seem to have been, overwhelmingly, men. But with the early advent of the illegal speakeasy, the night-club, and the cocktail bar, women appeared more and more frequently as consumers of illegal beverages, if not as producers and merchandisers. By 1925, the New York City Investigating Committee of Fourteen reported that the number of women in illegal establishments devoted to the sale of alcohol was "astounding." In 1929, the Assistant Attorney General admitted before a congressional committee that liquor could be bought by either sex at almost any time, day or night, in almost any place in the nation.

The defeat of Prohibition by 1929 and its repeal four years later constituted a devastating and perhaps culminating blow to a whole series of intertwined American traditions. A cynic might argue that Prohibition had been largely the work of the ethically-minded middle-class evangelical Protestant American women, their animus largely inspired by their exclusion from the pre-1919 saloon, and that once they had been invited into the cocktail bars of the twenties their ardor for abstinence rapidly cooled. But it is doubtless more accurate to say that what the nineteenth-century woman wanted was equality as much as masculine reform, and by the time she achieved it the ethical and moral system that had originally inspirited the dry crusade had been seriously eroded by the new urban-industrial values of the twenties. The hallowed place names of the dry crusade—Churchville, Vermont; Oberlin College; Westerville, Ohio—are redolent of the old American small-town system of values. But by 1920 this venerable tradition was in retreat before the challenge of a new society. In 1919, it had achieved one of its greatest triumphs, in the dry law. Ten years later, the flouting of the law marked its defeat and the erosion of its moral and ethical content.

The defeat of Prohibition was also a setback for the Protestant churches, particularly the Methodist, Baptist, and Presbyterian, which had so zealously supported the dry crusade. Protestantism in general was in grave difficulties during the decade. Its most vigorous manifestation during the first twenty years of the century, the social gospel movement, had lost most of its élan and many of its followers before the materialist challenge of the twenties. As this attempt to reconcile Christian ethics and capitalist economics waned, many of its renowned clerical leaders turned their attention to the causes of Prohibition and world peace, only to see the first defeated and the second become dubious of attainment. By the mid-twenties, the Methodist missionary societies reported that nourishing funds were diminishing yearly, and the Sunday plaint from the pulpit that the faithful were either in their automobiles or on the golf courses became customary. In 1927, the *Christian Century* reported that the evangelical churches had lost over a half million members in the preceding twelve months.

On the East Coast, a former Lutheran minister from North Dakota, Dr. Frank Buchman, was beginning to attract attention among the upper social and economic classes. Buchman's religious house parties, where in comfortable surroundings the initiates held something like a group confession, appealed particularly to the undergraduates of the Ivy League universities and to their social confreres. Divorced from practically all dogma or ritual, Buchmanism—or the Oxford Movement, or Moral Rearmament as it was subsequently known—stressed the ease with which the individual could secure "God guidance." The chief requirements after a personal "washing out" of sins were faith and a daily time of spiritual silence during which the believer could talk with the Creator directly.

In Los Angeles, Aimee Semple McPherson, ex-missionary, ex-schoolteacher, and ex-carnival barker, established her Four Square Gospel Temple, to which in droves came thousands of transplanted Midwesterners and Easterners to witness her "religious productions," replete with scenery, music, and theatricals and, as one unfriendly critic described it, full of sensuality and faith healing. Sister Aimee, like Buchman, made few demands on her rapidly growing congregation. As dogma, creed, and catechism were overlooked, the way to heaven was not particularly difficult. A "show for the Lord" and "a helping hand" for one's neighbors and friends, including Sister Aimee, was all that was needed. Buchmanism and McPhersonism were miles apart from the most modern of traditional Christian sects. Their almost complete lack of dogma and theology, their promise of a close and easy companionship with God, and the elegance of one and the sumptuousness of the other removed them far from the spare and hard-oak pew tradition of historic Protestantism. To that extent they reflected the new materialist, mass-consuming, sophisticated, pleasure-loving urban culture.

The defenders of the old traditions and morals, the agrarian-minded social conservatives and the religious orthodox, did not let this complex series of radical innovations in American society go without an angry and persistent challenge. The spate of movies and books in which sex was free and easy met with such a volume of state and local censorship laws that the film industry decided to establish its own control of morals and manners in self-protection. But what the Hays Office, named after the former Postmaster General Will H. Hays, succeeded in doing with its "two feet on the floor" rules for bedroom scenes was to substitute the suggestive for the explicit. By requiring that virtue must triumph, it also divorced the average movie from any connection with life. Book censors also took vigorous action, and in cities like Boston, where the new Catholics and the old Puritans were allied in the effort, even acknowledged literary masterpieces were denied a place in libraries or bookstores.

Some state legislatures and local councils, mostly in the West and South, attempted also to stem the tide of the feminine passion for short dresses and scant bathing suits. But police with yard-sticks to measure the required minimum coverage were not un-known, at least in the early years of the decade, on the big-city beaches of the Eastern shore. Here and there, divorce laws were tightened up, mature hostesses were installed in public dance halls to see that the proximity of the partners did not infringe the local standards of propriety, and occasionally local legislation went so far as that in Norphelt, Arkansas, which prohibited "improper and lascivious sexual intercourse," even among married couples.

The leaders of the evangelical Protestant churches, convinced that much of the prevailing immorality was a direct result of the flouting of the Prohibition law, demanded and often obtained, especially in the rural Midwest and the South, stricter enforce-ment legislation. But Bishop James Cannon, Jr., of the Virginia Methodists, and other prominent Prohibition leaders were handi-capped in marshaling their churches against the demon rum be-cause they were opposed on the issue by a large body of Roman Catholic sentiment, and because their own churches were split on a variety of issues centering on the conflict between modern and traditional Christianity.

By mid-decade, the idea that the ministry confine its attention to theology and avoid involving the church in matters of econom-ics and politics largely prevailed. Perhaps this led some activist ministers to the more venturesome theology of the modernist movement. This movement sought to reconcile the new views of science and psychology with traditional religion, an activity which was usually engaged in at the expense of a literal interpretation of the Bible and some of the venerated creedal views of particular Protestant sects. Modernism was met, however, with the same vigorous opposition that social Christianity had encountered. For the first time in years, the Episcopal Church held a heresy trial, and the Presbyterians forced the resignation of one of their most popu-lar and influential preachers, Dr. Harry Emerson Fosdick, from his pulpit in New York City.

The most bitter and most publicized clash between the modern-ists and the fundamentalists, however, came in the rural South.

Throughout the Southern states, the evangelical churches led a movement during the early twenties to prohibit the teaching of evolution in the public schools as an affront to the true biblical doctrines. The fundamentalists failed in North Carolina, but in Tennessee the state legislature responded and passed an anti-evolution act. The denouement of the issue came with the famous "monkey trial" at Dayton, Tennessee, where an inconspicuous high-school teacher, John Scopes, won for himself a temporary place in the national headlines and an imperishable one in history by being convicted of teaching evolution in his biology class. The trial might not have attracted national attention had not the old "peerless leader," William Jennings Bryan, become the principal prosecuting lawyer and had not a confessed agnostic, Clarence Darrow, of Chicago, the most brilliant criminal lawyer of the day, taken up the defense. The entrance of Nebraska's Bryan, the hero of the prairies, stout Prohibitionist and fundamentalist Christian, into the small-town Southern trial was at once symbolic and prophetic. Stripped of politics, the contesting forces at Dayton were those of 1896, the countryside versus the big city, the West and the South against the East, Anglo-Saxondom against the polyglots, traditional Protestantism versus the nonbelievers and the wrong believers, Prohibitionists against the sybarites, the simple innocents against the sophisticates. Although Bryan won in a technical sense, since the court found Scopes guilty, he lost the national argument in the newspapers by a country mile, and his death a week after the trial portended the eclipse of the cluster of values he so well represented.

From almost every angle, the old small-town-countryside Protestant culture was being assaulted in the twenties. The census returns indicated that its numerical superiority was past. Its religious, ethical, and moral values were being flouted at the same time that its economic underpinning was collapsing, with disastrously falling farm prices. Small wonder then that the countryside and its like-minded allies in the city responded to another crusade against its alleged enemies, a crusade growing out of frustration and impending defeat, and consequently one that could easily be perverted from the defense of its own disappearing values to the lynching of others. Historically, such folk movements have often led to bigotry, intolerance, and mass cruelty. The culminating battle of this American cultural struggle was to be no different.

The post-World War I Ku Klux Klan has usually been interpreted by historians as a traditional nativist movement fueled by the old American intolerance toward blacks, Roman Catholics, and Jews. There is, of course, truth to this point of view that may be documented from a variety of sources. The popularity of such books as Madison Grant's *The Passing of the Great Race* (1916) and Lothrop Stoddard's *The Rising Tide of Color* (1920) clearly indicated the swelling nativist sentiment that resulted in the Immigration Acts of 1917, 1921, and 1924. "America must be kept American," Calvin Coolidge observed as he signed the 1924 Act, which eventually limited all immigration to approximately 150,000 people a year. "The time has come," the Secretary of the St. Petersburg, Florida, Chamber of Commerce pronounced openly, "to make this a hundred percent American and gentile city as free from foreigners as from slums." And one has only to glance at a few symptomatic titles in the *Christian Century*—"Is the Future with the Catholic Church?" "Protestantism Has a Fighting Chance," and "Will Protestantism Destroy Itself?"—to mark the rising sensitivity of the traditional church to challenge and criticism. These sentiments taken together with the Klan's liturgy of hate would seem to indicate that the organization which at one time claimed over 5 million members was just another if not more violent installment of traditional outbursts against minorities and newcomers to the land of freedom.

That the Klan fed on intolerant attacks on minorities is unquestioned. But, in a deeper sense perhaps, this may have been the surface eruption of a much deeper and more widespread twentieth-century social malaise, with blacks, Catholics, Jews, and immigrants being unfortunate and convenient, if not accurate, symbols of what was troubling many Americans. The Ku Klux Klan was by no means entirely a phenomenon of the rural South. Its strength lay in the small and medium-sized cities of the South, Midwest, and West, though the largest groups of Klansmen were found in Chicago and Indianapolis. A recent study shows that Klan activity tended to be greatest in cities which had experienced considerable growth and social change, and that a substantial portion of the Klan members in at least one city—Knoxville, Tennessee—had resided there for at least ten years, and included white-collar workers as well as factory laborers.

Klan popularity does not appear to stem primarily from direct threats by racial or religious minority groups. Indeed, black militancy was almost nonexistent in the urban and rural South during the twenties, and the number of Roman Catholics was also small —at least outside of New Orleans and southern Louisiana, where the Klan was not successful. In the largest sense, the Klan fed on the anxieties, fears, and prejudices attendant to change, and the social and economic dislocations and uncertainties that occurred, or seemed just around the corner, in the nation's towns and cities. Most Klan violence in the twenties was directed against prostitutes, philanderers, and other moral transgressors, and Klansmen emphasized their Protestant religious affiliations and civic spirit. Like the European Fascists, the Klan was adamantly opposed to many of the manifestations of the new urban culture—its polyglot racial mixtures, its intellectuality, its leftist politics, its new standards of ethics and morality, and what was considered its sensual living.

In a long article in which he attempted to describe the nature and the purposes of the Klan, Imperial Wizard Hiram Wesley Evans admitted that the organization's membership was made up of "hicks and rubes and drivers of second-hand Fords," "plain people, very weak in the matter of culture," but representing "the old pioneer stock," the blend of the "Nordic race" which had given the world "almost the whole of modern civilization." They had been first "uncomfortable" and then "deeply distressed" at the dissemination of strange ideas in religion, politics, and morality by liberals and leftists and representatives of minority groups, ideas threatening their homes, their concepts of chastity, the sacredness of their Sabbath, and the right to teach their children in their own schools the "fundamental facts and truths." Economically, these pioneers had "outworked" the aliens, but the latter had so far "underlived" them that their patrimony was menaced. Moreover, "the intellectually mongrelized liberals" had convinced the country that the producers—the Nordics—"should carry the unfit and let the unfit rule them." What the Klan demanded, Evans concluded, was the "return of power into the hands of everyday, not highly cultured, not overly intellectualized, but entirely unspoiled and not de-Americanized, average citizen of the old stock." Its object, according to Evans, was to recreate a "native, white, Protestant America."

Obviously, the Klan represented a deeply troubled group of Americans, challenged and often bewildered by events, trapped along the edges of racially changing neighborhoods or in dead-end factory jobs, offended by new tastes and customs, haunted by the possibility that the world was proceeding in unfamiliar directions, and deeply sensitive to the destruction of their traditional values by the new mass-producing, mass-consuming culture. Like many politicians of the age, like Henry Ford and numerous other industrialists, they readily accepted the technology and the financial and selling techniques upon which the new mass culture rested, but they assailed its social results and possibilities. Because of the vulnerability of these nonwhite or non-Protestant groups in Southern and Midwestern society, they turned to the convenient black, Catholic, or Jew. Whatever its irrational qualities, the protest of the tradition-minded American during the twenties left its imprint on practically every major social and political debate of the decade. And both the forces of change and the defenses of tradition were increasingly centered in the nation's cities.

2

The Politics of Nostalgia

IF during the twenties the traditionalists were rapidly retreating on moral, religious, and social grounds, they at least won the outward trappings of national political power. In politics, a fear of the future, a desire to escape present troubles, and the urge to return to the values of a fancied Golden Age of the past combined to sound one of the two dominant chords of the decade. The other was the persistent Republican policy of accelerating the forces creating the new mass-production-consumption economy. This official policy led unerringly to one result: the rapid overturning of the social values ardently advocated by three Republican Presidents.

The almost universal social malaise following World War I was well calculated to inspire a "retreat to the past." The world in 1920 was anything but the peaceful and secure one that Wilson had promised for his war to end war and his peace with justice and without victory. In Europe, Ireland was in rebellion against British rule, Poland was waging a full-scale war against the Soviets, and Rumania had just ceased her military occupation of Hungary. With the franc falling disastrously, French cabinets were made and unmade with alarming regularity. Both the Communists and Mussolini's newly organized Fascists threatened the Italian government, and in Munich a Nationalist *coup d'état* had just missed being successful. Elsewhere, as Communist votes mounted, rightist dictatorships rapidly replaced the democratic governments sponsored by the peace settlements.

In the United States, the economic transition from war to peace was anything but smooth. With little or no reconversion plan, the government abruptly terminated war orders, almost before the ink on the armistice had dried, and rescinded much of the regulation in effect during hostilities. These actions created, first, unemployment and then ballooning prices as the pent-up demand for consumers' goods established a wild sellers' market. As wages fell behind skyrocketing prices, a wave of strikes further unsettled normal economic processes. Seeking to counter the rapid inflation, the Federal Reserve Board in late 1919 and 1920 tightened credit, an action which brought on a deflationary cycle. Well before the Presidential election, the country was in the first stages of the so-called primary postwar depression. During the summer of 1920, farm prices as well as the inflated values on agricultural land skidded dangerously, and by late fall, unemployment in the cities was rapidly rising.

For eighteen months before the election of 1920, the industrial scene had been violently disturbed by a bitter, protracted struggle for power between organized labor and capital. Attempting to protect and extend the gains made during the war, labor sought to organize the mammoth steel industry, as well as scores of lesser industrial opponents. But labor's challenge was met by a grim management determined to stop further organization and intent on returning the country, if possible, to the open-shop philosophy of the nineteenth century. The labor-capital issue was further inflamed by the baleful threat of the Russian Revolution and the rise of world radicalism. Despite the many attacks inspired by the West against the new Soviet state, its chance for survival appeared to be more than even in the summer of 1920.

With the publication of British Labour's 1919 program calling for nationalization of the nation's major industries, even that traditional home of conservatism appeared to be in danger of falling before the radical thrust. To frightened American conservatives, it seemed as if the United States was next on the radical timetable. In 1919, the Plumb Plan for modified government ownership of railroads was advanced by the Railroad Brotherhoods and supported by President Wilson's son-in-law, Secretary of the Treasury William G. McAdoo. Almost simultaneously, the striking miners voted overwhelmingly for the nationalization of the mines. In 1919, an American Communist Party was formally organized. Although not a party member at that date, William Z. Foster, a future Communist leader, was then heading the striking steelworkers in their battle against the industry's low rates and its standard twelve-hour day. Meanwhile, a wave of bombings aimed at a score of political and financial leaders swept the country.

The most frightening episode of the year's ominous harvest was the Boston police strike of September. If the police walked out, the question was repeatedly asked, what was to become of private property and social order? It was against such a background that Attorney General A. Mitchell Palmer organized his "ship or shoot" campaign against all alien radicals. Over twenty state legislatures passed criminal syndicalist laws providing for heavy fines and prison sentences for advocating or inciting assaults against public officials, destruction of real or personal property, and the overthrow of government. A committee of the New York legislature solemnly proposed that "every strike is a small revolution and a dress rehearsal for a big one." In such an atmosphere, it is small wonder that the leaders of the industrial and financial community were able to convince themselves and much of the public that the labor movement was crowded with agitators advocating the overthrow of the Constitution and asserting that the open shop was a basic ingredient of "the American way."

A good many other developments excited the imagination of the conservative and the timid during the election year of 1920. After five years of little immigration from abroad, over 400,000 immigrants entered the United States, and wild predictions appeared in the press that unless radical restrictions were made, from 2 to 5 million refugees from war-torn Europe would descend on the country in the following twelve months. The same stories invariably recalled that many of the radicals violently disturbing the domestic scene had European backgrounds.

Closer to home, a series of ugly race riots broke out in a number of Northern and Western cities. Migration from the rural South—stimulated by wartime economic opportunities—swelled the populations of black neighborhoods in the urban core and spilled into surrounding white residential areas. Blacks also competed for jobs and demanded a measure of political influence. The white response was often violent. A riot in East St. Louis, Illinois, in 1917 took the lives of at least thirty-nine blacks, and racial disturbances also occurred in Houston and other cities in the same year. Racially inspired bombings in Chicago, especially along the frontier of black settlement, were overshadowed by a major racial conflagration in July 1919. The drowning of a black youth at a public beach, after he was stoned by whites, unleashed a rash of attacks and beatings by both races. The state militia finally restored order, but not until twenty-three blacks and fifteen whites had died, and more than five hundred persons had been injured.

Black movement to the cities was accompanied by heightened racial consciousness. The challenges and opportunities blacks found in the cities led to widespread support for organizations like Marcus Garvey's Universal Negro Improvement Association, which enlisted thousands of working-class blacks under a banner of racial pride and militant self-help. The Harlem section of New York City, which contained the largest black urban population in the world, drawn from the Caribbean as well as from the Southern states, spawned a cultural movement stressing black traditions, art, and literature. The "Harlem Renaissance," and writers like Claude McKay, Jean Toomer, and Langston Hughes, created interest in African culture and emphasized the importance of Afro-American cultural identity and racial pride.

The revolt against prewar moral standards that marked the twenties was presaged at the beginning of the decade by Sherwood Anderson's *Winesburg, Ohio* and F. Scott Fitzgerald's *This Side of Paradise,* two works which ushered in the new jazz age. By midsummer of 1920, when the Volstead Act enforcing the Prohibition amendment was but six months old, it was already being flouted openly. Meanwhile, the automobile and the Hollywood movie, both enthusiastically received by the public, were rapidly contributing to the erosion of previously accepted manners and morals, especially among the young. The lure of mass entertainment and the emphasis on personal independence shaped much of the spirit and activity of the times.

Politics reflected, at least on the surface, a yearning for stability and older values. Leaving a Republican National Committee meeting in 1919, Boies Penrose, the cynical and outsized Republican senator from Pennsylvania, predicted that the leading issue in the 1920 elections would be "Americanism." When asked what that meant, Penrose was alleged to have replied, "How in the hell do

I know? But it will get a lot of votes." Uncommonly frank at times, Penrose was probably honest in voicing his perplexity over an exact definition of Americanism. But the senator was unerringly accurate in predicting the public's emotional response to the term and its value in vote-getting. Both national parties, in fact, sensed the nostalgic mood of the country, and in their platforms and their choice of candidates they honored Penrose's judgment. Neither party dealt in any realistic way with present or future problems; they contented themselves with arguments about past issues.

Like the party programs, the candidates also had an aura of prewar and even nineteenth-century America. Passing over the strong, prominent, or able men of the party—Newton D. Baker, William G. McAdoo, A. Mitchell Palmer, and the more than willing Woodrow Wilson—the Democrats selected the unexceptional James M. Cox, a Dayton newspaper publisher and governor of Ohio, pale of character and of political convictions. Only the energy and personal charm of the young and rather impetuous Franklin D. Roosevelt, the Vice-Presidential candidate, promised to lift the Democratic campaign above the mediocre. The Republicans likewise avoided choosing one of their party luminaries. Governor Frank O. Lowden of Illinois was passed over, as were General Leonard Wood, Hiram Johnson, and Herbert Hoover. By agreement among the managers of the party, particularly those from the senatorial wing, who were tired of being upstaged by an able and dominant President, the nomination went to Warren Gamaliel Harding, whose lack of qualification for the office was only surpassed by his ineptitude while serving in it.

Handsome, of imposing stature, modest, affable, kindly, and quite uncritical of his companions, Harding had made his way in the world almost totally by charm and by luck. Failing to graduate from a preparatory school, he managed to become owner and editor of a small country-town weekly newspaper. The Marion, Ohio, *Star* was, under his direction, uninspired, mediocre, and usually broke. His marriage to the daughter of the town's banker, over the opposition of her family, eventually offered financial support and social entree to the community's ruling circle. Harding soon found his proper milieu in Republican machine politics, where he allied himself with Senator Joseph Benson "Fire Alarm"

Foraker, "Boss" George Cox of Cincinnati, and finally with Harry M. Daugherty, shrewd and unscrupulous business lobbyist and political manipulator. Harding was elected state senator, lieutenant governor, and, after losing a race for governor, in 1914 United States senator. He contributed nothing to the Senate other than a reliable party vote on political matters and a bleakly conservative one on economic issues. He voted against war taxes on business because he thought they would weaken the country. But in party organizational affairs his star rose consistently, possibly because of his convivial habits and more certainly due to his ability to make resounding if meaningless speeches.

The Republican campaign was pitched to mark the sharp distinction between the character and policies of Woodrow Wilson and those of Harding. And its tone, including those notes imparted to it by the Vice-Presidential candidate, Calvin Coolidge, evoked the alleged American past with its folksiness, its stability and security, and its prosperity. Harding remained at home to conduct a front-porch campaign after the fashion of William McKinley. Mrs. Harding described her family as made up of "just folks," and the nominee declared that he was "just a plain fellow," "old-fashioned and even reactionary in matters of faith and morals." One of the advantages of keeping the candidate in Marion, Ohio, Senator Penrose observed, was that he would not be tempted to answer questions on difficult issues. The candidate obliged, confining himself to advocating the Golden Rule as the solution to the labor problem, arguing for the return of natural resources to the citizens, and uttering the hope that every American laborer would eventually become "a small business man." Otherwise, Harding was content to offer bromides such as "Stabilize America first, prosper America first, think America first and exalt America first."

But the voters in 1920 probably responded more to a mood than to specific issues and political stratagems. For all the jests at Harding's prenomination slogan of "back to normalcy," this and the rest of the Republican candidate's liberties with the language—"not heroism but healing, not nostrums but normalcy, not revolution but restoration, not agitation but adjustment, not surgery but serenity . . . not experiment but equipoise, not submergence in internationality but sustainment in triumphant nationality"—expressed precisely what many citizens wanted, or thought they wanted. The country was tired of chasing elusive, newly formulated high ideals on either side of the Atlantic, tired of the wrangling in the Senate over the League and of the leaderless and bad administration given to it in 1919–20, tired of the sharp price inflation and deflation, and of strikes, riots, and radicals. It was not a little apprehensive of what was happening to its moral standards and social institutions. The handsome and affable man sitting on his front porch in Marion, Ohio, talking in the back-yard language of yesterday seemed to offer an end to all its present troubles.

During the campaign, Harding had promised the country to appoint the "best minds of his party" to his official family, as well as to "play square" with the voters. Unquestionably, he tried to do both. Charles Evans Hughes, Herbert Hoover, and Andrew Mellon were selected for the Cabinet, and William Howard Taft was appointed Chief Justice of the Supreme Court. The President was in desperate need of expert advice, his own limitations being clearly marked in the tariff debate. "We should," he told a reporter without a trace of guile, "adopt a protective tariff of such character as will help the struggling industries of Europe to get on their feet." Hughes served the Administration well in foreign affairs; Hoover supplied most of the ideas for combatting the short depression of 1921. And if Andrew Mellon, of the multimillionaire Pittsburgh aluminum and banking family, ran the Treasury with nineteenth-century ideas, he did run it efficiently. Most of the administrative and legislative successes came from these men, although the President himself, with his benign and indulgent disposition, helped ease some of the rancor built up during the war and the struggle over the peace. He not only commuted Socialist Party leader Eugene V. Debs's federal sentence for antiwar activities but also met him at the White House with a cordial handshake.

Harding's real troubles came from two sources: his inability to stand firm against Congress, and his loyalty to the friends and cronies he had appointed to important positions. Although supported by some of the strongest and best-informed elements of his party, his recommendation for World Court membership was ignored, and he accepted the harmful Fordney-McCumber Tariff because he would not or could not stand up to small groups of intransigent nationalists and blocs of narrowly self-interested high-tariff partisans in Congress.

Hughes, Hoover, and Mellon, all of whom commanded respect in both the party and the country, were the leaders of his Administration. But it was apparent that Harding's golfing, drinking, and poker-playing companions, his real friends, made up as dubious a group of characters as had been seen in Washington since the Grant Administration. Albert B. Fall, Secretary of the Interior; Harry M. Daugherty, the Attorney General; Edwin Denby, Secretary of the Navy—as well as many lesser appointees—had been selected from the circle of the President's Ohio cronies and national political friends. Most of them were without a shred of qualification for office, and some were simply political innocents. But a great many were old-fashioned spoilsmen, political shysters, and just plain crooks. By the summer of 1923, while the President was on a trip to Alaska, rumors of corruption in the Administration were freely bruited about Washington. Apparently, Harding was told the facts during his trip, for he repeatedly asked his companions what a President did when he found that his friends had betrayed him. He died in San Francisco, at the close of the trip, fortunately spared the sordid revelation that through the machinations of the Secretary of the Interior the nation had been despoiled of some of its naval oil reserves, that the Veterans' Bureau and the Office of the Alien Property Custodian had been looted, and that some of the money had subsequently appeared in bank accounts controlled by the Attorney General and by the Republican National Chairman. Other revelations followed, Fall went to jail, and the Attorney General of the United States, on trial for fraud, escaped conviction by pleading the Fifth Amendment. Others in the group committed suicide or received long prison sentences.

For a time after Harding died, there was apprehension among the country's conservatives that the policies of the government might be given a new direction by Calvin Coolidge, who as Vice-President had been even more of a cipher than the usual incumbent in that somnolent office. But those who knew Coolidge hastened to assure their fellows that Harding's death was, if anything, a blessing; it would help remove the taint of corruption from the new Administration, which could be counted on to intensify the steady conservative drift of the government. "God is still in His Heaven," the president of the National Association of Manufacturers wrote, and he was precisely right. For if Harding was an amiable standpatter, Coolidge was both in personal life and in political philosophy an American primitive.

On August 2, 1923, Coolidge took the oath of office from his justice-of-the-peace father in a typical Vermont village dwelling and then proceeded to take much of this provincial and rustic atmosphere with him to the White House. There the whiskey-and-poker-game camaraderie disappeared overnight. So did much of Harding's kindness and feeling for human beings. As for past Administration policies, they were intensified to the point that politically the age of the twenties was the age of Calvin Coolidge. By the things he did, as well as by the many things he did not do, he left his stamp ineradicably on the decade.

A rather small man of 150 pounds, with sandy hair, a high forehead, and a prominent nose turned down at the end, Coolidge was not an impressive figure. He spoke with a harsh nasal twang and usually what he said was as uninspiring as the way he said it. Walter Lippmann commented that the President had a genius for "deflating interest" in almost any subject. Coolidge had scarcely been out of the United States and indeed seldom out of New England, where he had been raised and schooled and where he had pursued a political career. When he came to Washington, he brought with him a set of attitudes and ideas which he had picked up from his early life on a Vermont farm, from the small-town law office in Northampton, Massachusetts, and from Boston politics. His favorite poet, he confessed, was Whittier; his preferred music, martial and patriotic. His was a small-town mind, and if we are to believe his secretary, C. Bascom Slemp, he never changed his position on a fundamental public issue throughout his career.

Calvin Coolidge was a man of one piece, his political philosophy harmonizing closely with his basic personal characteristics. The important things in the universe, he felt, never changed much. This was especially true of human nature, which, on the whole, he viewed rather pessimistically. The historic American institutions, he believed, could be subjected to little if any just criticism, and any attempt to change them would probably result in far more harm than good. "Four-fifths of all of our troubles in this life would disappear," he once commented, "if we would only sit down and keep still." Coolidge was no friend of direct primaries or any of the other political reforms which had been a part of the progressive creed in the country since 1900. Direct democracy, he feared, might lead to popular excesses and unsound financial legislation resulting in "disorder and the dissolution of society." Neither was the President charitably disposed toward the regulatory state. Some regulation might be necessary, he admitted, but bureaucracy was an abomination—the element in American institutions that "set up the pretense of having authority over everybody and being responsible to nobody." The progressive attempt since 1900 to regulate business in fact had been devoted mainly to "destructive criticism." Throughout his Presidency, he wrote after he left office, he had attempted to substitute "positive policies" for the negative progressive philosophy.

The essence of Coolidge's positivism can be found in the man's almost mystical devotion, as William Allen White phrased it, to a business system untrammeled by government regulation or legal obstruction, and to the free accumulation of wealth. "Business should be unhampered and free," he reiterated many times, because the prosperity and the ethical and intellectual welfare of the whole nation depended on its profitable operations. The accumulation of wealth was of prime importance because it not only created large payrolls but also was the chief support "of all science, art, learning and charities. . . ." But there were even more hidden values interconnected with the business system, he told the New York Chamber of Commerce. "It rests squarely on the law of service. It has for its main reliance truth, faith, and justice. In its larger sense it is one of the greatest contributing forces to the moral and spiritual advancement of the race." The law of property, the President once observed, was "founded upon the constitution of the universe."

For such a mystical materialist, it followed that the proper end of government was to encourage and nurture the business world and to oppose its enemies. Harassing regulation should be mitigated or abolished, labor should be disciplined, critics confounded or silenced. Since income taxes bore most heavily on the wealthy, stringent government economy should be observed and taxes reduced. "Economy," the President said in his inaugural address, "is idealism in its most practical form." Government aid to any distressed nonbusiness classes was unthinkable. During the 1914 depression he remarked that the state was not warranted in furnishing employment to anyone, for anyone incapable of supporting himself was "not fit for self-government." During the twenties, he told the hard-pressed farmers to find their own way out of their difficulties. He remained unmoved in his position even in the face of national disasters. When the victims of a Mississippi River flood appealed for help, he replied, "The Government is not an insurer of its citizens against the hazards of the elements." Coolidge, in fact, was even doubtful about the social utility of many private charities.

The President's most trusted adviser was Secretary of the Treasury Andrew Mellon, and Mellon's policies of reducing government expenditures, lowering taxes, and paying off the debt received his enthusiastic support. By 1928, the highest surtax on incomes had been reduced from its 1920 level of 65 percent to 20 percent, and comparable reductions had been made in the inheritance-tax levels. The federal levy on gifts was abolished. Meanwhile, the wave of prosperity increased income, and as expenditures were curtailed, the total federal debt was sharply reduced, even though that of the states was mounting yearly. Under Mellon's direction, the Treasury was so lenient in administering tax rules and so ready to grant refunds to big taxpayers that the existing rate structure was in effect reduced further. Mellon and the President together consistently pursued one other policy that delighted the business expansionists. At least twice, when the Federal Reserve Board was inclined to contract credit by raising the rediscount rate, the President and his Secretary of the Treasury threw their weight against the move. Thus, the credit supply remained cheap and plentiful, fueling the expansionist and speculative boom. Even when it became obvious early in 1929 that much of the easy money was being used to speculate in stocks, the

President remarked that Wall Street prices were "not too high." Needless to say, as long as the boom lasted, Mellon was hailed by businessmen as "the greatest Secretary of the Treasury since Alexander Hamilton."

The policy of government by inactivity was further reflected by the President's unwillingness to recommend to Congress any major legislation of a positive stamp. This and his zeal for vetoing congressional enactments resulted in the smallest crop of important legislation in any Administration since the nineteenth century. A soldiers' bonus bill was passed over the President's veto by an insistent Congress facing the elections of 1924. Coolidge was sustained, however, in his two vetoes of the McNary-Haugen Bill, which would have granted aid to the hard-pressed farmers. The Immigration Act of 1924, a federal radio act, and two measures providing very modest financial support for Mississippi flood control and for the merchant marine constituted the major legislative harvest for six years. Without grass growing in the streets of Washington, federal negativism could scarcely have gone further.

Perhaps the most pervasive influence of the studied policy of inactivity was felt in the fields dominated by the federal regulatory commissions and by the federal courts. With almost unerring accuracy, Harding and Coolidge appointed men to the commissions who were opposed to strenuous federal regulation. The 1926 Coolidge appointee to the Federal Trade Commission, for example, announced that the old commission had been "a publicity bureau to spread Socialist propaganda" and that he intended to remedy that condition. Throughout the decade, consequently, the Interstate Commerce Commission, the Federal Trade Commission, and the Bureau of Corporations, as well as many other less important federal agencies, ceased to perform some of the functions for which they had been created.

Presidential appointments to the federal courts similarly changed the prevailing judicial attitudes toward the place of government in national life. In a little more than two years, Harding appointed four new men to the Supreme Court, all of them, including Chief Justice William Howard Taft, conservatives or reactionaries. During one of the first conferences of the new court, Taft announced that he had "been appointed to reverse a few decisions." The Taft court then proceeded measurably to narrow the permissible areas in the social and economic fields in which either state or national government could intervene. Within five years, the court had outlawed a national child-labor law, declared a District of Columbia minimum-wage law for women unconstitutional, and all but removed the power of the federal government to regulate effectively interstate power monopolies. During the twenties, the court invalidated twelve congressional acts as unconstitutional. Looking at the record of the Taft court, Senator Norris of Nebraska declared that the federal government had in name two legislative bodies, the Senate and the House, numbering over four hundred members. But in fact another had been recently constituted, the Supreme Court of nine men, who were "more powerful than all the others put together."

The court limited civil rights and restricted radicals and labor-union activity by vesting more power in legislative and administrative hands. By following the "clear and present danger" reasoning of Justice Oliver Wendell Holmes in the historic Gitlow case (*Gitlow v. New York,* 268 U.S. 1925), the court moved in a direction Holmes did not intend, and opened the way for Congress and state legislatures to pass security measures against radicals of all breeds which substantially narrowed the personal freedoms granted in the first ten amendments, provided it could be shown that the security of the state was in danger. The court subsequently upheld many of the numerous state "criminal syndicalist" enactments, which substantially abridged the Bill of Rights.

The willingness of the federal courts to grant sweeping labor injunctions also increased the administrative power of the federal and state governments. In obtaining a series of injunctions against strikes, unparalleled in both number and amplitude during the twentieth century, Attorney General Daugherty assumed massive power to intervene in labor relations and thus in the operations of the marketplace. On both civil-rights and labor cases, the Supreme Court usually followed the reasoning that although "governments exist for the protection of life, liberty, and property, the chief of these is property."

On foreign policy, Republicans during the Harding and Coolidge years were divided. There was nothing near the acceptance of the complete isolationism that some writers have depicted. Too much unfinished business from the war remained and the world was too intimately connected for a hermitlike program. One important wing of the Republican Party had, historically, never been isolationist. Instead, it had supported the acquisition of an empire and had tolerated Theodore Roosevelt's foreign ventures. Even during the League of Nations debate, the issue for many Republicans had not been isolation rather than internationalism, but international unilateralism rather than collective action. Only among the party's Western and more rural representatives was there strong "little America" sentiment decrying foreign ventures of any sort. And even this truly isolationist agrarian attitude was compromised by the obvious growing concern of Pacific Coast Republicans with Asia.

The United States refused to participate in any outright political discussions of the League of Nations. By 1924, even the Democratic Party apparently accepted this position by playing down the League as a campaign issue. Entrance into the World Court, recommended by both Harding and Coolidge, was defeated in the Senate. But the United States did not refrain from political relations with either Europe or Asia. The Washington Armament Conference, of 1921–22, in addition to prescribing reductions of naval armament by fixed ratios, also prescribed by a series of treaties between the world's great nations the new power relationships in the Pacific, which in effect diminished America's potential power in East Asia while restricting that of the Japanese in the South Pacific. And the country readily and enthusiastically signed the rather meaningless and completely impotent Pact of Paris of 1928, outlawing war. Over these years, the United States maintained four or five permanent officials at Geneva to represent the nation's interest and sent special delegates to over forty congresses sponsored by the League. What the United States consistently refused to do was to sign treaties of alliance or international agreements which contained a promise of support with arms.

A hint of the old militancy was conveyed by the Coolidge-Kellogg use of marines in Nicaragua to reestablish peace and support the claims of the conservative candidate for president against those of the liberals. The marines, in effect, supported the conservative administration until recalled by President Hoover in 1933. But even in the Western Hemisphere the penchant for using force when the real interests of the United States were involved was deemphasized in the twenties. When the Mexican Congress in 1924 acted to implement the nationalization clauses of the 1917 Constitution, threatening vast American holdings, the Coolidge response three years later was to send Dwight W. Morrow to Mexico City with instructions to negotiate. In 1924, the marines were withdrawn after a decade's stay in the Dominican Republic. And the last of the Coolidge years saw the formulation of the Clark Memorandum by the State Department, a document which in fact repudiated the Roosevelt Corollary to the Monroe Doctrine, and an action that laid the groundwork for the later "Good Neighbor" policy of Hoover and Roosevelt. Calvin Coolidge, as might be expected from his basic attitudes, was neither an imperialist nor an internationalist, but a man who wanted to avoid trouble, maintain peace, and keep the budget low.

The only problem threatening to disturb Coolidge's desire for composure during his six years arose from the continuing distress of agriculture. Increasing yields and falling farm prices, coupled with an overcapitalization of land values, high mortgages, and sharply increasing local taxes, contributed to the farmers' precarious existence, particularly in wheat- and cotton-growing areas. Two farm bills passed during the Harding regime, the Capper-Volstead Act and the Intermediate Credit Act, failed to grant substantial relief. In January 1924, the McNary-Haugen Bill was introduced, incorporating a radical scheme for government support for farm prices: a federal farm board would purchase surplus production of specified commodities from farmers and either sell the surplus on the world market or keep it until prices rose. Farmers would receive a higher domestic price (the international market price plus the tariff rate) and pay an equalization fee covering the difference between the world price and the fixed domestic price in the event the government lost money disposing of the surplus on the international market. The farm problem persisted into the Hoover years; Coolidge's opposition to any major government help for the farmer was adamant.

Coolidge's attitude helped to spur the political revolt of 1924, which resulted in the formation of the Progressive Party, supported by farm and labor groups, and led by Senator Robert M. La Follette of Wisconsin and Senator Burton K. Wheeler of Montana. The Progressive platform denounced the Coolidge-Mellon financial program, the Administration's sizable contributions to the growth of monopoly, and the corruption rampant in Harding's official family. It argued for support for the farmers and the right of labor to organize freely, and demanded government ownership of railroads and water-power resources, the ratification of a child-labor amendment, and the enactment of curbs on the Supreme Court's power of judicial review.

Since most of the Progressive following presumably would come from Republican areas, the La Follette challenge looked like 1912 all over again, with a Democratic victory possible. But, for a number of reasons, history did not repeat itself. The La Follette net was not cast nearly as wide as that of Roosevelt's in 1912. Personal qualities of leadership may have contributed to some of the difference. The temper of the country had also changed in the intervening twelve years. The United States was an urban nation in 1924 and many of its major unsolved problems lay in the cities. Though La Follette tried his best to appeal to the dissatisfied city voters, he was never able to convince the majority of them that he was more than an old-style agrarian reformer. Significantly, some of the very labor leaders who had helped organize the Progressive protest wavered in their support before the campaign was through.

As has been pointed out in recent studies, progressivism persisted throughout the decade and managed to score a number of legislative victories. The majority of these, however, were of a negative sort such as the congressional refusal to concur with Secretary Mellon's radical proposal practically to abolish taxes on wealth or to accept Presidential recommendations to sell the Muscle Shoals Dam and power facilities to private interests. But, aside from electric power, the real concerns of most of the congressional progressives of the twenties were intimately tied up with agriculture. Senators La Follette, Wheeler, Borah, Brookhart, Magnus Johnson, Shipstead, Norris, Hiram Johnson, and Walsh were all from Western states, and although the few urban radicals in

Washington sympathized with them, these Western leaders were unable to command either attention or support from most of the urban masses. Until progressivism could develop national leaders who were involved in the myriad problems of the nation's cities, it seemed as if it was doomed to a minority existence, and to a dying minority at that.

The Democrats, who ordinarily might have profited from the split in the Republican Party, contributed to Coolidge's reelection by engaging in a long and bitter convention struggle between the followers of Governor Alfred E. Smith of New York and William G. McAdoo. Smith was the darling of the Eastern city masses, an anti-Prohibitionist, a Roman Catholic, and a man who was sympathetic to many of the insistent social problems of the great metropolitan areas. McAdoo, born in Tennessee, Protestant, and one of the few remaining leaders of the Bryan-Wilson tradition in the party, evoked the enthusiastic support of the South and the West. After a sectional battle involving the Ku Klux Klan, Catholicism, the farm problem, and the issue of the countryside against the city, all of which were fought through 102 separate ballots, the convention wearily accepted a worthless compromise by nominating John W. Davis. An eminent international lawyer and Morgan partner, Davis was a political unknown whose appeal to the distressed farming regions of the South and West or to the urban masses was almost nil.

In a thoroughly standpat campaign, Coolidge turned most of his attention to La Follette, whom he depicted as a dangerous radical who, if elected, would turn America into a degraded "communistic and socialistic state." Coolidge's victory margin was impressive, the President polling almost 16 million votes to the 13 million collected by his two adversaries. Elated over the poll, Chief Justice Taft effused that this was no country for radicals but rather "the most conservative country in the world." Whether Taft was right or not, the farm problem would not down, and after being defeated in 1926 the McNary-Haugen Bill was passed by both houses of Congress in 1927 and again in 1928, meeting in each instance a blistering veto by the President on the score that the bill provided for government price fixing and thus would grant special privileges to one group of citizens at the expense of all the others.

Coolidge's vetoes of the McNary-Haugen Bill raised the hopes of the Democrats that in the 1928 Presidential election they might at last reverse the political tide that had been running so strongly against them for ten years. For though the prince of immobility was still in the White House, liberals, progressives, and radicals, long now in the minority, sensed an opportunity for a change in the nation's political temper. It is now obvious that, well before the great Wall Street crash of 1929, the mood of the country was changing. Already discernible was a growing dislike for the politics of statics and an increasing distaste for the narrow cultural and social outlook emanating from the White House. There was even a faint spirit of rebellion. In 1927, two anarchists, Nicola Sacco and Bartolomeo Vanzetti, were executed after their conviction six years earlier of murdering a guard at a Massachusetts shoe factory. This event elicited for the first time in the decade, as Malcolm Cowley has pointed out, an explosion of conscience among the intellectuals. Most of these rebels, moreover, were urbanites. In opposition to what they held to be a political lynching on the basis of very questionable and insubstantial evidence, hundreds of them collected money, wrote articles, and even marched to the Charleston prison gates to protest against the sentence of execution. Not for years had the intellectuals united for a social cause. Led by John Dewey, Paul Douglas, and Oswald Garrison Villard, they organized the radical League for Independent Political Action, looking toward increased social planning and increased social control. The organization soon had over 2,500 dues-paying members. Organized labor, torpid for long, began to bestir itself. At Gastonia, North Carolina, labor launched one of the most bitter and protracted strikes of the decade. Further to the left, the *New Masses,* an acknowledged Communist magazine, had been founded.

Even among the professional politicians there was disquiet, which may have had some relation to Coolidge's enigmatic remark in the summer of 1927 that he did not "choose to run" for the Presidency the following year. So as to quell their fears about a possible invitational quality in the President's remarks, the Senate passed an anti-third-term resolution the following January.

As if to mark further a change in traditional ways, the Democrats, gathering at Houston, Texas, nominated Alfred E. Smith with a minimum of conflict. Born in a tenement house near the wharves of the East River, Smith attended a Catholic school before he became, at the age of fifteen, a salesman in the Fulton Street fish market. He subsequently joined Tammany Hall and after eight years as a subpoena server was elected to the state Assembly, where he made a reputation by his support of social legislation. In 1918 he was elected governor, a position which he filled, except for a two-year interval, until 1928. The Smith record over the years was a mildly humanitarian one. Associated with such people as Robert Wagner and Frances Perkins, he was a friend, but perhaps not the advocate, of the immigrants and of the working people of the large cities. He defended civil liberties during the days of the Red hunt, and his civil-service reforms gave the state its first efficient bureaucracy. Though Smith advocated but never secured a minimum wage and state ownership of hydroelectric power, he was never an economic radical. In 1927 Walter Lippmann called the governor of New York "the most powerful conservative in urban America." Smith was important, however, not for the things he was for or against, but rather as a symbol. Although somewhat straitlaced in his personal life and aloof from his fellows, he represented the new gregarious breed from the melting pot of the large Eastern cities. Smith was not the first successful urban politician, as William Allen White wrote, but rather the first from the very bottom of the city who almost went to the top.

The Republican Party chose for its nominee in 1928 Herbert Hoover, who was Coolidge's Secretary of Commerce. Hoover was no less a child of fortune than Smith, although he had started life in a Quaker family on an Iowa farm and was soon orphaned. His career was also symbolic, not of a new but of an older breed of Americans. Through hard work and persistence, Hoover had worked his way through high school and an engineering course at Stanford University. Shortly after graduation, he became one of the world's top mining engineers, and much of his early life was spent in Australia and China. The outbreak of World War I found him wealthy and living in London, where he volunteered to supervise the repatriation of Americans from the war-torn continent. He was then asked to head the organization for relief of the Belgians and subsequently was called home by President Wilson to

administer the wartime food administration. So efficient was his
performance in all these endeavors that by 1919 both parties
talked seriously about nominating him as Presidential candidate.

Had Hoover run true to the nineteenth-century model of the
self-made man or to the engineering type, he might have been a
regular Republican, an ardent advocate of laissez-faire, and a narrow materialist, as suspicious of social theory and the cultivated
life as Calvin Coolidge. Instead, he was a Bull Mooser in 1912,
later a strong advocate of the League of Nations, and an ardent
follower of Woodrow Wilson. As a member of the Harding and
Coolidge Cabinets, he was one of the few activists and certainly
one of the most liberal-minded. Compared to most American
Presidents, Herbert Hoover was also a literate man. He read widely
and wrote extensively. Among his books are a translation of a
sixteenth-century text on mining and a volume entitled *American
Individualism*, published in 1922, containing a balanced and reasonable statement of political conservatism.

Although the future President believed that progress in historic
societies had been achieved by a small group of creative individuals and that any effort to enforce an equality of conditions and
rewards would destroy most of these creative impulses, he was by
no means an expositor of the economic law of the jungle. He could
write that the crowd, compared to the elite, "feels rather than
thinks but never creates," and that occasionally, operating on its
emotions, the masses could "hate, consume, and destroy." But he
balanced those judgments with the acknowledgment that many of
the impulses of the elite, impulses accounting in part for their very
creativity, their competitive appetites, their demand for adulation,
and their desire for power and wealth, were destructive of the
social fabric and had to be restrained. "No civilization," he wrote,
could be built or can endure "solely upon the groundwork of
unrestrained and intelligent self-interest."

Hoover's ideal elite, moreover, was not one selected by inheritance of either name or fortune, but rather a "natural" one based
on ability, in each generation selected after a fair start by "the free
running mills of competition." It was the government's job to
secure and maintain that equality of opportunity, the state of
competition, and the attraction of rewards that would make possi-

ble this fluid selective process. To do so, the government would have to place certain restrictions on the strong and dominant. But it followed that if government were to be effective in this task it could not be controlled by the very class it was supposed to regulate. A truly democratic process, therefore, was imperative in Hoover's ideal state, a democratic process that could not be influenced unduly by organized capital. In a society where the property group controls the state, Hoover wrote, "the individual begins to feel capital as an oppressor."

Hoover believed that contemporary American society had done an effective job of maintaining equality before the law. In fact, the United States had "gone further than any government" in securing an "equality of franchise," an "equality of entrance into public office," and a "government by the adult majority." And it had been far more successful than most other governments "in safeguarding an equality of opportunity through education, public information, and the open channels of free speech and free press." The nation's greatest failure lay in the economic field, where the rise of big industry and big labor was throttling individual initiative and making necessary the increasing role of government, which had become "the most potent force for the maintenance or the destruction of our American individualism." Already, Hoover admitted, industrial concentration and resultant governmental regulation had gone a long way toward the abandonment of Adam Smith's capitalism. Even though government regulation designed to promote social and economic justice had restrained individualism, it was entirely proper since "a fair division of the product was necessary if we were to keep the modern impulse of production alive." But governmental regulation, Hoover concluded, must be attuned to the major aim of the American system: "To curb the forces in business which would destroy equality of opportunity and yet maintain the initiative and creative faculties of our people are the twin objects we must obtain."

This was a conservative creed, but it was a reasoned and defensible one, drawing most of its presuppositions and insight from the best hopes of classical liberalism and applying them to the conditions of the day. If Hoover's argument had major faults in its reasoning, they lay in the assumptions that equality of opportunity had not seriously decreased since his own youthful ascent from orphan lad to world-famous engineer, that something like a fair division of the social product was then being made, and that concentrated wealth would not wield inordinate power in government. In the light of the tone and record of the Harding-Coolidge Administrations, these last two assumptions looked especially dubious. But for all its weaknesses, real or fancied, Mr. Hoover's credo was so far removed from that of most men surrounding him that it marked him as possibly the one positive force in the Coolidge Administration. It is little wonder that Coolidge's most devoted followers expressed anxiety at his nomination.

From the party platforms and the speeches of the contending candidates, it appeared that the election might be fought over the issues of farm relief, Prohibition, the granting of labor injunctions by the courts, and the interstate regulation of electric power. For although neither party satisfied the more zealous McNary-Haugenites, Smith seemed to promise the farmer more governmental action in solving his problems. And although the Democratic platform supported the Eighteenth Amendment, Smith early made it clear that he was a foe of the Volstead Act, whereas Hoover supported Prohibition as "a noble experiment." At contention, however, were two traditions, which seemed to be personified by the respective candidates. Al Smith, "the Happy Warrior," as Franklin D. Roosevelt had called him, was extremely articulate and, on the platform at least, gave all the appearance of being a sidewalk extrovert. Smith, a Wet and a Roman Catholic, wore a brown derby such as rural America had probably never seen outside a vaudeville act, and pronounced familiar words in the strange accents of Lower East Side New York. Herbert Hoover apparently embodied all the virtues of rural Iowa. He was shy, dour, and slow of speech, wearing high stiff collars that looked as if they had come from the village general store and were somewhat reminiscent of the Puritan Sunday dress. In reality, by training and experience he was much more sophisticated and cosmopolitan than Smith. But when Hoover spoke of "rugged individualism" he conjured up the pioneer past, with its alleged simple McGuffey Reader ethics. Smith, on the other hand, personified the teeming multiracial cities, from which, according to many Americans, arose most of the social problems which bedeviled the decade.

Although the candidates strove to keep religion out of the campaign, it was certainly an issue in both heavily Protestant and Roman Catholic districts. The most respected Protestant magazine, the *Christian Century*, sharply questioned whether religious tolerance should be exhibited to the extent that it tolerated an intolerant religion, and several high Protestant Church officials in the South let it be known publicly that they were supporting Hoover, although the nominal reason they gave for deserting the Democrats was Smith's attitude toward Prohibition. But probably an even more influential factor than either the religious or the alcoholic issue was the prosperity of the country, especially outside the agricultural regions. The Republicans naturally took credit for it, and Hoover promised that if the party was retained in office, even better things lay ahead. America's "final triumph" over want and poverty, he proclaimed, lay in sight.

Even with the most attractive and expedient candidate, the Democrats would have had a difficult time defeating the incumbent. And with religion, Prohibition, and the urban-farm issues added, the results were rather certain. Hoover received 21.4 million votes to Smith's 15 million, maintained a solid Republican supremacy throughout the Middle and Pacific West, and even won Texas and the upper South. About the only comfort the Democrats could draw from the election figures was that Smith had won Massachusetts and Rhode Island, two states usually found in the Republican column, and had increased the percentage of Democratic votes both in the Middle West and in the large cities of the country. If the future should turn out not so prosperous and if these voting trends should continue, Republican candidates would obviously be faced with trouble.

During the first seven months of his Administration, Hoover made it obvious that he was not content to follow the front-porch-sitting characteristics of his predecessor. Within weeks the new President had reorganized the White House secretariat, had reversed the Coolidge-Mellon easy-money policy by raising the Federal Reserve Board's rediscount rate, ordered publicity for large income-tax returns, and withdrew as many of the federally owned oil lands from further leasing to private firms as he was legally empowered to withdraw. True to his promise in the campaign, he also called a special session of Congress to deal with the farm problem and greeted it on April 16 with a proposal for the creation of a Federal Farm Board to secure the orderly marketing of farm products. A second message to Congress asked for higher tariffs on agricultural products. As journalists noted, a new spirit animated Washington: "The age of inactivity was over."

During the campaign, Hoover had indicated his opposition to the McNary-Haugen Bill. He now exerted himself to defeat a congressional proposal to incorporate into the new farm legislation the "export-debenture" principle, which would have granted a bounty on the export of domestic staples, in the hope of dumping American surplus production on the already disorganized world market. Instead, the Agricultural Marketing Act of June 2 created a Federal Farm Board with a revolving fund of $500 million which might be used to make loans to cooperative marketing associations and to privately managed stabilization corporations with the power to purchase, process, and store surplus commodities. Since the stabilizing corporations could purchase commodities at whatever price they chose and hold them off the market indefinitely, it was hoped that their operations would reduce the troublesome surpluses and thus raise the price of farm products. Government funds were thus to be indirectly committed to an attempt at price fixing.

The history of the Hoover tariff legislation was much more involved. Called for the purpose of enacting higher rates on agricultural goods, Congress soon busied itself with a general revision which by the traditional means of vote trading produced the Smoot-Hawley Tariff of June 1930, containing the highest rates in American history. Despite the fact that many American industries, including the automotive trade, and practically all the important academic economists protested against higher tariff schedules, the President did not intervene in the tariff fight until the bill had arrived at the stage of conference between the two Houses. At that point, the President managed to salvage a provision permitting him to reduce the existing rates on recommendation of the Tariff Commission by as much as 50 percent. The new Tariff Act, as predicted, set off a round of retaliatory increases by foreign countries, thus choking the channels of an already contracting world trade. The most Administration apologists could say for the Act was that Hoover, unlike Coolidge, would use the tariff-cutting provision in a substantial way.

Whether in normal times the effects of the Smoot-Hawley Act would have been mitigated and whether the Agricultural Marketing Act could have substantially helped the farmer were both academic questions by mid-1930. For in October 1929 the Wall Street crash and a world-girdling depression effectively ended normal times for at least two generations. From the fall of 1929 on, the entire world was to face one great crisis after another. And Hoover, who had been elected with a mandate to continue the good, fat, and soft days of the twenties, was now to be judged on how he met the first of these catastrophes.

If the President's record could be taken as a basis for prognosticating the future, there was to be trouble ahead. Secretary of Commerce Hoover had been engrossed in making the industrial productive system more efficient. In pursuit of this goal, he had encouraged industry through trade councils and other types of organizations to cooperate in self-government, a process which inevitably led to the critical diminishing of the individualism he was so fond of talking about. Yet he had evinced little concern for the other necessary half of the new economic system, the masses of consumers. He supported standardized industrial specifications set by the government, but was opposed or indifferent to grade labeling for the consumer. This apparent inconsistency was not very different from the response of most of the American leadership of the day. They were ardently for maintaining the old individualistic social ideals and values among the masses. But for themselves and their fellows, especially in economic matters, they had, to a rather startling degree, become collectivists dependent on a restricted kind of governmental paternalism. Hoover was the epitome of what many Americans of the twenties wanted: an able exponent of the new business system and a forceful expositor of the old rural social values and ethics. In good times, the ambiguities involved were neither so pronounced nor immediately harmful. But under the strain of a major depression these incompatible threads were to produce serious rents in the social fabric.

3

The End of Normalcy

OCTOBER 1929 marked a fateful month for the United States. A looming world economic crisis was suddenly given disastrous momentum by the New York stock-market crash. The resulting Great Depression upset governments, ignited revolutions and wars, fundamentally changed the nature of the dominant international economy, ended the careers of many widely known persons, and crushed the hopes and fortunes of untold millions of ordinary people.

Through the latter part of the 1920's there were numerous indications of ugly economic weather ahead. Since the collapse of farm prices in June 1920, agriculture and the communities it supported had led a precarious existence spotted with losses, foreclosed mortgages, and bankrupted financial institutions. The coal and textile industries were plainly in distress by 1927. The following year, a glut of petroleum products led to a ruinous wholesale-price war. By September 1929, the construction and building industry, which had contributed much to the great boom, had slumped 25 percent under the levels of the previous twelve months. In the face of these distressing facts, a few men voiced the prophecy that disaster might be imminent. Noting the extent of installment buying, Roger Babson warned a business conference that a recession was almost inevitable and a panic possible. As 1928 ended, an economist of the National Industrial Conference Board, citing the already "developing depression in basic industries," warned that the existing prosperity rested precariously on "a state of mind" rather than on basic economic facts.

Most people were unaware of the portents of the rising storm; since the United States had not had an extended depression since 1893, few had personal memories of such a disaster. Besides, they were daily beguiled by the hypnotic figures provided by the booming stock market. The market had not been without its temporary ups and downs. In February and again in June of 1928, the market broke violently, Bank of Italy stock dropping, for example, 160 points in one day. After every such break, the market rebounded with vigor, as millions of people sought to make quick fortunes on borrowed money. Politicians, journalists, businessmen, academic economists, and those who stood to profit most from the great boom—brokers and bankers—joined a national chorus of unbridled optimism. Twice before he left office, President Coolidge stated that stocks were "cheap at current prices" and that the huge amount of brokers' funds loaned to speculators, large and small, was not too high. The owners of *Time* magazine, reflecting the buoyant confidence, chose January 1929 as the time to start *Fortune,* their plush new journal devoted to business.

The new President, Herbert Hoover, talked about the possible abolition of poverty in the foreseeable future; Secretary of the Treasury Andrew Mellon agreed with the judgment of an expert economist that the country had reached a "permanent plateau of prosperity"; and the multimillionaire Chairman of the Democratic National Committee published an article in the *Ladies' Home Journal* entitled "Everybody Ought To Be Rich." Who could really believe the Cassandra-like voices of the few? Such pessimism, a leading New York banker declared, "was more to be feared than Bolshevism." Consequently, as thousands of new recruits daily invested their savings and all they could borrow, the market swept on to majestic heights.

By September 19, 1929, when the market stood at the highest point in its history, the paper profits of investors were measured in the billions. But, on October 3 and 4, stocks took measurable slides downward. Three weeks later, leading industrial issues lost from 5 to 90 points in one day. And then on "black Thursday," October 29, came chaos. As stocks plummeted by 50 to 100 points, millions wanted to sell to nonexistent buyers. For the next three years, the market ground inexorably downward, until 75 percent of the total value of the nation's listed securities, or some $90 billion, had been wiped out.

The effect of the great stock slide on the nation's financial structure was ruinous. Since much stock purchasing had rested on credit, the immediate calls for repayment in the plummeting market not only wiped out speculators by the thousands but also so tightened credit generally that business and industry were starving for funds. In this stringent situation, banks refused to make loans, businessmen to extend credit, and the general consumer to make purchases. As industry and commerce began to slow down and in some cases came to an almost complete stop, men and women by the millions lost their jobs. The end of an age was written in the little pink slips appearing with the weekly and monthly pay checks, announcing that the services of vice-presidents, managers, engineers, salesgirls, and manual workers were no longer needed.

The effects of the Great Depression were worldwide. Accelerated by the collapse of Austria's credit system in May 1931, fiscal disaster swept Europe and then the colonial world. In the aftermath of human suffering and insecurity, democratic governments, including that of Germany, fell before a rash of dictatorships. After Great Britain went off the gold standard in September 1931, the three-century-old world free market was replaced by a state-directed system of mercantilism, replete with exchange controls, export and import quotas, and managed currencies, all manipulated to gain commercial advantage from neighbor states. Unemployment, bankruptcy, and personal deprivation were almost ubiquitous.

In no nation were the economic and industrial effects of the Depression as sharp as they were in the United States. World trade figures fell by about 25 percent, but American imports and exports in 1933 were only one-third of the 1929 figures. The United States industrial collapse was of terrifying proportions. Total wages paid throughout the nation in 1932 amounted to only 40 percent of the 1929 figure, dividends to only 43 percent. It was estimated that American business wound up the year with a net loss of over $5 billion. Meanwhile, farm prices dropped even more disastrously, cotton falling from 17 cents a pound to 6 cents, and wheat from $1.05 a bushel to 35 cents. Before the mid-1930's, national unemployment statistics were a matter of guesswork. But estimates in 1932 placed the unemployed figure at one million for New York, 600,000 for Chicago. In the following year, the Lynds of *Middletown* fame found that only 42 percent of the workers in Muncie, Indiana, a town of 50,000 population, had regular jobs. By March 4, 1933, perhaps 12 to 15 million men, or one-third of the nation's working force, were without employment.

When it became apparent in late 1930 that the nation was faced with a major industrial depression, President Hoover appealed to employers not to cut wage scales. If the prevailing wage standards were maintained, Hoover predicted, the effects of the Depression would be limited. For a time the nation's manufacturers faithfully tried to meet the President's precedent-making request. But in the face of mounting deficits, and after reducing dividends and white collar salaries, the United States Steel Corporation on October 1, 1931, reduced wages by 10 percent. The example of the big steel company was soon followed by General Motors and United States Rubber. The rout of existing wage standards was on. By 1932, Pennsylvania reported that men were working for ten cents an hour and children in sweatshops for as little as one dollar for a fifty-five-hour week. Among the want ads in the *Saturday Review of Literature,* a request appeared for an English Department head for a "select college preparatory school" near New York. The offer promised room, board, and laundry, but no salary. A year later, among workers constructing a reservoir in Hollywood were farmers, ministers, actors, engineers, a school principal, and a pre-Depression president of a Missouri bank. The downgrading of labor skills could scarcely have gone further.

As soon as it became evident that the country was faced with an intense and possibly enduring industrial depression, all manner of alleged authorities came forward with cures for the great debacle. But by far the great majority of industrial and financial leaders of the country stood rigidly pat on their classic views. The business system was sound, they argued, and without need of basic reform. The decline was simply a product of the business cycle and probably was healthy, since it would prune away many of the inefficient elements in the industrial and commercial structure. If government abstained from intervention in the natural business process, the Depression would soon be over, probably within a year or two. Even after more than two years of public suffering, most industrialists and financiers had little to offer other than this negative program. They were as much opposed to any reform of the nation's productive and financial machinery as they were to attempts by government to alleviate distress through the dole, public works, or social insurance. During a Senate Banking and Currency Committee hearing of 1933, they still argued that government should reduce its expenditures, balance its budget, and otherwise fold its hands. Expansion of charitable activities at the local level, business leaders argued, would alleviate the distress arising from unemployment. As the months went by, as unemployment rolls grew ever longer and local contributions tended to dry up, the majority of them still refused to moderate their opposition to public relief supported by taxation. Into their remarks crept bitter statements against the unemployed which revealed a state of growing frustration and anxiety. Echoing Henry Ford's sentiment, the president of the National Association of Manufacturers in early 1932 ascribed the Depression and the growing unemployment to mass laziness. Most men without jobs, he said, either did not want to work or were "utilizing the occasion to swell the Communist chorus."

Business prestige and influence were among the major liquidations of the Great Depression. From their venerated position during the twenties, businessmen fell to objects of public hostility, suspicion, and ridicule, not so much because of the Depression but rather because of their unwillingness or inability to provide or support new solutions for the pressing problems of unemployment and growing poverty. Their doctrinaire hostility to relief and reform obscured their private charitable activities, fostered the public image of them as cold, indifferent, and greedy, and led to their social bankruptcy.

Organized labor in the early days of the Depression appeared to be almost as barren of ideas and leadership as business. Until 1931, William Green, president of the American Federation of Labor, contented himself with sterile criticism of business, and opposition to any scheme of public assistance or compulsory unemployment insurance as sure to turn the worker into a "ward of the state." Somnolent since the stirring days following World War I, organized labor seemed no more able than business to discern the reasons why the productive machine had slowed down or ways by which to accelerate it. Characterized by an almost total lack of leadership and besieged by mass unemployment and a rapidly falling wage scale, unions lost members in droves. By 1932, the union movement appeared to be on the way to oblivion.

Some outside the ranks of organized business and labor made public their own diagnosis of what had happened and what to do about it. A group of radical economists, anticipating some of the doctrines of John Maynard Keynes, argued that the basic cause of the Depression was the maldistribution of saving and spending under unregulated capitalism. David Cushman Coyle, Marriner Eccles, Rexford Tugwell, and Adolf A. Berle, among others, contended that in the old unplanned mass-production economy dominated by a few great industries and financial institutions, the few had siphoned off too many of the rewards, and the masses of people had obtained far too little. This maldistribution of national wealth had led to oversaving or overinvestment by the few and underspending or underconsumption by the many. The process had resulted in too many factories producing too many goods, with consumers unable to purchase enough to keep the industrial wheels spinning. This conclusion seemed to be borne out by one of the most influential scholarly studies to appear during the Depression. *America's Capacity to Consume,* published by the Brookings Institution in 1934, drew a picture of the distribution of the national wealth in 1929 which was profoundly disturbing to social conservatives. Eight percent of the nation's families had earned 42 percent of the national income, while 60 percent of the families had received only 23 percent.

Since private industry had been unable to preserve a balance of earning and consumption power sufficient to keep the productive machine working, the Keynesians argued, government would have to assume that task in one form or another. The more conservative among them, who desired to maintain capitalistic institutions as little changed as possible (as for example, Eccles), contended that this could be done by a change in taxation policies and by the government's taking up the slack in mass incomes during times of recession by extensive public works and construction programs. Tugwell, to the contrary, believed that the only way to salvage the situation was by a thoroughgoing system of government planning and control in which the separate identity of industry and government would tend to disappear. The future, he remarked in 1932, "is visible in Russia." He was joined in this radical outlook by such noted reformers as John Dewey and Charles A. Beard.

Among the more important reasons for the stock-market crash and the Great Depression were the major economic maldistributions arising out of World War I; a chaotic international financial policy, to which the United States contributed markedly by its insistence on high tariffs and on repayment of war debts; the speculative urge, which was probably as rabid on the European exchanges as it was in New York; the overextension of credit, which applied to families buying appliances as well as to businessmen and stock speculators; the downright dishonesty of some financial and business leaders, whose practices resembled those of the cardsharp; and the rigidity of the world and national price structure for industrial goods as compared to that for primary goods or raw materials.

But basic to the condition of the United States, as to the world, was the fact that some classes of people and some nations were obtaining too much of the rewards of industry and commerce, while others were receiving too little, to keep the highly industrialized machine devoted to mass production and consumption operating. Thus the primary-goods-producing nations were receiving too little to continue purchasing the manufactured goods of the industrially mature nations on a scale sufficient to maintain the vigorous exchange of goods. In the same way, the working masses of the industrialized nations were unable to maintain a level of purchasing sufficient to keep the factories operating on something near the level of full production. The new mass-production-consumption economy of the twentieth century apparently required either that men be rewarded more equitably by conventional pay checks or that government skim off a portion of the goods produced in order to utilize them for nonproductive pursuits such as armaments or war, or for disposition by gift or by dole. Years after he had left the White House, Herbert Hoover blamed the Depression on two major causes: the "weakness" and "wickedness" in the nation's financial system, and maldistribution of rewards.

There is some indication that Hoover appreciated the danger of maldistribution of income even while he was President. One of his first acts in meeting the Depression was to ask the industrial leaders of the country to maintain the existing wage scale. But Hoover did not go beyond requesting. To dictate on such matters was unthinkable. One of Hoover's most cherished ideals was freedom for the individual. Few, if any, of the other freedoms could be maintained if economic liberty was denied, because it supplied "the most nearly universal field for the release of the creative spirit of man." Consequently, he relied on private actions and individual decisions to cure the Depression; and he gave way to government activity reluctantly and only when he believed it was absolutely necessary.

The chief difficulty with the President's program was that business refused to provide the leadership he requested. This was made clear in the autumn of 1931 at a national conference of bankers. During the previous year, over two thousand banks, unable to collect from their debtors or pay their creditors, had closed their doors. The President asked the large banks to form a pool of their common resources to help the weaker institutions over the period of financial stringency. The bankers' reply that this was the government's business so discouraged Hoover that he returned to the White House thoroughly despondent. The growing realization that business would not act and the steadily deteriorating economy finally pushed Hoover to action. Already he had violated his major economic principles by agreeing to the Federal Farm Board's purchase of surplus wheat and cotton, a program given up the following year because it failed to raise agricultural prices. In his annual message to Congress in 1931, the beleaguered President asked for a revival of the World War I War Finance Corporation, with power to lend public money to privately owned banks and corporations. During the next two years, the Reconstruction Finance Corporation loaned $1.5 billion to financial institutions.

Despite these large loans to private firms, and the Administration's attempts to raise agricultural prices, the President was still adamantly against granting relief to individuals, even by indirect means. Hoover's willingness to aid agriculture and business but not the urban unemployed was due largely to his reluctance to make any individual a direct grantee of the federal government. Part of his opposition to unemployment relief may have come from his bias toward rural values and his antipathy to, or ambiguous feelings toward, the urban masses, among whom the need for relief was centered. In his more philosophical writings the President many times scathingly referred to the "mobs" of the French Revolution and the Paris Commune. Herbert Hoover, like so many of his friends and supporters, was a twentieth-century industrial man, but much of the cast of his social creed was molded by the values of West Branch, Iowa, from which he had come.

Hoover was neither a flint-hearted social Darwinist nor a blind believer in laissez-faire, even for the city masses. From the first days of the Depression, he called for massive private action to alleviate the distress of the unemployed. Repeatedly he asked utilities and railroads to expand their construction and thus afford work to the jobless. Simultaneously he encouraged the increase of private and local charity to provide for the needy. In October 1930, he created the President's Emergency Committee for Unemployment and supported this organization's national campaign to persuade homeowners, block by city block, to create work by repairing and adding to their properties. But beyond encouraging voluntary, local, and private efforts, the President refused to go. Federal grants for relief, even of the indirect kind, he argued, would be "a step toward a national dole," which would deprive the individual of a sense of responsibility, dry up "the precious charitable instincts" of the people, enfeeble local and state government, and make the unemployed direct and perhaps permanent wards of the national government. Relief in its most direct sense, Hoover reiterated many times, was the responsibility of local individuals and local government.

During 1930 and 1931, the President adhered to his position. He opposed a scheme for national unemployment insurance and rejected a suggestion by William G. McAdoo that the Federal Farm Board release its surplus wheat to the poor. If federal support were the last alternative to avoid starvation, Hoover would support it. But, he added, "I have faith in the American people that such a day shall not come."

Hoover's solution to the problems of unemployment and poverty might have been successful had the Depression been of short duration. But as grim month succeeded month and all the major economic indexes pointed steadily downward, the size of the problems ballooned while private funds and local efforts to alleviate suffering dwindled. Private industry had little recourse but to cut expenditures. From 1929 to 1932, the total of all private construction in the country fell from $10 billion to $1 billion. Public works followed the same pattern. Even though the federal government eventually attempted to take up the slack, huge cuts in construction by the states meant fewer jobs. From 1929 on, the total spent annually for public works declined steadily from $3.3 billion to $1.3 billion in 1933. As a consequence, work of any kind became more difficult to obtain and the number of families on public relief or on the charity rolls grew steadily. From 40,000 in the winter of 1928–29, the number increased to 500,000 by 1931–32, and many more were in need.

Compounding the bleaker aspects of the situation, states and local governments were running out of money. During 1931 and 1932, most states cut their relief appropriations. Michigan, where unemployment in the hard-hit automobile industry was acute, reduced its funds from $2 million in 1931 to $860,000 in 1932. In cities and towns, relief funds were as short. As people were thrown out of work, tax collections plummeted and public employees had to be laid off, or paid, like thousands of schoolteachers, in emergency scrip. Efforts to continue local public services through deficit spending were usually cut short by banks, which held city bonds and insisted on balanced budgets. Many communities were unable to care for their own citizens, to say nothing of the thousands of drifters looking for jobs or food. By 1933, an estimated million men and women were on the road, without permanent homes. During that year, the Southern Pacific Railroad reported that its guards had thrown 683,000 people off its freight trains. As the disparity between local resources and the size of the relief problem grew, the disposition increased to give all strangers short shrift. California first set up labor camps in forests and then posted guards at the state borders to turn indigent people away. Other communities, unable to care for their own citizens, simply escorted the drifters to the next county or city. Atlanta even placed the impoverished wanderers in chain gangs. A national survey by *Fortune* magazine in 1931 reported that the theory of local responsibility for the impoverished had completely broken down, simply because locally organized charity depended on "contributions of communities no longer able to contribute."

A number of alternatives were proposed to replace Hoover's reliance on local and private efforts to alleviate distress. With a view to the elections of 1930, the Democrats were of course bitterly critical of the Administration's program, but though long on criticism, the party as a whole was short on constructive measures. Among party leaders, only Senators Robert Wagner of New York and Hugo L. Black of Alabama advocated radical measures to soften the effect of the Depression. They were joined in 1931 by Governor Franklin D. Roosevelt of New York and by Democratic mayors like Tony Cermak of Chicago. Roosevelt was signally successful in passing his legislative program of raising income taxes and creating an emergency state relief agency, which spent $83 million on relief by 1933. As early as January 1930, Senator Wagner proposed the creation of a federal employment service, national unemployment insurance, and the expenditure of at least $2 billion on public works. Supporting Wagner's proposals was an important group of Western senators including Robert La Follette, Jr., George Norris, Bronson Cutting, Edward P. Costigan, William E. Borah, Hiram Johnson, Burton K. Wheeler, and Gerald Nye. The Democratic congressional victory of 1930 added further bipartisan support for the project. But even in the spring of 1931 the friends of direct federal relief did not have a majority in Congress, and opponents claimed that any such measures would merely waste federal resources, assume responsibilities more appropriately left to state legislatures, and undermine individualism. In March 1931, the President vetoed the Wagner Bill, which would have created a federal unemployment agency. Some months later, he mobilized a congressional coalition of Republicans and conservative Democrats to kill the La Follette-Costigan Bill, which provided for distribution of $750 million among the states for either public works or direct relief to the unemployed.

By the late winter and spring of 1932, however, the unemployment and relief situation had further deteriorated, especially in the large cities. In Philadelphia and Pittsburgh, one of every three adults was on charity rolls. Toledo had sufficient funds to grant only 2.14 cents a meal for relief applicants. By late February, Chicago, with over 600,000 unemployed, had spent all the relief funds budgeted for the entire year. Pointing out the danger of insurrection, Mayor Cermak demanded that the city get either "federal relief or federal troops."

Nineteen thirty-two was also a Presidential election year, and a good many members of Congress, who had previously been opposed to large federal appropriations, now changed their positions. Consequently, they supported a Democratic Party proposal to float a $2 billion bond issue to finance self-liquidating public works. Faced with congressional approval of this and possibly even more radical measures, Hoover capitulated and agreed to approve the compromise 1932 Emergency Relief Act, provided all other relief bills were pigeonholed. The Act extended the lending authority of the Reconstruction Finance Corporation by $300 million, which might be loaned to the states to bolster their relief programs. Considering the extent of the need, the sum was extremely small. Even so, the money would be spent cautiously, the President observed. Grants would be made to states only after evidence of their "financial exhaustion" had been produced and then only on a loan basis. Such monies, with interest, were to be paid back to the RFC by July 1935.

Hoover's reputation and political fortunes foundered on the shoals of the urban-relief question. It was not true, as was later charged, that his was a do-nothing, care-nothing Administration. By 1933, Hoover had gone far along the road to governmental intervention in the economic life of the country. With his approval, both the Federal Farm Board and the Reconstruction Finance Corporation had spent and lent billions, attempting to bolster the sagging economy. Moreover, the President had interjected the government into the private mechanisms of costs, wages, and profits to an unheard-of degree. Nor could it be said in 1932 that Hoover was indifferent or callous to the misery around him. The depths of his concern were written on his face, and few Presidents have worked harder or spent longer hours at the Presidential desk. But the very intensity of Hoover's efforts to overcome the Depression was to be used against him. If so much money and time had been spent to save banks and corporations, why not, the jobless man asked, a few pennies for the poor? Hoover answered with allusions to spiritual values and talk of freedom and responsibility, thus opening himself to the charge that he was the cold and uncaring servant of the ruling economic classes, as ready to help business as he was to sacrifice all other human values.

Most political commentators, even including many conservatives, recognized in 1932 that changes in the economic system were overdue. Walter Lippmann called for new economic motives "more disinterested and cooperative in their effects," while others assumed that the profit system would be altered or phased out altogether. Radicals agreed and were jubilant about the future. The Communist Party was certain that the crack-up portended the end of capitalism and opened the way for the dictatorship of the proletariat. But, in the midst of all the distress, the party had been able to recruit only some ten to fifteen thousand dues-paying members by 1932. Others offered a variety of schemes for dealing with the Depression, including suggestions that Americans retreat from the machine age and return to the land. On the other hand, the "Technocrats," drawing their inspiration from Thorstein Veblen, urged Americans to make their peace with modern production by junking capitalism and the existing political system and installing the engineer as governor of a new society. More of a danger to established institutions were the individuals and groups demanding a non-Communist dictator. During the twenties, much praise had been lavished on Benito Mussolini, and in 1932 Lawrence Dennis published *Is Capitalism Doomed?*, which argued openly for a syndicalist society on a Fascist model.

Here and there, private property and constituted authority were disregarded, suggesting that orderly society was beginning to disintegrate. In Seattle, empty lots were gardened with or without their owners' consent. In Pennsylvania and Kentucky, individual miners worked company coal seams, bootlegging their product to surrounding towns. In August 1932, Milo Reno's Farmer's Holiday Association barricaded the roads to Sioux City, attempting to prevent the sale of farm goods at the prevailing ruinous prices. In eastern Iowa, milk strikers met local authorities head-on in violent clashes, and, increasingly throughout the Middle West, sheriffs seeking to foreclose farm property encountered ragged lines of determined farmers armed with hunting rifles and shotguns. Meanwhile, thousands of men made "hunger marches" to state capitals and to Washington. The most significant march started from Portland, Oregon, in May 1932, a march of unemployed world-war veterans seeking to pressure Congress into passing a veterans' bonus bill, to which the President had already announced his opposition. By the time the Patman Bill was debated on the floor, 20,000 veterans were camped along Pennsylvania Avenue and later on the mud flats where the Anacostia River meets the Potomac.

Fear was rampant in 1932: the fear of the poor and unemployed that tomorrow would be no better, the fear of the rich that they would lose all they had, and the fear of the government that revolution was imminent. As organized labor cried that they had enough, and the head of the Federal Farm Bureau predicted a revolution in nine months unless something was done, wealth began to panic. Gold was shipped from the country to Switzerland; places of refuge were selected against the day the mob might start marching. A Hollywood director announced that he had gathered some old clothes together so that at the crisis he could "disappear into the crowd."

In this taut atmosphere, Hoover was confronted with the critical problem of the veterans camped along the Potomac. So far, the President and the District of Columbia authority, represented by General Glassford, had treated the veterans with consideration. Hoover had even supplied funds with which to ship the veterans back to their homes, and many had taken advantage of the offer. But when the bonus bill was defeated in the Senate, the remaining men grew restless. Some talked wildly, and a story circulated of the possibility of organizing the veterans into a khaki army representing the poor of the country. At that juncture, against the advice of Glassford, the President ordered General Douglas MacArthur and the army to remove the men from the capital. Calling the veterans "a mob . . . animated by the essence of revolution," MacArthur quickly accomplished the task. But the act probably settled the fate of the Hoover Administration. To the unthinking, the soldiers' bonus was confused with general relief. Many interpreted the action as a token of the government's intention to provide bullets instead of bread. Had not the coming fall election offered a promise of a change in Administration, the action at the Anacostia Flats might have ignited a disastrous social upheaval.

The selection of a Republican candidate and a program for the 1932 elections was little more than a formality. Unless the party wished to repudiate itself, it had to renominate Hoover and stand on his record. The Republican program was therefore a cautious document designed, according to one commentator, "to defend what was left of Prohibition and what was left of the country." The Democratic choice was another matter. Here the split between the conservatives and the liberal-minded had been widened by Franklin Roosevelt's speech of April 7, in which he charged the Hoover Administration with neglect of the ordinary American and expressed his sympathies with "the forgotten man at the bottom of the economic pyramid." Alfred E. Smith, who desperately wanted the nomination again, announced after the speech that he was ready to fight any candidate who persisted "in a demagogic appeal to the working classes." Newton D. Baker, an old Wilsonian internationalist, and Speaker of the House John Nance Garner were also conservative or moderate candidates.

Toward the left, but still not too far from the center, the governor of New York had rallied most of the liberals to his cause. Roosevelt's record of providing sizable relief funds, his support of public-power installations, and his opposition to a national sales tax (which Garner and the conservative Democrats had advanced in Congress) pleased the Democratic left. The forgotten-man speech won their affection. Roosevelt obtained the nomination, but the fact that he won through the support of many conservatives and as a part of the bargain had to accept Speaker Garner as the Vice-Presidential candidate indicated the very fine balance between the factions. The Democratic platform, which Roosevelt told the convention he accepted a hundred percent, also illustrated the relatively equal strength of the contending ideologies. The platform, Walter Lippmann observed, had been written by old Wilsonians and indicated their desire to return to the liberalism of

Cleveland and Wilson rather than to point the party toward a new collectivism.

Roosevelt soon showed himself a superb popular politician who did not fit easily into the ordinary American mold. His speeches were political masterpieces. Simple, concrete, and filled with homely analogies, they were understandable and infinitely appealing to the common man. He simplified even the most complex technical questions so that he had the ear, and apparently the understanding, of the masses. Yet Roosevelt never seemed to talk down to his audience. His warm and vibrant voice carried conviction and concern. And his superbly confident delivery in a cultivated Eastern accent seemed to lift his efforts far above the traditional vote-seeking. His personal demeanor contributed to the effect. He was one of the nation's few really lighthearted leaders, given to quips and cracks, carrying laughter around with him. But he never once demeaned his office or himself by vulgarity or absurdity. Roosevelt achieved that most difficult of public images—a man of immense zest, warmth, and at the same time dignity. With his large distinguished head held at a characteristic angle, his chin forward, a cigarette angled at the sky, and sometimes a cape flowing in the wind from his broad shoulders, the man exuded confidence and vitality. All in all, he was one of the most personable and attractive public figures the twentieth century has produced.

At the start of the critical campaign of 1932, there was little to indicate that Franklin Roosevelt would institute momentous changes in national policy. He had been an efficient governor of New York, but his accomplishments, except for public relief and an old-age security program, could scarcely be distinguished from those of his predecessor, Alfred E. Smith. Except for his "forgotten man" effort and the inevitable attacks against the Hoover Administration, his prenomination campaign was low-keyed. At the convention, he called for a legislative program which was neither radical nor conservative nor characterized by an "improvised hit-or-miss irresponsible opportunism."

During the campaign that followed, many of the respected party leaders talked straight conservatism. Alfred E. Smith advocated a balanced budget and a sales tax as the way to end the Depression.

Speaker Garner attacked Hoover's intervention in what should essentially remain nongovernmental affairs, and he trumpeted loudly for states' rights. The 1924 Democratic nominee, John W. Davis, assailed Hoover for "following the road to socialism." In many of his own speeches, Roosevelt sang in chorus with the party's conservatives and with the men who were largely responsible for financing his campaign: William Randolph Hearst, Bernard Baruch, John J. Raskob, Vincent Astor, and Joseph Kennedy. In his acceptance speech, Roosevelt paid vague tribute to the hallowed phrases—"liberal thought," "planned action," "the greatest good to the greatest number." He promised that the federal government would "assume" the responsibility for public welfare and "distress relief." But he also assailed Hoover for wasteful expenditures and pledged himself to a sharp reduction in taxes. "For three years," he reminded his audience, "I have been going up and down this country preaching that government—federal, state and local —costs too much. I shall not stop that preaching."

There were two and possibly more Roosevelts during the campaign of 1932: the Roosevelt associated with his financial backers, and the Roosevelt who gathered around him as intimates four professors who were later to become the core of the so-called "brain trust"—Felix Frankfurter of Harvard, and Raymond Moley, Rexford Tugwell, and Adolf Berle of Columbia. Each of these Roosevelts had an eloquent voice. Berle wrote much of the speech Roosevelt gave at the San Francisco Commonwealth Club. Arguing that the nation's industrial plant was probably overbuilt and that the creators of new railroads and factories "were as likely to be a danger as a help," the candidate described the fundamental task for the future as one of distributing the country's wealth more equitably and "of adapting the existing economic organizations to the service of the people." The major task of the government, he continued, was to assist in the development of a new "economic declaration of rights," which should include the right of all to a comfortable living and to own property. To achieve these goals, government would have to restrict "the manipulator and even the financier" and to restrain the "lone wolf," "the unethical competitor," and "the reckless promoter." In other speeches during the long campaign, Roosevelt promised to restore the farmer's purchasing power and to help save homeowners from loss of their properties and small banks from forced liquidation. But the Commonwealth Club speech was the only really radical one Roosevelt made during the campaign. He naturally attacked Hoover for a great many things, and by implication suggested that his own Administration would take the opposite tack. But if one focuses on his positive proposals, one can find little that would have antagonized the conservative voter.

Herbert Hoover was a sad figure during the election contest. Overworked, and bewildered by the persistence of the Depression, he did not campaign until October. Then came real disaster for the man and for his party. In his Des Moines speech he set the theme for the campaign and for the party for the next twenty years. Instead of centering his attack on Roosevelt's inconsistencies, he chose to depict his opponent as a radical who would destroy the American system. In his powerful Madison Square Garden speech, he charged that the New Deal would enslave the masses by the creation of a giant bureaucracy, run the government into ruinous debt, debase the currency by a ruthless inflation, undermine the national credit, and destroy the Supreme Court. This was no ordinary political contest, he warned in his parting shot, but rather a decision whether or not to depart from "a hundred and fifty years of American tradition," and one which would determine "the direction our nation will take over a century to come."

In drawing a fixed line where there was in reality little to mark, the President may have unwittingly shoved the New Deal further to the left. By adopting a position of rigid and doctrinaire conservatism, he confirmed his party in the narrow beliefs which were to help make it an impotent, impractical minority for the next two decades and to deprive the majority of a responsible opposition.

The discerning voter in 1932 was faced with a difficult choice. The Socialist Party, running Norman Thomas as its candidate, had dropped most of its ideology and had become an ineffective group with only 1,200 dues-paying members. The Communists, despite the country's years of hardship, were little better off. The minor parties, "Coin" Harvey's Liberty Party and Jacob Coxey's Farmer-Labor Party, were more a subject for jokes than for serious consideration. This left the alternative of the two major candidates—one who smilingly carried varying ideologies on both shoulders, and the other who, patently weary and disheartened, seemed to hark back to Adam Smith for his inspiration. Organized labor, which had denounced both major party platforms, refused to commit itself. And business, large and small, was more sharply split between the two candidates than it had been in years. The overwhelming Roosevelt victory was thus probably due to the majority's determination to vote against the ins and to cast a ballot for a hope and a very appealing personality. Whatever the cause, the election was a rout. Roosevelt defeated Hoover easily and carried with him sizable Democratic majorities in both houses of Congress.

The inconsistencies of Roosevelt's campaign, his appeal both to the right and to the left, presaged trouble for the future. His support ran from Tugwell and Berle on the left to Kennedy and Raskob on the far right. Both extremes, as well as the center of the party, claimed him after the election. In fact, he was the first President-elect since William Howard Taft about whom there was so much confusion among his supporters. It was such considerations that led Walter Lippmann to conclude before the campaign that Roosevelt had few if any really deep convictions. He was "not the dangerous enemy of anything," the journalist wrote; he was "too eager to please."

What then was Roosevelt on election day in 1932? Coming from an old, wealthy New York family, he had had the best education the country offered. But the nonacademic qualities that he thought educational institutions should promote are indicative of the man. Speaking in 1936, he maintained that proper education should instill, first, a "sense of fair play among men"; second, "a sense of equality"; and, finally, a devotion to "freedom in the pursuit of truth." The President was not a lover of books. He read detective stories and naval history, but otherwise spent his leisure sailing and collecting stamps. He had little interest in art and less in music, and, on the whole, was not very conversant with the world of contemporary ideas. When he was first introduced to Lord Keynes, the President was uncertain who the renowned British economist was. Another key to the complex Roosevelt mentality was his practical cast of mind, his love of the concrete. The questions he raised during his Presidency were not what this or that measure would do to the nation's ideology in the long run, but how the unemployed could be fed, the homeless housed. If Roosevelt retained something of the cultivator's practical mind, he also knew the city and its ways. A good portion of his life had been spent in New York City, and during his governorship the problems of the nation's major metropolis were always among the most pressing he had to face. In the early part of his life, it is true, Roosevelt had been an urban aristocrat and something of a snob. But sometime, probably during the period when he was struck down with infantile paralysis so severe that he would never walk unaided again, he acquired a pervasive sense of sympathy for his fellow beings.

Confident of man's power and will to change himself, and tolerant perhaps to a fault of man's minor vices, he was an incorrigible optimist—almost a shallow one, some said. Perhaps this peculiar neohumanist spirit lay at the base of the New Deal. In the face of human need or deprivation, all other values were secondary. "The only real capital of the nation," he once said, was "its natural resources and its human beings." Federal relief to the masses might lead to corruption and bureaucracy, he acknowledged. It might create a huge federal deficit and upset the budget. But these were minor evils compared to the specter of hungry men. No decent democracy could afford "to accumulate a deficit in the books of human fortitude."

As a young man in the 1912 campaign, Roosevelt spoke of the necessity of establishing a social system in which both competition and cooperation were essential ingredients. How much of each a society needed at any one time depended on what it had to do to provide a decent living for its citizens. In his 1929 inaugural speech as governor of New York, he said he was prepared to preach the doctrines of laissez-faire and private enterprise. Two years later, he launched the state on a vast relief and social-security program. He remained all his life scornful of social absolutes and theoretical constructs that limited a society's attempt to achieve a good life for its citizens. What economic and social doctrines he stressed at any time depended much on what was happening. Had a sharp recovery taken place in the fall and winter of 1932–33, the New Deal, as we know it, might never have been conceived. Instead, a banking crisis occurred, bringing the country to the brink of a social abyss. That crisis, widespread unemployment, and increasing personal want created the famous "hundred days," as well as much that came afterward.

4

The New Deal and
the Politics of Urbanism

THE New Deal has often been characterized as a sort of Santa Claus political movement. Enormous expenditures of federal funds offered something tangible to almost everyone—businessman, miner, farmer, laborer—and to almost every section—East, West, urban, rural, big city, and small town. By gross definition, it was all of this. But the New Deal Administration was also the first one that became intimately concerned with urban life and city problems, in spite of Franklin Roosevelt's belief that most American strengths and virtues resided in the countryside. The cities received billions of dollars in aid, primarily because most of the country's citizens and problems—unemployment, hunger, and disrupted public services—were concentrated there. The patrician President, inclined toward almost any scheme to renew agriculture and even to resettle the urban jobless on farms, entered reluctantly into many of the programs that shored up the cities, funneled aid to urban minority and recent immigrant groups, and made the big cities crucial to the New Deal political coalition. But the New Deal marked the beginning of a new era in relations between Washington and the cities, and produced programs and policies that would influence and shape urban America for decades.

Prior to 1933, one wing of the Democratic Party had been based in New York, Boston, and Chicago political machines, which in turn rested on racial, religious, and immigrant minorities. But in Philadelphia, Pittsburgh, Chicago, and elsewhere, dominant Republican machines turned in approximately the same political results. The big-city machines of both parties were built on local loyalties for favors received locally, were often quite independent of the national organizations, and were most often obsessed with controlling local court and statehouse. New Deal ideology and activities bound minorities to other middle-class and lower economic groups to form an impressive Democratic majority in practically every large city, irrespective of its past political tradition. During the financial chaos of the Depression, urban leaders renounced the goal of local political independence ("home rule") that had enjoyed the support of bosses and reformers alike in an earlier era, and looked to the state and federal governments for assistance. When most states did nothing, mayors came directly to Washington for help and formed lobbying groups and other national associations—most notably, the United States Conference of Mayors—to make their interests known to congressmen and bureaucrats in the major government departments. By 1938, the main support of the New Deal Democratic Party lay in the nation's cities.

The urban emphasis of the New Deal did not develop immediately and were never joined in a conscious and effective urban policy. In the early Roosevelt years, more universal problems had to be faced. Among them was the breakdown of the national banking system. Despite the improvements made by the Federal Reserve Act, the banking system during the 1920's remained chaotic. Numerous state banks, weak in resources and relatively unregulated, existed outside the Federal Reserve System. Even within the system, there was no effective way to pool regional or national resources so as to aid institutions embarrassed by frozen assets. The London *Economist* characterized the American system as "unregulated, unstable, and unsound." Throughout the twenties, the number of banks closing their doors rose steadily, especially in the depressed agricultural regions. By 1929, almost seven thousand banks had closed. After the market crash, the pressure on banking institutions increased by the month. In 1931, President Hoover asked the major institutions to pool their resources to aid weaker units. Turned down by the financiers, the President recommended the establishment of the Reconstruction Finance Corporation, creating machinery whereby the government might lend money to distressed banks. Although the RFC acted with dispatch, providing more credit to banks than the President was willing to offer to public relief, the pressure continued to grow. In December 1930, the first important large-city bank, the Bank of the United States, had closed its doors in New York. Thereafter, public distrust of banking strength created runs all over the nation. In 1932, failures rose to the rate of forty institutions a day, tying up on the average $2 million of deposits per institution. Before the election in October 1932, the governor of Nevada instituted a bank holiday to save some of the state's banks from disaster. The holiday movement spread rapidly after Michigan's governor closed all Detroit banks on February 14, 1933. Within three weeks, bank holidays were declared in many states.

Faced with the awesome possibility that the economy's circulatory system would suddenly stop, Hoover tried desperately to avoid impending chaos. But big-city bankers, fearful for the solvency of their own institutions, could only suggest that the government deposit money without security in banks tottering on the brink. The lame-duck Congress—many of its members already defeated in the election—passed the problem to the President, as did the Federal Reserve Board. Hoover then tried to get an agreement with the incoming President, which would have limited Roosevelt's freedom of action to what the Hoover Administration considered sound financial practices. But Roosevelt was not to be entangled with Hoover's troubles until after inauguration day on March 4. Receiving little help from anyone, the harassed Hoover did little or nothing. As a result, on the eve of inauguration day, more than half of the nation's financial institutions were closed and those remaining open faced the peril of massive runs. Fear, gradually smothering the productive resources of the nation, had reached continental proportions. Practically the entire nation, including the so-called captains of industry and finance, looked to Washington and the new President as a last resort against calamity.

New Presidents in their first week in office are usually freer to make decisions than at any other time in their careers. Because the Democratic Party had been out of office for so long, Roosevelt was even freer than most of his predecessors. What really liberated the President from ordinary restraints was the depth of the crisis he and the nation faced. In March 1933, the majority of citizens and probably Congress would have followed Roosevelt along any path he chose that gave promise of mitigating their woes and their fears. The common peril stilled criticism, invalidated normal procedures, and even suspended constitutional doubts.

Roosevelt soon made it evident that he was aware of the extraordinary situation freeing him from platform and campaign promises, and from normal congressional opposition. "The only thing we have to fear," Roosevelt said in his inaugural address, is "fear itself—nameless, unreasonable, unjustified terror which paralyzes needed efforts to convert retreat into advance." Of the many things the new Administration did during those hectic days from March to June, commonly called in retrospect the "hundred days," perhaps the most important was to animate the government and the country with a sense of action, if not of precise purpose. On March 4, Roosevelt boldly told the country that he expected unusual speed and action from Congress, but that if Congress should fail, he was prepared to seek extraordinary emergency powers of a wartime nature to confront the desperate situation.

On his first day in office, the President, without grant of authority, closed all the nation's banks. Five days later, he presented to Congress a draft banking bill which, when passed in a few hours, went far to preserve banking assets and to restore public confidence in the financial structure. Observing on the following day that many liberal governments had been "wrecked on rocks of loose fiscal policy," he asked for and obtained wide powers to economize on veterans' pensions and to slash pay rates to federal employees. But within the next six weeks he secured the passage of a spate of measures involving the expenditure of billions of dollars. Half a billion was made available to the states for direct unemployment relief. Three billion was appropriated for a gigantic public-works program. The creation of the Civilian Conservation Corps and the farm and home loan policy to rescue distressed mortgages obligated the government for billions more.

The gigantic New Deal relief program, which in its entirety and over an eight-year span touched almost one-third of the nation's workers, was at once the most controversial and the most popular of the Administration's efforts. The conservative and parochial-minded objected, of course, as much to Roosevelt's assumption that to every man was due the opportunity to work as to the federal government's direct efforts to provide the jobs. They denounced the New Deal reasoning that by such "pump priming" the economy might be restored to something near normal, and they even opposed the extensive public-works program which Hoover had accepted in a much less generously financed version. The insistence of Secretary of Interior Harold Ickes, director of the Public Works Administration, that the public buildings, dams, schools, and highways to be built be of palpable use and initiated locally did little to soften the more conservative criticism, even though the extent to which private contractors and the building industry would profit was obvious.

But far more opposition arose to the many relief projects headed by the former director of social work in New York State. Harry Hopkins rapidly became for many Republicans the New Deal *bête noire,* perhaps because of his single-minded devotion to Roosevelt, but perhaps also because his ruthless energy and amazing efficiency were wedded to a bundle of intensely held social convictions. He was, observed a colleague, "a high-minded holy roller in a semi-religious frenzy."

Hopkins became public champion of the "immediate work instead of dole" approach for the unemployed, even though many of the projects amounted only to leaf sweeping and grass cutting. The public ridicule of the relief worker on the Federal Emergency Relief Administration's payroll as a man leaning on a shovel and of the project as "boondoggling" deterred Hopkins not at all from combining a deep concern for human dignity with the administration of public relief. Embedded in the philosophy of the New Deal's "permanent" relief agency, the Works Progress Administration, was the injunction against downgrading labor. Trained men were not asked to do manual labor if it was possible to arrange for them to pursue their own skills. Out of this approach, as well as Mrs. Franklin D. Roosevelt's concern for intellectuals and the arts, came projects for writers, artists, musicians, and dancers. The young were provided for by the National Youth Administration, which kept many of them in school and more in pocket money.

New Deal relief projects were devised for the countryside as well as for the city. But because the great bulk of unemployment was urban, and because many of the more conservative-minded rural places refused to accept federal grants, a large proportion of relief funds went to the cities. And thus the recent immigrants and the racial minorities profited disproportionately from the federal largesse. Since such people were traditionally the last hired and the first fired, they were natural candidates for relief rolls. The persistent affinity of racial, religious, and national minorities for the New Deal was not all explained by relief checks, but the election slogan in Harlem, New York City, "Ham every day on the WPA instead of a turkey [on Thanksgiving Day] with Tammany," was eloquent of a new order of politics.

The New Deal's legislative program during the hundred days was just as paradoxical as its actions on economy and spending. Although the President had spoken of driving the money changers from the temple and of substituting "social values" for "monetary profit," his financial proposals were characteristically far more temperate than his language. The financial acts of 1933 prohibited commercial banks from trading in securities. They gave the Federal Reserve banks far more power over their members in regulating the rate of interest charged and the volume of loans made. They transferred many decision-making powers from the twelve regional banks to the national Federal Reserve Board, and made the latter more responsive to the President. The Securities Act provided for rigorous regulation over what had been a self-governing, and sometimes chaotic, free market. But though these acts signaled a shift of power away from private entrepreneurs to the government and made possible for the first time a managed currency, they abolished neither private ownership of the nation's basic financial institutions nor monetary gain as the impelling force of the economy.

The Administration's programs for agriculture and business were radical, when measured by historic standards. Inspiration for the Agricultural Adjustment Act came principally from Henry Agard Wallace, who managed *Wallace's Farmer* after his father left the editorship in 1921 to become Secretary of Agriculture under Harding and Coolidge. Throughout the twenties, the younger Wallace preached the doctrine that the farmers would have to manage their production as capital and labor did. During the lean year of 1931, Wallace asked for voluntary crop reduction and government crop insurance, and coined the phrase the "ever normal granary." Other ideas for the new plan came from the McNary-Haugen proposals, the experience of the Hoover Federal Farm Board, from George N. Peek of the old War Industries Board, and from the agricultural economist John Black, who had studied a scheme of crop control in Germany.

The essential idea behind the AAA was to pay farmers for curtailing production of major crops in order to achieve a balance between supply and demand. Production of important staples was to be limited until their prices reached "parity"—defined as the price ratio existing during the years 1909–14—with nonagricultural prices. This "ordered harvest," it was hoped, could be secured by an elaborate plan of setting marketing quotas for individual farmers, who would be paid for their reduced output by a tax on the processers of farm goods. The necessity for approval by two-thirds of the farmers involved gave the plan a democratic aura. The AAA abolished neither private holdings nor the profit motive in farming. But it did emphasize group ends and objectives at the expense of the individual. As violations of both the spirit and the letter of the Act grew, so did the necessity for increasing restrictive and coercive measures. Eventually, production quotas for some crops were assigned to particular acreage plots, and the right to grow and sell specific produce at the going market price without penalties was frozen to the ownership of particular land parcels. Agricultural planning thus introduced a host of regulations which substantially curtailed the freedom of the individual husbandman.

The New Deal's major hopes for recovery lay in the National Industrial Recovery Act, the essential ideas for which came from organized business. Arguing that unfair and unregulated competition had in part destroyed prosperity, Gerard Swope, president of the General Electric Company, proposed a vast scheme for the self-regulation of business, which he hoped would "stabilize production and prices" and lead to recovery. This idea, supported by the United States Chamber of Commerce, appealed to the planning-minded Administration, which also saw it as a way to stabilize wages and spread existing work among more men, and at the same time as a vehicle to forestall much more radical labor legislation being proposed in Congress. At a press conference on April 12, Roosevelt said the NIRA's aims were to spread employment among a large number of people, to prevent any individual from working too many hours, and to stop the drift toward industrial concentration. The President described it as a national scheme for "the regulation of production." To achieve these diverse and contradictory ends, the congressional act set aside the antitrust laws and provided for the adoption of industrywide codes of business conduct. A national code prohibited the employment of anyone under sixteen years of age and established a minimum-wage scale of forty cents an hour.

In the hurried development of 557 separate industrial codes, adopted by representatives of various industries, small business had some voice, labor had little, and the consumer almost none. Some of the codes sought to curtail production by limiting the use of machines—spinning machines in the case of cotton textiles, for example—to a maximum number of hours a week. Others sought to establish minimum prices for industrial products by a complicated system of computing production costs. Practically all of them sought to abolish "unfair competition" by regulating the branding of products, the granting of credit terms, rebates for volume buyers, and other discriminatory sales practices. Inherent in the codes was the obvious desire to apportion markets, limit production, and to a degree eliminate price competition. Although the revolutionary scheme was described as one of self-government by industry, it was apparent that the codes were essentially made by the large industries and favorable to them. Hailing the advent of the codes, one Wall Street publication stated that in the long run the "large aggregates of finance capital" stood to benefit from the new regime. But even large business had to pay something for its new freedom from competition and antitrust laws: Section 7(a) of the NIRA gave labor the legal right to organize unions.

The NIRA also introduced the power of government into industrial matters where it had not existed before. Although the Administration hoped that the real enforcement of the Act would come from public pressure, punitive measures were written into it, and eventually Administrator General Hugh S. Johnson and his 4,500 fellow employees used them against violators. Never before in peacetime, except in antitrust actions for distinctly different purposes, had the government proceeded against individual businessmen in matters concerning hours of labor, prices, and selling methods.

During the hundred days, the business community had to submit to another great incursion of governmental power into what had been considered an essentially private domain. The Tennessee Valley Authority Act instituted not only regulation but outright government competition in the production and sale of electric power. The rise of the interstate electric-power industry had been one of the amazing business phenomena of the twenties. Technically, American industry led the world, and the spread of electrical lighting and appliances throughout cities and farmsteads effected a virtual revolution in American life. But the industry, essentially unregulated during the twenties, had become the plaything of corporate manipulators, who, piling holding company upon holding company, contributed little to efficiency and much to profit for the few.

Led by Senator George W. Norris of Nebraska, a small band of congressional reformers sought unsuccessfully in the twenties to bring the interstate aspects of industry under effective public control. They did manage to defeat the efforts of Presidents Coolidge and Hoover to sell the publicly constructed Wilson Dam on the Tennessee River to private interests. Norris's long struggle was partially successful in April 1933, when Roosevelt proposed and Congress passed an act creating the Tennessee Valley Authority, a public corporation with wide powers to plan for the full development of the natural resources of the Tennessee River valley, comprising most of the upper South. Ostensibly, the TVA was established to engage in flood control and to further navigation of the river, tasks in which it succeeded admirably. But a subsidiary clause in the Act empowered it to sell power, and within a few years the manufacture, transport, and sale of electric current from its twenty newly constructed dams became its major concern. In proposing the Act, Roosevelt had spoken of creating a federal yardstick by which to measure the costs incurred and profits won by private industry. At the eventual cost of over a billion dollars, the New Deal created a vast industrial complex publicly owned and publicly operated, competing directly with private enterprise.

The greatest New Deal challenge to business prestige and power came about through Section 7(a) of the NIRA. Neither inspired nor particularly wanted by the Roosevelt Administration, Section 7(a) had been added to the Act by organized labor's friends in Congress as a minimum payment for their support of the industrial measure. While the President was gravely concerned about the plight of millions of workingmen out of jobs, he spent little time and thought on the languishing labor organizations. In fact, the NIRA without Section 7(a) would probably have weakened the unions, since it established, by government mandate, minimum-wage and maximum-hour regulations, objectives which the unions had been unsuccessful in obtaining for their members. But Section 7(a) asserted that labor had the right to organize and bargain collectively "through representatives of their own choosing." It also outlawed the yellow-dog contract and stipulated that men could not be forced to join a company union as a condition of employment. Although these were simply declarations without means of administrative enforcement, the union movement became so inspirited during the next few months that a National Labor Board was created to mediate strikes in August 1933, with the staunchly pro-labor Senator Robert F. Wagner as chairman. Within two years, membership in organized labor rose by over 25 percent.

Toward the end of the hundred days, a perplexed reporter asked the President at the newly reinstituted news conference whether the government was embarked upon a program of economy or spending, on one that would lead to the restoration of capitalism or to nationalization and socialism. Roosevelt's answer that the government was bent upon feeding the hungry and restoring prosperity did not clarify the issue much. But a look at the record of the three months should have supplied the answer. Except for the TVA, there had been nothing really revolutionary in the New Deal program. Direct relief and managed agriculture were radical in terms of the past; but the NIRA had been conceived by the business community and on balance, even with its wage and hour controls and Section 7(a), its immediate, if not long-run, consequence was to bolster the health of big business. During 1933 and the early months of the following year, the business and conservative community interpreted it that way. The U.S. Chamber of Commerce, the *Magazine of Wall Street, The Wall Street Journal,* and independent conservatives like David Lawrence agreed that thus far the New Deal's actions had been "inventive," "courageous," and "fair." During the latter half of the year, the most trenchant criticism of the Administration, in fact, came from labor and from those on the left, who demanded revolutionary action. The remobilization of the defeated and scattered right against the New Deal was mostly a matter of politics. During 1933, Republican leaders agreed that the New Deal program was so popular they could ill afford to be openly critical. But the 1934 congressional elections, which resulted in the most stunning defeat in history for the Republican Party, seemed to indicate that if the party were to survive it had to draw a line of distinction between itself and the New Deal. Herbert Hoover, looking backward as well as forward, led off the attack in 1934 by publishing his *Challenge to Liberty,* the tone of which was indicated in its first few pages. The New Deal, he wrote, represented "the most stupendous invasion of the whole spirit of liberty that the nation has witnessed since the days of Colonial America."

In part, the opposition to the New Deal came from a reviving business community. By the opening of 1934, the economy had climbed out of the pit of 1932 and 1933. Industrial production, which had stood at 56 percent of the preceding five-year average in March 1933, reached upward to 93 percent in June, and although wavering from that time on, the economy continued to inch forward. Aided by the drought and sizable government subsidies, farm prices were even more responsive to the general upturn: the average by 1935 was 66 percent higher than that of 1933. Corporation balance sheets looked better, and even the stock market showed signs of optimism. With returning health, the business community regained its confidence and its voice. Relatively docile while desperately sick, it now began to scan the bill for medical fees and was shocked to realize how much it had paid and was likely to pay in the future for the New Deal treatment.

The basic business principles clustering around such phrases as rugged individualism, competition, private enterprise, the profit motive, sound currency, and the gold standard had been cardinal tenets of the American businessman's faith. Now, if they had not been swept away, most of them were in the process of being radically modified. From being public heroes, businessmen had become whipping boys, or at least the subjects of common jest. The once awe-inspiring title "banker" had become "bankster" in common argot, and the allusion to Al Capone and his gangsters measured the extent of his fall from grace. The 1934 elections made it apparent that a real shift in social power from the business to the political community had occurred. Politicians and bureaucrats were setting rules for the new game and enforcing them.

Business anxiety was not without justification, even though during his first term Roosevelt usually talked a good deal more radically than his subsequent actions warranted. In the four years after 1933, the President proposed at one time or another what amounted to a new bill of rights, which if enacted into law would have insured the creation of a semisocialist economy. He referred to the right to work, the right to adequate food, to housing, a decent education, clothing, and recreation. At other times, he suggested expanding the TVA concept to include all the great river systems of the country.

F.D.R.'s so-called brain trusters were given, even more than their chief, to loquacious radicalism. Henry Wallace published a book in 1933 entitled *New Frontiers,* in which he argued that since the days of American expansion were past, the keynote of the new age would be cooperation instead of competition, social inventions instead of mechanical ones, "the worship of beauty and justice and joy of spirit" instead of the worship of "power and wealth." A. A. Berle, Jr., in the *Saturday Review of Literature,* claimed that the collapse of private enterprise in 1929 was as significant in human history as the collapse of feudalism, since it inevitably meant a transfer of many individual transactions into "a public process." But of all brain trusters, perhaps Rexford G. Tugwell produced the most fearful hobgoblins for the business community. In his book *The Industrial Discipline and Governmental Arts* (1933), Tugwell predicted a great augmentation of "government compulsion" to spur industrial production, widen public access to goods, protect wage scales, limit price rises, and direct capital investments. "We need," Tugwell concluded, "some kind of compulsion to efficiency to adhere to a common purpose." Since Wallace, Berle, Tugwell, and Raymond Moley were commonly supposed to be the drafting architects of the New Deal's future—as expressed by a chant going around the country: "Tugwell, Berle, Moley—Holy! Holy! Holy!" —it is small wonder the disciples of private enterprise were shaken by the prospect.

With some justification, conservatives saw the specter of revolution everywhere during the first four years of the New Deal. After their dismal performance in the elections of 1932, the Communists were flexing their muscles, assaulting every political movement to their right. On the moderate left, Midwestern farmers demanded more action in defense of their homes and living standards. Meanwhile, California had produced two movements, both of which were far more radical in their aims than the New Deal's. Under the leadership of the old socialist Upton Sinclair, the "End Poverty in California," or EPIC, organization demanded the flotation of a gigantic bond issue with which to establish state-owned farms and workshops where the unemployed could be put to work in useful production. Simultaneously, a former Long Beach health official, Dr. Francis E. Townsend, respectable churchgoer and foe of radicalism, organized a movement to give every citizen over sixty years of age a pension of $200 a month, provided the pension scrip was spent in thirty days. His scheme, Townsend argued, would take care of the superannuated workers laid off during the Depression, remove them from the labor market, and restore prosperity. Fueled by distress among the aged, the Townsend movement took on some of the character of a religious crusade, presumably supported by some 2 million voters organized in five thousand local clubs spread across the nation. The appeal of the scheme for Townsend followers was indicative of the widespread destitution among the older age groups; it was also eloquent of the changing values of the traditionally conservative older generation. The Puritan injunction to work and save had now been transmuted into an injunction to retire and spend, at government expense.

Since 1930, Father Charles E. Coughlin, priest of an impoverished parish near Detroit, had been promoting on his radio program a mixture of religion and politics. Son of a poor Irish laborer, who had earned a doctor's degree from the University of Toronto at the age of twenty-three, Coughlin developed an impressive radio personality, and by 1931 he was broadcasting every Sunday evening on a national hookup of twenty-two stations to an audience estimated in the millions. Blasting Communism, Fascism, the Wall Street millionaires, and the prevailing monetary system, Coughlin supported Roosevelt in 1932. By 1934, he was disenchanted with the New Deal and organized his National Union for Social Justice. Among the more radical elements of the Union's creed were proposals for the nationalization of "important natural resources," the control of private property for the public good, abolition of the Federal Reserve System, establishment of a government-controlled bank, and conscription of wealth as well as men in wartime.

All that was needed in 1935 to bring these diverse groups together in a new radical party was a skillful leader, a master politician of the radical tradition. In 1935, it looked as if that man was Senator Huey Long of Louisiana. Long arose out of the poverty and illiteracy of the rural South. As champion of the poor white, but unlike so many of his kind in the South never a Negro-baiter, Long was elected governor of Louisiana at the age of thirty and United States senator four years later. Once governor, he built modern roads into the back country, provided free school books for everyone, handsomely increased the physical resources of Louisiana State University, and constructed an impressive state hospital where, he promised, anyone in Louisiana could be treated free of charge. Long paid the bills for his program by income and inheritance measures and by a severance tax on oil. In passing his program, he met bitter opposition from the influential and wealthy elements which had hitherto controlled the state with an awesome disregard for conventional methods of politics and for the provisions of the state constitution. He dictated to the state legislature (even resorting to intimidating its individual members), ordered the university to construct buildings though there was no money for them in its budget, and surrounded himself with a bodyguard of gunmen in Al Capone fashion.

When Long left for the United States Senate, he fired the properly elected lieutenant governor so that he could place his own man in the governor's chair. A flabby, pudgy, red-nosed individual, with a vocabulary profane, earthy, and ungrammatical, he impressed his fellow senators as a man of inordinate energy and ambition. His major program was the "Share Our Wealth" movement. "There is no rule," he declaimed, "so sure as that the same mill which grinds out fortunes above a certain size, grinds out paupers at the bottom." If the wealth at the top was curtailed and properly distributed, he promised, a republic might be built in which every man was a king but no one wore a crown. Delighting to call himself the Kingfish of the movement, he elaborated his program after 1933 by promising everyone a minimum income of $2,000, a house, an automobile, and a radio, free homesteads, and free education. With a view to attracting Townsend and Coughlin support, he vigorously attacked Roosevelt. "The New Deal," he roared on the floor of the Senate, was "headed just as straight to hell as a martin ever went to a gourd." He assaulted international bankers and promised a pension to everyone over sixty-five. Townsend and Coughlin responded favorably to these invitations. In the spring of 1935, James A. Farley, Postmaster General and Roosevelt's able political adviser, took a secret poll which showed that Long might get as many as 4 million votes in 1936 and thus hold the balance of power between the two old parties.

While the radicals were mobilizing in 1935 to imperil the New Deal's tenure in Washington, so was the conservative right. The American Liberty League, organized in August 1934 in Miami, Florida, to "teach the necessity of respect for the rights of persons and property," was from the beginning identified with the big money, Wall Street, and large corporations. Among its founders were Al Smith, John W. Davis, John J. Raskob, William S. Knudsen, and Pierre du Pont. Simultaneously, a group of conservative Democrats including Davis, Al Smith, Governor Eugene Talmadge of Georgia, and William Randolph Hearst organized the Jeffersonian Democrats, whose object, it was rumored, was to defeat Roosevelt in 1936 by splitting the Democratic vote. The scheme for a third party was later vetoed by Smith and Raskob, but the organization's unwavering opposition to

Roosevelt was clearly and publicly expressed in 1935 and 1936.

The New Deal's difficulties in 1935 included more than political ones. Three years of experience with the AAA indicated that additional regulation, often of a coercive type, was needed to reduce the production of some crops without increasing the supply of others. Between March 1933 and January 1936, the federal government appropriated over $3 billion for public works and direct relief. Although many unemployed had been shifted from direct to work relief, in 1935 over 2.7 million people were still on direct relief and over 6 million were receiving some benefits from the government. The relief program, considered in 1933 as a temporary means to meet an emergency situation, now began to look as if it might be permanent.

Industrial affairs were, if anything, more chaotic than conditions in agriculture and relief. The desire of workers to have unions of their own was ignored by employers and a wave of strikes broke out in 1934, including some very bloody ones in the Southern textile regions. The National Industrial Recovery plan, the New Deal's major hope for economic health, was coming apart at the seams. Labor branded the NIRA a creator of industrial monopoly, and small business rapidly joined the opposition. The Administration was forced into more coercive measures, big industry became increasingly disenchanted with the program, and many experts decided that the NIRA was actually hurting expansion by raising prices and dampening demand. In the famous Schechter chicken case, the Supreme Court gave the NIRA the *coup de grâce* by unanimously declaring the Act unconstitutional on the two principal grounds of an improper delegation of legislative power and an unwarranted use of the interstate commerce powers of the federal government. Of the two, the latter was far more significant, since the distinction the court made between the direct and indirect effects of intrastate transactions on interstate commerce seemed to imperil many other important New Deal measures.

The future of the New Deal was doubtful during the spring of 1935. Many of its major programs were not producing the promised results. The Schechter decision imperiled the constitutional base for others. Politically, it was assailed by both the right and the left, within and without the Democratic Party. With the 1936 elections impending, the New Deal obviously needed a major blood transfusion if it was to remain politically healthy, but during much of 1934 the President acted as if his major reform work was finished. He called for no crusades and spoke out for few reforms.

After the elections of 1934, events began to push Roosevelt the politician back into action. The organization of the Liberty League and the Jeffersonian Democrats, the attacks of Long and Coughlin, the threat of Upton Sinclair and Townsend made it appear as if the American electorate were being rapidly divided between antagonistic left and right groups, as had happened in many European countries. Roosevelt was thoroughly aware of the rising discontent among liberal leaders of his own official family and equally sensitive to the hostility of the organized right. In his message of January 1935 opening Congress, he made a verbal attempt to consolidate his leadership of the reformers. He confessed that the New Deal had not as yet "weeded out the overprivileged" or "effectively lifted up the underprivileged." And he hinted strongly as to what course he would likely be following during the coming Presidential election: Americans "must foreswear" the acquisition of great wealth, which had created "undue private power over private affairs and to our misfortune over public affairs as well." During the next four months, however, the President did little to interfere with Congress, where a vicious battle was being conducted between the partisans of further reform and the conservatives. It was during those four months, also, that the Supreme Court killed the NIRA, that organized business for the first time voiced its unequivocal opinions of the New Deal, and that the Liberty League and the Jeffersonian Democrats began to attack the President personally.

Roosevelt consequently shifted sail and initiated a revitalization of the New Deal that some historians have called the "second hundred days." In June 1935, he called on Congress to pass a new tax bill that by raising income and inheritance taxes would stop the transmission of vast fortunes from generation to generation, a process "not consistent with the ideals and sentiments of the American people." The bill also sought to place a graduated tax on corporations, instead of the flat rate they were then paying. Popularly known as the "soak the rich" bill, it was a partial answer to Huey Long's proposed "Share Our Wealth" plan, and it obtained support in Congress on that basis.

Roosevelt's support of the Wagner Labor Bill, which outlawed company unions and guaranteed labor's right to organize and bargain collectively, was perhaps animated as much by his desire to retain the confidence of the laboring man as it was by his rising antipathy to big business. When the Wagner proposal first came to him in May 1934, he agreed that it might be helpful against "autocratic employers," but he observed that there were people on the labor side who were just as autocratic. Until mid-1935, the President showed little enthusiasm for the Wagner Bill. Irritated then by industry's adamant refusal to cooperate with organized labor, and sensitive to the rising business criticism of his Administration, he called on Congress to pass the bill, which would prevent the destruction of organized labor's independence and guarantee for every worker "freedom of choice and action." Nevertheless, Roosevelt never became an unreserved admirer of unions. He consistently felt that the National Labor Relations Board was far too pro-labor in its administration of the Wagner Act. His 1937 angry "plague on both their houses" expostulation against labor and business indicated his fundamental distrust of any organized private economic group.

The President's support of the Social Security Bill was probably a labor of affection and not mainly inspired by politics. As governor of New York he was heartily in favor of old-age and unemployment insurance. But it should be noted that the Social Security Act dealt a deadly blow to Dr. Townsend's more radical schemes. The Utilities Holding Company Act, requiring interstate power-producing firms to divorce themselves from their nonoperating structures, also contained principles that Roosevelt had previously supported. But his attack on private utility companies at this specific time was extremely useful throughout the South in countering Huey Long's charge that the New Deal had become the creature of private corporations.

In some ways, the second hundred days of the New Deal were almost as significant for the future of the country as the first hundred had been. The gift and inheritance-tax features of the "soak the rich" taxation bill probably changed somewhat the future division of wealth. The Wagner Labor Act obviously altered power patterns in the nation's industrial and commercial complex. During the first hundred days, the power of government had been sensibly increased at the expense of the business community. By the operations of the Wagner Act, organized labor was to win a significant portion, though not the lion's share, of the total power remaining to industry and commerce. The Social Security Act removed many economic hazards that once threatened the individual in a traditional capitalist society. And it unquestionably accelerated the change in American loyalties from the old rural nineteenth-century virtues of personal thrift, self-reliance, and individualism toward the new mutual-help and collective goals of midcentury.

The major reforms of the second hundred days enabled Roosevelt to beat back the challenge from the radicals—Long, Coughlin, and Townsend. They also practically predetermined the nature of the 1936 campaign, since it was obviously impossible after 1935 for the President to regain his pre-1935 pose of being above the battle of the left and the right and above the struggle of labor and capital. Roosevelt wrote to Roy Howard, the newspaper-chain owner, that with the passage of the Utilities Holding Company Act a breathing spell for business was at hand. But by that time conservative opposition had become so virulent that there was no chance of turning back to the moderate center position.

Few Administrations seeking reelection have received such a savage enfilade from so many different quarters as did the Roosevelt regime in 1936. The assassination of Huey Long spared the New Deal his rancorous voice. But Father Coughlin and his farmer-labor allies made up in part for the missing Long. The New Deal, Coughlin said in one of his wildest moments, had both of its feet of sordid clay mired, "one in the red mud of Soviet Communism, and the other, in the stinking cesspool of pagan plutocracy." From the right, the Liberty League shouted equally fervent denunciations. Roosevelt and the New Deal, it charged, had overturned the Constitution, sacrificed freedom, abolished private enterprise and individual initiative, and destroyed the American way of life. Even more sober conservative voices took up this chorus after ex-President Hoover alleged that the New Deal had introduced into the United States personal government based on F.D.R.'s "collectivist theories" and "the foreign creeds of Regimentation, Socialism and Fascism." The Chicago *Tribune's* attack was less qualified. "The Red New Deal with a Soviet seal, sired in an alien land" was a sample of the poetic efforts of this paper, warning readers daily in a front-page box that they had only so many days in which to save their country.

One might have expected the 1936 national Republican convention to have written a platform and chosen a candidate that would have been palatable to the old guard of the eighties and nineties. Actually, it did neither. Bridging the gap between the party's passion and its sense of expediency, the convention borrowed the New Deal program while denouncing its philosophy, promising that the Republicans would provide the same services but with less ideology and much more efficiency. The convention then proceeded to nominate a pair of Theodore Roosevelt progressives, Governor Alfred M. Landon of Kansas and Frank Knox, the Chicago newspaper owner and publisher.

Fortune shone on Roosevelt during 1936. It was a good year economically. The volume of industrial production almost doubled that of four years before, farm income rose from $4 billion in 1932 to $7 billion, and unemployment dropped by over 4 million from the figure of the previous Presidential election year. Even the Supreme Court's action in denying the constitutional validity of one important new program after another brought unexpected dividends. When the court declared the Agricultural Adjustment Act unconstitutional, the Department of Agriculture announced a new subsidy program to stop soil erosion. Almost immediately thereafter, a series of violent dust storms, following a persistent spring drought, threatened to blow away most of the topsoil on the Great Plains.

By his 1935 legislative program, Roosevelt had annihilated his radical opposition. The organization of the American Labor Party in New York and of Labor's Non-Partisan League nationwide, both pledged to Roosevelt, was the direct political result of the Wagner Act. Even the American Communists, following the Moscow directive to support popular-front governments against the

Fascist threat, muted their campaign against the New Deal. Roosevelt was also fortunate in his opposition. Though the opposing candidates were not agents of reaction, many of their vocal supporters resorted to clichés so divorced from reality that the official candidates were overlooked.

Roosevelt did not run against Landon and Knox. He ran against Hoover, the Liberty League, the United States Chamber of Commerce, the National Association of Manufacturers, Robert R. McCormick's Chicago *Tribune,* the Hearst newspapers, and most of the American press. In his acceptance speech at Philadelphia, he described his enemies as "economic royalists" who had created "a new despotism," a new "industrial dictatorship" that was depriving the majority of Americans of freedom and the pursuit of happiness. Freedom, he observed, was no half-and-half affair. The average American, "guaranteed equal opportunity in the polling place . . . must have equal opportunity in the market place." He concluded with a call for his generation of Americans to meet their "rendezvous with destiny" in a great reform crusade. In September, the President said he hoped to achieve "an ordered economic democracy." In his last speech of the campaign, in Madison Square Garden in New York, he went even further in his challenge to the industrial and conservative opposition. Never before, he exclaimed, had these forces been so united in their opposition and in their hatred of a candidate. He welcomed their hatred, he retorted, and if in his first Administration "the forces of selfishness and lust for power met their match," he hoped that during his second they would "meet their master." Pointing out that the New Deal was accused of wanting improved conditions for workers and farmers, increased income for consumers, protection for the crippled and the blind, and food for the poor and the jobless, he admitted to the particulars of every charge and ended with a promise: "For these things too and for a multitude of things like them, we have only just begun to fight. . . ."

The election results of 1936 were hardly credible. Roosevelt won by 11 million votes, the largest popular plurality on record up to that time. He carried every state except Maine and Vermont. The Republican delegations in the Senate and the House were reduced to the almost unbelievable figures of 17 and 89, respectively. The elections were notable for other reasons. Never before had the United States been so sharply divided on economic lines. Return after return indicated that wealthy and upper-middle-class neighborhoods were mobilized almost solidly for Landon, the slums and lower-class areas almost solidly for Roosevelt. The important newspapers of the nation, except in the South, almost unanimously supported the Republican candidate. With them were the solid ranks of business magazines and business organizations. Union organizations, on the other hand, were almost all for Roosevelt. A radical shift of power had taken place in the country between 1932 and 1936. Business prestige and the influence of wealth were probably never at a lower ebb than in November 1936. Predictions were numerous that the Republican Party would die. The prestige of Roosevelt, of the reformers, of the planners, and of organized labor was never higher.

New Deal history is full of paradoxes. But possibly none is so striking as the contrast between Roosevelt's campaign promises and the legislative results following each of his canvasses. Although he promised little during the campaign of 1932, Roosevelt then proceeded to harvest one of the most comprehensive reform programs in American history. During the 1936 campaign, he predicted that the period of social pioneering under the New Deal aegis had just begun. Since one-third of the nation was still "illhoused, ill-clad, and ill-nourished," he observed in his second inaugural address on January 20, 1937, the present was no time for pausing on the reform road that lay ahead. Given that statement of intention and the overwhelming New Deal victory of 1936, it was reasonable to expect that Roosevelt's second four years would be punctuated with as many important legislative measures as the first. That exactly the contrary happened was due to many diverse and complex reasons; but, admittedly, the first decisive check of the New Deal and the start of its decline lay in the Supreme Court struggle.

The 1933 court was largely the conservative body that it had been during the twenties. Charles Evans Hughes, the onetime progressive, had replaced William Howard Taft as Chief Justice in 1930. But, according to an estimate of *Time* magazine, "the pure white flame of Liberalism had burned out in Hughes, to a sultry ash of conservatism." On the liberal side of the bench, Benjamin Cardozo had replaced Oliver Wendell Holmes. Otherwise, the court was identical to the court of the twenties, dominated by the Harding and Coolidge appointees, with Louis Brandeis, Harlan Stone, and occasionally Owen Roberts as a protesting minority. After the first hundred days of the New Deal, Bertram Snell, the Republican House leader, talked with Chief Justice Hughes about organizing resistance to the reformers. Hughes apparently cautioned him that the time had not yet arrived when Republican and conservative leaders could safely crusade against the President's program. Subsequently, in 1934, the Chief Justice joined a 5–4 majority of the court in finding constitutional both a Minnesota act giving courts the right to postpone the foreclosure of mortgages and a New York law setting minimum prices for milk. But Hughes's general dictum in these cases that, while the emergency of the Depression might "furnish the occasion for the exercise of power," it did not create additional powers, gave the conservatives heart; the court, they hoped, was preparing a position from which to attack the more radical New Deal measures.

They were not disappointed. By a unanimous decision in May 1935, the court in the Schechter case overturned the NIRA, a finding which few people regretted. The court found the law unconstitutional because of the federal government's limited power to regulate interstate commerce. Only those matters that had a direct effect upon interstate commerce, it declared, were susceptible to federal power. If the court were to hold that only goods in transit across the state borders fell within their restricted definition of interstate commerce, then, as the President pointed out at the time, much of the New Deal legislation was in danger. During 1936, the court justified Roosevelt's fears. With either Hughes or Roberts or both joining the majority, the court struck down the Agricultural Adjustment Act and the Guffey Act regulating the production and hence the price of coal. At the same time, by a 5–4 decision, it invalidated a New York State minimum-wage law for women on the grounds that such a law violated the freedom of contract guaranteed by the Fourteenth Amendment. Thus it looked as if neither federal nor state government could regulate the fundamental conditions of labor. If that was so, it was likely that the Wagner Labor Act and even the Social Security Act were threatened.

During its previous 140 years of existence, the court had held only some sixty federal laws unconstitutional; now in 1935 and 1936 it found eleven New Deal measures void. Justice Stone, one of the minority, felt that the session ending in June 1936 had been the most disastrous in the history of the court. Moreover, the lower federal courts had caused as much devastation to the New Deal program. Within three years, circuit and district courts had issued over fifteen hundred injunctions against administrative officials of the numerous New Deal agencies, injunctions which at times almost brought to a halt important operations of such federal administrative bodies as the TVA and the National Labor Relations Board.

Roosevelt and the New Deal had a perfect opportunity to challenge the court before the electorate and utilize the 1936 campaign as a referendum on the issue. But neither the President nor his chief aides spoke out during the campaign. The Democratic platform promised only that if the New Deal was invalidated by judicial action, constitutional means would be found to reverse the decisions. The overwhelming election victory of 1936 would have proved a heady wine for any politician. And it proved so for Roosevelt. The very size of the victory probably led to an entrapment.

When, on February 3, 1937, Roosevelt submitted his judiciary reform bill to Congress, he could rightfully be accused of having acted cavalierly toward the democratic process. The bill would have empowered the President to appoint a new federal judge whenever an incumbent, on reaching the age of seventy, failed to retire within six months; it limited the number of such Supreme Court appointees to six, thus enabling the President to increase the size of the court to fifteen. The measure was prepared in secrecy. Most of the Cabinet and the Democratic congressional leaders were unaware of its existence until its presentation. It was accompanied by a justification based principally on the argument that old and infirm justices were impeding the judicial process and contributing to the crowded dockets. Since it was clear that what Roosevelt wanted was new judges who would agree with the New

Deal, the disingenuous explanation hurt the proposal as much as did the secrecy with which it was prepared.

Dismayed by the President's refusal to consult them on the court bill and by his later rather blunt use of patronage to gain his ends, many liberals in Congress joined their conservative colleagues in opposition. A similar movement of moderate and liberal opinion stirred throughout the country. From sources that hitherto either had supported the President or had treated him with consideration came sharp judgments of censure. "Lack of good faith," "lawless legality," "political sharp practice," and "intent to deceive," were just a few of the phrases that must have stunned the overconfident Roosevelt.

Within a few weeks, it was clear that the President had for the first time lost control of Congress. But the most devastating blow to the court-packing scheme was probably delivered by the court itself. With Hughes and Roberts palpably shifting their constitutional views, the court on March 29, 1937 *(West Coast Hotel v. Parrish),* declared a state of Washington minimum-wage statute valid in such broad language that the legality of any reasonable state regulation of wages and hours was assured. Less than a month later, in a series of cases featured by that of *NLRB v. Jones and Laughlin Steel Corporation,* the court agreed to an even more astounding reversal of their recently enunciated doctrine on the interstate-commerce power. By viewing commerce as a unified stream from the manufacturing to the selling of goods, and not merely the transit over state borders, and by declaring that the federal power was applicable to all parts of the stream, the court in a 5–4 decision, with Hughes and Roberts assenting, opened the way for a vast augmentation of federal power over the nation's economic life. Quickly thereafter, the court upheld the Social Security Act, and in May, Justice Willis Van Devanter, one of the most unreconstructed conservatives, resigned. Almost simultaneously, the Senate Judiciary Committee defeated Roosevelt's bill, and eventually a weak compromise was agreed to, denying the President the right to pack the court but making possible by procedural changes quicker hearings and appeals on actions questioning the legality of administrative regulations. By its strategic retreat, the Supreme Court had saved much of its prestige, while losing a good deal of power. Roosevelt, on the other hand, had won much of what he was contending for, but at the expense of considerable prestige.

Within a short time, he was to lose even more. Throughout 1937, the new industrial unions employed the sit-down strike as one of their chief weapons against their more stubborn industrial opponents. This threat against property rights set off choleric spasms of "I told you so" from inveterate opponents of labor. But the sit-down technique also worried a good many moderates. Books with such titles as *When Labor Rules* conjured up ominous specters of the future, and the numerous and prolonged strikes in the automobile, rubber, and steel industries worried even a great many liberals. A more damaging blow to New Deal strength was the depression of 1937 to 1938. As the major indices fell off rapidly, the stock market plunged downward. Unemployment reached the 8 million mark. Forgetting the balanced budget it had earlier promised, the Administration asked for greatly increased relief appropriations. There was to be no turning back to the selfish creed of the twenties, Roosevelt said—"this nation has definitely said yes—with no 'but' about it—to the old Biblical question, 'Am I my brother's keeper?' " Most needy people were provided with relief, and the economists coined the new term "recession" to describe the retrograde movement. But though Roosevelt would never admit to the existence of the economic plunge, the "Roosevelt depression," as it was called by many, undermined many Administration claims at the same time that it dimmed the luster of the word "planning."

Meanwhile, the New Deal was meeting with constantly growing congressional opposition. At the opening of the 1937 session of Congress, the President outlined a major reform program, along with his historic court plan. Among the measures passed were the important Wagner Housing Act, providing federal funds for low-cost housing; a bill regulating the production of coal; renewal of a Trade Agreements Act; and a proposal to grant federal loans to farm tenants. But when Congress adjourned in August, no action had been taken on a bill to create seven regional TVA's, a wage-and-hour bill, a new farm program to replace the AAA, and an executive-reorganization scheme. All bore Administration tags, and all were reintroduced in 1938. But the conservative opposition, emboldened by the existence of the "recession," was even more vocal and more numerous than in the preceding year.

The nature of this new conservative bloc was defined by Representative Martin Dies of Texas. It should not be called a Southern bloc, the congressman declared, because it had "the support of nearly all small-town and rural congressmen. . . ." The enemies of the new coalition, he concluded, "are the men from the big cities which . . . are politically controlled by foreigners and transplanted Negroes, and their representatives in Congress have introduced insidious influences into the New Deal." The New Deal Democratic Party had been shaped by a Northern urban–Southern rural alliance, but the traditional and rural-minded South grew increasingly restive and, by 1938, seriously questioned its allegiance to the party's reform-oriented legislative program. For the first time, commentators noted the formation of a lasting alliance between Republicans and conservative Southern Democrats, a combination that was to plague Roosevelt the rest of his days.

Won from an obviously reluctant Congress was a new AAA act, a reactivation of the WPA and PWA, and a much-amended wage-and-hour bill. But despite most intense pressure from the White House, the executive-reorganization bill was defeated, and the regional TVA proposal never got beyond the committees. Meanwhile, from the conservative wing of his own party in Congress, Roosevelt heard charges of "executive domination," "tyranny," and even "dictatorship." The long-prevailing liberal wind turned in 1938, and with it the fortunes of the New Deal. The last important reform measure was the wage-hour bill of 1938. But, from then on, the liberal forces simply did not have enough votes to carry a major reform measure through Congress.

The President tried to meet the challenge in the primary elections of 1938 with his famous purge. Singling out a number of the most recalcitrant Democrats, including Senators Walter George of Georgia and Millard Tydings of Maryland, he attempted to defeat them in the primaries. Other conservative Democrats he obviously ignored, giving cheer and comfort to their opponents. The results of the purge, undertaken against the advice of many of the President's friends, were meager. The only marked success Roosevelt scored was in defeating New Yorker John O'Connor, chairman of the House Rules Committee. Elsewhere, his opponents won resounding victories and returned to Washington confident and resentful. The 1938 congressional elections also proved a turning point in the hitherto dismal fortunes of the Republican Party. Republican numbers in the House and the Senate had been regularly decreasing since 1930, and with each election it appeared that the party was headed for extinction. But in 1938 the Republicans almost doubled their numbers in the House, from 88 to 170, and gained eight seats in the Senate. Among the new Republican senators was the son of a former President, Robert Taft.

The New Deal as a militant reform organization killed itself with its own practical successes. By 1939, business had recovered from the recession of the previous year and was in a relatively healthy state compared to its condition in 1933. The farmers were buoyed by government subsidies. Both groups resented and feared the growing power of labor, especially after the sit-down strikes of 1937 and 1938. Despite the millions still unemployed, the Social Security Act had introduced at least some protection against vicissitude for the laboring classes. As a degree of economic health returned to an increasing number of people, the inclination for further social surgery diminished. A majority was still ready to defend the New Deal's past, but fewer had the incentive for further reform.

What had the New Deal accomplished? While it made no really revolutionary changes, it so accelerated existing trends that the years 1933–37 can be considered the most eventful in domestic politics since the Civil War. Among its many achievements, perhaps the most noteworthy was saving the nation from chaos in March 1933. Its success in inspiring confidence in the financial structure was critical in the history of the country. Only slightly less important was its recognition of the necessity for feeding the needy, supplying work for the jobless, and protecting the owners of homes, farms, and small business from foreclosure and bankruptcy. For all such relief work, the New Deal spent some $8 to $10 billion in nonrecoverable funds, an expenditure which despite the accompanying inefficiency and corruption was one of the best the nation ever made. Had deflation been permitted to run its course, as Secretary of the Treasury Andrew Mellon proposed, much of the middle class might have been wiped out. The New Deal attained what few democratic governments have been able to achieve in such periods of acute social stress. It was creative enough to retain the loyalties of the majority without forcing either the left or the right into violent opposition. Except on the labor-capital front, where the action was often local and almost never pointed toward government, there was less violence from marching men after 1933 than before that date.

By its economic and labor reforms, the New Deal shifted power somewhat from the reigning business classes, some of it to the newly inspired labor unions, but most to the government itself. The prestige of big business took a severe beating during the Depression and New Deal years, a pummeling that accounted for much of its choleric attitude toward the Roosevelt Administration. To a slight degree, the owning classes may have lost a fraction of their inheritance. The business classes also lost some of their power to make decisions vital to the economy—setting interest rates, determining how securities were sold, deciding the number of dwelling units in a community, establishing wage and salary scales and prices for electricity, coal, oil, and even farm goods. After 1933, such decisions were invariably influenced and sometimes controlled by the federal government. The New Deal did not, however, hamper the growth of large corporations or discourage the development of stronger ties between far-flung corporate enterprises and the federal government. The proliferation of new regulations and agencies actually created closer bonds between government and the largest economic entities and helped pave the way for the emergence of the military-industrial-governmental complex of the post-World War II era.

Economically and socially, the most significant failure of the New Deal was its inability to achieve recovery and a reasonably efficient economy. After six years of reform and spending, 8 to 10 million workers were still unemployed in 1939. Per capita income was still considerably below the 1929 figure. The economy did not recover its 1929 productiveness and did not absorb all the stagnant labor power until the government primed the pumps with billions for preparedness and war.

The New Deal also failed to develop an effective and comprehensive urban policy, and many governmental measures actually contributed to intensifying the long-term urban crisis. Public-works projects and housing programs were created mainly to generate employment and provide a spur to the economy, rather than to rebuild the cities or redirect their growth, or provide decent living conditions for millions of lower-class urban dwellers. The Federal Housing Administration, created in the Federal Housing Act of 1934, underwrote private loans primarily for new housing outside the inner cities. While this enabled thousands of families to purchase homes, it also stimulated the suburban-development boom and central-city decay, and provided support mainly for private construction and real-estate interests. Federal highway policies were equally shortsighted and were not coordinated with housing measures and other government programs which directly affected the cities. Public housing was initiated during the New Deal, but Roosevelt's reluctance to move in this direction, and rising conservative opposition toward the end of the decade, severely limited its impact. Thus, the dilemmas and failures of the nation's cities in the sixties and seventies were results, in part, of the negligence and confusion of federal policies dating back to the thirties.

The New Deal made almost as many substantial changes in the political system of the 1920's as it did in economic life. During its first four years, practically all important legislation originated, not in Congress, but in the executive branch of the government, the Wagner Labor Act constituting the principal exception. Throughout the hundred days, Congress virtually abstained from changing important features in the draft legislation presented to it. Often during this hectic period, newly created administrative agencies were empowered to issue their own regulations, which would have the same legality as if enacted by Congress. This tendency to delegate substantial legislative power to executive agencies was somewhat curtailed by the NIRA decision. But, by the end of the New Deal, Congress had almost ceased to be a legislation-initiating body in important matters and had become a reviewing, modifying, and negating agency.

Although Roosevelt's contest with the Supreme Court diminished his personal prestige, it also resulted in a substantial loss of power both for the court and for the several states. By radically broadening the federal power over interstate commerce, the court seriously limited its own power to declare federal economic regulation unconstitutional, as well as that of the state to intervene in economic matters. The residual powers of the states were also steadily reduced by the numerous New Deal subsidies, for along with each subsidy ran the mandate of the federal government. To help pay the mounting bills, the federal government invaded the traditional sources for state taxes, notably such consumer items as gasoline and automobile tires.

But probably the most potent force in the erosion of state power lay in the proliferation of direct beneficial relations between the federal government and the individual, which before 1933 had been rare. By 1939, the federal government and its agencies were making money payments to farmers, to men on relief and federal works projects, to college and high-school students, to the aged, to the unemployed, to widows, to dependent children, and to the needy blind. It was also making loans directly, or guaranteeing them at low interest rates, to homeowners, farmers, sharecroppers, and small businessmen. Hundreds of thousands of citizens took advantage of government-financed housing projects, school and college buildings, parks and playgrounds. As these ties became more numerous, and as the national pattern of movement from state to state in search of climatic or economic opportunity was accelerated, state and parochial loyalties withered and Americans looked more and more to Washington for solutions.

In the realm of politics, the New Deal scored perhaps its most astounding success. From 1894 to 1930, the Democratic Party had been distinctly a minority one, winning only three congressional elections in the thirty-six years, with two of those occurring in 1912 and 1914, when Theodore Roosevelt had split Republican unity. But after 1932 the New Deal fashioned a coalition of urban voters, composed largely of the underprivileged classes and minority ethnic groups, which, when tied to the South and other distressed rural areas, produced a majority in six successive congressional elections and in seven of the following nine. The new majority was, of course, a disparate one, full of conflicting and anomalous elements. By 1937, despite the Administration's extensive aid to agriculture, rural America was obviously alienated by the urban parts of the New Deal program. This was especially true of the South, whose attitude toward the racial and immigrant minorities in the Northern cities was intensely influenced by its own racial history. But so strong was the people's memory of the Depression, and so vivid the remembered contrast between Republican passivity and New Deal action, that the victorious coalition held together long after its reason for being had disappeared.

The interaction of the Great Depression and the New Deal left many other marks on American attitudes. Some nineteenth-century folk convictions were badly eroded during the twenties by the mass-consumption society, with its emphasis upon mass sales, mass advertising, and installment buying, and by the hedonistic appeal of the automobile, the movies, and the radio. The Depression and the New Deal rapidly speeded up that process. By the mid-thirties, it could be questioned whether the majority of Americans believed that work was altogether good and idleness or leisure necessarily bad, that any man could really find a job if he looked for one, that a man who worked hard got ahead, that personal security was the responsibility of the individual and not of society, that saving was therefore a good and spending at or beyond one's income an evil. If their votes meant anything, the American people were adopting a new set of individual and social mores, which contradicted many of those the majority had held in the past. Apparently, they were content to accept subsidies, however offered, and most were unworried by large debts, whether governmental or personal. They were also acclimated to a bewildering variety of governmental regulations and controls. This process of trading individualism for a collective mentality, of developing social consciousness instead of the individual conscience, for investing in the common security at the expense of individual freedom, was well advanced by 1940. During the following decade, it was to be accelerated by the demands of war and a succession of foreign crises.

5

The Totalitarian Challenge: Foreign Policy, 1933-41

I N his first and second inaugural addresses, Franklin Roosevelt scarcely mentioned foreign policy. During March 1933 and January 1937, he was preoccupied with domestic problems. Yet, within ten months after his second inaugural, he declared in a major speech given at Chicago that the peace, freedom, and security of the United States and of the world were being jeopardized by aggressor nations. He proposed to quarantine such nations from civilized world society. He did not specify particular countries, but even the most untutored citizen was aware that he was talking about Japan, Italy, and Germany.

Japanese armed forces continued to ravage Manchuria and China in spite of League of Nations censure, and Mussolini had invaded and conquered Ethiopia. Hitler's rearmament of Germany, which in 1936 was extended to the Rhineland in clear violation of the Versailles peace terms, constituted another severe blow to the tottering prestige of the League and to the concept of a world ruled by law instead of force. The virulent antidemocratic propaganda emanating from Hitler and Mussolini and the beginnings of the Rome-Berlin axis in 1936 and 1937 challenged not only international stability but also democratic institutions. Hitler's and Mussolini's joint aid to Franco's forces in the Spanish Civil War indicated that they were not content to assault their European neighbors with words but were ready to translate their aggressive vocabulary into armed deeds. By 1937, international pundits were already predicting that a nationalistic and rearmed Germany, aided by Italy, would soon challenge the Versailles settlement and attempt to remake the map of Europe. In East Asia,

111

it was obvious that Japan sought nothing short of dominance. As the President spoke in Chicago, a second and greater world war was clearly in prospect.

Franklin Roosevelt's 1937 proposal for an international quarantine revived and intensified many slumbering feelings of hostility and loyalty. Since the defeat of Wilson's League, the lines of cleavage within the country on foreign policy had remained exceedingly complex and did not reflect any exact geographical, party, or occupational basis. There remained perhaps slightly more devotion to the idea of internationalism among Democrats than Republicans, and on the whole it was apparent that except for the Democratic South, more friends of international action were clustered in the urban areas than in rural regions. The international trading and financial communities produced more internationally minded people than the industrial ones. And the rural Midwest was perhaps the center of the most intense isolationism. The President's suggestion, therefore, was once again calculated to change the existing political patterns in the nation. It certainly was made in the face of a dominant isolationist majority in both parties and in all sections of the country.

In 1937, the American people not only were opposed to any new armed adventures outside the Western Hemisphere but also regretted such episodes in the past. To the 1937 Gallup poll question of whether it had been a mistake for the United States to enter World War I, 70 percent of those queried answered yes. Novels, poetry, and most movies and plays of the twenties and thirties were almost unanimous in condemning America's entry into World War I and in questioning whether any modern war was worth fighting. From Hemingway's *A Farewell to Arms* and Dos Passos's *Three Soldiers* to Maxwell Anderson's *What Price Glory,* one conclusion emerged: peace under almost any circumstances was preferable to war.

Americans devoted much literary and scholarly effort to ferreting out exactly what had drawn their nation into the struggle. Some writers blamed Wilsonian idealism, while others pointed to British and French propaganda. A more popular explanation, especially after the Great Depression, designated international investors, traders, shippers, and the producers of war goods—especially the munitions makers—as the principal culprits. When it became known that certain American steel and munitions firms had attempted to wreck the London Naval and Geneva Disarmament Conferences, both House and Senate committees—the latter under the chairmanship of Senator Gerald P. Nye—began investigations into the profits and the influence of the munitions industry. The Nye Committee concluded, simplistically, that the international bankers, munitions makers, and businessmen had really been responsible for the nation's participation in World War I.

Whatever the role of international business profits in encouraging American involvement in the war, the public demand that profits be taken out of armaments was based on the unrealistic notion that this would insure insulation from foreign wars. As a result, the Pittman Neutrality Resolution passed both houses of Congress and was rather reluctantly signed by the President on August 31, 1935. The resolution prohibited the export of munitions from the United States and the shipment of arms on American vessels to foreign powers engaged in an international war. It also empowered the President on the outbreak of a war to warn American citizens against traveling on ships flying the flags of belligerents.

The Neutrality Resolution put into place the last arc of an unfortunate circle. American intervention in World War I had upset the balance of power in favor of the Western Allies. The American withdrawal from Europe during the twenties consequently reduced the strength of the remaining victors. And America's announcement of her probable neutrality in the event of another European war almost insured a readjustment of the Versailles settlement either by diplomacy or by warfare.

Although Franklin Roosevelt had hedged during the twenties and early thirties on the issue of international cooperation for peace, there was little question where his sympathies lay. He cheered the early Ethiopian successes in the Italo-Ethiopian war and was indignant at the Hoare-Laval Plan to settle the conflict by giving Italy a portion of Ethiopia. When Germany occupied the Rhineland in 1936, he denounced the country's reverting to the "law of the sword" and claiming, by assuming the preposterous title of "master race," to be the arbiters of human destiny. Two years later, he protested against the Nazi persecution of the Jews and confessed he could scarcely believe such things could happen in modern civilization. During the Spanish Civil War, he privately labeled the actions of Germany and Italy as "armed banditry." Though extremely cautious in committing the nation to international action, Roosevelt took as many steps toward cooperating with the League of Nations and the Western democracies as he believed Congress and the voters would support. As earlier Presidents had done before him, he urged American membership in the World Court, only to see the proposal again defeated in the Senate.

The President was never happy with the Neutrality Resolution, stating repeatedly that it was "impossible for any nation completely to isolate itself from economic and political upheavals in the rest of the world. . . ." Both he and Secretary of State Hull were particularly opposed to an automatic embargo upon all parties to a foreign war. Instead, they supported a measure to give the President an option to impose an embargo on either one or both of the belligerents, thus making it possible to discriminate against a supposed aggressor and to cooperate with the League of Nations' sanctions. But as both Congress and the country were against this tying of America to the League, Roosevelt retreated. He signed the measure with the observation that the inflexible provisions might precipitate the country into war. Since there was little or no opportunity for America to trade with Ethiopia, the President applied the embargo provisions to arms for Italy with enthusiasm and even wished to extend them to other commodities, including oil, copper, and steel. In September 1935, both the President and Hull supported an amendment including these items, but again, in face of stubborn congressional opposition, the President backed away from a full-fledged fight. The elections of 1936 were too near to take such a risk. He therefore contented himself with denouncing those who made profits from the Italian war trade and asking for a moral embargo against the shipments to Mussolini's forces, an effort which at least proved that little could be accomplished by such voluntary schemes, as American trade to Italian Africa increased about twenty times.

During the campaign of 1936, Roosevelt was particularly sensitive to the pacifist sentiment in the country. His famous "I hate war" phrase probably allayed the doubts of many voters. But the President had not changed his foreign-policy persuasions. In his opening message to the Congress of 1937, he asked for major modifications in the expiring Neutrality Act. Again, Congress insisted on a mandatory embargo and even added provisions barring loans to belligerents and arms to the League of Nations if it should apply sanctions against an aggressor. Almost from the first days of the Spanish Civil War, Roosevelt understood that it was an international contest, and his sympathies were entirely with the Loyalist government. But Hull and the State Department strongly supported cooperation with the British and French Non-Intervention Agreement, which handcuffed the democracies while ignoring Russian aid to the Loyalists and German and Italian aid to Franco. The Anglo-French agreement also violated the long-acknowledged right of all existing governments to import arms with which to put down a rebellion. Since the Spanish war was technically a rebellion, the terms of the Neutrality Resolution did not apply, and Roosevelt's application of the Act was probably inspired as much by State Department pressures as by political reasoning. Later, when the Fascist triumph was imminent, Roosevelt thought of lifting the embargo. But he did not act, possibly because he felt such an attempt would cost the Catholic vote in the 1938 elections. American policy, together with that of Britain and France, went a long way to insure the eventual defeat of the Spanish Republican forces.

The United States had followed the British and French lead on the Spanish question, with disastrous results for the future of democracy and peace. Subsequently, Great Britain and France offered to follow the American lead in Asia, with approximately the same outcome. The Japanese armed invasion of Manchuria in 1931 had drawn the strongest words of censure both from President Hoover and from his Secretary of State, Henry Stimson. Since Japan had clearly broken the Nine Power Treaty of Washington, Stimson urged collective retaliatory action by the United States and the other signatory nations. But the President, appreciative of congressional and popular opposition to any warlike actions in the Orient, rejected even a proposed economic embargo and confined his response to words. After it became apparent that the League of Nations was not prepared to offer any more resistance than had the United States, the Japanese turned to the much bigger game of China. Following the Marco Polo Bridge incident near Peiping in July 1937, the Japanese army launched a full-fledged campaign to defeat Chiang Kai-shek and conquer North China.

In the context of these European and Asiatic developments, on October 5, 1937, Roosevelt delivered his famous "quarantine speech," obviously designed to warn Americans of the awful realities of the world, as well as to measure the domestic support he could command for an effort to stop the drift toward chaos. If the "present reign of terror and international lawlessness" were to continue, Roosevelt solemnly warned, even the Western Hemisphere would not be spared armed conflict. If words meant anything, the President sought to impose an international embargo on Japan, Germany, and Italy.

Twenty-four hours after the quarantine speech, the League of Nations condemned Japan as an aggressor and proposed that the signers of the Nine Power Treaty of 1921 meet and consider collective action. Eager to win American support in Europe, Great Britain and France welcomed the suggestion of a conference, approved Secretary of State Hull's suggestion of Brussels as a meeting place, and indicated—along with other nations—that they would support the United States in any reasonable initiatives, including sanctions against Japan. By November 3, 1937, the opening day of the conference, no positive American policy had been formulated, primarily because Congress and the American people were determined to avoid any international action that might lead to war. The response to the quarantine speech was largely unfavorable. Roosevelt and the State Department were accused of warmongering. A poll indicated that two-thirds of the Congress were opposed to participating in sanctions against Japan, and a subsequent Gallup poll revealed that over 70 percent of Americans favored a complete withdrawal from the Far East, an action that would presumably leave even the Philippines to a dire fate. Against such odds, the President retreated. The Brussels conference disbanded with a pious statement of support for the Nine Power Treaty principles.

Roosevelt continued his efforts to secure an international understanding to counter the dominant pattern of aggression. Early in 1938, he proposed to the British Prime Minister, Neville Chamberlain, a plan to change treaties without the use of force and to assure all peoples access to raw materials. Chamberlain replied that a conference for this purpose would obstruct his developing policy to grant "a measure of appeasement" to Italy and Germany. By the spring of 1938, it was evident that a majority of the people of the United States, Great Britain, and France were prepared neither to go to war nor even to risk war in any cause other than their own immediate national security. The world policies of the three powers differed only to this extent: Britain and France were willing to bargain with Germany, Italy, and Japan, while the United States would do nothing either to bargain or to seek other means of restraint.

In March of 1938, Hitler marched into Austria. That fall and winter, he precipitated a world crisis by demanding and obtaining at the Munich conference the westernmost provinces of Czechoslovakia and the Sudeten Mountain land, without which the defense of the country was practically impossible. Faced with the threat of a world war, Britain and France ignored the French treaty with the Czechs, as well as Russia's promise of aid. Excluding the Czech and Russian representatives from the bargaining table at Munich, they agreed to the German acquisition in return for Hitler's promise to respect what was left of Czech territorial integrity.

Though Chamberlain and French Premier Édouard Daladier came home to cheering crowds acclaiming them as men who had secured "peace in our time," the results of Munich were catastrophic for the democracies. Czechoslovakia, with the best army in Central Europe, was alienated from and embittered against the West. What was left of the French position in Central and Eastern Europe was destroyed. More suspicious and sullen than ever, and nursing the suspicion that Munich opened the way for a German attack eastward with British and French blessing, the Russians no longer argued for collective security at Geneva but retreated into an isolationist position. Maxim Litvinov, Russia's most insistent defender of collective security during the thirties, was recalled to Moscow. All of Central and Eastern Europe lay helpless before

Hitler. In March 1939, he indicated exactly what his signed word was worth by overrunning and subjugating the rest of Czechoslovakia.

Germany's breaking of the Munich pledge ended all talk of appeasement in Britain. Rearmament was speeded up, defensive alliances were hastily offered to Poland, Turkey, Rumania, and Greece, and as a new German propaganda campaign against Poland was instituted, Britain and France even approached Russia, proposing a defensive alliance against the Nazi menace. Since the first Russian price for an agreement was a guarantee of hegemony over Eastern Europe from the Baltic to the Bosporus, with the further understanding that Russian troops might occupy any or all of the territory in furtherance of the agreement, the negotiations at Moscow understandably went slowly. Additionally, Poland and Rumania feared Russia as much as they feared Hitler. Meanwhile, Russia and Germany were negotiating in Berlin, where if good faith in future performance was at a lower premium, the immediate price offered the Soviets seemed to be better. On August 23, 1939, the German and Russian Foreign Ministers signed a treaty of nonaggression, by which both agreed to refrain from attacking the other. They also agreed secretly that if the boundaries of Eastern Europe were changed, Germany was to obtain Lithuania, East Prussia, and Western Poland, and Russia would be compensated by the acquisition of parts of Eastern Poland, Finland, Estonia, Latvia, and Rumanian Bessarabia. Having isolated the Western powers from Eastern Europe, Hitler increased his demands on Poland and on September 1 invaded that stubborn and unhappy country. Two days later, Britain and France declared war on Germany.

Although the United States did not participate officially in the Munich negotiations, the President called on both sides to arrive at a peaceful settlement. Roosevelt had few illusions about the permanence of the Munich agreement. In response to the 1937 revival of Japanese naval construction, he had requested a sizable increase in appropriations to start the construction of a "two-ocean navy" capable of protecting both the Atlantic and the Pacific coasts. Immediately after Munich, the President increased expenditures for armaments, and in his January 4, 1939, message to

Congress he requested a defense budget of almost $2 billion, most of it for the construction of ships and airplanes. Despite the criticisms of pacifists, the money was voted.

Congress remained opposed, however, to changing the Neutrality Act, despite Roosevelt's argument that the Act, operating unevenly and at times unfairly, was helping to bring on war instead of stopping it. During the early spring of 1939, the Administration made its last urgent effort to repeal the neutrality legislation. Roosevelt let it be known that he had given up his intention of purging the Democratic Party of its conservative anti-New Dealers. He invited many congressmen and senators to the White House. In a direct encounter at the White House, Roosevelt and Hull argued with the foreign-policy leaders of the Senate that the outbreak of a European war seemed imminent and that repeal might possibly stop the world's descent into a maelstrom. But all this activity was futile. After making a count in the Senate, Vice-President Garner told the President he did not have the votes, and that was that.

When Hitler marched into Poland, Roosevelt assured the American people that, as long as he could prevent it, there would be "no blackout of peace in the United States." "The nation will remain a neutral nation," he further promised, "but I cannot ask that every American remain neutral in thought as well. Even a neutral has the right to take account of the facts. Even a neutral cannot be asked to close his mind or his conscience." The nation was far from neutral, for the American conscience had already moved, as Roosevelt realized. Immediately after Munich, American opinion was so fragmented and so torn between a sense of relief that war had been avoided and fear that it might still be on the next leaf of the monthly calendar, anger at the dictators for their brutal demands, and disgust at Britain and France for their weak submission, that it was impossible to speak of a consensus. But Hitler's seizure of Czechoslovakia, his barbarous campaign against the Jews, and his invasion of Poland convinced the majority of Americans that Hitler and Germany were responsible for starting another world war. In the autumn of 1939, a national poll indicated that, when asked what countries they blamed most for starting the war, 82 percent named Germany and only 3 percent named Britain and France. But the currents of isolationism ran deep and drew strength from doctrinaire pacifism, disillusionment with World War I idealism, some pro-German and pro-Irish sentiment, and a strong belief that America should stay out of European wars. An overwhelming majority of 96.5 percent in the same poll still felt that the United States should stay out of war.

Immediately after the declaration of war, Roosevelt traded on this strong partiality toward the Western democracies by again asking Congress to revise the Neutrality Act, so that Britain and France might purchase war goods in the United States. The kaleidoscopic events of 1939 revealed the embarrassing position into which neutrality legislation had placed the country. The "cash and carry" provisions of the Act, permitting export of American-made arms provided they were paid for in cash and were shipped on a foreign vessel, expired in 1939, leaving mandatory an embargo against shipments of war goods to Britain and France, whom the country so patently favored. But it permitted such shipments to Russia, whose diplomatic *démarche* of August had helped bring on the war and who was now an alliance partner of the Nazis.

The President was acutely aware of the fact that over 90 percent of the American people wanted peace. He therefore asked only for a reinstitution of the "cash and carry" provision and supported his appeal by argument that this would mean noninvolvement in the war. The struggle in Congress was long and bitter. Roosevelt's assumption that a British and French victory was essential to save Western civilization, and that therefore this country, in its own self-interest, should do everything necessary to insure that victory, was well known only to a very few intimate friends. The President therefore kept very quiet during the debate on the Neutrality Act, which became law, as amended, in November. The new Act reinstituted the "cash and carry" provisions but barred loans to belligerents, prohibited the arming of American merchant ships, and forbade American citizens from traveling on the ships of belligerents in war zones. The President continued his silent policy after the passage of the Act, only very occasionally reminding the populace that there was a great difference "between keeping out of war and pretending that this war is none of our business."

For the world and for the United States, 1940 was a momentous year. During the early fall of 1939, the German war machine overran Poland, and that country was divided between Germany and Russia. A short time later, Russia invaded Finland and eventually dictated a peace. In the following month, Germany invaded neutral Denmark and Norway and occupied Holland. These events helped tumble Neville Chamberlain from power in Britain. But Winston Churchill's new government was powerless to stop the tide of German might. By June, the British had achieved their incredible evacuation of Dunkirk, but the army came back to Britain defeated, dispirited, disorganized, and without equipment. France fell, and Mussolini entered the war to grab the jackal's share of the spoils. On August 12, three superb mechanized German armies were poised on the Channel in view of England, while overhead the Luftwaffe of 1,800 planes struck at the Royal Air Force in the Battle of Britain. Against these formidable men and machines, the British fought with an outnumbered air force, the fleet, the indomitable spirit of the people, and the leadership of Winston Churchill.

During those months, when the fate of Western civilization was in balance, the Presidential elections of 1940 were being fought out. Sometime in 1939, Franklin Roosevelt decided that he might run for a third term, despite the fact that every poll showed a majority of voters opposed to breaking the two-term tradition. His fears that the Republicans might nominate and elect a reactionary who would destroy the New Deal probably played a part in his decision, as did, undoubtedly, his own lively ambition and fondness for power. Whatever the combination of emotions, fears, facts, and fancy that impelled his course, he let it be known that he did not want the nomination and would not run for the office, but never once said definitely that he would decline it. He encouraged a number of his chief supporters, including Harry Hopkins, Alben Barkley, Paul McNutt, and Cordell Hull, to work for the honor, but he never gave any of them substantial help, and he did intrigue behind the scenes to obstruct the campaigns of Vice-

President Garner and James Farley. His unwillingness to announce his intentions kept all candidates in a most awkward position, and by the late spring of 1940 it was evident that the nomination was his for the asking. Since he would not ask, a draft movement was rather clumsily devised, and the convention nominated him for a third term despite the opposition of the conservatives led by Farley and Garner, the latter being replaced as the Vice-Presidential candidate by Henry A. Wallace.

As soon as the Republican Party nominated Wendell Willkie, Roosevelt knew that 1940 was not to be another 1936. For the big, broad-faced, tousled-haired Willkie was a difficult man for Roosevelt to attack. Willkie was a Wall Street man and a utility executive who had fought the TVA to the last ditch. But he was no antediluvian business reactionary. Able, literate, and energetic, he had been a Democrat until 1938 and had supported many New Deal measures. Moreover, he was no isolationist; he stood for all possible aid to Britain short of war. He was a committed man arguing, with a hoarse voice that carried conviction, against New Deal regulations that crippled private enterprise and against the third term, with its implications of dictatorial ambitions.

Against Willkie, Roosevelt ran on his record and used the mounting Nazi terror in Europe to its utmost, insinuating that any change during these perilous days would necessarily be for the worse. But the great German crisis building up over the English Channel carried with it grave political liabilities as well as opportunities. In June, during the death agonies of France, both French Premier Paul Reynaud and Churchill pleaded for massive aid to shore up the crumbling democratic cause—France for American armed intervention, and Britain for destroyers. Roosevelt promised all the material aid he could muster, but both military intervention and the gift or sale of destroyers were matters for Congress, and it was not a propitious time to ask. With France defeated and Britain tottering on the brink, however, the state of both the home defenses and those of the British Isles became even more critical. In Congress, a bill for compulsory military service, the first of its kind in peacetime, met intense opposition not only from the Republican leadership but from many Democrats. For a long time, the President did not commit himself to "selective service," but on August 2, when it was apparent that without his support the bill would languish for months in debate and perhaps face defeat, Roosevelt publicly defended the selective-service measure.

The President also desperately wanted to grant Britain fifty over-age destroyers, but he was almost certain that Congress would not agree, and he was keenly aware of the great political risk he would take in even broaching the subject. All his political instincts warned him against a destroyer deal immediately before the elections. But on September 3 he announced a bargain with Britain transferring fifty destroyers by Presidential edict in return for the lease of naval bases on British Western Hemisphere possessions. Although the deal could be defended as a measure of national defense, it also made the President vulnerable to a charge of dictatorship in bypassing Congress and of committing the country in defiance of the Neutrality Act to an unneutral position and possibly to war.

The destroyer deal, as Roosevelt predicted, unleashed a tornado of criticism in Congress and throughout the country. Even Willkie characterized the deal as "the most dictatorial and arbitrary" Presidential act in American history. Willkie's supporters and the isolationist press were much less restrained. For the remainder of the 1940 campaign, the President was depicted as a would-be tyrant and a warmonger ready to sacrifice the lives of millions of Americans in another futile Wilsonian crusade. In the last week of the canvass, Willkie charged that Roosevelt's reelection would result in the country's entering the war within six months. Under the opposition attack, the New Deal coalition seemed to be dissolving. Isolationist and pacifist criticism appealed especially to liberals and the farming Middle West. Incensed because he felt that the President had not accorded the CIO enough support, John L. Lewis returned to his original Republican allegiance, while labor generally seemed to be wavering. Unemployment was still high and the economy in an uncertain condition. The American Communist Party depicted Roosevelt as the militarist leader of reactionary capitalism. The charge seemed to carry weight particularly with young men, who were obliged to register on October 16 under the

Selective Service Act and to stand ready for possible induction into the armed forces by the operation of the first national drawing, scheduled just a week before the election.

In the face of narrowing odds, Roosevelt retreated from the high ground of principle and once again became the politician. During the last week of the campaign, he continued to strike out at the opposition Republican leaders, who, he said, were playing politics with national defense. But he also reacted perceptibly to the charge of warmongering. Up to that time, he had repeatedly promised that American soldiers would engage in battle only in national defense. On October 30, at Boston, he struck out the qualifying phrase already written into his speech and flatly promised, "Your boys are not going to be sent into any foreign war."

Despite the fact that Willkie carried only eight states, in popular votes the election was the closest one since 1916. Though foreign affairs had bulked large in the campaign oratory, and though New Deal support was radically diminished among Italian and German groups, the nation was obviously still voting in patterns based on economic and social classes. Roosevelt carried every large city with over 500,000 population, his support there in the main coming from the poorer neighborhoods. But if the New Deal magic was still potent politically, and if Roosevelt was still the hero of the underprivileged groups, his party, as it had in 1938, received something less than unqualified support. The Democrats only succeeded in gaining six seats in the House over their totals of two years before, and in the Senate they lost a total of three.

Once the elections were out of the way, the President returned to the fundamental problem of how to aid the British without antagonizing the majority in Congress. By this time, Roosevelt was committed to aiding Britain, even if that meant war and the violation of his preelection pledge. So were many top army and navy officials and most of the Cabinet, including the two internationally minded Republicans, Secretary of the Navy Frank Knox and Secretary of War Henry Stimson. But the President was mindful also of the grave danger of leading a divided nation so close to war that any untoward event might push it, in a strong reaction, to a decision for peace at any price, the results of which would be a catastrophic blow to his own leadership, to world democracy, and to the eventual security of the United States. Just how close the Administration came to this perilous situation was revealed in August 1941, when the Selective Service Act was extended by the margin of one vote in the House. Roosevelt therefore defended all his openly announced policies with the argument that they would help insure the maintenance of peace, though he was often aware that they were bringing the country closer to participation in the war.

Such too was his strategy in proposing the Lend-Lease Act. By the fall of 1940, it was apparent that while Britain would protect her island, she could not much longer protect her empire, to say nothing of mounting a victorious attack against her enemies, without massive assistance from the United States. North Africa was endangered, with it Suez, and, as a consequence, most of Asia. Britain was also running out of available funds with which to purchase goods in the United States. Either the "cash and carry" provisions of the Neutrality Act had to be amended or the fall of most of the non-American world to the Fascists would become even more likely. At this grave juncture, Roosevelt proposed that the nation become the "arsenal of democracy." He suggested to Congress that the President be empowered to lend or lease supplies and munitions to those countries whose preservation he considered vital to the continued security of the United States. Since the bill proposed that the United States freely give munitions to one side and deny them to the other, this was a highly unneutral policy, even a quasi-belligerent one. The President was aware of the implications and so were the members of Congress. To placate public sentiment, Roosevelt argued that the proposal would not violate the Neutrality Act but would, instead, tend to insulate the country from actual war.

The lend-lease proposal brought to a showdown the struggle between two large groups of Americans separated by the convenient but very inexact labels of "isolationists" and "interventionists." Like the great foreign-policy questions of the past, the issue cut across traditional party lines and basic political and social attitudes, the strangest of bedfellows being found on both sides of the conflict. Supporting the isolationist position were those who disliked anything Roosevelt did (a major group by 1941) and those who feared that lend-lease was a certain step toward war and that war would bring a dictatorship to America, or that it would mean the end of reform and a wave of reaction comparable to that experienced in the twenties, or that it would be used by Roosevelt to embark on all sorts of wild socialist schemes. Bitter-end Republicans, pro-Fascists, and anti-Semitic groups found themselves leagued with the Communists, the ardent pro-Irish group, many socialists, dedicated pacifists, Anglophobes, pro-Germans, and followers of the old Midwestern progressive tradition. On the opposite side were the people ready to support Roosevelt in almost anything he proposed, professional Democrats, convinced internationalists, a majority of the Jewish and Scandinavian peoples, liberal and conservative anti-Fascists, Anglophiles, and many high military officials. Clustered on the membership rolls of the America First Committee, dedicated to keeping America out of war, were the names of Herbert Hoover, historian Charles A. Beard, Robert Wood (president of Sears, Roebuck), the two La Follette brothers, Charles A. Lindbergh, and Father Coughlin. Although not members, Earl Browder and Gerald L. K. Smith were also in the opposition. At the opposite pole, supporting the program of the William Allen White Committee to Defend America by Aiding the Allies, was an equally improbable collection of names including General Pershing, Harold Ickes, Owen D. Young, John Dewey, Frank Knox, Henry Stimson, and Harry Hopkins. Throughout the country, the issue disrupted old political patterns, while domestic matters were more or less forgotten. Although there were enough exceptions almost to defy analysis, opinion polls showed the contending groups had different geographical bases. Except for the Scandinavians, the rural regions of the North and the West tended to be isolationist. Except for the South, traditionally wedded to Wilsonian idealism, internationalism drew its largest following in the urban East.

In Congress, many Democrats and most Republicans disagreed with Roosevelt's lend-lease proposals. The debate over lend-lease was as bitter as it was protracted. But the majority of Congress and the American people saw in this measure a possible means of reconciling their contradictory desires—of remaining at peace and of preserving the democratic world. By substantial majorities in both Houses, lend-lease became law on March 11, 1941, and very soon a sizable flow of American-made munitions was on its way across the Atlantic.

Roosevelt subsequently pursued his policy of aiding Britain by indirection, by subterfuge, and even by misrepresentation of the Administration's policy to Congress and the country. Damaged British warships were repaired in American harbors. British fighter pilots were trained in the United States, and American technical specialists flew in combat flights against Germany from British airfields. The American and British General Staffs met in January 1941 in a secret full-dress conference in Washington. Although the President specifically denied on May 27, 1941, that the United States was convoying merchantmen in the Atlantic, within a few months this was being done. In September 1941, the U.S. destroyer *Greer*, patrolling off Iceland, discovered and followed a German submarine, meanwhile periodically radioing its position to nearby British forces. When the submarine attacked with two torpedoes, the *Greer* replied with depth charges. Roosevelt reported the incident to the American people as an attack on an American naval ship, without mentioning the preceding provocation. Within a few days, the navy was ordered to convoy British, American, and neutral ships as far as Iceland and to attack German warships and submarines on sight. We did not want a "shooting war," Roosevelt remarked on October 27, but if such a war should start, the American people could be certain who had begun it. By that time, the United States and Great Britain were alliance partners against the Axis, engaged in a shooting war on the North Atlantic.

By October 1941, many high army and navy officials, some of the Cabinet, and perhaps even Roosevelt wanted open participation in the world struggle. But there appeared to be no expedient way to enter it. Germany refused to counter American activities in the Atlantic with a full-scale attack, and the Administration realized that Congress and the American people would only be activated to support an all-out war by a major enemy assault. This attack came, finally, not in the Atlantic but in the Pacific.

After the 1937 Brussels-conference fiasco, Japan continued the invasion of China, checked only by Russia. During the summers of 1938 and 1939, the two powers fought major but inconclusive engagements along the Manchurian-Siberian border. A short-lived peace came to the northern area by virtue of the Russo-German pact of August 1939 and the Japanese-German alliance a year later. Subsequently, Japanese attention was momentarily focused on Southeast Asia, where after the fall of France and Holland opportunity beckoned to seize French Indochina and the Dutch East Indies. The June 1941 Nazi invasion of Russia eliminated the Soviets for a time as a major Asiatic power. Consequently, only the United States remained as a counterpoise against Japanese ambition to become master of East Asia. After Germany's invasion of Poland, American policy was consistently aimed at maintaining an independent China and protecting the French, British, and Dutch empires in East Asia. But such a policy meant rising conflict with Japan, and war in the Pacific was the last thing the Administration wanted. Time was needed for American rearmament and for supplying of Britain. Moreover, the main interest of the United States was in the struggle for Europe, rather than the diverting conflict in the Orient.

Throughout 1940 and 1941, the United States attempted to restrain Japan through diplomatic and economic pressure. In order to be effective, this had to be automatically increased as British, French, and Dutch strength waned and as Russia became totally preoccupied with the German attack. As early as July 1940, the United States embargoed shipments of aviation gasoline and scrap metal to Japan. A month later, a loan was made to the hard-pressed Chinese government, and in October 1940, after Churchill had reopened the Burma Road, American supplies began to move across the Himalayas to the forces of Chiang Kai-shek. Facing this potential check to Japan's territorial ambitions, ruling circles of that country divided into contending groups. The first, led by the army leaders, demanded that the empire expand to its utmost limits, at the risk of war with the United States. Included in their plans were French Indochina; the Dutch East Indies, possession of which would assure Japan of adequate oil, tin, and rubber; and possibly Malaya and Burma. A second group of naval and civilian officials, led by Premier Fumimaro Konoye, were fearful of defeat in a contest with the United States and were more moderate. If the United States was willing to acknowledge the Japanese occupation of China, renounce its embargo, and stop its support of Chiang Kai-shek, they would be ready to accept the continued independent existence of French Indochina and the Philippines.

While the two groups jockeyed for control, almost continuous negotiations were conducted with the United States. Matters came to a head in July 1941, when, after the German invasion of Russia, Japanese forces occupied the military bases of French Indochina. In retaliation, the United States froze all Japanese funds in this country, closed the Panama Canal to Japanese shipping, and called Philippine reserve forces to active duty. On Roosevelt's return from the Atlantic meeting, both he and Churchill underlined these menacing actions by stating that, in the event of further Japanese aggression, the United States would protect its interests by all available means. Only if the Japanese retired from Indochina would the President be willing to continue the discussions.

Prior to Roosevelt's blunt statement, Premier Konoye had proposed a personal meeting with the President to settle by negotiation the growing differences between the two countries. He now redoubled his efforts to persuade his associates that more could be gained by discussions than by war. As an advance tender of good faith, the Japanese government, on August 28, promised that no further advance would be made in South Asia and that it would withdraw its troops from Indochina as soon as the "China Incident" was settled. The Konoye government even hinted that Japan might ignore its treaty arrangements with Germany if the United States should be drawn into "a defensive war" with Hitler. Along with this tempting offer came the unofficial warning through Ambassador Grew that, if this overture was turned down, the Konoye government might fall before the demands of the military expansionists.

For a time, Roosevelt was inclined to accept the Japanese offer of August 28 as a basis for a personal meeting with Konoye. But on the State Department's judgment that Japan would again back down if pressed, and would not resort to war, he replied that he would consent to attend such a meeting only if a prior agreement was made about China. On the issue of China, the last hope of avoiding war was shattered. During the next six weeks, Premier Konoye repeatedly asked the President for a conference and even proposed to his government that Japan withdraw its troops from China. But his suggestion was overruled by the army chiefs, and on October 18 the Konoye government fell, to be supplanted by a group of militarists headed by General Hideki Tojo. Although negotiations with Washington continued, the new Cabinet, on November 5, won the Emperor's consent to prepare for an attack if the United States refused to change its position on China.

The developments of November and early December were simply an epilogue, for events were already determined. Since neither country would yield on the Chinese question, the special Japanese mission of Saburo Kurusu to Washington as well as Secretary of State Hull's proposal for a ninety-day truce were useless. Both governments were well aware of the fact. An intercepted Japanese message indicated on November 21 that war was impending at any time after November 29. The President and the State Department were mainly concerned about a possible response to a Japanese attack on British and Dutch possessions in the Pacific. On November 24 and again on the 27th, the day after the Japanese fleet had left Japan on its way to Pearl Harbor, American commanders in the Pacific area were warned that a Japanese assault on Guam and the Philippines was probably imminent. But neither the Administration nor the army or navy believed that Japan would have the temerity to strike at Hawaii. As American commanders had taken few precautions against attack, on Sunday, December 7, their naval and air units were as concentrated and as unprotected as if on parade. Within ninety minutes, the major part of the Pacific fleet, including eight battleships, had been either sunk or disabled while it slept in the warm Hawaiian morning sun. On nearby airfields, the remains of American air power lay shattered and smoking. Hours later, General Douglas MacArthur's bombing squadrons were destroyed in the Philippines.

By the greatest defeat in American military annals, Washington's perplexities about how to answer the Japanese challenge were dissolved. Feeling that they had been ruthlessly attacked for little or no cause, the American people stopped their debate over foreign policy and demanded retaliation. With only one dissenting vote, Congress passed the declaration of war against Japan on December 8.

Nothing official had been said so far in Washington about Germany and Italy, but on December 11, Hitler, committing another of his colossal mistakes, declared war against the United States. Had he not done so, American opinion might have insisted that the nation concentrate its energies in the Pacific, and the President would still have been confronted with the question of how to deploy forces against Germany. Congress answered Hitler's declaration of war on the same day with one of its own, and a thoroughly united nation grimly turned to fighting a global war.

Almost as soon as the shock of the Pearl Harbor debacle had subsided, Congress demanded an investigation of the apparent negligence that had made the disaster possible. Some former isolationists charged that the President himself had been remiss in not warning the armed forces, and the insinuation was clear that Roosevelt had goaded Japan into the attack to achieve his objective of entering the world conflict. After the war, not a few writers and historians expanded these insinuations into charges that Roosevelt had secretly committed the nation to the British cause in the Atlantic sector and had contrived by arbitrary and unconstitutional methods to bring on war with Japan in order to achieve his ultimate aims. In most of such writings, the conclusion, even if not precisely stated, was that the future would have been far happier had events in Europe and the Pacific been allowed to run their course without American intercession.

It seems reasonably clear that Roosevelt wanted to join and would have joined the war against Germany at a much earlier stage had not public opinion and Congress restrained him. The record also indicates that the President cut his constitutional corners rather close in the destroyer deal. He withheld information from both Congress and the people and at other times even deliberately misinterpreted some of his more warlike actions so as to soften the attack of the isolationists. It is also clear that Roosevelt and Hull never really took either Congress or the people into their confidence in the delicate negotiations with Japan. A pragmatist, Roosevelt was never too concerned about means when he was convinced of the desirability of the end. Americans would later largely support F.D.R.'s prescience in committing the United States to the Allied cause and against the European and Asian dictatorships. An American agreement with Japan in the Pacific might have been possible in 1941, but United States intervention in Europe was doubtless necessary to the survival of a relatively free and decent society. The nation was not subsequently very well served, however, by the precedent of military steps initiated by the White House, presumably in the national interest but with little or no public discussion or congressional approval.

6

The Divided World:
Foreign Policy, 1941-60

THE problems of the peacemakers in 1945 and 1946 were far more complex than those confronting the statesmen of Versailles in 1918 and 1919. In 1918, the Western democracies for a few moments of history had a virtual monopoly of power. Except for Japan, scarcely any significant organized power existed to contest their judgment. But in 1945 and 1946 Russia bulked ominously, not only because of its major contribution to victory but also because of its central position in the European-Asiatic land mass, directly confronting the majority of the world's population. Russia also represented a new and as yet relatively untarnished revolutionary faith, whose promises to the impoverished masses were as unlimited as its demand for orthodoxy and its hostility to the underlying social assumptions of the West.

In 1945, the world was in violent flux. The successive fall of France, Holland, Italy, Germany, and Japan, and the rapid decline of the British Empire, created profound changes in the power structures of Europe, Africa, and Asia. As the Europeans withdrew from their vast empires, Asian and African nationalism became quickly identified with both race and color, compounding the confusion.

By the end of the war, the United States had mobilized over 16 million men and had extensively deployed them on every populated continent save South America. The total force represented by its land, air, and naval components was staggering. Measured either by its firepower or by its reach, nothing like it had hitherto been experienced.

Since its factories were producing over 45 percent of the world's

133

total armament, the United States was able to supply impressive amounts of weapons and other equipment to all of its allies. By the end of the war, the country had shipped under the Lend-Lease Act some $42 billion worth of material, of which 69 percent went to Britain and 25 percent to Russia, including locomotives, oil refineries, and rolling mills. Throughout the North African campaign, after the landings in Morocco and Algiers, up the Italian peninsula, on the beachheads of France, and in the Pacific, the weight of both men and material was contributed by America.

Consequently, even though the United States had entered the war almost two years after Great Britain had stubbornly faced the Nazi challenge virtually alone, American opinion weighed heavily at the British-American council tables planning the strategy of the war and the peace to follow. At Casablanca (January 1943), Quebec (August 1943), and Cairo (November 1943), where the United States, the British Empire, the Free French, and other allies had concluded their formal agreements, the judgments of Franklin Roosevelt, his Chief of Staff, George Marshall, and his Secretary of State, Cordell Hull, tended to prevail. Prime Minister Winston Churchill, backed by superb British staff work, was a formidable figure. But on most points of conflict, and there were not a few, the view of the United States prevailed. One important exception, however, was the decision not to launch the cross-Channel attack that Russia had been pleading for in either 1942 or 1943. Despite the consensus among American military leaders that an attack was necessary to relieve the hard-pressed Russian armies, Roosevelt reluctantly, but probably wisely, agreed with the British leaders that such a gamble before 1944 was too hazardous.

Conversely, one of the more important military decisions affecting the shape of postwar Europe was contrary to British desires. From 1942 on, Churchill had argued for a British-American thrust in the Eastern Mediterranean against the "soft underbelly of Europe," in the hope that a victorious campaign through Yugoslavia, Greece, or the Balkans might seal off the territory from the Russians and thus save the entire region from occupation by Communist troops. On American insistence that the military objective of destroying the German army was paramount to all other considerations, including the postwar political situation, the plan was dropped. This decision, coupled with the rapid advance of Russian troops in 1944, contributed to the Soviet domination of Eastern Europe. As a compromise, partially meeting the Russian demands for relief and Churchill's plans for Southern and Central Europe, the North African and the succeeding Sicilian and Italian campaigns were fought.

Despite such conflicts the relations between Britain and the United States were remarkably smooth, partly because of the determination of Roosevelt and Churchill to agree, and partly because their goals for the postwar world were generally similar. No such harmony characterized either the British or the American relations with Russia. After agreeing on January 1, 1942, in Washington, not to make a separate peace with the Axis nations until victory was won, the three powers also pledged their support to the principles of the Atlantic Charter, a document previously signed by Roosevelt and Churchill. Among the first principles of the Charter were those of self-determination for all nations and peoples and a pledge against territorial aggrandizement. Nevertheless, on May 20, 1942, Soviet Foreign Minister Molotov demanded as the price for a British-Soviet alliance Britain's recognition of the Russian conquest of the small Baltic states, as well as large and vaguely defined parts of Poland, Finland, and Rumania. Supported by the United States, the British refused the demands but still persuaded the Russians to sign the declaration. Regardless of Russia's temporary acquiescence, however, the fact that they had so promptly entered a territorial bill of demands foreshadowed a stormy future for relations between the partners in the Grand Alliance.

Relations between the three powers were strained as plans for the second front were repeatedly postponed. Stalin was clearly unenthusiastic about both the North African and the Italian campaigns and adamant against the British proposal for a thrust through the Balkans. As plans for a cross-Channel invasion matured, the Russian temper improved perceptibly. At a Foreign Ministers' meeting in Moscow in October 1943, the three powers apparently saw eye to eye on an American plan for the treatment of postwar Germany—the plan that, apart from precise territorial arrangements, became the basis for future policy. During the first meeting of Roosevelt, Churchill, and Stalin, at Teheran in November 1943, relations continued to improve. A second front was definitely promised for 1944, further conversations were held on Germany with the result that a proposed partition of Germany won informal agreement, and Stalin even seemed to approve of Roosevelt's general plans for a United Nations organization to police the world in the postwar era. The personal relations among the three leaders at Teheran were excellent, and Roosevelt believed that he had won Stalin away from his suspicious and cynical attitudes of the past.

The peak of cooperation between the three allies was reached at the Yalta conference in February 1945. By that time Western troops were near the Rhine, and Russian forces were only fifty miles east of Berlin. The Yalta conference was held to make definite arrangements, in anticipation of Germany's early collapse, for occupation zones to separate Russian from Western troops and thus prevent accidental conflict, and for the restoration of order in the occupied territories stretching from the Mediterranean to the Baltic. For eight days in Yalta, Roosevelt, Churchill, and Stalin, accompanied by a crowd of diplomatic and military officials, met and worked out a host of agreements which were to go far to settle the future course of European and world affairs.

The three on whom the ultimate decisions rested were a remarkable trio. The affable squire and democratic politician from Hyde Park, on whose aging features the marks of a final sickness were already etched, was faced by Churchill, the cultured aristocrat, a realist with a long historical memory, and by Joseph Stalin, ruthless revolutionist and dictator, whose mind and personal appearance bore the stamp of the Russian peasantry.

Frequent disputes arose during the week at Yalta, but on all sides the spirit of compromise seemed to override the conflicts. The Yalta agreements provided for the division of Germany into three spheres, the eastern half to be occupied by Russia, the western by the United States and Britain. A restored Poland was to share in the division of East Prussia with Russia, and Russia was further to obtain sizable portions of what had been East Poland. Poland was to be compensated by annexations of portions of Eastern Germany, the exact boundaries left unspecified. On all these territorial matters, the Russians won a reluctant consent from Roosevelt and Churchill. But Russia did agree, contrary to its previous stand, to permit France to share in the occupation of Germany and to participate in the combined control commission which was to oversee and unify occupation policy. Both Roosevelt and Churchill refused to accept the Soviet proposal that $20 billion be exacted from Germany as reparations, but they consented to use the Russian figure as a start for further negotiations and, indirectly at least, sanctioned the use of German prisoners for forced labor inside Russia and the removal of industrial facilities from Germany to Russia.

Russia also retreated on the issue of the new Polish government. In 1943, Russia had severed relations with the democratically oriented Polish government-in-exile in London, and had organized their own Lublin provisional government. In the face of Roosevelt's and Churchill's adamant demands, Stalin at first offered to include representation of the London group and even to reconstitute the provisional government so that it would reflect "all democratic elements" in Poland and abroad, and to hold an early "democratic election" to determine the permanent nature of the government. On the last day of the Yalta conference, the American delegation's proposal to extend the principles of the Polish settlement to all the liberated states in Eastern and Central Europe was adopted without discussion or debate. On the other hand, the Russians and the British had also previously agreed, at the Moscow conference in 1944, that Britain was to have a preeminent role in Greek affairs, Russia a similar one in Bulgaria and Rumania, and the two powers would cooperate in the restoration of Yugoslavia and Hungary.

A separate agreement, not published for over a year, was made between the United States and Russia on the Far East. In addition to the Kurile Islands and the southern half of Sakhalin, Russian influence in Outer Mongolia and Manchuria was assured by the promise to return all the concessions she had lost in the Russo-Japanese War. In return for these bountiful grants, Russia was obligated to recognize Chinese sovereignty in Manchuria and to conclude a treaty of alliance with the Chinese Nationalist government. But the greatest quid pro quo that the United States obtained by the territorial concessions was the Russian promise to join the war against the Japanese within three months after the German surrender.

Returning from the Yalta meeting, Roosevelt and other high American officials were elated at what had been done there. Certain they had obtained a Russian commitment to cooperate in the building of a peaceful, stable world, Roosevelt remarked on March 1 that never before had "the major allies been more closely united —not only in their war aims but also in their peace aims." Harry Hopkins stated that all the American delegates were "absolutely sure they had won the first great victory of the peace. . . ." "The Russians," he observed, "had proved that they could be reasonable and farseeing. . . ." After a visit to Moscow in April, General Eisenhower wrote: "Nothing guides Russian policy so much as desire for friendship with the United States."

This general jubilation over the Yalta results, however, was remarkably short-lived and was replaced with growing criticism that eventually swelled into a chorus of denunciation. Triggering the first doubts was the secret character of the agreements. When the news of these provisions leaked out, and subsequently the facts of the Far Eastern settlement were published, political opponents of the President asked what other portions of the treaty were still undisclosed. Turning over Chinese territory without Chiang Kai-shek's consent smacked of Munich, it was said. More important, Yalta had definitely prescribed the fundamental shape of the postwar settlement both in Europe and in East Asia without either the advice or the consent of the Senate. The President and his aides had ignored the constitutional treaty-making powers and presented Congress with a fait accompli in much the same way as Woodrow Wilson had. Even so, the deluge of criticism did not appear until after Eastern Europe had fallen to the Soviets and the Communist forces prevailed in China. In 1950, Senator Robert Taft, looking ahead to the Presidential campaign of two years later, wrote that the Yalta conference "handed Stalin the freedom of Eastern Europe and prepared our present peril."

The territorial settlement in the Far East was tied in with military plans that had to be kept secret if they were to be effective. Still, members of Congress and especially some representatives of the opposition party should have been taken along to Yalta and consulted before commitments were given. Roosevelt's approval, implied or otherwise, of the Russian plan to use German prisoners of war as virtual slaves indicated a callousness that was shocking. But as for the remainder of the Yalta pact, it probably gave the West more than could have been reasonably hoped for.

On the surface, the Far East arrangements looked like the granting of territory and concessions to the Soviet Union without a proper return. But all the territory, as well as the concessions, had been taken from Russia in the 1905 Peace of Portsmouth. In return for the reestablishment of a Russian naval base at Port Arthur and the joint Chinese-Russian operation of the South Manchurian and the Chinese Eastern Railroads, a Russian alliance with the Chinese Nationalist government insured that the Soviets would not recognize or support the Chinese Communists, whom, even before Japan's defeat, Chiang considered his major enemy.

As of February 1945, another major advantage accrued from the bargain. Japan had not yet been defeated, and most American intelligence reports indicated that victory in the Pacific would have to be won by an invasion of the Japanese home islands. According to the calculations of Generals Marshall and MacArthur, the American General Staff, and Winston Churchill, the assault on Japan would probably cost a million to a million and a half casualties. (The eighty-three-day battle for the island of Okinawa, which started April 1, 1945, was to result in almost 50,000 American casualties, including 15,520 dead.) It was obvious that if the Russian armies were to engage the Japanese-Manchurian forces, the cost in British and American lives would be materially reduced. Only after Japan's capitulation was it fully revealed that the submarine campaign had sapped the strength of the island empire to the extent that her early defeat was inevitable, a defeat that was further speeded up by the atomic bomb. But in February 1945 the work on the bomb was known only to a very few high American and British officials, and a good many of those who knew never expected it to materialize.

The European end of the Yalta bargain was also probably a good deal more than the Western allies could reasonably have hoped for. In February 1945, Russian troops were deployed along a much-indented line running south from Budapest and north to within fifty miles of Berlin; the Allies were still west of the Rhine, three hundred miles from the German capital. American military policy insured that the Russians would reach Berlin first and occupy Prague and Dresden. Since the Nazis were using most of their rapidly dwindling strength in the East, the Russian forces were held up at the Oder River for weeks, and Eisenhower could easily have entered Berlin and occupied Prague. Despite Churchill's plea to take Berlin, General Eisenhower argued that the city was no longer a military objective and chose, without consulting either Roosevelt or Churchill, to send his motorized forces into Bavaria. From there, the capture of Prague was still possible before the Russians arrived. But after having first ordered General Patton to proceed to Prague, Eisenhower revoked the command. Ignoring Churchill's reiterated pleas to "shake hands with the Russians as far east as possible," and backed by Washington, he withdrew his troops to west of the Elbe River, permitting the Soviet forces to liberate Czechoslovakia, all of Eastern Germany, and Berlin.

Though Roosevelt had undoubtedly placed too much trust in Stalin (and too much faith in his persuasive powers over the Soviet leader), and Roosevelt's successor failed at first to see the importance of East-West strategic alignments in shaping the postwar world, Russia was bound to have a major hand in ordering the destinies of the newly reconstructed states of Eastern Europe. The Soviets had suffered over 6 million battle deaths, compared to a total of just over 650,000 for the United States and Great Britain. Although the aerial devastation of Great Britain was appalling, Russia had been invaded, at a cost of at least 10 million civilian casualties and heavy property losses in most of the prime industrial and agricultural parts of the Soviet Union. At the end of the war, Stalin was alleged to have said that the British contributed time to the Allied victory, the United States supplied the goods, but Russia paid in blood. Indeed, the major part of the German army was destroyed on the Russian steppes.

In demanding at Yalta that the governments of Poland, Czechoslovakia, Hungary, Yugoslavia, Rumania, and Bulgaria be "friendly" governments, Stalin was doing no more than any Western power would have done in similar circumstances; in fact, exactly what they did do in Greece and Italy, where the governments were threatened by Communism. In agreeing to the phrases that were supposed to govern the development of peacetime governments in Eastern Europe, the Russians were badly outmaneuvered, and sacrificed vital national interests. Whatever the explanation, Roosevelt and Churchill won a victory at Yalta that was perhaps too astounding to endure. Among leading Western statesmen, only Churchill was inclined to be gloomy about the future, probably because of his superb insight into what was and was not possible in foreign relations.

Predictably, the good will generated at Yalta lasted scarcely longer than it took the various representatives to return to their countries. Essentially, what dashed the high hopes that had been raised were the developments in the liberated countries of Eastern Europe. As Poland, Hungary, Rumania, and Bulgaria were invaded by the Russians and the Nazi-dominated governments driven out, a tripartite Allied control commission was set up in each instance, but weeks after Yalta these commissions were not working as the Western powers believed they should. The Russians ended the Radescu government in Rumania and replaced it with one dominated by Communists, without consulting the Control Commission. No democratic additions were made to the Lublin government in Poland, and Western representatives of the Control Commission were not permitted to observe what was being done outside Warsaw. At the same time, however, American and British representatives in Italy, although disputing among themselves about the nature of the new central government, were carefully, if subtly, excluding Communists from participation in it. In Greece, Western domination was neither careful nor subtle. British troops stopped native Communist forces in a pitched battle in Athens, and afterwards sixty thousand British troops joined in a nationwide campaign against the Communists.

Both the American and the British governments protested vigorously against the developments in Rumania and especially in Poland. Roosevelt pointed out to Stalin that the Yalta agreement was "breaking down." Stalin admitted the deadlock, but charged that the two Western powers had equally violated the agreement in Italy and Greece. By the time of the Potsdam conference of the three powers, in July 1945, on the question of Eastern Europe, the deadlock was complete. In Potsdam, Churchill made his famous charge that the Soviets had placed an "iron fence" around the British and American representatives in Eastern Europe, a remark which eventually was to pass into the vocabulary of the Western world as the Iron Curtain separating the East from the West, Communism from democracy, autocracy from freedom. It was also at Potsdam that the Russians, showing an increasing appetite for territory, as well as a lack of appreciation of the rising storm in Asia and Africa against Western imperialism, demanded a share of the Italian colonies.

The term "cold war" was not used until 1947, but its antecedents actually go back before the Potsdam conference. During the last few weeks of his life, Roosevelt was exasperated with Russia's actions in Eastern Europe and more so by Stalin's veiled accusation that he and Churchill were seeking to make a separate peace with Germany. Stalin was equally irritated by Western criticism of his Eastern European policy. For a time, Russia refused to send Molotov to the scheduled San Francisco conference, where it was hoped that all the nations allied against Germany would establish a world organization based on the agreements made at Dumbarton Oaks. The tension between the Western allies and Russia rapidly increased after Roosevelt's death on April 12, 1945. In major part, this was due to the diverging and perhaps irreconcilable interests of the former alliance partners; in part, it was due also to the conditions surrounding Harry Truman's succession to the Presidency.

Neither Roosevelt nor congressional leaders had ever seriously expected that Harry Truman could attain the Presidency. By no means without ability, Truman in his previous political career in Missouri and in the United States Senate had been successful but not outstanding. His nomination as a candidate for the Vice-Presidency had been compounded of compromise and expediency. When Southerners and conservatives objected to the renomination of Henry Wallace in 1944, a combination of big-city machine Democrats, ardent New Dealers, and labor leaders, who were running the convention for Roosevelt, found in Truman the almost-perfect candidate to recement the quarreling factions. No politician in either party disliked the jaunty and friendly senator from Missouri. He was a convivial fellow without personal complexities, always ready to help a colleague of either party when he could, and never known to take an extreme stand or to offend anyone, save on the stump or on the floor of the Senate when debating a party issue. By family he had Southern connections, and his rise in politics had come largely through the support of the Pendergast machine in Kansas City. In his early career he had been conservative on economic issues, but he was such a good organization Democrat that his voting record in the Senate was almost straight New Deal. Roosevelt's opinion of Truman was indicated by the fact that he rarely saw the Vice-President and seldom asked his counsel. And what Harry Truman thought of himself is obvious from his statement, when he first learned of Roosevelt's death, that "the moon, the stars, and all the planets" had fallen on him.

Truman rapidly gained a measure of self-confidence. He very naturally relied on his advisers in the State Department, where Russian policy was largely determined by the information sent in by the American representatives from Moscow. There Ambassador W. Averell Harriman and his most trusted adviser, George F. Kennan, perceived a rising Soviet threat to Western interests, though Kennan saw this threat primarily in economic and political rather than in military terms. Other advisers to the President emphasized the dangers of Russian Communism, in very blunt terms, and Truman brought his own personality and determination to these issues and to the shaping of American policy. Within a week of his inauguration, the new President had come to the conclusion that American dealings with the Russians had been a "one-way street," and he made up his mind that the pattern "could not continue." At the Potsdam conference in August 1945, and afterwards, the President apparently accepted the thesis that by the terms of the Yalta agreements the United States and Britain were entitled to act unilaterally in Greece and Italy, whereas Russia was bound by her word to obtain Western consent for the reinstitution of civil governments in Eastern Europe. When the Soviets ignored the West in their dealings with Rumania and Poland, Truman concluded that the Russians were "not serious about the peace" and "were planning world conquest."

The President was a remarkably stubborn man and a highly partisan one. Once having taken a position, he was rarely inclined to back down and accept a compromise. His favorite way of meeting opposition was to attack it head on, and so he did with the Russians. On the reconstruction of Southern European governments after Potsdam, there was little or no consultation with Russian representatives. Immediately after the defeat of Japan, American lend-lease shipments to Russia were stopped abruptly, whereas those to Western European countries continued. Prior to the summer of 1945, there had been extended discussions in Washington about the possibility of American aid in the repair of Russian war damage. Nothing was done, whereas a large loan was made to Britain. On the basis of experience in Poland and Rumania, Truman decided that he would not allow the Russians any part in the control of Japan. Although the term was not yet current, the "cold war" had been declared. Each side distrusted the motives of the other and each sought to profit at the expense of the other.

In the meantime, Russia was hastening to organize all the governments of Eastern Europe, and through native Communist Parties sought to subvert Western European democratic regimes. In the United Nations it attempted, by consistent use of the veto, to thwart all efforts to revitalize economic life in Europe and the Middle East. An unreconstructed Lublin regime became the official Communist government of Poland, which, by a unilateral agreement with Russia, was given all the former German territory east of the Oder River. Since Russian troops occupied Eastern Germany, the process of Soviet domination went on there faster than in the so-called independent states. The Czechoslovakian government, which up to June 1948 still contained remnants of democratic parties, was remodeled under Russian pressure, as was the Hungarian government.

As early as 1945, Josip Broz (Tito) had instituted his own form of Communism in Yugoslavia, and in Rumania all chance of opposing the ruling Communist regime was dissipated by the abdication of King Michael on December 30, 1947. In Greece, the government had been able to survive against armed Communist bands only by massive British support. The Greek Communists, a United

Nations investigating committee reported, were being regularly supplied from neighboring Bulgaria, Yugoslavia, and Albania. With British support, the tottering Turkish government was just able to stave off Russian pressure against the Straits. And in Iran a Russian scheme to set up a separate Communist state in the province of Azerbaijan was foiled by a United Nations threat to investigate and by severe American pressure.

Future Russian policy was clearly indicated as early as February 1946, when an ominous shift took place in both military and economic planning. Demobilization of the army was abruptly stopped, and the emphasis in the current five-year plan was changed from consumers' goods to armaments. In the spring of 1946, when the American army was hard put to find adequate personnel for the occupying forces in Japan and Germany, the Russian army numbered at least 4 million men. At the diplomatic bargaining table, Soviet strategy consisted of repeating the arguments supporting its case ad infinitum. At numerous Foreign Ministers meetings provided for by the Potsdam conference, peace treaties with Italy, Bulgaria, Hungary, and Rumania were finally accepted, the first on mostly pro-Western terms, the rest on those of Russia. But on the problems of German borders, German reparations, and the ultimate nature of the German state, no agreement was possible. Similar deadlocks were encountered in the Security Council of the United Nations, where Russia could impose a veto. In the General Assembly, the Soviets resorted to a walkout when the debate was critical of Russian policy or the vote on important matters seemed likely to go against them.

Despite American credits, loans, and outright gifts of $11 billion to rehabilitate the economic life of Western Europe, deprivation and want was the normal state of millions in the Low Countries, Western Germany, France, Italy, the Balkans, and the Middle East. Throughout Europe, millions of refugees were seeking new homes. Millions more returning to their old homes found nothing but destruction. Children were without families and women without men. Because of the catastrophic destruction of productive and transportation facilities, hunger was the normal lot—a condition which, of course, led to severe erosion of whatever social and personal ethics had survived the war. Even in Britain, the destruction of material and spiritual resources had been so great that both the ability and the inclination to rebuild society were at a perilous minimum. As Winston Churchill observed, Europe was "a rubble heap, a charnel house, a breeding-ground of pestilence and hate."

After the war, American policy was premised on the assumption that, after an initial period of short duration, Europe would be able to rebuild its own economy. American troops might have to remain in Germany for some time, but apparently no American leader seriously thought that either American arms or American financial aid would be necessary for a long period of reconstruction. Consequently, the demobilization of America's troops went on with almost indecent haste as both soldiers and their families at home put pressure on Congress for their speedy return. By 1946, American armed strength had dwindled to a minimum of 2,200,-000 men, which was scarcely enough to provide adequately for the occupation forces in Germany and Japan. It was at this juncture that American leadership began to perceive that American hopes and ambitions for the postwar world would not be so easily attained. The United States would have to be prepared to actively intervene when necessary to promote the development of a stable capitalist world order that was at the core of long-range American interests.

During the perilous years of 1946 and 1947, Harry Truman became President in fact as well as in title. Few men in the history of the United States have been confronted with such awesome problems with so little preparation for them. And few men have risen so resolutely to meet the occasion. Repeatedly, the President asked Congress for a new Selective Service Act, a request distinctly not popular in the postwar climate of opinion. Congress first responded with a limited one-year extension of the wartime act. In 1947, acknowledging the rising tensions, it reluctantly passed a much stronger measure. But the most drastic changes in American policy were still to come. They were sparked by Russia's growing militancy and by Europe's utter inadequacy to meet either the exterior challenge of Soviet force or the interior threat of Communist subversion.

Washington was, of course, informed about the mounting peril to Europe. But the full extent of the impending disaster was not recognized until Britain told the United States, in early 1947, that because of her critical domestic situation she would have to recall all her troops from Greece and stop whatever aid she had been giving to Turkey. The probable result, the British note intimated, was that the governments of both countries would collapse before the Communist thrust. With the lend-lease program of 1941 as a model, the President, on March 12, asked Congress for a $400 million appropriation with which to supply the two endangered countries with economic and military aid. But this step, revolutionary in itself, was just a beginning. Speaking at Harvard University on June 5, Secretary of State George Marshall called for a massive aid program for the harassed European democracies, with the purpose not of relief but of rebuilding Europe's productive resources. Any government willing to assist in the task of reconstruction, Marshall promised, would be welcome.

Neither aid to Greece and Turkey nor the proposed $17 billion reconstruction program for Western Europe went through Congress without stiff opposition from a variety of sources. Led by Henry Wallace and Senators Pepper of Florida and Taylor of Idaho, one group saw in the so-called Marshall Plan a scheme to wreck all chances of cooperation with Soviet Russia and to establish a new type of American imperialism. Labeling it a "martial plan," Wallace warned it might well lead to war. Supported by domestic Communists, some pacifists, and others on the left, this group attacked the reactionary nature of the Turkish and Greek governments and argued that any such aid should be channeled through the United Nations. On the right, a group of Republican senators led by Robert Taft of Ohio, Kenneth Wherry of Nebraska, and George W. Malone of Nevada argued that the revolutionary scheme would lead either to war or to national bankruptcy. The new Republican House of Representatives elected in 1946, the first since 1928, was especially sensitive to economic arguments and was eager to balance the national budget and reduce taxes. In view of the pent-up domestic demand for goods, it was argued, a further drain-off by Europe would produce unmanageable inflation. An extreme nationalist note was sounded to the effect that if the plan was successful, it would build up in Europe competitors for American foreign trade. Still another bloc deplored the exclusive concentration on Europe and insisted that stopping Communism in Asia was just as important, if not more so.

Most of the Republican congressional exponents of these arguments came from either the isolationist or the unilateral nationalist pre-Pearl Harbor traditions. These groups, stemming in large part from the trans-Appalachian West, had been defeated in the 1940 Republican national convention by the internationalist-minded and for the most part Eastern Republicans. Again in 1944, when the issue was more sharply drawn, they were thwarted by the nomination of Thomas E. Dewey. But they still had substantial strength throughout the country and probably even more in the newly elected Republican Congress. Had it not been for the leadership of Senator Arthur H. Vandenberg of Michigan, both Greek and Turkish aid and the Marshall Plan might have been lost. A leading conservative and noninterventionist in the prewar years, he nevertheless favored the Marshall Plan and pledged the support of the Republican organization in the Senate.

After six weeks of debate, Congress, which had already voted aid to Greece and Turkey, passed the European Recovery Program. By 1955, over $13 billion had been spent under its provisions. The results of the plan were remarkable. The Western European transportation system was restored, agriculture was mechanized, new mines were dug, and hydroelectric dams and factories were built. Between 1945 and 1950, Western European industrial production had increased by 60 to 70 percent, that of agriculture by 25 percent. Within five more years, the per capita production of the area exceeded the prewar level, an event that set the stage for a subsequent wave of prosperity exceeding even that of the palmy days of 1928 and 1929. Under the Truman aid program, Greece and Turkey were strengthened. The *Economist* described the Marshall Plan as "the most straight-forwardly generous thing that any country has ever done for others": but it was not entirely altruistic. Fundamental to U.S. interests was a stable and restored Europe, productive and resistant to Communist influence and far-reaching social change. A strong Western Europe would be a first line in the containment of Soviet power to the East as well as a market for American investment and an engine for economic development in much of the rest of the world. The Marshall Plan succeeded beyond the wildest expectations for it: by 1960, Western Europe had been so invigorated that it was challenging the United States for economic and political leadership.

Even while the Marshall Plan was being debated, two other schemes for the strengthening of Western Europe were vigorously supported by the United States. The first envisioned the unification of Germany as a step toward the restoration of self-government and industrial productivity. The second, much more radical and daring in scope, looked toward a unified Western Europe bound together by both economic and defense agreements. Unquestionably, the industrial heart of prewar Europe had been Germany, and Western European economic recovery could never be complete unless it included a revitalized Germany. This objective could not be achieved as long as the conquered country was divided into four occupation zones.

American policy in 1946 was pointed toward the objective of the unification of Germany, its industrial restoration and its reintegration in the economic life of Western Europe. This was an exceedingly touchy problem. The British had not forgotten or forgiven the German bombings, and the French fear of a revitalized Germany was understandable. But the greatest obstacle was Russia, whose fear of a united Germany was and remained almost pathological. Many times approached on the subject, the Russians demanded as a price for their agreement a major voice in the control of the new state and in the future development of the Ruhr Valley, which contained the great iron and coal complex basic to the economy of Western Europe. Significantly, the Russians did not offer the Western Allies a share in the control of the Silesian coal and iron district which lay in the Russian sector.

Since Soviet intervention in Western Germany and the Ruhr was too high a price to pay, the Western countries, in February 1948, agreed to unite their three zones of Germany without Russian cooperation. Subsequently, a German constitution was adopted, and in May 1949 the German Federal Republic was recognized and included in the scope of the Marshall Plan. Russian reaction to this *démarche* was quick. Throughout Eastern Europe, the Communist Parties launched a campaign to eliminate all opposition. The Czechoslovakian government was completely dominated by the Communists. In Hungary, bourgeois and peasant parties were declared illegal, and so much pressure was brought on Yugoslavia to follow the Russian line that Marshal Tito severed relations with the Soviets. To culminate the counterattack, the East German People's Republic was organized.

In April 1948, the Soviet Union curtailed the overland traffic between West Germany and Berlin, where two million people were threatened with starvation or a dependence on Russian supplies. Militarily, the Western position in Berlin was poor, since neither at Yalta nor at Potsdam had the West obtained guarantees of land transit across Russian-occupied territory. But to write off Berlin meant acquiescence before a Russian show of force, and was both militarily and politically unacceptable. Although both American and British air commands had warned their governments that supplying Berlin by air was an impossible feat, the airlift ordered by President Truman actually increased the quantity of Berlin's supplies throughout the following winter and led to Russia's lifting of the blockade in May 1949.

Months prior to the Berlin blockade, the United States had encouraged Western Europe to combine in a mutual-defense pact providing for a common army. But to implement the agreement the United States had to promise that it would join and support the united effort. As a result, the President announced, on March 18, 1949, the ratification of the North Atlantic Treaty, by which Canada and the United States, in association with ten Western European countries, agreed to create a common army for the defense of Europe. The North Atlantic Treaty Organization was as much a revolutionary step for the United States as it was for the participating European countries. In pledging the United States to help resist an attack against any member state, it violated long-cherished foreign-policy doctrines, and the pact was not accepted without violent protest from congressional traditionalists.

As a counterproposal to the North Atlantic Treaty, Senator Taft and ex-President Hoover argued for a massive air and naval buildup on the North American continent. In case of Communist aggression, this force might be utilized if the facts warranted. The Taft-Hoover doctrine, variously called "continentalism," "fortress America," and "the principle of the free hand," attracted the support of a rapidly developing neo-isolationist–unilateralist group in the Republican Party, as well as that of the so-called Asia Firsters. The latter group was not isolationist but advocated using America's strength in Asia rather than in Europe. Despite all criticisms, the North Atlantic Treaty was approved by the Senate by a vote of 82–13, and the United States had merged its future security for an indefinite period of years with that of Western Europe.

If a measure of peace and stability had been won for Western institutions in Europe, as much could not be said for Asia. For centuries, Asia had been characterized by overpopulation, hunger, and autocratic government. Great portions of the continent in the nineteenth century had to submit to Western imperialism, which extracted both the wealth and the self-pride of the native population, at the same time introducing them to, but not giving them, Western technology. During World War II, the myth of Western supremacy had been shattered by the Japanese. At the end of the war, it was doubtful whether the once-great European nations were any longer powerful enough to hold their Asian empires. Consequently, a nationalism evolved, closely identified with a racial mystique born of resentment against the West and fed by the expectation of an economic and technological development sufficient to provide something better than the marginal life most of the continent's population had experienced in the past. Compounding the Asian confusion at the end of the war was the rapid destruction of old political units and the rise of innumerable new ones, unstable by nature and even explosive.

With the defeat of Japan and the increasing withdrawal of British, French, and Dutch power, one of the few familiar native prewar governments with a chance of exercising enough authority to continue its existence was that of Chiang Kai-shek's Nationalist regime in China. But even Chiang's government was weak and in danger of falling before the explosive fury of one of the new forces sweeping the continent. Whether because of its upper-class origins or because it had been continually attacked by Western imperialism, foreign foes, and native warlords, Chiang's Nationalist movement had scarcely made a dent in China's massive problems. By 1943, the Communist forces under Mao Zedong had established a government in Yenan and from that point were fighting both the Japanese and the Nationalists. So threatening had they become that by 1944 Chiang was using almost half a million troops against them.

Prior to 1945, American policy had been directed toward getting the two Chinese factions to cooperate in fighting the Japanese. In Asia as in Europe, the immediate military problem took precedence over long-run political objectives. But after numerous attempts to win an agreement between Chiang and the Communists had proved futile, a bitter dispute broke out among American advisers in China and Washington. Some of the military, exasperated at Chiang's use of arms against the Communists instead of the Japanese, and appalled at the corruption, inefficiency, and weakness that characterized the Chungking regime, argued that the Nationalist government was impossible to deal with. They were joined by a substantial section of the diplomatic advisers on China, especially after a group of American journalists returned from the Yenan Communist headquarters with glowing reports of the contrasting honesty, efficiency, and singleness of purpose that they found there. The Yenan group won further American support when it was described in State Department reports as not being really Communist in nature but only "agrarian." Despite this growing disposition to look on the Yenan Communists with favor, Roosevelt concentrated all American support behind the Nationalists, and at the end of the war Chiang's forces were excellently equipped with American arms.

By December 1945, the Yenan Communists also had gained much strength. In the opinion of the American commander in China, General Albert G. Wedemeyer, Chiang's government and army were no match for the Communists without substantial American help. Wedemeyer further insisted that a victory for the Yenan group would be a victory for world Communism and would imperil America's position in the Orient. The United States was faced with three alternatives: (1) to extend major aid to Chiang and possibly participate in the civil war to insure a Communist defeat; (2) to attempt to get an armistice agreement between the two warring factions and organize a coalition government with representatives of both sides participating; (3) to retire from the field completely and permit the issue to be settled by the continuing civil war.

After much discussion, Washington decided on the middle course, at the same time maintaining a sizable aid program amounting to $700 million in two years for the Nationalists. In December 1945, General Marshall went to China to try to secure peace and establish a coalition government. For almost thirteen months, he worked assiduously at his task and at one time actually arranged a cease-fire, as well as an agreement for a coalition government pending a constitutional convention elected by democratic means. But a lack of good faith on both sides wrecked the agreement, and in January 1947 Marshall quit China for good and returned to Washington as the new Secretary of State, angrily denouncing both the Communists and the Nationalists. After Marshall's return to the United States and the evacuation of American forces, the Nationalist position steadily deteriorated. Although superior in equipment and numbers, the Nationalists were no match for the dedicated Communist armies. In a few months the battle for China had become a rout, whole Nationalist divisions, many of them supplied with American equipment, deserting to the other side. By October 1949, Chiang Kai-shek had fled to Formosa. Immediately after their victory, the Chinese "agrarian Communists" began a crusade to eliminate all Americans and American influence from East Asia, meanwhile boasting of their fidelity to Marxian Leninism and to Moscow.

The Chinese Communist victory was an especially bitter dose for many Americans to take. China had been a favorite arena for American missionary efforts and commercial initiatives, and during the war Roosevelt had worked toward the construction of a powerful postwar China that could offset both Japanese and Russian power in Asia. Possessing a major portion of the world's land surface and population, China was potentially the greatest power in the Orient. But this great potential was now turned against a *pax Americana* and in the direction of the "liberation" of millions of Chinese and other Asians from the vestiges of Western imperialism.

Many Americans, and especially the Republican opposition in

Congress, lamented the "loss" of China as the result of either colossal stupidity or a criminal Communist conspiracy, or possibly both. The situation was much more complex than that, however, no matter how distressing America's diplomatic defeat. Many factors were involved: inexperience, misjudgment, insistence on immediate military gains irrespective of future political developments, and the reluctance of the American people to become involved again in a major Asiatic war. There was also the corruption of Chiang's regime and the lack of popular support for the Nationalist forces, as well as the strength and revolutionary zeal of the Chinese Communists. Whatever the causes, the outcome in China embarrassed the Administration in Washington and fanned the flames of anti-Communism both within the government and without.

Many of the ideas behind the revolutionary Truman foreign policy came from a variety of advisers, but the ultimate responsibility for all of them belonged to the President, though before he succeeded to the office he had apparently been little concerned with affairs outside of the nation. In its totality, the Truman program contained almost every controlling principle characterizing American policy in Europe through at least the succeeding Eisenhower and Kennedy-Johnson administrations. In essence, it was an aggressive policy of defending every Western European state either from direct challenge by Russia or from the subtler menace of internal subversion. It further sought to increase the power of the West by organizing a unified Europe, both militarily and economically. The Truman policy did not seek by force to convert once-held Communist lands to a non-Communist life. It was essentially a policy of "containment"—a word first used by George Kennan in 1947—a policy that recognized in fact, if not explicitly, the settlement made at the end of the war by the occupying armies. Western political and economic institutions were to dominate the western and southern parts of Europe, while Soviet institutions were to dominate the East.

Containment in this sense also suggested, however, that the world was essentially divided into two blocs: a "free" world led by the United States, and the oppressed Communist nations dominated by the Soviet Union. Soviet expansionist moves had to be resisted at all costs, especially the clever subversion that used democratic freedoms to destroy democratic governments. The simplicity and limitations of this world view would gradually be revealed: nationalism, rather than Marxism or capitalism, was the major operative force in much of the Third World; the Communist bloc was united more in rhetoric than in fact (as the cases of Yugoslavia and the People's Republic of China demonstrated); and some pro-U.S. dictatorships were part of the "free" world only in the loosest sense of the term. But during Truman's Administration, and into the fifties, the Communist threat shaped both American foreign policy and, to an increasing degree, domestic politics. American anxieties on this score accelerated after the Soviets successfully detonated an atomic bomb in August 1949, the same month in which Mao Zedong proclaimed victory in China.

On April 7, 1950, a top-secret memorandum from the National Security Council, labeled N.S.C.-68, was delivered to President Truman. Containing the basic ideas of Secretary of State Dean Acheson and Paul H. Nitze, who replaced George Kennan as Policy Planning Staff Director in the State Department, N.S.C.-68 embodied the harshest outlines of American cold-war policy: a large increase in defense spending, higher taxes to support the military buildup, global resistance to Communism in all its forms, much more emphasis on internal security, and the assumption that basic Soviet policy was aimed at Communist world domination. These policies and assumptions became even more influential throughout the government after the Korean crisis.

The invasion on June 25, 1950, of South Korea by a well-equipped army from the North led to a far more extensive conflict than the "police action" that it was initially termed. Due to a temporary Russian boycott of the United Nations, the Security Council was able to act without the inevitable Soviet veto. On June 25, one day after the invasion of South Korea, the Security Council unanimously branded the North Korean attack as aggression and demanded that the Communist troops be recalled. President Truman announced twenty-four hours later that American land and naval forces would be sent to Korea. The Security Council also adopted the American resolution calling on all member states to contribute forces to the conflict against the North, and by the end of the war some sixteen nations were contributing token forces of men and supplies to an international army. By the time the war ended in the armistice of July 1953, it had cost the United States over 35,000 dead and missing soldiers, over 100,000 wounded, and expenditures of over $22 billion. Save for the expenditures, these figures were dwarfed by the South Korean military and civilian casualties.

After the Chinese Communists entered the war, a grave question divided the nations: whether to attack Communist China and thus involve the United States and cooperating nations in a major war that could turn into a world war, even an atomic one, if Russia chose to come to the aid of her Communist partner. With both the Marshall Plan and the North Atlantic Alliance just being established in Europe, Britain and France, faced by millions of Russian soldiers east of the Iron Curtain, were determined to localize the conflict. General Douglas MacArthur wanted nothing short of complete victory. During his triumphant march up the Korean peninsula in the autumn of 1950, MacArthur repeatedly asserted, despite Communist warnings to the contrary, that the danger of Chinese participation was minimal. The Chinese action not only proved him dead wrong but also demolished his promise to end the war by Christmas. The disastrous retreat of the United Nations forces into South Korea was a blight on MacArthur's brilliant military record, and during the wearisome campaign to regain lost ground his hopes for victory were again abruptly curtailed, this time by the United Nations and by his own government. Fear of full-scale Chinese participation and eventual Russian support led to an agreement between the United States and its allies that the Chinese bases across the Yalu River from the North Korean border were not to be bombed and that the United Nations troops were not to proceed beyond the thirty-eighth parallel, the prewar boundary separating the two Koreas. MacArthur protested vigorously. But in making his objections public and relaying them in writing to a Republican congressman who later read them from the floor of the House, he was guilty of insubordination to his Commander in Chief, the President. The general also had challenged one of the basic safeguards of democratic government, that of civilian control of the military. There was little else that a strong President could do but to relieve the general of his command.

The dismissal of MacArthur in April 1951 brought to a climax all the furies of partisanship. The loss of China, the less than enthusiastic European contributions to the war, and the United Nations' intent to limit the war to Korea had already aroused Republican tempers in Congress to such an intense pitch that in the resulting welter of charges of incompetence, subversion, and conspiracy the nation almost lost its poise. Although many Republicans were extraordinarily inconsistent in signing the Taft-Hoover manifesto on continentalism at one moment and in the next indicting the Administration for losing Asia, the Truman-Acheson policy in the Far East did nevertheless appear to sacrifice much of Asia in order to save the gains made in Western Europe. The rapid development of the Asia First, anti-United Nations, go-it-alone groups of Republicans was a natural evolution, and the Administration's Asia policy a splendid target. The recall of General MacArthur supplied emotional fuel to an already in-flamed cause consisting of zealous patriotism and intense partisanship, and undoubtedly contributed to the Democrats' loss of the Presidential campaign.

The uncertain struggle in the Republican Party for the 1952 Presidential nomination threatened for a time to make for a real shift in American foreign policy. Before the Republican national convention, most of the conservative and nationalist elements in the Republican Party had rallied around the candidacy of Senator Robert Taft. Supporting the Ohio senator were the continentalists and fortress-America groups, the old isolationists, the go-it-aloners, anti-United Nations people, the Asia Firsters, and the extreme, Red-baiting nationalists, who for one reason or another preferred to spend their energies catching domestic Communists rather than confronting grave international problems. It was a formidable if paradoxical group, but Eisenhower was the perfect riposte to the Taft coalition. Supporting him in the party were the followers of the Willkie-Dewey-Vandenberg tradition, and although a good many other elements entered into the decision, Eisenhower's first-ballot nomination and subsequent election in the race against Adlai Stevenson constituted a major step in committing the Republican Party to internationalist principles. At times during the campaign, General Eisenhower, in his assault on the Truman policy, sounded as if he were something less than a fervent supporter of the international viewpoint. But his flirtation with the Asia Firsters, Senator Joseph McCarthy, and the Taft supporters was only an affair of reasonable political expediency and never a commitment to marriage. After Eisenhower's well-publicized New York "harmony" meeting with Taft, the Ohio senator admitted that "differences" still existed between the two in matters of foreign affairs.

Eisenhower's appointment of John Foster Dulles as Secretary of State was testimony to his persistent international viewpoint. Few men have ever had Dulles's training and experience before coming to the State Department. And few Secretaries of State have had such a wavering record on foreign policy. Though he had been a Wilson internationalist, Dulles was a convinced noninterventionist by 1940. He contributed to the America First Committee. But after America's entrance into World War II he again became an internationalist. During Truman's Administration, he negotiated the Japanese peace treaty for the State Department, and he acted as Dewey's foreign-policy adviser in the campaign of 1948.

As Secretary of State, Dulles was given almost a free hand by Eisenhower, and at times it appeared as if he were radically re-shaping the nation's foreign policy. His attack against the Acheson containment philosophy and his promises of liberation for the Russian-dominated states of Eastern Europe threatened the unwritten agreement between the West and the Soviets supporting the territorial status quo along the Iron Curtain. Dulles's threat to engage in an "agonizing reappraisal" of American commitments in Europe was aimed at France and the other NATO members reluctant to contribute their promised share of mutual-defense costs. His critical speeches on Indian, Yugoslavian, and Egyptian neutralism added up to the old maxim that those who were not for us were against us. And his references to "massive retaliation" and "going to the brink of war," as well as his advocacy of armed American intervention in French Indochina, were redolent of the anti-United Nations and Asia First factions in the Republican Party.

But in actuality the Eisenhower-Dulles foreign policy was not so different from that of Truman and Acheson. Some slight modifications and changes in emphasis resulted in a U.S. alliance with Fascist Spain, the signing of the Southeast Asia Treaty, and the abortive Middle Eastern Treaty with which the Secretary of State unsuccessfully attempted to force the noncommitted Arab states into an anti-Communist alliance, ancillary to NATO. Despite Senator William Knowland's charge that Eisenhower had negotiated a Korean peace "without honor," the armistice commission finally agreed on a territorial status quo ante along the thirty-eighth parallel, exactly what Truman's actions in limiting MacArthur had foreshadowed. And though the U.S. refused to intervene and aid the anti-Communist rebellions in East Germany, Poland, and Hungary, a fervent global resistance to Communism and the Soviet Union continued to be at the core of American foreign policy.

Dulles's practice of this doctrine was sometimes restrained by Eisenhower's realism. After a series of disastrous French reversals in Indochina, Dulles argued for armed American intervention, even if unsupported by her Western allies. But in the end Eisenhower, out of approximately the same considerations that moved Truman to avoid a major war with the People's Republic of China, decided against the commitment of American forces. As a result, at the Geneva conference of 1954, Indochina was divided into North and South Vietnam, and the sovereignty of Laos and Cambodia was recognized. By undertaking not to overturn the agreement, the Eisenhower Administration implicitly recognized its legitimacy. But out of deference to Dulles's sensibilities the United States did not lend her consent to the accord, and this may have contributed in part to the failure of the subsequent elections and provisions for peaceful reunification of the country which the agreement set forth.

Secretary Dulles subsequently negotiated the Southeast Asia Treaty, resulting in an organization promptly labeled SEATO, but it was not, in strength at least, analogous to NATO. No military organization was formed, and indeed, India, Ceylon, Burma, and Indonesia refused to join even this largely consultative organization. But the increasing worldwide struggle between the two nuclear powers, and America's increasing propensity to intervene against Communist movements in South Asia, were among the considerations that led to the calling of the Bandung conference of April 1955.

Bandung was a milestone in the evolution of the tortured postwar world. Gathered there were twenty-nine nonwhite representatives from Asian and African nations, including delegates from Communist China, for the purpose of discussing the future of the non-European world. Neither the United States nor the European nations nor the Soviet Union had been invited. Predictably, therefore, the keynote of the Bandung conference was an attack on colonialism. But the most important development was the formulation of the doctrine of "neutralism," an affirmation that a large part of Asia and Africa would not ally itself with either side in the cold war and that the underdeveloped nations of the world needed independence from the economically advanced nations. Incorporated in the neutralist doctrine were demands on the rest of the world for political liberation, for the recognition of racial equality, and for massive economic and technological aid to assure the Orient and Africa a living standard approaching that of the West. Also implied in the Bandung doctrine was the intention of playing the two major power groups off against each other. After Bandung, the going price for Asian support was to appreciate rapidly.

From Asia, neutralism spread quickly to the Middle East and Africa. Since Egypt and adjacent regions had long been dominated by the British and the French, and since American money had to a large degree been responsible for the astonishing rise of Israel, neutralism came naturally to Egypt's young dictator, Gamal Abdel Nasser, as it did for the heads of other Arab states, who could use the doctrine additionally for prying more returns out of the Western companies exploiting the fabulous oil basins scattered around the Persian Gulf. Denied the lucrative oil revenues of the southern Arab states, and beset with mass poverty and a calamitously rising birth rate, Nasser sought a solution for Egypt in the construction of a gigantic dam and irrigation works along the Nile, to be engineered and financed, he hoped, with Western skill and money. A treaty granting Egypt the necessary credit was on the point of being ratified in 1956 when Secretary Dulles publicly denounced the agreement because of Nasser's refusal to reduce his purchases of Russian arms.

In an angry protest, Nasser secured a promise of funds and technical assistance for the construction of the Aswan High Dam from the Soviets and subsequently nationalized the Suez Canal, the majority of whose shares were held by France and Britain. In response to the rapid Egyptian rearmament with Russian supplies and the seizure of the Suez Canal, Israel, France, and Britain came to a secret understanding. On October 29, 1956, as Israel invaded the Sinai Peninsula, France and Britain attempted, with lamentable preparation and execrable execution, to overthrow the Nasser regime and retake the Suez Canal.

These surprising developments threatened utterly to destroy American policy in the Middle East, which had as its major aims (1) the exclusion of Communism from the area; (2) the protection of the gigantic American oil concessions; and (3) the maintenance of Israel as an independent state. Prior to the Suez explosion, the United States had attempted to rationalize its complex Middle Eastern policy by supporting the status quo between Israel and the Arab states. But in November 1956 the British-French action in the Suez forced the United States to make a choice between the continuation of that policy and the alienation of Britain and France. To support the Western allies might antagonize the Arabs to the point of endangering American oil concessions and possibly pushing Nasser into the hands of the Russians for protection. Egypt certainly would have become a Russian client. Involved also were the anticolonial sensibilities of the uncommitted nations of Africa and Asia. Support for Nasser and Egypt, on the other hand, meant a deep rupture in and possible collapse of the Western European Defense Community, encouragement of further Arab seizure of foreign property, and the loss of thousands of Jewish votes for the incumbent Administration. Since the U.S.S.R. had threatened the Western partners with rockets if they did not retire from Egypt, American pressure against its allies might be interpreted by the Kremlin as an indication that the United States would not risk open conflict with the Soviets and thus might invite further Russian expansion. It was a difficult choice, and one that might have been avoided if American policy prior to the Suez Canal seizure had been more enterprising and imaginative, more energetic and more definite. But the choice had to be made among the thorny alternatives, and Eisenhower and Dulles forced Britain, France, and Israel to retire from Egypt.

The baneful results of the Suez fiasco quickly became apparent. Throughout the Middle East and Africa, Nasser's prestige soared, and Dulles's attempt to organize a Middle Eastern Treaty Organization to ward off Soviet pressures was shattered. The explosive Arab nationalist and neutralist movement propelled Syria into a short-lived union with Egypt; the pro-Western government of Iraq was overturned in a violent revolution; and only the landing of United States troops at Beirut stopped a radical Lebanese revolution. The Suez incident also gave impetus to the independence movement in Africa and strengthened the bloody Algerian campaign for independence, a campaign that in the summer of 1958 helped destroy what remained of the reeling Fourth French Republic and on the threat of an armed rebellion brought Charles de Gaulle to near-dictatorial power in France. Although de Gaulle was far from being a neutralist, he was not an ardent supporter of American-European policy, and the Suez affair impelled him toward a policy of substituting French for American leadership in Europe.

In its eight years, the Eisenhower government strongly supported the inherited policy of encouraging Western European unity both politically and economically. The objections of France to the rearmament of West Germany were overcome by persistent efforts, and in October 1954 the seven NATO members agreed to accept Germany into their defense community. The addition of West Germany to Western defense, the armament of East Germany by the Soviets, and particularly the death of Joseph Stalin in March 1953 were new and important counters in the grim struggle for the future of Europe.

For a time, the succession of Nikita S. Khrushchev, dictator of Russia, appeared to portend a radical change in Communist policy. Khrushchev's denunciation of Stalin, his cordial spirit at the Geneva summit conference with Eisenhower in July 1955, and his apparently tolerant attitude toward developments in the client

Eastern European states, all suggested that the Russian temper had changed. But the bloody suppression of the Hungarian anti-Russian uprising in October–November 1956, occurring simultaneously with the Suez crisis, clearly indicated that, though Russian leadership had changed, Russian policies had not. Khrushchev reiterated his desire for "peaceful coexistence" with the United States, but he also boasted of the ultimate superiority of the Communist system and bluntly warned, "We will bury you." The subsequent competition between the Americans and the Soviets in the Congo, Southeast Asia, Berlin, and Cuba revealed just how dangerous to civilization a period of "coexistence" could be.

The reluctance and inability of the Eisenhower Administration to aid the Hungarians in their revolt, as well as Khrushchev's formula for coexistence, are explained by the so-called balance of terror, Churchill's apt phrase. By 1955 and 1956, Russia and the West realized that each possessed enough atomic armaments to destroy the other, and perhaps the rest of the civilized world as well. On November 1, 1952, the United States had exploded the first hydrogen bomb, a weapon of incalculable power even when contrasted with the awful force of the atomic bomb. Russia countered with one of its own in August of the following year. This situation, unparalleled in human history, was frightful enough to cause even the most impetuous statesman to pause. The further development of intercontinental rockets and of world-girdling satellites capable of carrying atomic warheads intensified the deadlock. The alternatives to mutual destruction were either an increase in the pace of development of technological achievement and competition in the hope of securing a margin of destruction, or an attempt to abolish the possibility of atomic war by the renunciation of such weapons under an international agreement. But whether within or outside the structure of the United Nations, the two powers, both repeatedly declaring their desire to abolish the awful weapons, failed to agree on exactly how that end was to be achieved. By the early 1960's, talk of atomic disarmament was almost academic. Britain and France had joined the atomic club, and the People's Republic of China and India were soon to achieve membership. The bomb had become an international status symbol, replacing imperialism and colonialism.

Before 1949, the United States had had an atomic monopoly; after that date, the Russian bomb ended that basis for a *pax Americana*. Moreover, rising Chinese power in the Orient spread U.S. resources ever more thinly around the perimeter of the Communist-dominated world American leaders wanted so much to contain. By the middle fifties, neither the United States nor Russia had the degree of control they once held within their respective orbits. The growth of Asian and African neutralism, the rise of China, and the resurgence of France, Germany, and Japan marked the end of the period dominated by the two great superpowers. Just as the Soviet Union was experiencing increasing difficulties in its relations with even small satellites like Rumania, the United States was troubled by a Communist-inclined Cuba and by a balance of international payments problem brought on by her foreign-aid program. Although the Chinese-Russian clash and the French-American conflict over European leadership tended to reduce the strain between the two principal nations, the movement toward fragmentation of world political power seemed hardly reversible. And if the past was any guide to the future, the growing multiplicity of claimants for leadership meant more turmoil rather than less. By 1960, when the balance of atomic terror demanded peaceful coexistence, the prospect of a world diplomatic revolution with accompanying conflict seemed imminent.

The increasing difficulty of shaping the world to America's liking, of stopping the spread of Communism and revolution, and of winning new allies in a struggle overshadowed by the prospect of nuclear annihilation led to rising confusion and frustration at home. Congress showed a growing disposition to question the efficacy of foreign aid, either for economic or for military development. Of particular significance for both party and world politics was the increasing reluctance of Southern Democratic representatives, once pillars of internationalism, to supply funds for foreign activities. Among the general public there were also indications of a sense of disillusionment with a world that stubbornly refused to conform to the pattern America expected of it. Beginning to arise from this maldisposition was a public inclination to turn inward and a frustrated demand for stronger action abroad uncomplicated by the desires of America's allies. Often irrationally combined, the two conflicting sentiments expressed themselves in demands for quitting the United Nations, abolition of all foreign aid, and, if necessary, the use of force to stop Communist encroachment.

Such feelings were not confined to the advocates of either party, but since the proposed program had obvious appeal to the once solidly Democratic South and Southwest and was very close to the program supported by the embittered Western Republicans of the Taft tradition, it seemed certain in 1960 that the normal patterns of domestic politics would be shaken.

7

Prosperity and Pessimism

MODERN war makes more drastic changes in society than any other social phenomenon except revolution. Such changes often become permanent. Within two years after Pearl Harbor, the compulsions of war had remade American society as the New Deal had not done in six. Unemployment had practically disappeared; total production, as measured by the gross national product, had increased by over 60 percent; the customary rights and privileges of most individuals had been seriously altered; and taxes and the national debt had risen as they never had in the years from 1933 to 1938.

Among the more permanent changes was a massive uprooting of people from their traditional homes. Over 15 million servicemen were moved to military camps located mostly in the Southern, Eastern, and Western parts of the country, and similar migration was made by civilians attracted to the fantastic multiplication of ship and airplane construction facilities. Other war-born industries, and the increasing tempo of conventional production, triggered an equally important movement of people from the countryside and the small towns to the larger cities. During the war years, almost a million blacks moved North to locate in the large industrial complexes where wages were high and opportunities for a better life appeared greater. The increasing urbanization of the nation, which had slowed almost to a stop in Depression days, again picked up speed during the war and postwar years. Whereas the urban population had increased by only .3 percent from 1930 to 1940, the comparable figure in a 1950 census index was 2.5 percent, and in another was 7.5 percent. Meanwhile, the total farm population had diminished by over a million people. The war and its immediate consequences had contributed to a vast urbanization of the nation's people, which would, in turn, eventually make important changes in their social and political attitudes. In addition, the war materially affected the relationship between government and corporations, as well as contributing to significant changes within corporate structures.

Government expenditures during World War II made the New Deal's pump-priming efforts look puny and archaic by comparison. By 1944, approximately one half of the nation's production went directly into the war effort, and during the following year federal expenditures amounted to more than $100 billion, compared to the largest New Deal expenditure of $8.5 billion. From 1941 to 1946, the government became the direct or indirect employer of most of the nation's working force and the owner of over $16 billion worth of industrial facilities and of millions of tons of strategic raw materials. In large part, the facilities were leased to private operators, and after the war most of these were sold outright to private concerns.

For a short time after the end of the war, government expenditures were cut back sharply. But then the cold war, the Korean War, foreign-aid programs, the multibillion-dollar missile, and the space efforts made the federal government again the country's prime purchaser. In 1962, federal, state, and local government expenditures amounted to about $170 billion, a figure representing almost one-third of the total gross national product. Over half of this amount was spent by the federal government.

Had federal purchasing been spread evenly over the national industrial plant, the results of the spending would not have been so marked on either the government or the private sector of the economy. But a preponderant share of the vast amounts went for direct or indirect military programs, many of which dealt with intricate atomic and space problems. By 1960, the immediate donor of most such funds was the military bureaucracy in Washington, the immediate grantees a few hundred firms commanding enough technical facilities and research intelligence to deliver what was wanted. Just before leaving the White House, President Eisenhower warned the nation of the peril involved in the ever increasing identity of interest between the opulent military patrons and their industrial suppliers, the "military-industrial complex." Two years later, a knowledgeable journalist published a book entitled *The Warfare State,* in which he argued that the main support for the postwar American economy had been the enormous annual defense expenditures. He also contended that it was of direct interest to the military as well as their chief suppliers and subcontractors to maintain the huge military program, which now included within its ranks many of the nation's topflight scientists and engineers. Since expenditures of the postwar magnitude could not be defended in a relatively peaceful world, the danger was obvious that the series of sustaining international crises might become institutionalized as necessary to the existing economy.

The amount of federal expenditure, as well as the extent of governmental control over capital, labor, and the general public from 1940 to 1960, were roughly measured by the degree of foreign peril, either real or fancied. During the war, the countless agencies headed by the War Production Board not only decided what should or should not be produced but also rationed raw materials, transportation, labor, and many articles of general consumption. They set prices and controlled rents, and more indirectly attempted to determine wage scales and profit rates. Since little opposition to the war existed, little effort was needed to regulate men's minds. The removal of the Japanese-Americans from their West Coast homes to interior camps, even though their record of loyalty throughout the war was almost unimpeachable, indicated what might have been done with any large group of dissenters.

Immediately after the war, a reaction similar to that of 1919 and 1920 occurred against governmental intervention in the normal private activities of citizens. But while many powers were wrested from Washington by an insistent Congress and a militant citizenry, the series of international crises in the forties and fifties caused the pendulum to swing in the opposite direction. During the Korean War, the controls of World War II were partially reestablished. To stop one crippling railway strike, President Truman temporarily nationalized the railroads, but his attempt to do the same with the steel industry was thwarted by the federal courts. In the midst of his 1960 Presidential campaign, Vice-President Nixon brought official pressure on the steel industry to assure the workers a wage raise. Through stockpiling of strategic materials and by continuing agricultural marketing controls, the government was also a major force in determining prices for a long list of commodities and raw materials that ranged from structural steel to sugar beets, from platinum to peanuts.

Government was only one of several major forces in the postwar period contributing to a centralized economic life. The changing structure of both organized industry and organized labor substantially contributed to the process. In 1941, 45 percent of all defense contracts had been given to just six corporations. During the next four years, although the vast volume of war orders and subcontracting led to spreading the orders among many more companies, the percentage of contracts given to the hundred largest corporations increased. Since peace and reconversion never really came, the policy of granting government contracts to the largest companies continued despite the efforts of the Smaller War Plants Corporation and numerous House and Senate committees.

The new postwar technology gave further impetus to the growth of industrial gigantism. With the development of supersonic air transportation, atomic power, and intercontinental and interplanetary missiles, the costs of research, retooling, and development became enormous—often quite beyond the means of the smaller firms. The enormous distance that industry had spanned in a half century, as well as the scientific, managerial, and capital demands made on it, is illustrated by a comparison of the Wright brothers' airplane assembled in a bicycle shop (1903) with the intricacies of the supersonic jet plane of 1960.

By 1960, approximately five hundred corporations accounted for two-thirds of the nation's industrial production. Consequently, the character of their controlling bureaucracies was of utmost importance. As A. A. Berle, Jr., noted in *The Fictions of American Capitalism: Power without Property* (1960), the corporate trends already evident during the twenties had now matured. The old owner-manager of the large corporation had practically disappeared. Corporations were now headed by a new professional managerial class, many of whom were college-educated. Although few managers owned any significant number of the corporation shares, they possessed enormous power. Since most of the new capital they required was generated internally from profits and depreciation accounts, they were no longer dependent on banks, insurance companies, or individual investors. Thus, finance capital and Wall Street control of the major corporations, as well as the power of stockholders, tended to wither away. The publicly held securities of the average large corporation amounted to such vast sums that ownership was extremely diffuse. The capital structure of the American Telephone and Telegraph Company, for example, was so great that no individual owned as much as 2 percent of the voting stock. The remainder was spread among 200,000 investors, whose very numbers made effective control by stockholders impossible. Consequently, the top managerial group tended to become a self-perpetuating directorate which, though not owning, controlled. They were, in a fashion, trustees, but trustees remarkably free from restraints.

During the war, the organization of labor unions closely paralleled the structure of corporations. A flood of war orders created an unnatural demand for labor, and the ability of corporations to charge back rising costs to the government dissipated executive hostility to rising wage scales and union organization. In this benign climate, union membership rose rapidly. As growth continued after the war, total membership in 1955 amounted to 17 million, or about one-quarter of the total work force. With ample membership fees and pension funds, union bureaucracy grew larger, and power steadily drifted from the shop and the city federation to the national headquarters, from the constituent unions to the national federation. Local strikebreaking by national labor organizations was not unknown. And a precedent was set in 1953 when the president of the AF of L refused to back down before the threat of the Carpenters Union to disaffiliate. After a previous failure to unite, the AF of L and the CIO finally merged in 1955.

As unions grew larger and their power more centralized, their relations with business and government underwent a marked change. During the war years, labor policy was controlled in Washington by labor leaders who dealt directly with the government and with the many corporation executives on the wartime boards. The advantages of the arrangement were apparent to the participating partners, and in a postwar period characterized by administered prices at home and a succession of foreign crises abroad, the tendency to settle major labor disputes on a national basis became almost habitual. Involved in many such settlements were considerations of internal politics, national security, and the eventual costs to consumers. Increasingly, labor policy became a part of national policy, far removed from the shop and the control of the members.

As the American economy in the postwar period became more tightly controlled by relatively small groups in government, the great corporations, and the labor unions, it also became and remained, at least for almost two decades, incredibly productive. Many reasons were advanced for the continuation of the great boom. Initially, it was triggered by the $150 billion saved by individuals during the war, which constituted a deep pool of deferred purchasing power. Thereafter, huge defense expenditures arising from the cold war and the Korean War became a permanent prop to the economy. From 1947 to 1957, security costs of the government, not including veterans' payments, totaled $325 billion, a sum that exceeded the amount spent by private industry for new plants and equipment. In one very real sense, defense expenditures could be considered a peculiar type of national dole. They resulted in a vast augmentation of purchasing power without an increase in the production of useful goods and an actual decrease in useful labor. Millenniums before, the Pharaonic pyramid construction must have had similar effects on the Egyptian economy.

A high birth rate, which was to diminish in the sixties and seventies, further stimulated industrial growth. Government policy of easy credit rates, and almost yearly budget deficits, pumped additional purchasing power and inflationary pressure into the economy. The relation of the more or less controlled inflationary policy to the continuation of economic growth was evident in the early sixties when a short-lived deflationary period brought lower industrial indices and sharply increased unemployment. Of importance second only perhaps to the government's multifarious activities was the adoption by industry of Henry Ford's formula of the twenties: mass production, low unit prices, and high wages. Business was eager for mass production, but numerous government indictments for price fixing seemed to indicate a willingness of many industries to charge as much as they could. Though labor supported high wage standards, it fought the introduction of labor-saving devices, and when defeated encouraged featherbedding, or the maintenance of unnecessary positions. But because of the thrusts and counterthrusts of organized labor, capital, and government, because of competitive elements still operating in the economy, and because of the new character of corporate management, production sales and wages mounted and prices, despite the inflationary trend, were maintained at a reasonably low level.

The gross results of this great "surge to abundance" were scarcely believable. By 1955, the American economy, with about 6 percent of the world's population, was producing almost 50 percent of the world's goods, a ratio that was substantially reduced after that date by the renewed prosperity of Western Europe and Japan. The median family income rose from $3,083 in 1949 to $5,657 in 1959, a rise which, when corrected for inflation, still amounted to 48 percent. Accompanying this rise in income and the consequent torrent of consumers' goods, there was much talk about a "classless society." But despite all the bounteous wealth, the census figures reported that over 13 percent of families had an income of less than $2,000, a figure far below the subsistence standard. The greater portion of these unfortunates was made up of nonwhites, the national median for such family groups being only 54 percent of the yearly income of white families.

By 1960, other trouble spots had appeared in the economy. One of the most ominous during the early sixties was persistent unemployment of the unskilled and overemployment of the highly trained. While an estimated 5 to 6 percent of the labor force in 1960 was unemployed, 7 percent of the available work was done on overtime. The widespread introduction of automated factories and offices, inspired by high wage costs and a decreasing need for unskilled labor in a sophisticated technology, partially explained the continuing unemployment. Equally important, perhaps, was the fact that industry and business were probably faced with the more fundamental problem of overabundance that had dogged agriculture for decades. Economists noted elements of "consumer satiety" among the more fortunate groups.

Probably no other capitalist society has been as resourceful in employing men, machines, and materials for the production of what are essentially nonsalable goods. Millions of man-hours and dollars were poured into surplus agricultural production, surplus armaments, surplus capital, and consumer goods. The agricultural items were either downgraded (e.g., potatoes used for fertilizer) or sent abroad at ridiculously low prices subsidized by the government; armaments were prodigally scattered among so-called friendly powers; and industrial goods and whole factories were given to underdeveloped nations. Simultaneously, the fraction of the labor force in the total population was reduced. The ratio of the old and the retired increased as longevity rates rose and pension plans multiplied; that of the nonworking young was raised by the maintenance of relatively large military establishments and by a sharp increase in the number of students attending institutions of higher education.

In the "affluent society," the care and feeding of the consumer was a continual preoccupation of the business world. He was daily cajoled by advertising, frequently consulted as to his wishes by market surveys, and his future inclinations to buy or not to buy were intently studied by research organizations. A marginal decline in his purchasing expectations was often enough to curtail inventories and cause the stock market to waver. Stimulated by the government's easy-money policy, the consumer was flooded with credit. The extent to which purchasing on credit had become universal in American life was dramatized by the announcement in 1960 that the largest retail concern in the country, Sears, Roebuck, had over 10 million credit accounts on its books, or one for every five American families. Credit cards valid throughout the world were issued in abundance, and a lien on future earnings was utilized for such transient items as holiday travel. During the fifties, private debts rose from $73 billion to $196 billion. By 1960, eighteen cents of every dollar earned after taxes went to pay back previously contracted installment and mortgage debts. But despite all these devices, unemployment refused to decrease measurably, and this fact, plus the rising burden of private debts, perhaps indicated a maldistribution of income which might eventually imperil the continued efficient functioning of the economy.

Whatever the future of the economy, its record was an astonishing one. Both foreign and domestic commentators reached far for adjectives to describe the new productive machine: "neo-capitalism," "welfare capitalism," and "democratic capitalism." But if "democratic" implied control from below, it missed the mark entirely. Most of the population was supplied and some groups even inundated with goods. But the classic competitive process, as many influential economists admitted, had virtually disappeared. So had any sustained effective control of the great corporations by their legal owners, the stockholders. The individual consumer had about as much effective power in the marketplace as the small manufacturer or a solitary worker attempting to influence the actions of his union. Economic policy had, on the whole, become national policy determined by the bargaining of governmental, corporate, and to a lesser extent labor elites. Only when the masses were moved to concerted action, in mass buying or mass refusal to buy, was there a profound impulse from below. Generally, that sort of impulse came in moments of either euphoria or fright generated by the actions or the words of the controlling elite.

Many significant changes in social patterns took place during the postwar years, some the result of long-time trends in American society, some arising from more recent ones. The shift from the farm to the city continued, and by 1960 fewer than a third of the population lived in towns, villages, and on the farms. The traditional mobility of the nation was accelerated by shifting populations within cities. As the newcomers, many of them blacks, Puerto Ricans, or Mexicans, moved to the cities, a large fraction of the previous urban population went to the suburbs. This two-way traffic created ever larger metropolitan areas, with sprawling suburbs on the fringe and increasingly intense and compacted problems in the inner core. To the suburbs went a great proportion of the city's educated middle class—and a corresponding proportion of the city's tax revenues—and they were followed by many commercial and cultural institutions that had given the city its urbanity. The decaying central areas, on the other hand, were racked with violence, unemployment, and poverty, and bred a new kind of proletariat with few attachments to traditional American values. A major emphasis of urban public policy was on control of the new proletariat—and all others among the poor and unfortunate who posed a potential threat to the established order —through police, courts, and the welfare system.

The national population shift from the colder to the warmer climates of the country was responsible for the sharp growth of the Pacific Coast, the Southwest, and Florida. Often overlooked as a vital factor in the changing folkways was the vast amount of American travel abroad. The millions of soldiers transplanted abroad during the war, the continuing shifting of government personnel during the cold war, and the annual swarms of tourists to Europe and Asia added up to an impressive number of Americans who encountered foreign cultures. Social parochialism along with political isolation appeared to be things of the past.

Major movements took place within the employment structure. The reduction in the number of common laborers, from 11 million in 1900 to 6 million in 1950, was speeded up by automation. Feminization of the nation's working forces continued. By 1960, more than one-third of the women of working age were either employed or looking for work. And within some age groups as high as 28 percent of the married women were working for wages. But perhaps of much more importance in indicating the future social drift was the movement of a major portion of the working force away from the actual production of goods and into the so-called service, amusement, and leisure industries. Despite the great increase in production, by 1960 fewer people were employed in manufacturing establishments than in 1945. By the latter date, more than half of the nation's employees were engaged in nonindustrial pursuits, especially in sales, distributive, advertising, and secretarial services, and in amusement and leisure enterprises. Thus, the number of people involved in actual production was contracting at a rather rapid rate. In this new mass-consumption society, the old equation of man confronting materials and making something new of them had been changed to man confronting man and persuading him to act. A latter-day Emerson might have written: man was in the saddle and rode mankind.

Advertising was one of the basic supports of postwar mass culture. In *The Affluent Society,* John Kenneth Galbraith, one of the nation's leading economists, commented that the volume of goods needed to ward off mass unemployment and a possible racking depression was only sustained by a "synthesis of desire" which was "sold" to the public principally through the medium of advertising. Advertising's main objective, as one of its leading devotees admitted, was to make the consumer unhappy with what he had, and to consider it "obsolete."

Long before 1960, the advertiser and his colleague, the public-relations expert, had moved into the field of manipulating public opinion about more important matters than consumer goods. The campaign of 1960 and 1961 of the American Medical Association to defeat the Medicare proposal, a scheme to subsidize medical care for the aged, was directed by a skilled public-relations organization. Almost every federal department or commission of consequence had its own staff. In the 1952 Presidential election the Eisenhower organization was advised by one of the leading public-relations firms on how to establish a proper public "image" for their candidate. By 1962, even gubernatorial and senatorial candidates had public-relations experts on their staffs, and the word "image" became a political as well as a business stereotype. What was sought, of course, was not a true or mirror image but a synthetic one that would hide blemishes and project hidden or nonexistent virtues. In business and politics, the objective was to manipulate the public mind.

A rapidly growing monopoly movement in the daily press also contributed to the specter of a managed electorate. Whereas in 1910 practically all cities had two or more competing newspapers, the Hutchins Commission report revealed that, by 1955, 40 percent of the large dailies held a local monopoly and in ten states not a single city had rival newspapers. Television, which in 1960 was in 87 percent of American homes, mitigated to some extent the drying up of diverse opinions in the daily press. Federal regulation requiring equal time for political candidates and containing a vague injunction to pursue the public interest kept the expression of opinion on television somewhat freer than in the press. But in some ways television was organized in a more concentrated fashion than the press. Since national programs were so extensive and advertising receipts depended on the number of viewers, its operators concentrated on securing the largest possible audience. Although both sides of questions supported by major groups were invariably presented, marginal opinion, minority taste, and strange ideologies were rarely reflected on the screen. A toleration of acceptable variance was shown, but social heresy was either avoided or depicted so as to make it repugnant. When exhorting the public to consume, television certainly outstripped the newspaper in irrationality and in untruth. Some of its national quiz shows were rigged, most of the applause of its live audiences was contrived, and the utter nonsense, insidious deception, and barefaced falsity of much of its advertising material were obvious. Although television's potential in raising the nation's cultural level was enormous, most of its programs were trivial and banal.

"No art form, no body of knowledge, no system of ethics is strong enough to withstand vulgarization," one critic of America's mass culture despairingly wrote in 1958. In as pessimistic a mood, other commentators noted the nation's aspiration for conformity, which demanded a similarity not only in dress, food, housing, and automobiles but in ideology and philosophy as well. A plethora of books with titles such as *The Organization Man* and *The Man in the Grey Flannel Suit* played variations on the theme. Most such volumes were inclined to link this compelling desire for sameness to basic economic institutions. But at least two authors found deeper reasons for the alleged fear of individualism. David Riesman suggested that under the impact of modern urban and industrial culture the average American had changed his character from "inner-directed," responding to a cluster of internal personal values, to "other-directed," or responding to the mass values held by his neighbors. Erich Fromm, the noted psychiatrist, attributed the sheeplike character of the masses to an impelling desire to escape from the painful necessity of making choices and a resulting willingness to accept the values imposed by the group. In other words, the urge was to escape from individualism and freedom to the security and regimentation of the herd.

Most critics doubtless overemphasized both the uniformity of the day and the individualism of the past, or of other cultures. What had changed most in America, as also in Europe, was man's attitude toward man and his individual place in society and in the universe. Nowhere was this more clearly defined than by the creative artists, particularly in literature. This reestimation of man and his place in the universe started not at midcentury but during the twenties and the thirties.

In *A Farewell to Arms,* one of Ernest Hemingway's characters observes that the world breaks almost everyone, and those that it cannot break, it kills. "It kills the very good, the very gentle, and the very brave impartially. If you are none of these you can be sure it will kill you too, but there will be no special hurry." This terrifying and sardonic statement, imputing to either society or nature or both a basic malevolence toward the good, the gentle, and the strong, was written some ten years after World War I, and before the Great Depression, by a man who had lived through the relatively peaceful and lush days of the 1920's and who had acquired a considerable reputation as a novelist. Yet its statement about man and his relation to his fellows and to the universe can be taken with some modification as a reasonable reflection of the sentiment of most other gifted non-Marxian American writers of the twenties and the thirties. From Sherwood Anderson's tales of an Ohio town, published in 1919, to John Steinbeck's novel (1939) of the Depression-born migrants from Oklahoma, the writer's general image of man and the human condition is almost a constant. If there were individual exceptions, like Robert Frost, writing from a slightly more optimistic angle of vision, there were many who disagreed with Hemingway solely on the possibility of finding much goodness, gentleness, or bravery in the human race. If one looks at Anderson's aberrant rustics, Fitzgerald's glittering, brittle youth, Dos Passos's lost urbanites, Eugene O'Neill's Freudian cast, Faulkner's Southern monsters, and Nathanael West's shrouded characters from a planetary insane asylum, the sum is a frightening, even terrifying one.

In the world view of America's major novelists, human virtue was a rare commodity; in part, perhaps, because it did not pay. In F. Scott Fitzgerald's short story "Dalyrimple Goes Wrong," a young, idealistic war hero comes home to great cheers and a pitiful clerkship. His honesty leads from one trouble to another, until he determines to cast his moral restraints aside. He commits a robbery, becomes a solid citizen, and as the story ends is elected state senator. Faulkner made much the same point, but with a signifi-

cant variation toward irrationalism, in *Sanctuary*. By the false witness of the nonvirtuous heroine, Temple Drake, an honest boot-
legger is killed by a mob while the real gangster, Popeye, dies at
the hands of organized justice for a crime he does not commit. In
Faulkner's later works, while the good and the bad seem to be
punished impartially in the end, in the short run at least, victory
almost always resides with the most repugnant characters. As the
few families with long-developed codes of behavior steadily disintegrate, the South is taken over by an incredible swarm of the
barbarous, amoral, avid Snopeses. Of them, one perceptive villager
charitably remarks: "There's some things even a Snopes won't do.
I don't know just exactly what they are, but they's some, some-
where."

According to most of these authors, very little could be done to
stop the triumph of evil. There seemed to be, beyond man's power
to reverse, a grim and remorseless tide running toward pain, tragedy, and death. Free will was an eschatological fantasy. Hemingway's heroes are men to whom things are done, and as one of his
characters remarks, "Madam, there is no remedy for anything in
life." This pattern of the hero-victim became so standard in
American literature that the hero as a victor practically disappeared.

Post-World War II literature continued, with some variations,
the pessimistic, irrational, and tragic themes of the twenties and
thirties. Writers found society just as inimical to man. It was some
"strange sentient organism," John O'Hara wrote, "with a dull
implacable hostility" to the individual. The institutions compos-
ing it were of the same genus. Created by man, they had become
his master. The new machine techniques, Norman Mailer's General Cummings observed, demanded that a master class rule with
an iron hand so that the masses be made "subservient to the
machine." Both the natural and the social worlds were irrational,
and what looked like the good and safe course of human action
often turned out to be the bad and disastrous. In his novels, James
G. Cozzens reiterated that human freedom was "the knowledge of
necessity," but the "necessary" was often impossible to detect
even by his most rational heroes. Men were buffeted, according to
Cozzens, by a never ending series of unreasonable, relentless, in-

exorable forces; there was no exit save death. "The victor was, of
course, the vanquisher of all men, those forces ever victorious of
circumstances."

With such a conception of man's relation to the world, it was
not surprising that many writers departed from the existing formal
literary structures of the past. The slice-of-life pattern invaded the
novel and the play, and much modern poetry was written with as
little regard for rhythm and cadence as for intelligibility. The
author no longer attempted to order the world for his audience;
that would have been an exercise in superstition. Instead, he retreated into his own private realm of fantasy, where there were
few if any symbols of common understanding. Heroes, or rather,
antiheroes, rarely struck out at the world as Hemingway's characters had. Instead, they were shadowy and passive, tossed here and
there like chips on a wild stream. Sometimes they acted scarcely
at all either on their fellows or on nature; they simply talked.
When the characters of modern literature did act, it was seldom
in the traditional pattern of high effort and high passions, but
more often in the vein of sustained nastiness, as in Katherine Anne
Porter's *Ship of Fools*. Action was often limited to the field of sex,
where, casting aside human understanding and dignity, the characters sought to destroy their victims to gain another meaningless
trophy for their transient desires.

While the literature of the twenties contained some satire, the
persistent note of the fifties was pity—for man's loneliness and for
his inability to communicate with his fellows, and basically, an
involved self-pity of the author. There was also pity for man's
limited resources—"the corrupted unsound mind in the unsound
body, both unnerved by aging"—and pity for the odds against
which he fought. The reiterated plaint was that man got a very raw
deal in life in a universe which might have been put together "by
some idiot." One way out was to stop being a man. Across the
Atlantic, Samuel Beckett's degraded tramp observed without passion: "I have been a man long enough, I shall not put up with it
anymore." Characters in American literature who either committed suicide or seriously thought about it were numerous. This
mass withdrawal from life was the ultimate vote of no confidence
in man, his beliefs, and the structure of his society.

Social critics were almost as gloomy in their estimate of man and his institutions as were the creative writers. As in creative literature, the rapid decay of the earlier optimism had started in the twenties. The sharply changing views of Walter Lippmann and Reinhold Niebuhr may perhaps best illuminate this remarkable intellectual transit over the years. For fifteen years after the Peace of Versailles, Lippmann served consecutively as an assistant editor of the radical *New Republic,* as editor in chief of the liberal and literate *New York World,* and as a distinguished columnist for the conservative and influential *New York Herald Tribune.* These changes in employment corresponded to changes in his thinking. As a young man in 1914, Lippmann contended that science offered society the possibility of substituting controlled change for disordered growth. Eleven years later, in *Phantom Public,* he seriously questioned the possibility of progress and wondered whether man could ever really know his environment well enough to control it. It was a mark of his maturity to recognize "the vast indifference of the universe to his own fate." Lippmann examined traditional liberal democratic aspirations and clearly exposed his disbelief in the ability and fitness of the masses to rule. Liberalism, he ruefully remarked, had been an instrument of the universal conscience for the freeing of men, but it had not been, and probably could never be, an effective instrument of control once the masses were enfranchised. After the Scopes anti-evolution trial in Tennessee, he wrote in 1926 that it was "no longer possible to doubt that the dogma of majority rule contains within it some sort of deep and destructive confusion." His dreary conclusion to *Men of Destiny,* published the same year, was to the effect that eighteenth-century democratic theory was in permanent eclipse. "Its assumptions no longer explain the facts of the modern world, and its ideals are no longer congenial to modern man." By 1929, in discussing the limits of the attainable for humanity, he had adopted a stoical position: since man could no longer achieve what he desired, "he must want what he can possess." Lippmann had started his long search for instruments to control the enfranchised masses and to mitigate their excesses.

One of the major difficulties, he later wrote, in seeking controlling sanctions was that most of the traditional principles or "the great fictions" of the past have been eroded by "the acids of modernity." In the search for viable substitutes, he discounted traditional religion. In *A Preface to Morals* (1929), he could only produce as a possible substitute for the old discarded myths a "High Religion," basically humanistic in nature, the controlling principle of which was disinterestedness. Later, but before 1941, he suggested the possibility of the formation of a new cultural and political elite, and still later, a reformulation of the eighteenth-century principles of natural law.

From 1915 to 1928, Reinhold Niebuhr occupied a Detroit pastorate, after which he became a faculty member of the Union Theological Seminary. He had been an ardent member of the social gospel movement, believing intensely in the innate goodness of man. But during the twenties he began to shift the grounds of his theological and philosophical speculations. In *Does Civilization Need Religion?* (1928), he was still persuaded that the chief function of religion was to assert "the dignity and worth of human personality in defiance of nature's indifference and contempt." In an article entitled "The Confessions of a Tired Reformer" (1928), he questioned whether racial prejudice was not more the result of the universal characteristic of man than, as the liberals thought, of the viciousness of particular individuals or groups. From then, his flight from theological liberalism was at full gallop. By 1932, after the onslaught of the Depression, he observed that the very best that could be expected of man was a wise rather than "a stupid self-interest," and referred to history as a "perennial tragedy."

Niebuhr was by this time also striking at one of the central doctrines of religious liberalism or modernism by denying that it was possible to find a rational solution to the multiple crises threatening modern man. Reason, he contended, remained a menial servant of man's passions and of nature's caprices, and the way back to a relatively peaceful and humane society could be found only through the use of what he called the "ultrarational" faculties. A comprehensive statement of his ultrarational views (which many of his opponents called irrational) is to be found in his 1941 Gifford Lectures at the University of Edinburgh, entitled *The Nature and Destiny of Man.* By some mental alchemy, Niebuhr remained a political radical and a reformer. But his theological views in the space of some ten years made a 180 degree transit from religious liberalism to a neo-orthodoxy, from the rational to the ultra or irrational, from engendering hope about the immediate future of the world to a dark and deep pessimism.

It is fascinating to speculate why this massive and profound shift in the thinking of American creative writers and intellectuals took place at the time it did. Most historians concerned only with its immediate political nature, and unmindful of the philosophic depth of the change, have ascribed it to the disillusionment resulting from the war, America's failure to join the League of Nations, and the triumph of reactionary and materialist politics during the Harding and Coolidge Administrations. Others have explained it as an accumulating response to the series of crises suffered by American society since 1917, an explanation which does not account for the sharp intensity and the wide latitude of the shift before 1929. Some have tried to relate it to the doctrines of Sigmund Freud and to the new scientific theories of indeterminacy, emanating mostly from biology and physics, which challenged the assuring and comforting nineteenth-century mechanistic explanation of the universe. Still others have seen it as a tidal reaction against the business culture of the twenties.

What few historians have mentioned as a major cause of the shift in attitudes is the intellectual's deep antipathy to the rising masses and the rapid evolution of modern mass culture. The early 1920's was precisely the time when the vast crowd of lower-middle- and working-class people made their first appreciable impact on democratic industrial and urban life. The tastes and distastes of the buying millions in many ways soon dictated the form, the design, the content, and levels of quality not only of consumer goods but also of many cultural intellectual, and political institutions.

As early as 1915, Randolph Bourne, the little hunchback intellectual of Washington Square, perceived what was coming. He was gleeful at the demise of the so-called genteel culture of the nineteenth century presided over by millionaires and academicians, but he was not at all happy with what was being substituted for it, a "low-brow snobbery" of the masses which was just as "tyrannical and arrogant" as the aristocratic spirit that had preceded it. "It looks," Bourne concluded, "as if we should have to resist the stale culture of the masses as we resist the stale culture of the aristocrats." But even Bourne, who died during World War I, might have been shocked had he experienced the full impact of the masses on educational and cultural institutions and on national standards of taste. It required H. L. Mencken to register the soaring temperature of indignation. "The American people," he wrote in one heated but not atypical outburst, "taken one with another, constitute the most timorous, snivelling, poltroonish, ignominious mob of serfs and goose-steppers ever gathered under one flag in Christendom since the end of the Middle Ages." Mencken has often been described as a sport, an exceptional nihilist, or simply as a bad boy sticking his tongue out, whose opinions represented no one but himself. If that is so, one is hard-pressed to account for similar phrases uttered by scores of other writers, critics, artists. The evidence clearly suggests that Mencken was not alone in his attack upon the "booboisie."

From these various strands of contempt for and fear of the masses, of doubts about democracy and progress, and of pessimism about the ultimate destiny of man, one might have expected the weaving of a rather thoroughgoing cultural and philosophical conservatism. As a matter of fact, many of America's intellectuals found other ways of release from their anxiety and frustration. Some fled to London and Paris as a way of showing their disenchantment with their own culture. Some indulged in a feverish hedonism, while others found a retreat in extreme aestheticism. George Jean Nathan, co-founder with Mencken of *The American Mercury*, announced that social and political problems did not bother him one iota. What concerned him alone was art, himself, and a few close friends. "For all I care," he concluded, "the rest of the world may go to hell at today's sunset." Still others—Max Eastman, John Dos Passos, and Edmund Wilson—were attracted by the Russian experiment.

The difficulty that most of the intelligentsia faced in outwardly embracing conservatism during the twenties was that hitherto most of them had been ardent radicals. For years before 1920 they had been rebelling against a culture dominated by the post-Civil War millionaires. In that fight, their chief ally had been the economic and political radical. To expect them to say farewell to old friends and join the enemy across the political spectrum was perhaps asking too much too soon. But perhaps even more of a barrier was the fact that political conservatism in the United States had been and continued to be dominated during the twenties by a class whose narrow materialist views included colossal ignorance and even a suspicion of high culture. Calvin Coolidge and Henry Ford were the reigning conservative heroes—Coolidge, whose views on culture were either totally obscure or nonexistent, and Ford, who confined his "artistic" efforts to collecting old vehicles and McGuffey Readers. Between the intelligentsia and Coolidge and Ford there was nothing in common except hostility. The antagonism was further strengthened during the Depression by the Roosevelt Administration's energetic efforts in support of the arts and the conservative attack on practically all of the New Deal's intellectual ventures from the Writers' Project to the Federal Theater. As long as the conservatives continued to view state aid to the creative arts as something akin to subverting the foundations of the republic, the chances for even a mild flirtation between the two groups was minimal.

Even though the creative mind on the whole continued to regard the political conservative during the twenties and the thirties as its natural enemy, it had nevertheless established the preconditions for the eventual rise of a new political and social outlook. By questioning the doctrine of progress, the intellectuals were tending to sap the reforming élan. By deflating man's claim to moral excellence, they were casting doubt on the possibility of personal reformation. Their assumption that both nature and human society were subject to powerful irrational and uncontrollable forces questioned the validity of much social planning. And their generally pessimistic estimates of the qualities of the masses bred doubts about the worth of extending democracy.

After World War II, the intellectual's path toward philosophical conservatism was made much easier by a number of factors. The Soviets' nationalist policy and Stalin's insistence that the Russian artists cut their creative ideas to fit the Communist Party's measurements disabused most Westerners of the hope for a cultural renaissance under Russian socialism. New Deal reforms had achieved many of the aspirations of the onetime radical intellectuals, and thus their programs for social change had arrived at a dead end. But neither the labor unions nor the masses showed the deference expected of them by the intelligentsia. Instead, the masses, increasingly concentrating on consuming the multitude of goods and services produced by postwar industry, appeared to the intellectual as colossally indifferent to truth, quality, liberty, and ethics. "Production, consumption and profit," Edmund Wilson wrote with asperity, "have come to play the role that religion played in our grandfather's generation." Such things could not even be discussed, since "they have taken the place of the book of Genesis and the divinity of Jesus Christ. . . ."

In the postwar years, some onetime militant radicals and liberals took long and strange journeys. Although many continued to support liberal causes, some, like Max Eastman and John Chamberlain, for example, became contributors to the bleakly conservative *National Review,* whose editor had pronounced that "all that is finally important in human experience is behind us. . . ." Edmund Wilson toyed with the idea of selective breeding as an antidote to suffocation by the rising mediocrity. The radical journalist Max Lerner described man as "an animal with bestial impulses that can be multiplied by the multiple cunning of his brain." And that consistent apostle of rationalism, Walter Lippmann, labeled the materialist-worshipping masses as the "new barbarians" who were "in" but not "of" Western culture.

Lippmann summed up these antiliberal and antidemocratic sentiments in *The Public Philosophy* (1955). When mass democracy informed through mass communication ruled, Lippmann wrote, no individual confrontation was possible, and consequently, by a sort of Gresham's law, the irrational statements drove out the more rational. All so-called truths produced by such a system were "self-centered and self-regarding"; all principles were "the rationalization of some special interest." There were "no public criteria of the true and the false, of the right and wrong beyond that which the preponderant mass of voters, consumers, readers, listeners happen at the moment to be supposed to want." Where mass opinion so formed dominated the government, Lippmann concluded, nothing could result but a "morbid derangement of the true functions of power."

Punctuating this pessimistic chorus were many proposals from both left and right for the restructuring of society. Some critics, among them Reinhold Niebuhr, saw the need for a return to religion and Judaic-Christian values. Others proposed a reconstitution of natural law and natural rights as antidote to the prevailing materialist relativism. Walter Lippmann and Raymond Moley, among many others, argued for natural overriding principles "to command the will and obedience of man." Max Lerner and other radicals preferred to reach back to humanism and traditional socialism for principles of the proposed social reorganization. A few on the extreme right—John Chamberlain, for example—saw "a self-adjusting" natural order in the free market and free capitalism.

Whether from the political right or the left, most critics of the social order hoped to achieve a reconstruction through the creation of a new hierarchical elite that would presumably replace business, labor, and governmental groups. The character of the new elite was almost as varied as its sponsors, but not one of the proposers explained how they could be forged and how they could elicit from the masses the deference necessary to their dominance. Impractical as these elitists were, their large numbers indicated vast disquiet among the intelligentsia with modern mass materialist and relativist democracy, and a building impulse for social control. This flight from traditional liberal-radical values added a massive conservative leavening to postwar society which the character of politics was soon to reveal.

8

The Politics of Statics,
1941-60

WORLD War II tended to mute the more strident tones of
domestic politics. The flood of war orders providing work for
long-dormant industries and more jobs than there were men and
women to fill somewhat soothed the dispositions of both capital
and labor. The abolition of the Works Progress Administration,
the New Deal's virtual refusal to propose radical social measures
for the duration of hostilities, and the inclusion of thousands of
businessmen on the controlling war boards in Washington also
helped to suppress temporarily the rancor existing between the
supporters of the New Deal and most of the business community.
Farmers, faced with unlimited markets for their produce and a
government-set scale that insured them more than parity prices
for many commodities, were prosperous. And though price, wage,
production, and rent controls irritated many people, the great majority accepted them as necessary to win the war. Patriotism and
prosperity thus acted as solvents for some of the bitter quarrels of
the past decade, solvents which in time were to change the balance
of the parties.

The war sharpened the already growing conflict between the
President and Congress. Wars have offered Presidents an ample
opportunity for the assumption of near-dictatorial powers, and
Roosevelt was not timid in seizing the chance. From 1941 on, the
President, often by necessity, made critical decisions after consultation with a few executive officers. Less and less were senators
and congressmen called to White House conferences, and increasingly the President asked Congress for immediate action in a per-
emptory way reminiscent of his first hundred days in office. In

1942, after waiting four months for Congress to act on a price-control bill he had recommended, Roosevelt tartly warned the legislature that if they had not acted by October to remove the threat of economic chaos to the country he would. "In the event that Congress should fail to act and act adequately, I shall accept the responsibility, and I will act. . . ." Eighteen months later, the President described a pending congressional tax bill as entirely unsuited to the spirit and purposes of the times. He demanded a law that would abolish all "unreasonable profits," limit personal incomes to $25,000 a year, and provide $10 billion in additional receipts for the government. When the Democratic-controlled Senate passed a bill supplying only an additional $1 billion and ignored his other requests, Roosevelt replied with a sharply censorious veto, which prompted Senator Alben Barkley, one of the President's most loyal supporters, to resign temporarily his position as the majority leader of the Senate.

The timing of Roosevelt's tax demands in 1944 recalled his "soak the rich" program before the election of 1936. His correlative requests for a postwar bill of economic rights, including the right to a job, a decent home, a good education, adequate medical care, and social insurance, raised the suspicion among his opponents that he was willing to run for a fourth term. These requests also ended the wartime moratorium on the discussion of divisive social issues. Roosevelt refused to campaign for the renomination. When the well-organized Democratic Party convention met, however, he was selected on the first ballot. But the growing opposition to Presidential dictation as well as to further reforms was made evident by a rebellion of delegates representing big-city machines and the South. With Roosevelt's halfhearted acquiescence, they nominated Harry Truman as the Vice-Presidential candidate instead of the liberal incumbent, Henry Wallace.

Republican prospects had been steadily improving since the 1938 elections. Although Wendell Willkie had lost in 1940, Roosevelt's margin in popular votes had been much less than in either 1932 or 1936. Moreover, Republican candidates for Congress had fared extremely well in 1940 considering that the party lost the Presidency. Republican resurgence was further marked in 1942 when the formal Democratic control of the House of Representatives was reduced to a mere five votes. Consequently, there was no lack of would-be Republican candidates in 1944. But after Governor Thomas Dewey of New York defeated Wendell Willkie in the Wisconsin primary, his nomination was almost automatic.

Since Dewey was an internationalist and promised to preserve the major social gains of the New Deal, few issues were debated in the campaign of 1944. In his few speeches, Roosevelt scarcely acknowledged that he had a competitor. When he did depart from his subjects of war and peace, he identified the Republican Party with Herbert Hoover and the Depression. Once again, the outcome was scarcely in doubt, but though the President rolled up his customary huge electoral vote, his margin in popular votes—about 3 million—was the smallest for any Presidential campaign since that of 1916. What might eventually have happened to the fortunes of this political wizard was forestalled by his death in the late spring of 1945. Both the complex problems of the peace and the highly explosive domestic issues surrounding demobilization and reconversion were left in the inexperienced hands of Harry Truman.

Perhaps the new President's greatest liability in 1945 and 1946 lay in the public's low estimate of his abilities. He followed one of the ablest politicians who had ever held the office, a man who commanded almost fanatical adoration by the majority at home, and who by 1945 was a world figure of imposing stature. By almost any concrete measurement, Truman shrank by comparison with Roosevelt. Physically inconspicuous, he had neither the personal charm nor the assured, cultivated manner of his predecessor. His past record was, by comparison, almost a blank one, and he lacked that almost indefinable charismatic quality that a successful Presidential campaign often confers temporarily on some of the most ordinary politicians.

Truman's inherited Cabinet thought of him in condescending terms. Consequently, during his first few months in office, he was obliged to establish his authority. Few Administrations since Jackson's have been punctuated by so many personal quarrels. Henry Wallace, Louis Johnson, and J. Howard McGrath were all dismissed from the Cabinet. Henry Morgenthau, Jr., left in a huff, and later James Byrnes and Harold Ickes made public their differences with the President.

Truman's old companions in the Senate also had considerable doubt as to whether he would measure up to the Presidency, and some were not entirely despondent at the prospect. After fourteen years of submitting to the White House, both the Senate and the House were eager to reestablish their authority. This anti-Presidential mood was intensified by the growing conservative complexion of the Congress and the country. The decline in Democratic congressional majorities from 1938 on had come largely at the expense of the liberal wing of the party. Rising Republican votes in the East and the Midwest had defeated many reliable New Dealers; death had also taken its toll. With the departure of liberal-minded Northern Democrats, control of the congressional party by traditionalist Southerners became intensified. At one time during Truman's last four years, the president pro tempore of the Senate, the Speaker of the House, and the two party whips were all Southerners. Moreover, the chairmen of eighteen of the Senate's thirty-three standing committees were from the South, a number that included most of the more important committees such as those on appropriations, foreign relations, armed services, and banking and currency. Although the Democratic Party commanded a national majority during four of the six Truman years, its controlling group in the national legislature was predominantly from one of the two most rural sections of the country, and one that represented less than a third of the nation's total population, and perhaps no more than a fourth of its total voters.

These same years witnessed a similarly striking change in the composition of the Republican Party in Congress. In 1938, the Middle and Far West Republican senatorial delegation was studded with names like La Follette, Norris, Borah, Johnson, and Capper. By 1950, death and defeat had removed all these old symbols of revolt against traditional Republican doctrines. During these years, a new type of Republican senator had appeared in the East (especially in New England)—internationally minded and not irrevocably opposed to the interests of labor and minority groups inhabiting the large industrial cities. But the control of the congressional party was dominated by Republicans from the West, whose thinking lay much closer to the old Republicanism than it did to that of this new Eastern species. The Republican leaders who came into power after the congressional victory of 1946 came from nonurban states or those, like Ohio, with a long tradition of conservative control. And though Robert Taft of Ohio—the new majority leader of the Senate—supported housing legislation, the group as a whole tended overwhelmingly to espouse traditional pre-New Deal economic and social theory.

After 1938, many Southern Democrats in Congress combined with the Republican minority to stop social and economic legislation favoring mass urban groups. During the postwar period, the control of both congressional parties by groups largely representing the South and the Middle and mountain West facilitated a developing coalition probably animated more by the opposition of its constituent parts to the political desires of the urban masses than by positive common principles. The interior of the nation with almost three-quarters of total rural inhabitants was thus in control of Congress.

Both by birth and by associations, Harry Truman was closely identified with the controlling congressional groups in each party. Had he chosen to follow his earlier convictions, his relations with Congress might have been far less stormy. But as a Missouri politician and as a senator, Harry Truman was one man; and as a President, another. From his wide reading in political history he had acquired a profound respect for the office of the Presidency as well as a Jacksonian attitude toward it. The President, he wrote later, was the "only lobbyist the whole people had in Washington. Almost every aspect of their welfare and activity falls within the scope of his concern. . . ." As the master politician that he was, Truman might have added that the President and the whole people are intimately concerned with one another at the ballot box. He had not spent years living with the Pendergast machine for nothing, and he recognized that a Democratic candidate could not hope to win the office without preserving in some form the four-times-victorious coalition of farmers, laborers, and urban minority groups that Franklin Roosevelt had fashioned.

Truman felt pledged to carry out the foreign and domestic policies of his predecessor. He therefore asked Congress for the first peacetime universal training law and for higher taxes to meet the expanding costs of his foreign policy. Congress honored neither of these requests, nor did it fully meet Truman's demand for a workable price-control law to stop the spiraling inflation. An eventual price-control compromise failed either to halt ascending prices or to encourage enough immediate production to meet demand. Consequently, black markets reappeared and housewives found themselves unable to obtain meat at their usual shops. The sharp rise in prices brought about numerous labor demands for wage increases, and in 1946 a national railroad strike was threatened hard on long labor stoppages in the automotive and soft-coal industries.

Fearing economic chaos, the President seized the railroads, and when labor walked off the job in lieu of accepting a compromise wage scale, the President personally appeared before Congress to demand the proclamation of a national emergency under which he might draft the strikers into the army. Fortunately, the strike was settled before Truman finished his speech, but his proposal to draft strikers into the army alienated organized labor temporarily, and public dissatisfaction with inflation, black markets, and price controls—emphasized skillfully by the Republican slogan of "Had enough?"—produced the almost inevitable result. In the elections of 1946, both houses of Congress went Republican. *Life* magazine predicted that Congress, which had for years been a "rubber stamp and whipping boy for the White House," would now assume direction of political life. The returning Republicans attempted that and more. Many of them, in fact, saw the election as the equivalent of the Republican victory of 1920 and rejoiced at the opportunity "to repeal the New Deal." Meeting before the opening of Congress, a conference of Republican leaders agreed on a program of radical reductions in government expenditures, lower taxes, a return to states' rights in health and welfare measures, and the abandonment of government interference with business and labor.

The new congressional leadership started out bravely if inconsistently with their announced program. The passage of the Taft-Hartley Act outlawing the closed shop empowered states to pass right-to-work acts, allowed employers more latitude in speaking against unions and in petitioning for shop elections, and gave the President limited powers to enjoin strikes that imperiled the national security. The Act also prohibited the use of union dues in political campaigns and required a non-Communist oath from labor leaders using the facilities of the National Labor Relations Board. The President called the Act "a slave labor measure," but it was promptly passed over his veto. Against Presidential opposition, the new Congress also reduced taxes and passed a farm support measure that substituted a flexible scale of price supports for the old rigid formula of 90 percent parity. It did, however, despite much criticism, support the President's European foreign policy.

But the Eightieth Congress by no means took the play for public attention away from the White House. Starting with his annual message in January 1947, Truman fairly peppered the national legislature with requests for basic social reform. His demands for a broad extension of social security, for a scheme of federally supported public medicine, for extensive aid to education, for further aid to agriculture, and for the repeal of the Taft-Hartley Act were all ignored by the Republican majority precisely as they would have been had the Democrats controlled Congress. But the President was perhaps not so much interested in securing reform legislation as he was in securing his election in 1948 and a Democratic victory. The President's game, of course, was to place the responsibility for the lack of benefits to farmers, laborers, and minority groups on the Republicans.

The Republican convention did its best to defeat the Presidential strategy by denying the nomination to Senator Robert Taft, the man who best represented the principles of the party's officeholders. After General Eisenhower declined to be considered, on the grounds that the "wise subordination of military to civil power will be best sustained when life-long professional soldiers abstain from seeking high political office," the prize again went to Governor Dewey of New York, already on record as an internationalist and a supporter of most New Deal reforms.

The party platform also clashed with the professions of Republican congressional leaders. It advocated a broad extension of the social-security program, federal aid to housing, a "just" system of price supports for farm products, the abrogation of state poll taxes, and fair-employment legislation. Only in the platform's demand for government economy did the convention defer to the principles of its officeholders. But by doing so it cast some doubt on its zeal for the reforms it had already proposed.

The Democrats had difficulty in finding many principles which were acceptable to even a bare majority of the party. Aroused by Truman's adamant stand against Russia, extreme left-wing Democrats broke away to organize the Progressive Party, led by Henry Wallace and Senator Glen Taylor of Idaho. The more moderate left, including Americans for Democratic Action, was equally opposed to the President, because they believed he had deserted the New Deal by eliminating Wallace, Ickes, and Morgenthau from his Cabinet. A civil-rights program supported by Hubert Humphrey, mayor of Minneapolis, and by the President resulted in the defection from the convention of over thirty Southern delegates. These "Dixiecrats" later held a convention at Birmingham, formed the States' Rights Democratic Party, and nominated two Southern governors as their candidates. Even the usually dependable big-city bosses, fearing certain defeat with Truman, attempted without success to interest General Eisenhower in the nomination. Organized labor was unenthusiastic about a second term, and the Midwestern farmer had allegedly returned to his normal Republican affiliation. The party gloomily went through the familiar motions and prepared itself for defeat.

The following campaign was one of the most startling in recent history. Since the public-opinion polls all showed Dewey as a certain winner, the Republican candidate was rather nonchalant in his electioneering efforts. His relatively few campaign speeches were dignified and almost noncontroversial. Dewey challenged neither the premises of the Administration's European foreign policy nor the basic reforms of the New Deal, and contented himself with the argument that his party would carry out the existing foreign and domestic programs with far more efficiency and economy than could "the tired, confused, strife-ridden and politically minded" Democrats. Dewey left the vulgar aspects of the campaign to his more partisan colleagues.

The President, however, would not participate in a gentlemanly front-porch campaign redolent of the Harding and McKinley tradition. Almost deserted by the higher-ranking members of his party and lacking the plentiful finances of his opponent, he waged an intensely partisan and astoundingly individual canvass, most of which was aimed at bread-and-butter issues. Calling attention to the social-welfare promises of the Republican platform, he recalled Congress into an unprecedented July session, demanding that the Republicans live up to the professions of their official program. When the session adjourned without accomplishment, Truman labeled it a "do-nothing Congress," one of the worst in history. The President followed this partisan ploy with an old-style cross-country campaign in which he repeatedly read a partisan record on the Eightieth Congress. In the cities, he called the Taft-Hartley measure a slave-labor act and asked labor whether it thought it would be better off under a Republican or a Democratic President. Before recent immigrants, he flayed the "anti-Semitic, anti-Catholic" immigration bill passed by the Republican Congress. He reminded Jewish voters of his recent and speedy recognition of the State of Israel. In agricultural regions, he asked farmers whether they proposed to vote for the Republican sliding scale of subsidies or for the Democratic 90 percent plan. And almost everywhere he characterized his opponents as the party of the oil and power lobbies.

In a more positive vein, "give 'em hell Harry" Truman elaborated his Fair Deal, which included programs for extensive public housing, for federal aid to education, for publicly supported medicine and hospitalization, particularly for the aged, a long-range scheme for agricultural-price supports, the freeing of labor from the Taft-Hartley measure, the extension of social security, and the passage of a broad civil-rights measure insuring "equal status to the Negro and other minority groups." But acute politician that he was, Truman relied mainly for success on the past record instead of on future promises. His political philosophy was summed up in his observation late in the campaign that the farmers and laborers would be "the most ungrateful people in history" if they turned the Democrats out and voted the Republicans in.

To the consternation of the polltakers and the surprise of most politicians, Truman won, although by a very small popular major-

ity. While he lost the densely populated Eastern states of Connect-
icut, New York, Pennsylvania, New Jersey, Delaware, and Maryland, and four states in the Deep South, his victories from Ohio
westward helped make up the winning total of electoral votes.
Unable to explain the results in rational terms—Senator Taft remarked that it defied "all common sense for the country to send
that roughneck ward politician back to the White House"—most
interpreters regarded the election outcome as just one more victory
for the coalition of voters that the New Deal had put together.
Enough farmers and laborers and members of minority and fringe
groups, they explained, were still letting their memories of the
Depression-ridden thirties dominate their political thinking. But
despite the fact that Truman carried virtually every major city in
the country, he won most of them by an extremely small margin:
New York by only 300,000 votes, Chicago by 200,000, Los Angeles
by 8,000, and Philadelphia by fewer than 7,000. Obviously, the
urban voter was no longer as enchanted with the Democratic Party
as he had been since 1932. And had not the Southern racial ex-
tremists aided Truman with the Northern black community by
opposing him, the election might have had a different outcome.
Otherwise, the Truman victory depended on the support he received from the normally Republican territory from Ohio to the
Pacific.

The President regularly throughout the next four years recommended his Fair Deal program to Congress, but not even a majority of his own party was inclined to support much of it. Some
expansion of social security was obtained. Modest funds were
voted for public housing and slum clearance. By executive measures, the civil rights of minorities were somewhat extended. But
the conservative coalition of Southern Democrats and Midwestern
Republicans blocked most efforts at further reform. Moreover, a
series of spectacular developments relating to foreign affairs practically obliterated most domestic issues from the public mind.

In 1949, Russia exploded its first atomic bomb, just after two
Americans were charged with cooperating with the Russian espionage system. The rumor gained currency that the rapid Soviet
perfection of the bomb had been made possible by secret information leaked from official American sources. Since Alger Hiss, one

of those charged with Communist connections, had been a member of the State Department under Roosevelt and Truman, the Hiss perjury trials and the spy trials rapidly created an atmosphere of partisan politics. Some Republicans who had already charged Truman with being soft on domestic Communists saw in Hiss's conviction proof that the Administration and particularly the State Department were honeycombed with traitors. After the victory of the Communists in China and the beginning of the Korean War, the Republican charge was made repeatedly that subversives in the State Department had planned the American debacle in Asia.

Leading the Republican campaign to tar the Administration with the brush of Communism was Senator Joseph McCarthy of Wisconsin. Defeating the incumbent Senator Robert La Follette, Jr., in 1946, McCarthy was practically unknown until he made the public charge in February 1950 that the State Department was "thoroughly infested with Communists." The senator added that he had a list of 205 Communists in the State Department, although a month later he reduced this number to "fifty-seven card-carrying members of the Communist Party." When asked for specific names, McCarthy was unable to produce one. But he maintained himself in the daily newspaper headlines by completely unverified attacks in the same vein on a series of important Administration leaders, the most prominent of whom were Secretary of State Dean Acheson and his predecessor General George Marshall.

The official Democratic reply to the McCarthy charges was made by President Truman. McCarthy's activities, as well as those of the House Committee on Un-American Activities, he said, were "red herring," designed to win votes rather than to protect the country from subversion. The President pointed out that long before McCarthy had taken up the subversion cry the Administration's own loyalty boards had been operating, but on the traditional basis that precluded "character assassination" by the widespread publication of rumors and unverified facts. Truman concluded that the desperate Republicans, unable to win by any other means, had descended to the irrational issue of a Communist internal conspiracy and were, by their wild and unfounded accusations, destroying reputations and careers for the sake of winning the next Presidential election. Radicals and liberals also accused the Red hunters of attempting to destroy the New Deal heritage by smearing its proponents. But as an increasing number of respected Republicans approved of the anti-Red campaign and as new revelations of Russian espionage in the United States, as well as in Canada and Great Britain, were published, the voters increasingly tended to believe the charge that an internal subversive threat existed and that the Truman Administration was incapable of dealing with the conspiracy.

The Administration ran into other difficulties before the elections of 1952. The President's firing of General MacArthur was necessary if civilian supremacy over the military was to be preserved. But the general's removal was not popular, and the Administration's continued failure to bring the Korean hostilities to an end was also a liability. Although a majority probably agreed that a limited war was preferable to an attack on China, with the possibility of Russian atomic retaliation, it was difficult to give up the hope for victory and to support an endless war. Almost as damaging to the Administration's reputation was the revelation of fraud in the Bureau of Internal Revenue and "influence peddling" in other important agencies.

The Democrats probably selected their strongest candidate in nominating Adlai Stevenson. His apparent reluctance to become a candidate and his refusal to see most public questions in black-and-white terms permitted his opponents to charge him with indecisiveness. His careful prose and cultivated wit also opened him to the charge of being an "intellectual" at a time when that class was under popular suspicion of being, at best, impractical and, at worst, of harboring subversives. But Stevenson had been a very able governor of Illinois, and in appearance, mentality, and political instincts he was far removed from Truman. To a party split between Americans for Democratic Action on one pole and states' rights Southerners on the other, these qualities were a distinct advantage. Even so, after the Republican nomination, almost all chance for a Democratic victory vanished.

The contest for the 1952 Republican nomination emphasized that the party had no more cohesion than its opponents. With the death of Senator Vandenberg, Robert Taft had become the official spokesman of the congressional party on both domestic and foreign affairs. His consistent anti-New Deal record and his advocacy in January 1951 of an "oceanic" foreign policy, which would have protected the island nations of the Atlantic and the Pacific from Communist aggression but would have stopped short of maintaining an American army on either the European or the Asiatic continents, had won the support of a good many Republican officeholders. The Taft formula was the first offered by the party that would have greatly limited American commitments abroad and yet could not be labeled isolationist. Both as a foreign-policy statement and as an economy measure, it appealed to the Midwest, precisely the section that had supplied most of the victories for the party in the long, lean days since 1932. The senator was hailed as "Mr. Republican," and during the early months of the nomination campaign, a Taft victory seemed inevitable.

The Taft candidacy did not go unchallenged. Liberal Republicans, and especially the internationalists in the party, started a search for alternatives. Led by Dewey, Harold Stassen (then president of the University of Pennsylvania), Senator Henry Cabot Lodge, and Governor Earl Warren of California, these groups had a distinct East and West Coast flavor and were recruited mainly from the noncongressional elements of the party. Eventually, most of the anti-Taft men came to support General Dwight D. Eisenhower, at the time commander of the NATO forces in Europe, who in late 1951 retracted his nonpolitical position of four years before.

Eisenhower had many advantages for a divided party whose thirst for victory had been so long unslaked. Except on foreign policy, he was without a political record. Few knew until January 1952 that he was even a Republican. Born in a small Texas town and raised in another in Kansas, he had much appeal for the old-stock rural Americans. His brilliant military career endeared him to many conservative businessmen and made his patriotism unimpeachable, even to the most ardent nationalist. Moreover, the man exuded integrity, personal warmth, and charm, along with other virtues not ordinarily connected with the military profession —modesty and tolerance. Eisenhower's enormous popularity was well attested to by the public-opinion polls. Well before the conventions met, a Gallup poll showed that he would likely defeat either of the leading Democratic candidates, whereas Taft was shown trailing them both. The Taft managers did not help their candidate by attempting to secure votes in the convention by the old political methods. But, in the last analysis, Eisenhower was selected by a slim margin on the first convention ballot because of the prevailing feeling that he alone of the Republican candidates might win.

Eisenhower attempted to appease Taft by inviting him to a September conference in New York, after which Taft announced that the general and he agreed on all important issues except foreign policy. It is also possible—though denied by Eisenhower —that the two men also agreed that the senator and not the President would be the real leader of the congressional Republican Party. The Republican nominee also courted the favor of other important dissident Republicans. There was to be some retreat from an internationalist foreign policy. But in some ways the comments of Eisenhower and his chief adviser, John Foster Dulles, were much more militant in their foreign interventionism than those of their opponents. On domestic issues, the nominee sounded almost as conservative as a Midwestern right-winger might hope for. Although he declared that he was for the "broad middle way" and that most of the New Deal's social gains should be preserved, he denounced an excess of government intervention and in almost Taftian tones suggested that "if all that Americans want is security, then they can go to a prison." He supported Senator McCarthy in Wisconsin, commenting that while their methods might differ, their ends were the same. He appeared with the reactionary Senator Jenner in Indiana, and of course he attacked the Truman domestic record with wholehearted enthusiasm, as predicted. Eisenhower was elected by an impressive margin, losing in only nine Southern states.

The Eisenhower Cabinet was acclaimed by the party's regulars. Although not, as one of the Administration's critics described it, composed of "nine millionaires and a plumber," it was a very wealthy and conservative group and included at least two strong Taft supporters. The State Department's meek acceptance of McCarthy's demands in 1953 cheered the ultranationalists. And the Taft-sponsored legislative program resulting in a reduction in taxes, the grant of the tidal oil lands to the states, and the reduction in the level of government payments to farmers was meat and drink to the party's conservatives. They were equally pleased by the Administration's refusal to permit the TVA to build and operate a coal-burning power-producing station and by the contracts awarded to private companies for the development of hydroelectric power in Hell's Canyon, on the Snake River.

Senator McCarthy continued his rumor-filled inquiries into domestic subversion as chairman of the Committee on Government Operations and its Permanent Subcommittee on Investigations. Government officials were brought before the committee and subjected to questioning about their collegiate political affiliations and to innuendo and condemnation by association. The leading political groups—Republican and Democratic—were reluctant to interfere with such a vigorously "patriotic" activity, even though many considered McCarthy's methods crude and ineffective, if not actually dangerous. In 1954, McCarthy's committee began hearings on Communist subversion in the U.S. Army, and in this endeavor the Wisconsin Red-baiter clearly overextended himself. Eisenhower withdrew even his tacit support, and conservative groups in the Congress and abroad in the country also abandoned him. Though radical-right groups like the John Birch Society hovered on the fringes of the nation's political life, and virulent anti-Communism continued at the core of national institutions like the Federal Bureau of Investigation, McCarthy's excesses resulted in his censure by the Senate and the termination of his "investigations."

Despite the President's occasional denunciation of "creeping socialism" and the apparent reversal of the national conservation policy, the record of Eisenhower's first term was not an unmixed one. Especially after Senator Taft's death in 1953, the censure and deflation of Senator McCarthy, and the Democratic congressional victory of 1954, the Administration's tendency was away from accepted Midwestern Republican principles. During the 1952 campaign, Eisenhower had declared his leaning toward conservatism in economic matters and toward liberalism in social concerns. But during the recessions of 1953 and 1954 the Administration used both fiscal and monetary policies to reinflate the economy and suggested it was ready to resort to broad public spending if necessary to stop a downward plunge. In 1954, the President even boasted that by controlling the economy the government could practically guarantee the continuance of prosperity; "the fear of a paralyzing depression can be safely laid away." No New Dealer had claimed more for governmental intervention.

In his second state-of-the-union message, the President described his goals as "first, to protect the freedom of our peoples; second, to maintain a strong growing economy; third, to concern ourselves with the human problems of the individual citizens." He proposed during the remainder of his first term the extension of social security to workers in small establishments and to the self-employed, extensive increases in funds devoted to public housing and to education, and a highways bill that contemplated the construction of over forty thousand miles of superhighways, financed by both state and federal funds. Despite Secretary of Agriculture Benson's laissez-faire views, payments to support agricultural prices actually rose during the Eisenhower years.

Not all of the President's recommendations were accepted by Congress, which was as thoroughly dominated by the Southern Democratic-Midwestern Republican coalition as its predecessors had been. Certainly on issues of foreign policy, and to a lesser extent on domestic questions, the President received more congressional support after the Democratic victory of 1954 than before. At various times, starting with his campaign of 1952, Eisenhower had labeled his brand of politics as "liberal conservatism" and then successively as "dynamic conservatism," "moderate progressivism," and "progressive moderation." Well before the Presidential election of 1956, Eisenhower had used the term "new Republicanism," which he later modified to "modern Republicanism." And for a period the President acted as if he were about to give his party strong executive leadership in an effort to remodel it. Under strong pressure, the President eventually canceled the Dixon-Yates contract that had bypassed the TVA and awarded the construction of a power station to a private concern. And during the election campaign of 1956 he strenuously supported his proposals for more federal aid to schools and pressed for his highway-building program and for a soil bank that would decrease agricultural production by removing marginal lands from cultivation.

The Eisenhower record was not, however, generally dynamic or innovative, and was most frequently characterized by political commentators as either conservative or middle-of-the-road. The President himself was not particularly energetic or ambitious. As Presidents go, Eisenhower was rather old when he took office, and during his tenure he had two serious illnesses. Even when feeling well, Eisenhower was scarcely engrossed in the political details of his job. He took frequent vacations, left many of the Presidential chores to his subordinates, and avoided partisan politics and politicians whenever he could. The truth was that the President did not like his job very much and freely confessed his distaste to his personal friends, who, for the most part, were selected from outside the ranks of professional politicians.

The various policies of the Eisenhower Administration that affected cities were time-serving at best and destructive and confusing at worst. Albert Cole, whom Eisenhower appointed to head the Housing and Home Finance Agency, had actually voted against the Housing Act of 1949 as a congressman from a rural Kansas district, and he condemned public housing as a threat to free enterprise. Senator Hubert Humphrey of Minnesota charged that this nomination was "like putting the fox in charge of the chicken coop." Eisenhower did not end public housing, but he provided little sympathy or support for it. Urban redevelopment, which had the support of the business community, on the other hand, also enjoyed Eisenhower's endorsement and was enacted in the 1954 Housing Act. This measure contained the basic outlines of urban renewal, and a number of innovative features as well, but its basic attraction to business lay in the provisions for government assistance to private interests in the clearance and development of the downtown areas of American cities. In his second term, Eisenhower cut back on most urban programs as part of a general budget slashing and thus severely impaired the Administration's relations with the nation's mayors, most of whom were Democrats.

The election results of 1956 were among the most anomalous in history. Eisenhower defeated Stevenson by almost 10 million votes, carrying all but seven states in the South and, even more surprising, winning a margin in each of the four largest cities of the country. The Eisenhower victory in New York, Chicago, Philadelphia, and Los Angeles, to say nothing of traditional Democratic cities like Jersey City, indicated that the longtime alliance between the Democratic Party and the minority and laboring groups in the large cities had at least temporarily ended, a major political revolution that unquestionably would be taken into consideration by the party managers four years later. But despite the President's immense popularity, the Republican Party failed to win control of either the House or the Senate and lost more gubernatorial races than it won. For the first time in history, a winning President was to be confronted with a hostile Congress during its opening session. Analyzing the results, commentators remarked that the Democrats had been beaten in a popularity contest but had won an election.

Without the President's personal popularity, the Republican Party was still a minority one, a fact that spurred Eisenhower, in vigorous post-election efforts, either to reshape or replace it. Both in his second inaugural address and in a talk to the National Committee he emphasized that the party was doomed unless local and state organizations showed more willingness to adopt the principles of what he called "modern Republicanism," which in effect would moderate its hostility to government intervention in economic life and to reforms appealing to the urban masses. When his appeals to the National Committee for party renovation were ignored, the President for a time thought of founding a new conservative party, but gave up the scheme as impractical. And as his liberal recommendations to Congress were treated with no more respect by the Republican minority, he gradually lost interest in party reform and turned his major attention, as Roosevelt and Truman had done before him, to foreign affairs. The congressional elections of 1958 continued the existing pattern of nominal Democratic control with real power located in the Southern and Midwestern coalition, a Democratic-Republican alliance that had frustrated his predecessors in office and was to thwart the plans of his successor.

But if Eisenhower did not remake the official Republican Party, he nevertheless sensibly altered it, certainly modified its public presence, and quite possibly saved it from oblivion. A few more Presidential defeats and the party, dominated by the remaining Adullamites in Congress who had either withdrawn from the modern world or who had never entered it, and committed to hopelessly outdated, anti-New Deal, anti-urban, anti-international principles, might well have disappeared as a vital political force. Republican platforms since 1936 had given lip service to many New Deal reforms, and individual Republicans, mostly from urban areas, had greatly contributed to the enactment of both social and civil-rights measures. But most Republicans in the Senate and the House before 1953 denied by vote and voice any relationship with the party's published programs, except possibly for those portions dealing with agriculture. The plaint of an Eastern Republican congressman as he declined to run for office again illustrated the almost intolerable tension existing between the party's professions and its actions. He could not, he declared, continue to talk conservative enough to be nominated, liberal enough to be elected, and reactionary enough to succeed in his party's permanent organization.

By 1960, civil rights had become a dominant issue in American politics, and one that threatened once more to disrupt and possibly revolutionize historic party patterns. For historic reasons, the black vote, until 1932, had been largely Republican. But then the New Deal's relief, federal work, and social-security programs had converted it almost overnight. After World War II, the opposition by conservative property owners in the cities to high relief costs and Truman's civil-rights policy kept most blacks in the Democratic ranks. By executive order, Truman had abolished segregation in the armed forces, and he twice requested Congress to pass civil-rights legislation empowering the federal government to secure voting rights for Southern blacks as well as equality of public rights. In both instances, Southern resistance had blocked legislation and Southern schisms had threatened the unity of the Democratic Party.

Even Roosevelt and Truman refused to alienate with radical civil-rights programs large blocs of the coalition that had sustained them in power, and they looked on a number of black demands as unrealistic and premature, if not unreasonable. This reluctance on the part of leading white politicians and the glacial pace of change in the traditional patterns of race relations led, along with rising black impatience and determination, to a variety of challenges to racial discrimination throughout the nation, especially in the South, and also threatened black allegiance to the Democratic Party.

In 1954, the United States Supreme Court, headed by Chief Justice Earl Warren, an Eisenhower appointee, reversed the fifty-eight-year-old ruling permitting school segregation provided the facilities were equal. The landmark decision—*Brown v. Board of Education of Topeka, Kansas*—which grew out of sustained legal efforts by the National Association for the Advancement of Colored People (NAACP) and other groups in state and lower federal courts, declared school segregation unconstitutional as a violation of the equal-protection clause of the Fourteenth Amendment. The next year, the court ordered that school desegregation proceed "with all deliberate speed."

Although a few of the border states sought to comply with the Supreme Court ruling, it was met with the most vigorous opposition in the rest of the South. In March 1956, more than one hundred Southern congressmen called for "massive resistance" to the *Brown* decision and to racial desegregation in general. At Little Rock, Arkansas, in September 1957, the opposition led by Governor Orval Faubus eventually forced Eisenhower to send federal troops to enforce a court order for the desegregation of the public schools and to protect black students from the violence of mobs and local authorities as they attempted to attend the previously all-white Central High School. Spurred by Presidential requests, Congress passed a civil-rights measure in 1957, under which the Attorney General started suits to obtain black voting rights. Even though a second civil-rights measure was passed in 1960, by 1962 fewer than one-fourth of Southern blacks had registered to vote, and in nine years after the court decision, only 8 to 10 percent of Southern black children were attending desegregated schools.

But blacks had determined to settle for nothing less than their full constitutional rights, though the task, especially in the face of violent white opposition, was not easy. In December 1955, a black

woman named Rosa Parks refused to give up her seat on a Montgomery, Alabama, bus to a white man, as required by the segregation laws, and she was arrested. The black community protested
the action by boycotting the city's bus system and successfully
challenging the segregation statute in the federal courts. Two years
later, the Reverend Martin Luther King, Jr., who had first achieved
national notoriety as a local black leader during the Montgomery
bus boycott, formed the Southern Christian Leadership Conference with other black leaders in ten Southern states.

Racial bombings, beatings, and harassment reached a crescendo
in the following decade, as did the movement to achieve black civil
rights. Most of this activity was concentrated in the South, but it
reached northward as well. World War II had brought another
great wave of blacks to the North, and the massive migration
continued, until blacks constituted a major population group in
practically all large Northern cities. They were in the majority in
Washington, D.C., and Newark, New Jersey; they formed a quarter or more of the population of Chicago, Cleveland, Cincinnati,
Detroit, Philadelphia, and St. Louis. By 1960, they were a million
strong in New York City. Because of poverty and white restrictions, they usually settled in all-black slums in the central districts,
where they suffered disproportionately from unemployment, poor
housing, ill health, and hunger. By 1960, the question of equal
rights had become the major political and social issue in both the
North and the South, and its impact helped to redirect the currents
of national politics.

At the end of Eisenhower's second term, all indications pointed
to the possibility that the nation was headed for a major political
reorientation. From 1938 on, both major parties and Congress had
been dominated by conservative and rural majorities. Essentially,
the situation had come about because of two special situations.
First, apportionment had historically given the rural communities
an increasingly disproportionate share of representation in state
governments, party machines, and in the Senate of the United
States. Second, the dominance of the South in the Democratic
Party and of the Middle West in the Republican, chiefly because
they were safe districts for the incumbent officeholders, led to the
control of Congress by an informal but real coalition. At the same

time, however, an urban nation was becoming rapidly more so. By 1960, 70 percent of the American people lived in towns or cities, a political fact that showed up regularly every four years in Presidential nominations and elections.

Because the President was elected by popular vote, he was the chief representative of the underrepresented urban majority, and as a consequence the postwar conflict between the White House and the Congress rapidly increased in intensity. The situation was a major cause for the increased prestige of the President, the administrative wing of the government, and the Supreme Court in the postwar era. Since the thinking of Congress was not in harmony with that of the majority of the country, many significant and necessary adjustments had to come through the action of the Chief Executive or by the judiciary.

Because the official parties had ceased to represent the majority of the voters in several crucial areas, the parties themselves were rapidly losing prestige and strength, a fact attested to both by the rapidly growing numbers of independent registrations and by the almost unprecedented election of 1956, which produced a President from one party and a congressional majority from another. The critical struggle over civil rights also betokened a change in the traditional makeup of the parties. In 1960, both parties stood in a paradoxical relationship to the civil-rights issue. The Democrats, whose hopes for national victory lay in the minority groups and with labor, were permanently embarrassed by a South apparently determined to maintain as many attributes of white supremacy as possible. As the traditional conservative party, the Republicans were as perplexed as their rivals, for much of twentieth-century conservative strength lay in the rural regions. Any attempt to base the party on the new urban majorities would ipso facto change its fundamental nature. Urbanism and civil rights had thus become the fueling forces for significant political change.

Tension was also increasing between the technical and cultural elite and the passive adherents of the standards of the mass-production-consumption society. The rapid evolution of new technology demanded an ever more rigorously trained intelligentsia, but at the same time, the chief engines of mass culture, education, and information—radio, television, movies, the stage, the publishing industry, schools, newspapers, and the periodical press—were under constant pressure to adjust their standards to the tastes and the comprehension of the masses. Part of the pressure was self-applied; part of it was from advertisers and those desirous of reaching a mass audience and market; and part stemmed from the "democratization" of culture apparently demanded by the wider public. By 1960, educational reform had excited much talk and some action. But whether the secondary schools and the multi-universities could accommodate themselves to staggering increases in enrollment and still continue to educate the highly trained, technically proficient experts needed to run the new society was still an open question. In 1960, the reorientation of American life was yet a matter for the future, even though the latent forces of change had been accumulating rapidly for twenty years. Partially because of rural political overrepresentation, as well as because of urgent foreign problems, little had been accomplished in meeting the manifold and intricate problems created by a burgeoning urban and technical civilization, the geography of which often ignored state boundaries, and the demanding standards of which were frequently beyond the comprehension of the masses. But the static quality that had characterized American politics from 1945 to 1960 could not continue indefinitely. The pressures were too insistent and the stakes too high. By 1960, significant change seemed to be a necessity if the new and vigorous urban society were to endure. Just as many of the old cherished agrarian social virtues had given way to the new, urban values had to evolve to meet the needs of a new and very much changed nation.

9

The Politics of Turmoil
at Home, 1960-69

THE young President stood hatless in a chill wind to deliver his inaugural address. The message was of new challenges and old verities. "Let the word go forth," John Fitzgerald Kennedy declared, "from this time and place, to friend and foe alike, that the torch has been passed to a new generation of Americans—born in this century, tempered by war, disciplined by a hard and bitter peace, proud of our ancient heritage."

In January 1961, most Americans looked ahead with high expectations. Cold-war anxieties remained and the issue of race loomed dangerously, but the economic signs seemed promising. The millions of young people born just after World War II who entered college and adulthood in the 1960's expected a time of peace and prosperity. Virtually no one imagined the entanglements abroad and turmoil at home that would curse the decade and in one way or another destroy this new President and two of his successors.

There was never much doubt that Richard Milhous Nixon, a two-term Vice-President, would be the Republican nominee for President in 1960. But John F. Kennedy's rise among the Democratic hopefuls—Lyndon B. Johnson, Hubert H. Humphrey, and Adlai E. Stevenson—was something of a surprise. Kennedy blunted the impact of his Roman Catholic religion by a forthright speech to the Greater Houston Ministerial Association, and his victory over Humphrey in the West Virginia primary was a turning point in the Democratic campaign. At the convention in Los Angeles, Kennedy won on the first ballot. Perhaps even more surprising was Johnson's acceptance of the Vice-Presidential spot, which some observers believed was offered only out of courtesy.

But Johnson had strength in places, like the South, where Kennedy was weak.

The issues that separated the candidates, aside from personal style and appearance, were Kennedy's charges that the Eisenhower-Nixon Administration had permitted the internal economy to languish and the nation's defense to slumber. Kennedy's campaign promises to "get the country moving again" and to eliminate the "missile gap" with the Soviets were integrated and complementary.

In a series of unprecedented television debates with Nixon, style more than substance seemed to prevail, with the younger, more dashing candidate making the best impression. Possibly, Kennedy's "New Frontier" rhetoric and his economic and defense postures won him a few votes, as did his obvious appeal to youth, and his Catholic affiliation. But it is more probable that the old irrational New Deal coalition of the South and the big-city machines based on ethnic groups won him his extremely narrow 112,803-vote margin of victory, the smallest of the twentieth century. The Democrats retained their dominance in Congress, though they lost seats in both Houses.

John F. Kennedy was something new and puzzling to the pattern of the American politician and indeed of the contemporary leaders of the world. At forty-three, he was the youngest of all American Presidents and internationally a veritable stripling among old men —Adenauer, de Gaulle, Franco, and even Khrushchev. The first Catholic President, he represented at least in the minds of many of his supporters the new immigrant stock. Yet he carried the cachet of a Harvard education, of having published a book, and of being impressively articulate. He was also independently wealthy, supported by the millions acquired by his businessman father who had guessed right before the crash of 1929.

Politically and ideologically, Kennedy was also something of an enigma. Remarkably independent in his senatorial career, he had never belonged to the Democratic "club" headed by majority leader Lyndon Johnson. Nor did he intimately attach himself to the party's liberal wing. Although he selectively supported welfare issues, he was not outspoken on the question of civil rights for blacks, nor had he been an opponent of Joseph McCarthy.

Kennedy had a public reputation for reform, but personally he was a conservative, pessimistic about curing human and national ills by legislation and cautious on budgetary matters except for defense expenditures, where he was ready to match the Russians gun for gun and missile for missile. From his appointments, one would gather that Kennedy was an educational and cultural elitist. He surrounded himself with some of the best and brightest minds from the country's most prestigious universities, and his official guest list while in the White House (actually drawn up by his beautiful wife Jacqueline) was replete with luminous figures from the scientific and artistic worlds. No wonder the new Administration was dubbed Camelot.

As the Kennedy Administration pursued variations of cold-war policies abroad, much of the legislative New Frontier at home also turned out to be well-traveled country. The young President did secure from Congress an increase in social-security payments and a more generous minimum-wage law (which incorporated, however, so many congressional exceptions that it proved remarkably ineffective for agricultural and domestic workers and many other low-wage earners). A pollution-control act addressed the nation's massive problems in securing clean air and water. The Administration's housing act appropriated for the first time generous sums for urban-renewal projects. An area-redevelopment act provided funds for regions of high unemployment, with particular emphasis on Appalachia. But Kennedy's proposals for job training and stopgap employment for youth, and medical care for the aged, ran afoul of congressional opposition, as did other education and welfare measures.

Following a rise in unemployment in the spring of 1962, the President was far more adventurous in dealing with the national economy. For the first time in American history, he proposed a deficit budget in times of relative prosperity. With a threat to cancel government contracts, he forced the giant United States Steel Corporation to roll back a price increase on its basic products, and also suggested in a public speech that he might investigate the company's tax records.

The emphasis in the Kennedy Administration was more on competent management than on sweeping social reform. In case after case, the Administration proceeded a bit further than its predecessors in certain directions and then trimmed sails quickly in the face of harsh political winds. Robert S. McNamara, the Ford Motor Company president whom Kennedy appointed Secretary of Defense, did promote certain new policies, but he was most famous for his computer cost accounting and management systems. For all its expert advice, the Administration approached economic management awkwardly. The general tax cut Kennedy proposed included a 20 percent reduction on corporate rates, did not remove the most serious inequities, and was probably not necessary to reduce unemployment. In any event, it was not passed until after Kennedy's death. But the tax-cut proposal and Kennedy's support for the Trade Expansion Act and huge defense contracts did raise his stock considerably in the business community.

Like all political slogans, the New Frontier referred more to symbol and aspiration than to substance; but it was less well defined than the New Deal as a political program or an array of legislation. In fact, the Kennedy Administration had difficulty getting any bills through Congress, and the major pieces of legislation were not passed until the early years of Johnson's Presidency.

The most dramatic events, the thorniest moral and legislative issues, to confront the Kennedy Administration at home concerned civil rights. The ultimate consequences of the *Brown* school-desegregation decision of 1954—which potentially imperiled racial discrimination throughout the society—were driven home in the 1960's, not so much by haggling in the courts as by courageous and persistent nonviolent protest. Blacks and sympathetic whites, who persisted in their demands for equal rights even when Washington counseled moderation or patience, were the driving force in the movement, always pushing it forward until the basic objectives had been achieved.

As the decade opened, most of the South was still rigidly segregated, from separate rest rooms, drinking fountains, and seating in theaters to schools, parks, and even Bibles in some courtrooms. To some things, like lunch counters and hotels, blacks often had no access at all. On February 1, 1960, four black students began their protest against such laws at the lunch counter of Woolworth's in Greensboro, North Carolina, where they were refused service.

They sat patiently, suffering the jeers of angry whites. This "sit-in" movement spread across the South, involving tens of thousands of blacks and whites, and dramatizing the drive for racial equality. Martin Luther King, Jr., was arrested at an Atlanta sit-in, and John Kennedy's telephone call during the campaign to King's wife, Coretta, offering his sympathy and moral support, may have secured enough black votes to account for his narrow victory.

The Kennedy Administration fully supported civil rights, but also believed that this was a problem of deeply rooted Southern white prejudice that could be resolved one step at a time, logically and gradually, through constitutional action. The Kennedy family had little direct personal experience with blacks or the South, but they did know that virtually every elected official in the region stood staunchly for segregation, and the depth of white popular feeling on the issue had already been demonstrated by the resistance that forced Eisenhower to call out the troops in Little Rock, Arkansas. Southern whites had developed a strategy of "massive resistance" to any changes in the racial system, challenging every effort of blacks and the federal government. But the Kennedys also believed that this pattern could be changed, especially when blacks had equal voting rights. The Administration was, however, unprepared for the outburst of white reaction against black protests.

On May 4, 1961, less than four months after Kennedy's stirring inaugural address, a group of "Freedom Riders" led by James Farmer of the Congress of Racial Equality (CORE) left Washington, D.C., by chartered bus to test the public-accommodations laws in the Deep South. Ten days later, whites burned one of the buses outside Anniston, Alabama, and a second bus that managed to make it unscathed to Birmingham was met by a white mob wielding baseball bats and chains. The riders were dragged off the bus and beaten for fifteen minutes until police arrived. The city's Commissioner of Public Safety, Eugene "Bull" Connor, was a committed opponent of civil rights for blacks, and he passed the word to his officers not to interfere too quickly in the violence. The policy of rational, nonviolent, gradual change seemed quite inadequate in the face of this madness.

The Attorney General of the United States, Robert Kennedy,

emerged as the foremost champion of the civil-rights movement within the Administration. Speaking by telephone to the Freedom Riders in the Birmingham bus station and with Alabama Governor John Patterson, Kennedy attempted to find a peaceful solution. Somewhat naïvely at first, he looked to Southern authorities to enforce the law and preserve order. He also tried to persuade the Riders to call off their protest: their lives were in danger, and they had made their point. But the Freedom Riders were determined to carry on. When they arrived in Montgomery, the capital of Alabama, on May 20, they were again met by whites and attacked. A white mob surrounded a church where civil-rights demonstrators had gathered, including Farmer and Martin Luther King, Jr., and that night actually kicked in the door of the building. They were finally driven off by a small contingent of United States marshals, sent by Kennedy, and kept at bay by eight hundred National Guardsmen reluctantly called out by Governor Patterson.

Under National Guard protection, the Riders continued their journey the next day. When they reached Jackson, Mississippi, they were arrested and jailed for forty days. Remarkably, no one had been killed during the protest. With pressure from Attorney General Kennedy, the Interstate Commerce Commission issued a firm directive prohibiting racial discrimination in facilities and accommodations that came under its jurisdiction.

The story of the Freedom Riders outlined the struggle for civil rights during the next several years. Blacks persisted in demanding their rights, even at grave personal risk to themselves. Whites resisted, in some cases violently. Robert Kennedy worked to protect the protesters, tried to persuade Southern officials to obey the laws, and argued for strong national civil-rights legislation in Washington. The style and pace of the protests were controlled by civil-rights leaders and organizations, and the Attorney General responded to situations they had created. Sometimes federal authority was too little and too late. In 1962, James Meredith, a black, entered the University of Mississippi. Governor Ross Barnett, who spent most of his time publicly denouncing desegregation, encouraged troublemakers, and a riot resulted which took the life of one

French journalist and left the campus wreathed in tear gas. Three thousand troops and a corps of United States marshals were required to quell the violence.

The civil-rights campaign reached new intensity in 1963, with a series of demonstrations in Birmingham, Alabama, organized by the Southern Christian Leadership Conference (SCLC). Dr. King was jailed on April 12 for violating a city ban on protest marches, but this did little to stop the movement. King used this time to write his famous "Letter from the Birmingham Jail," which defended his movement and the strategy of nonviolence and criticized white moderates for standing in the way of social progress and ignoring the desperate need for change. "Actually, we who engage in nonviolent direct action are not the creators of tension," King wrote. "We merely bring to the surface the hidden tension that is already alive. We bring it out in the open, where it can be seen and dealt with." Without nonviolence, "many streets of the South would, I am convinced, be flowing with blood." One day, the demonstrators would be recognized as the "true heroes" of the South. "Oppressed people cannot remain repressed forever. The yearning for freedom eventually manifests itself, and that is what has happened to the American Negro."

During the first week in May, demonstration leaders launched a "children's crusade" against segregation, sending thousands of students on nonviolent marches through the city. Even though the city commissioners had been voted out of office in a public referendum establishing a new mayor-council form of government, "Bull" Connor and his colleagues retaliated against the demonstrations with fire hoses, police dogs, and club-swinging legions of police that filled the jails with protesters and the front pages of newspapers around the world with lurid photographs. On May 10, when a tentative agreement easing segregation practices was announced between black and white city leaders, Dr. King's motel was bombed. A settlement was eventually reached in Birmingham, as white businessmen overcame their fear of negotiating with blacks. The Birmingham demonstrations provided vital national pressure for the passage of a federal civil-rights act. But the violence ended on September 15, with one of the worst crimes of the decade, when four black children attending Sunday School were murdered in a Ku Klux Klan bombing of the Sixteenth Street Baptist Church.

In June, Alabama Governor George C. Wallace, who entered office proclaiming "segregation now, segregation forever," staged a theatrical "stand in the schoolhouse door" at the University of Alabama to prevent the admission of black students. By prearrangement with federal officials, he made a speech and stepped aside. The riots of a year before at the University of Mississippi were not repeated, but the difficulties encountered by blacks at all levels in the South were again demonstrated for all to see. The next day, NAACP leader Medgar Evers was gunned down in front of his home in Jackson, Mississippi.

Violence in the United States was not confined to blacks or civil-rights workers. On November 22, during a visit to Dallas, President Kennedy was shot to death as he rode with his wife in a motorcade. The nation was stunned and appalled that a young, vital leader could be struck down so suddenly. Investigations into the tragedy began immediately and continued off and on for years. The first official commission to probe Kennedy's death, chaired by Chief Justice Earl Warren, reported that a lone assassin, Lee Harvey Oswald, a former defector to the Soviet Union who returned to the United States and supported various leftist causes and was arrested in Dallas on the day of the shooting, was responsible. Since Oswald was himself shot and killed by nightclub owner Jack Ruby, many questions remained unanswered. A congressional panel concluded some fifteen years after the event that Kennedy's death was probably the result of a conspiracy, though no other individuals were named.

At the moment Kennedy was declared dead on an emergency-room table in Dallas, Lyndon Baines Johnson became the thirty-sixth President of the United States. He formally took the oath of office that same afternoon aboard Air Force One, with Jacqueline Kennedy standing at his side.

The new President, whose selection as Vice-President many Kennedy men had considered a mistake, seemed totally alien in Camelot. Johnson shared with his predecessor both a towering ambition and an awesome personal vitality; but in other ways the two were as alike as cheese and chalk. Kennedy had been born to the economic purple and had had the best education money and a first-class mind could provide. His introduction to politics came from his maternal grandfather's Irish wards of Boston and the Court of St. James's, where he assisted his father, the ambassador, during the immediate pre-World War II period. Johnson sprang from the dry hills of southwest Texas, ranching country, but until the New Deal raised the price of beef, a relatively impoverished area. His education came from the public schools and from the then struggling teachers' college at San Marcos, innocent alike of any cultural pretensions and of scholarly reputation. He learned politics as a secretary to a Texas congressman during the New Deal days and as a five-term member of the United States House of Representatives. Elected to the Senate in 1948, he soon became the acknowledged leader of his party in that body.

Johnson announced that there would be no changes in policy and that his total efforts during the following year would be devoted to securing passage of the legislation already proposed by the martyred President. This he did with efficiency and dispatch, undoubtedly aided by the general reaction of remorse over Kennedy's death. But in civil rights, poverty and relief legislation, and tax matters, Johnson's prodigious energy, his intimate knowledge of Congress, and the many debts owed him for past congressional favors undoubtedly were also responsible for his signal success. Under Johnson's adroit handling, the Congress that balked under Kennedy turned into a productive legislative mill. The new President pushed Kennedy's tax-reduction bill through, and also other legislation, including the food-stamp program, aid to mass transit, and hospital-construction legislation. But the first priority was civil rights, to which Johnson brought a depth of personal conviction as well as loyalty to his predecessor's desires.

The need for a civil-rights law was dramatized in late August 1963 when more than 200,000 demonstrators joined the March on Washington for Jobs and Freedom, organized by Bayard Rustin and A. Philip Randolph. Speaking from the steps of the Lincoln Memorial, civil-rights leaders lamented the legacy of brutality and fear that had been the blacks' throughout American history. Martin Luther King, drifting into the rhythmic cadence of the Southern preacher, focused on the future: "I have a dream that this nation will rise up and live out the true meaning of its creed, 'We hold these truths to be self-evident: that all men are created equal.' "

With a rising national demand for action, and Johnson's skilled prodding, cloture was finally invoked, for the first time, to end seventy-three days of filibustering in the Senate against a civil-rights bill. In June 1964, a bill stronger than the one Kennedy had introduced was enacted, and President Johnson signed it into law on July 2. The Civil Rights Act of 1964 was to be amended repeatedly in the future, but it remained the cornerstone of the nation's efforts to secure, to the extent that federal legislation can secure, substantive equality for all of its citizens. The Act outlawed discrimination on racial, sexual, and religious grounds in employment and public accommodations; strengthened voting rights for blacks; authorized the Attorney General to sue for the desegregation of public facilities and schools; provided a threat of cancellation of federal funds to discriminatory projects and activities within districts and even entire states; and continued the existence of the Civil Rights Commission, though its powers remained weak. The law also barred busing as a device to overcome de facto segregation created by housing patterns, which was a typical condition outside the South.

The Civil Rights Act was almost immediately strengthened by two factors: the continuation as Attorney General of Robert Kennedy, a committed foe of racial injustice, and the funding of President Johnson's "War on Poverty," which provided billions of dollars that could be used to persuade local and state governments to comply with the civil-rights statute.

Poverty was truly a national problem—urban and rural, black and white—as civil-rights workers and politicians discovered in the backwoods of Mississippi and the back alleys of the Bronx. Whole families eking out a bare existence in one-room sharecropper's cabins in the South, children with distended bellies from malnutrition and semistarvation, and ignorance so deep that hope was impossible did indeed exist in the richest nation on earth. But like so many other national problems, poverty was concentrated in cities, not only on skid rows but in declining neighborhoods, run-down tenements with peeling paint and no utilities, and even abandoned and condemned buildings. This realization was power-fully conveyed in a best-selling book by Michael Harrington, *The Other America,* published in 1962.

The nation's cities had always been crucibles of social change and social problems. The pace of urbanization after World War II, the accelerated migration (almost one and a half million people in the 1950's alone) of Southern, mostly rural blacks to Northern and Western cities, and the impact of new technologies and various federal policies and programs created uneven patterns of develop-ment within metropolitan regions and cities that were growing *and* decaying, providing opportunities for some citizens and confining others to squalid, dead-end slums.

The figures were troubling. Millions of Americans lived below the poverty level, and in most cases they could hardly be blamed for their failure. Old people and children comprised most of the poverty-stricken, and in some cities one-third or more of the fami-lies below the poverty line had household heads who were actu-ally employed full time. Through the 1950's, unemployment rates had risen, and the relative incomes of people at the bottom of the income scale actually decreased. The American Dream clearly had not worked for large numbers of Americans, and the extent of these failures suggested that something was basically wrong with the system. The burden of proof could no longer so easily be placed on the shoulders of the poor. The facts also showed that blacks were thrown into poverty in gravely disproportionate num-bers, yet another demonstration of the legacies of racial discrimi-nation.

In January 1964, in his state-of-the-union message, President Johnson declared an "unconditional war on poverty," and on Au-gust 20 signed into law the Economic Opportunity Act. Growing out of the various programs and ideas dealing with juvenile delin-quency, mental health, urban renewal, and job training initially developed during the Kennedy years, Johnson's poverty program established a framework for planning and coordination, provided for experimental approaches to the problem on a national basis, and relied to a greater degree on the principles of self-help and local control. The Act's most controversial provision, as it turned out, was a clause calling for the "maximum feasible participation" of the poor themselves in directing and developing these programs.

The Act established an Office of Economic Opportunity (OEO) and a variety of programs. Manpower and job-training programs like the Job Corps and the Neighborhood Youth Corps focused on preparing young people in disadvantaged areas for employment and enhancing their job opportunities. Head Start, Follow-Through, and Upward Bound were individual improvement programs that assisted youth of various ages in remedying educational deficiencies and building up self-confidence. Community Action Programs and Volunteers in Service to America (VISTA) were community-involvement programs designed to encourage local participation and citizen activism on behalf of community projects and development. Income-maintenance programs comprised the largest federal outlays for the War on Poverty (social security, unemployment compensation, Medicare, the GI Bill, etc.), though most had existed previously and were not funded through OEO. OEO itself had an annual budget that never rose to more than $2 billion, which did not go very far in meeting the needs of from 30 to 40 million poor people.

The emphasis was on providing opportunity, in the faith that the system was basically sound and simply out of balance. Many programs were aimed directly at youth, in an effort to interrupt the cycle of poverty at the earliest possible stage. Community Action Agencies—with local leadership drawn from public officials, members of private leadership groups, and the poor—became the umbrella organizations administering many of these programs directly. Rather than forging the political consensus among various local groups that OEO intended, however, the tripartite administrative arrangement revealed deep-seated conflicts at the local level, and suggested that the system was in need of more than just fine-tuning.

The poor increasingly came to consider themselves a separate political force, with interests different from those either of the traditional political leadership or of humanitarian and welfare organizations. Established authorities and welfare agencies resisted this new assertiveness by the poor, and as they became increasingly militant, it seemed that the federal government was in effect supporting widespread, organized resistance against itself and local government as well. An amendment to the law in 1967 gave state and local governments authority to designate Community Action Agencies and mandated that the tripartite arrangement be applied strictly, thus limiting representatives of the poor to no more than one-third of the total.

The ultimate impact of the War on Poverty is not entirely clear. Beyond question, thousands, even millions, of poor people were helped in one way or another, and the emotional fires of the ghettoes were somewhat soothed. But the effort never lived up to expectations, in part because the expectations and rhetoric used to express them were inflated, in part because the Southeast Asian conflict eventually distracted the nation's attention from poverty and urban problems. The small success of the War on Poverty was also attributable to the fact that other established federal programs were responsible, at least in part, for creating and sustaining the problems of the poor. Federal housing programs, dating back to the New Deal, encouraged a building boom in the suburbs while neglecting the cities and actually reinforcing the barriers of racial segregation that confined blacks to urban slums. Public housing, invariably located in inner cities alongside other low-income housing, continued on a shoestring. More than half of all housing constructed in England after World War II was publicly subsidized. In the United States, the figure was well below 5 percent.

Urban-renewal and redevelopment programs, growing out of the Housing Act of 1949 and the 1954 amendments, intended to rid the cities of unsightly slums and provide a rebirth of neglected urban lands, actually reduced the supply of low-rent housing, dislocated thousands of poor families, increased rents, and provided a financial bonanza for private business interests from slum clearance and construction loans and subsidies. Some slums were indeed eliminated, but the process of decay was merely shifted to other areas and the poor were in some ways even worse off than before. Blacks and other minorities suffered more than others. Urban renewal became known as "Negro removal."

The Interstate Highway System, begun with the legislation of 1956 and not coordinated with these other programs, had similar results. Great swaths of limited-access highway destroyed the delicate fabric of inner-city neighborhoods, encouraged a real-estate boom on the urban outskirts, and helped to scatter jobs on the metropolitan periphery, where they were even further out of the reach of the urban poor.

Urban decentralization tended to further fragment and segregate cities by race and income level. Autonomous suburban enclaves kept minorities and poor people out through zoning laws and other devices, and inner cities usually lost the tax revenues of wealthier people who resided outside and often worked inside the city limits. At the same time, the social-service demands generated by a rising proportion of low-income people increased. A United States Supreme Court ruling, in the case of *Baker v. Carr* (1962), helped correct the traditional political disadvantage of cities by requiring the apportionment of state legislatures on the basis of one man–one vote. But the cities were now usually outvoted in the state capitol by rural-suburban coalitions.

The urban crisis of the 1960's and 1970's obviously grew out of fundamental social and economic forces that were endemic and highly resistant to change. Basically, resources were funneled where they could earn the most on the private market (suburbs and expensive inner-city developments) rather than where they were socially most needed (the downtown core and solid inner-city neighborhoods, which were gradually deteriorating). But few recognized either the source or the severity of the problems, and most officials were surprised when widespread violence erupted in the inner cities.

On August 11, 1965, rioting broke out in Watts, a section of Los Angeles. From scattered looting and rock throwing, the conflagration grew in intensity over the next five days, eventually leaving thirty-five people dead, more than four thousand under arrest, and more than $200 million in property damage. Fourteen thousand National Guardsmen were called in to assist city police in containing the disturbance. No single major incident or grievance led to the rioting, and city officials were hard put to explain what had happened.

There were some hints, however. Watts was mostly a black area, with a male unemployment rate of 30 percent and a falling median-income level, in a region of the country where economic prosperity was everywhere to be seen. Violence was directed against the police and firefighters, but was largely confined within Watts itself. Much of the rioting involved looting of stores, and millions of Americans watched TV news film of rioters carrying furniture, clothing, TV sets, and electronic equipment out of shattered businesses. Many of the rioters had no previous criminal record. Some social scientists termed the events in Watts and other American cities "commodity riots," in which attention focused on the material goods of an affluent society that paraded its bounty in omnipresent advertising and denied opportunity to gain such bounty to substantial numbers of its citizens.

The remainder of the decade witnessed so many instances of urban violence that city officials came to dread the approach of each new "long hot summer." The next major riot broke out in Newark, New Jersey, on July 13, 1967. Twenty-six persons were killed, fifteen hundred injured, and more than a thousand arrested. Only a few days later, on July 23, there was a week of violence in Detroit, where economic conditions were much better and the local government was responsive to black demands. Nonetheless, the violence was intense. Eight thousand National Guardsmen and 4,700 United States paratroopers were brought in; forty-three people died, two thousand were injured, and five thousand were left homeless as fires raged through the area; and property damage approached a quarter of a billion dollars.

President Johnson appointed a special commission, chaired by Governor Otto Kerner of Illinois, to investigate the riots. The National Advisory Commission on Civil Disorders reported on March 2, 1968, that the United States was a nation divided into white and black, fragmented by the venom of white racism, and it recommended an array of new programs to deal with the problem. Actually, the federal government was already responding to urban violence by funneling funds into the riot-torn areas, putting more people on the welfare rolls, directing the forces of the War on Poverty to inner cities, and developing new programs to instill community pride and provide jobs in black ghettoes across the country. The riots had clearly been effective in getting Washington's attention; blacks gained through the fear of violence what was not likely to be gained otherwise. But the riots were not conscious, organized political acts, no matter how much they were responses to "oppression." Once the incidence of urban rioting declined, and virtually vanished, the government officially declared the urban crisis to be over.

The War on Poverty and the efforts to prevent and control urban violence were part of what President Johnson called in 1964 his Great Society, a program that produced the greatest outpouring of legislation since the New Deal. The list of major new legislation in 1965 included Medicare, which paid part of the medical expenses for persons sixty-five and over; housing assistance, including a new program of rent supplements; expanded federal aid to education; an Appalachian Development Act; an increase in funding for OEO; and the creation of a Department of Housing and Urban Development. Some of these, of course, were initially generated during the Kennedy Administration. The following year, Congress passed the Model Cities program, which was intended as the beginning of a major comprehensive effort to concentrate resources in the most seriously troubled inner-city communities, and created a new Department of Transportation.

For all its apparent novelty, the Great Society was essentially an extension of the spirit and programs begun in the New Deal, during Johnson's formative political years. In civil rights, Johnson went far beyond anything seriously contemplated by the White House during the 1930's. But in most respects the debts owed by the Great Society to the New Deal were heavy. Medicare, after all, was an extension of social security; rent supplements were new variations of old policies; and the analog of the Civilian Conservation Corps was obviously in mind when some of the OEO agencies were developed.

The Great Society also reflected the basic political philosophy of the New Deal, which held that American society was essentially sound but in need of adjustment and repair. The system could be made better and more equitable for disadvantaged groups, but a major redistribution of wealth and power was not needed and was, in fact, dangerous. The biggest challenge was to achieve political consensus (one of Johnson's favorite phrases) in support of programs to benefit the majority of people through greater opportunities for individual success. Federal intervention in the economy would work closely with major economic interests in a process of "managed capitalism," and the national government would serve as a broker among competing interests. The Great Society also had very specific political purposes—to defuse social discontent, dampen campus and urban radicalism, and forge the coalition necessary for Johnson's election in 1964.

One major difficulty of broker state politics is that interests must usually be organized and influential in order to be heard. The nation's poor had never been an organized political force, though some movement occurred in this direction during the 1960's, and blacks had generally been neglected even when they were organized. By 1964, blacks, most of whom were poor, began to be an effective political force. The civil-rights movement had already won some significant victories, particularly the Civil Rights Act of that year, and additional triumphs were in the offing.

"Freedom Summer" 1964 brought hundreds of volunteers to Mississippi to work in civil-rights projects, especially voter-registration drives and establishing Freedom Schools. Southern white authorities violently resisted in many ways, from petty harassment to beatings, but nowhere more brutally than in the deaths of three young civil-rights workers—two white and one black—at the hands of law-enforcement officers and other whites in Philadelphia, Mississippi. In all, fifteen people were murdered in the state during this period. The FBI was often sent in by Attorney General Kennedy to investigate, but J. Edgar Hoover believed the civil-rights movement was Communist-inspired, and he had little enthusiasm for the task. Civil-rights leaders complained that their workers were not protected by laws or constituted authority, as indeed in many cases they were not. But the nonviolent movement continued to draw national and international attention and sympathy, and the crust of segregated institutions was gradually crumbling. In December, Martin Luther King, Jr., received the Nobel Peace Prize.

The civil-rights revolution could only be secured, in the view of King and other leaders, by the ballot. Blacks could then protect and advance their interests through sheer political strength, especially in areas where they were already in the majority. Again, the resistance of Southern white authorities helped shape public opinion for national action. On March 7, 1965, Alabama state troopers and county deputies carried out George Wallace's orders and stopped a voting-rights march on a bridge in Selma, Alabama. On national television, the public saw helmeted officers attacking the marchers, clubbing old women and just about everybody else in their path. The nation was aroused. Under the protection of National Guardsmen, King led the renewed march from Selma to Montgomery, and on March 25 reaffirmed the rights of blacks to vote from the steps where Jefferson Davis had taken the oath of office as president of the Confederacy more than a century before.

On March 15, President Johnson had used the words of the most famous civil-rights anthem—"We Shall Overcome"—in a speech to Congress promising submission of a voting-rights bill. Johnson signed the bill into law on August 6. The Act insured the right of all adult citizens to vote, outlawed literacy tests and other tools used to disqualify black voters, and placed elections in the Southern states under the routine surveillance of federal authorities. In one sense, the struggle for basic civil rights for blacks and other minorities had, with this step, been won.

The civil-rights movement revealed how deep and widespread racial prejudice was in America. Economically, blacks suffered much more than whites, and centuries of discrimination had created deficiencies that would take perhaps generations to overcome. In the efforts to redress these grievances, blacks had renewed their sense of racial pride. Some younger blacks, especially, grew suspicious of all white institutions and turned to Afro-American history and culture for their identity and values. Mostly, this was reflected in a burgeoning of African dress and black literature, poetry, and song. Another result was the emergence of "Black Power," a slogan first used during a Mississippi march begun by James Meredith in June 1966. Among the civil-rights leaders who joined the march, Stokely Carmichael and other members of the Student Nonviolent Coordinating Committee (SNCC) were the most vocal, raising fists in the air and chanting "Black Power."

The Black Power movement divided the advocates of civil rights. The paramilitary Black Panther Party in California, which engaged police in direct confrontation and pledged to meet violence with violence, broke the nonviolent solidarity of the movement for black rights. And since Black Power implied the superiority of black institutions and values, and the necessity for blacks to depend only on themselves, the goal of racial integration was called into question. The great majority of blacks did not join this new wing of the movement, though even moderates recognized the need for blacks to flex their political and economic muscles. Black Power certainly pointed to the continued existence of tensions and problems, especially in the economic sphere, even after the basic legal rights had been won.

Ever since Lyndon B. Johnson became President on that bleak day in Dallas, he had looked to the 1964 campaign, seeking election to the office. The Democrats conferred their nomination on him in an emotional convention in Atlantic City that included a lengthy tribute to the memory of John F. Kennedy. Johnson selected Senator Hubert Humphrey, a liberal from Minnesota, as his running mate.

The Republicans, after a good deal of ideological infighting, chose Senator Barry Goldwater of Arizona. Goldwater was a decent man of strong opinions, the darling of conservatives across the country, but he was not an effective national campaigner. He spoke his mind, regardless of the audience or the sensitivity of the issue. On visits to old-age homes, he criticized Medicare and social security. He went into the Tennessee Valley to condemn TVA. In his acceptance speech, Goldwater played into the hands of the Democrats, who sought to capture the political center, by declaring: "Extremism in the defense of liberty is no vice . . . moderation in the pursuit of justice is no virtue."

The campaign was rough-and-tumble. The Democrats took advantage of Goldwater's ideological position and his strong support for American military strength and portrayed him as a radical right-winger. Television commercials unfairly linked Goldwater with the careless use of nuclear weapons, and presented Johnson as the "peace candidate." Johnson promised: "We are not about to send American boys nine or ten thousand miles away from home to do what Asian boys ought to be doing for themselves."

The strategy worked. Johnson carried forty-four states and

gathered in some 43 million votes to Goldwater's 27 million, the greatest winning percentage (61.1) in American history up to that time. The Democrats retained control in both Houses of Congress. The election not only disproved the belief that Americans would vote for a strong conservative if given a clear choice: many political pundits began to speak of the disappearance of the Republican Party.

Johnson's stunning mandate promised a productive, dynamic, and highly successful term, one that might well be extended for another four years. Johnson had improved even upon the New Deal Democratic voter coalition, and the Voting Rights Act would help insure a return of the South into the Presidential Democratic fold. That the overwhelming victory and hopeful prospect turned so quickly sour was due, not to the continuing urban crisis or failures of Johnson's domestic policies, but to mounting disaster overseas.

By 1967, the Vietnam War had become the most controversial national political issue. Protests against American involvement in Southeast Asia had become increasingly radical and widespread, and involved segments of the middle and working classes as well as students, professors, and those on the left. The war became a heavier and heavier political burden for the Democrats to bear, and threatened to wipe out the initiatives for civil rights, public welfare, and urban salvation that had been begun at such great cost. Resistance to Johnson and his foreign policy thus developed even within his own party.

In November 1967, Senator Eugene McCarthy of Wisconsin announced that he had agreed to run as a "peace candidate" against Johnson in the nation's first Presidential primary in New Hampshire. Senator Robert Kennedy, the first choice of the anti-war forces, declined the invitation on the grounds that his running would be interpreted as an act of personal vindictiveness. Kennedy and the President had been at odds, personally and politically, since before John F. Kennedy's assassination. Kennedy was also almost certainly concerned about the prospects of winning a primary campaign against a powerful incumbent President. In any case, the New Hampshire results astounded the Administration. McCarthy took 42.2 percent of the vote on March 12, to

Johnson's 49.5 percent. The political landscape had been dramatically altered and the President's vulnerability was revealed.

As Johnson saw support for the war collapsing at home, he reached a momentous personal decision that shocked the nation. On March 31, 1968, in a television address, he announced a cutback in the bombing of North Vietnam as a gesture toward peace, and calmly declared that he would not run for reelection. With the President out of the race, the nomination fight boiled down to a contest between a regular Democrat loyal to Johnson and one or more of the antiwar candidates. The two major challengers to the Administration's policies were McCarthy and Kennedy, who formally entered the race a few days after the New Hampshire primary. McCarthy continued to show strength against Johnson. In Wisconsin, he outpolled the President 56.2 to 34.6 percent. He faced Kennedy for the first time in the Indiana primary, where Kennedy won with 43 percent of the vote and McCarthy trailed in third place behind the governor, a Johnson stand-in. A short time later, Kennedy also won in Nebraska.

Kennedy's reluctance to enter the race lost him considerable support among his college-student constituency, which now made up the bulk of McCarthy's strength. Kennedy's appeal to youth was most marked among teenagers, and these forces joined with his strength among blacks and urban ethnic voters. McCarthy conducted a principled, almost rarefied campaign, and the candidate's lack of intensity seemed highly refreshing to some. Kennedy, on the other hand, exhibited all the family characteristics of activism and personal commitment, and a measure of charisma that seemed far removed from his old image as "ruthless Bobby," the younger brother who knocked heads and collected political debts. Kennedy's campaign organization was also highly organized, well financed, and very effective.

As the campaign progressed, tragic news came from Memphis, Tennessee. Martin Luther King, Jr., who had been leading a strike of city sanitation workers for better wages and working conditions, was shot to death on a motel balcony on April 4. Riots erupted in black sections in hundreds of cities across the country. The worst violence occurred in Chicago and Washington, D.C. Nationwide, 55,000 federal troops and National Guardsmen were called out, and forty-six people died. President Johnson went on national television to mourn for King and plead for calm. Robert Kennedy quoted memorable lines from Aeschylus, and reminded a tearful crowd of stunned blacks that his brother had also been assassinated. A single killer, James Earl Ray, was eventually arrested, convicted of murder, and sentenced to life imprisonment. Many suspected a conspiracy, but none was ever proved.

The Presidential campaign moved inexorably on to Oregon, a state without many black or ethnic voters. Here the Kennedy machine was finally stopped with a McCarthy victory. McCarthy and Kennedy now both set their sights on California, the nation's largest state and the most critical for their chances. Kennedy campaigned tirelessly and his vaunted organization swung into action. McCarthy was clearly outclassed. On election night, there was joy in Kennedy headquarters. The candidate himself appeared briefly for a conciliatory victory speech at the Hotel Ambassador in Los Angeles. As Kennedy walked from the room through a hotel kitchen, a disturbed Jordanian, Sirhan Sirhan, pulled out a pistol and fired.

Robert F. Kennedy's death, coming after the assassination of his brother and only weeks after the shooting of Dr. Martin Luther King, Jr., was almost too much for the nation to bear. It seemed to confirm a national return to violence and death as political means, and the elimination of the major political leaders who could build bridges between the majority and the disaffected minorities. The campaign continued in lackluster fashion with Vice-President Humphrey, hand-picked by Johnson for the nomination, as a front-runner.

On the Republican side, Richard M. Nixon made a dramatic political comeback. Defeated in his bid for election as governor of California in 1962, Nixon had moved to New York City. Amassing political debts in his efforts on behalf of Goldwater, he gained the reputation of being a good "party man." By 1968, the groundwork had been laid. During a well-orchestrated Miami convention, the Republicans nominated Nixon and accepted his choice for Vice-President, the rather obscure governor of Maryland, Spiro Agnew. The party that had almost been written off after 1964, with a candidate who seemed in 1962 destined for political oblivion, was now rushing confidently toward the White House as the Democrats foundered and chopped each other to pieces.

The Democratic national convention in Chicago in 1968 was one of the most dramatic and controversial political gatherings in American history. The forces and conflicts that had been building for years, and especially in the preceding six months—hard-hat blue-collar workers against antiwar protesters, police against college students and counterculture dropouts, the old politics against the new—were now focused on Chicago. Demonstrations had been planned by various student and antiwar groups for months, and Abbie Hoffman's yippies promised a series of political pranks to reveal the absurdity of the Democratic Party and the war. Thousands of young people showed up simply to be there and make known their support for McCarthy and in memory of Robert Kennedy. Awaiting this throng was the Chicago police, who had been instructed by Mayor Richard Daley to maintain order at all costs. Daley resented the protesters' efforts to make his city look bad, and he had nothing but contempt for McCarthy supporters, Hoffman's yippies, and the rest. As the "last big city boss in America," Daley was himself one of the leading symbols of the old politics.

Inside the convention halls, under heavy security, the delegates clashed over the platform, and especially the Vietnam War plank. The struggle between Humphrey and McCarthy underlay these debates, with Humphrey virtually certain to win. Outside, other confrontations occurred. In a city choked with delegates and visitors, hundreds of young people camped out, illegally, in Grant Park near the convention headquarters hotels. Chicago police swept the park repeatedly in efforts to clear it: they were often met with rocks, and responded with billy clubs and tear gas. After several nights of this, the evening for the balloting arrived.

As candidates were placed in nomination, the police attacked a crowd of demonstrators in the street in front of a downtown hotel. Officers indiscriminately clubbed demonstrators and spectators, drove one group of people through the plate-glass window of a bar, and pounded hundreds of unresisting people before dragging them away to paddy wagons. All was recorded on national television. A special commission appointed to investigate this incident subsequently termed it a police riot. At the same time, some convention speakers lashed out against Daley and his police. Daley cursed from the convention floor, and his supporters, who packed the galleries, shouted down opponents on the platform. As predicted, the nomination went overwhelmingly to Humphrey, who celebrated his victory while tear gas wafted in the streets and into the hotels; films of the police attacks on the demonstrators ran over and over again on the national TV networks. Incredibly, the band played "Happy Days Are Here Again."

Humphrey worked tirelessly during the campaign, though without complete success, to overcome his dilemma: he needed to stick close to Johnson and the traditional Democrats, and issues like law-and-order, while also moving away from the President's doomed Vietnam policy and the themes that threatened to drive McCarthy and Kennedy supporters from the polls. Humphrey tried to strike a note of optimism, of faith in the future, of new efforts to solve social problems, of his willingness to seek and achieve peace. His greatest asset, as it turned out, was his running mate—Senator Edmund S. Muskie, a steady man of quiet integrity and chiseled features who stood in stark contrast to his ungainly Republican counterpart. Nixon said nothing of substance at all and was, amazingly, permitted by the press and the public to avoid the Vietnam issue altogether by simply stating that he had a secret plan to end the war which could not be revealed until after the election.

It looked at first like a Republican runaway in the polls. The main concern was whether George Wallace's American Independent Party could deflect enough electoral votes from the major contenders to force the decision into the House of Representatives. But as November approached, the traditional elements of the Democratic coalition began to reassemble. A last-minute blitz by the Humphrey campaign, underwritten largely by labor unions; the second thoughts many voters had about Nixon; and Johnson's halting of all bombing of North Vietnam in late October brought the contest down to the wire. Nixon won with 43.4 percent of the vote to Humphrey's 42.7 percent. Wallace received 13.5 percent, a very creditable tally for a third-party bid. Nixon's support lay largely in the West and in the Southern and border states. He did not carry a single major city, and the Republicans never threatened to take control of the Congress. The main result of the election was to reveal the nation's disenchantment with Johnson and his policies.

History is not neatly packaged into decades, but the 1960's appear to have a certain distinctiveness. Opening with the confidence and high expectations of John F. Kennedy, on the tide of the postwar baby boom, they ended in turmoil and the ascension to power of the very man Kennedy had defeated and sent toward retirement nearly ten years before. A decade following the apparent innocence and conventionality of the 1950's ended with bizarre symbolic acts—the vicious murders of actress Sharon Tate and others in Southern California by Charles Manson and his family cult, in which blood, personal magnetism, sex, mysticism, and politics were strangely and tragically mixed.

The 1960's were years of prosperity and poverty. The gross national product roughly doubled, and median family income and the consumer price index rose almost as much. Measured by the quantity and variety of consumer goods, and in the proportion of the world's total resources used (about half), the United States was unquestionably the richest country on the globe. Yet, even after the War on Poverty and the social programs of the decade, some 27 million people (roughly 14 percent of the entire population) lived in poverty, by the government's own reckoning in 1970. Government programs to aid the poor, the cities, and the jobless were increasingly stifled, mostly by the avalanche of funds needed for the war in Southeast Asia and by the new popular emphasis on law and order and property rights. Two able leaders who helped shape the decade, and who could have shaped a better future—King and Robert Kennedy—were gone from the scene, leaving legacies of hope, frustration, and bitterness.

After 1960, especially, domestic and foreign affairs were inextricably linked. Guns and butter, overseas war and opposition at home, America's mission and human rights abroad, arms sales to the world and the military-industrial complex, foreign aid or programs to save American inner cities were only a few of the matters that linked the nation's destiny with its role in the world. And the prospering of United States-directed multinational corporations in the nurturing climate of the Marshall Plan so mingled foreign and domestic affairs that they were all but inseparable. The United States was no longer isolated or insulated from cataclysms and turns of events elsewhere in the world; Democrats and Republicans alike readily admitted the international dimensions of American destiny. The debate at home, however, centered increasingly on whether the American role in the world was that of a shining example of democracy and freedom or of a counterrevolutionary giant determined to defend its entrenched interests at the expense of weaker, developing nations.

10

The Politics of Turmoil Abroad, 1960-69

THOUGH Kennedy's inaugural address contained some hints that the cold war would become less frigid, the foreign policy of his Administration followed the cold-war blueprint. The protection of American interests and allies and the containment of Soviet influence throughout the world were still the twin pillars of the nation's international posture. Kennedy introduced a number of variations on this theme, particularly in creating the Peace Corps, which enlisted American volunteers to assist others around the world, especially in developing countries and remote areas. But in the crises of Berlin and Cuba, Kennedy brandished the saber in a fashion that would have unnerved even John Foster Dulles.

Kennedy charged in the 1960 campaign that national security was endangered by a growing disparity in armaments between the United States and the Soviet Union. As a matter of record, the missile gap never existed. Even Secretary of Defense McNamara realized this shortly after taking office. But Kennedy pursued a major arms-building program nonetheless. The supply of United States intercontinental ballistic missiles rose by five times between 1960 and 1967. Along with this, American military forces were expanded and diversified in order to lessen the degree of dependence on the nuclear deterrent and to permit flexible response to military situations. Counterinsurgency forces, like the Green Berets—an elite antiguerrilla combat unit—became a central element of Kennedy's defense policy, though most United States soldiers continued to receive conventional military training.

The Kennedy Administration had scarcely settled in before it was confronted with the first of a long series of foreign-policy crises that eventually took the nation to the brink of an atomic holocaust. The Bay of Pigs fiasco had its genesis under Eisenhower, though Kennedy had promised during the campaign to take steps against the revolutionary government in Cuba. Fidel Castro, who led the forces that after years of struggle toppled the dictatorial Batista regime in January 1959, had nationalized many American holdings, instituted sweeping reforms in housing, education, and the economy, and adopted a socialist form of government. The United States severed relations with Cuba in January 1961.

When Kennedy took office, a secret force of arms and men had been assembled by the CIA in Guatemala and plans for the landing to free Cuba from Castro were set for sometime in the early spring. Two critical questions remained: Would the Cuban people rise up against Castro as they had against Batista; and should the entire operation be called off as too risky? Eisenhower had stipulated that American forces were not to be used, and Kennedy maintained that position and allowed the operation to continue as clandestine and nonofficial.

United States ships transported the invasion force from Central America to Cuba, and on April 17, 1961, the landing by 1,400 troops was launched. Earlier, B-26 air attacks, flown by Cuban exiles, had failed to knock out the Cuban air force, and the invasion quickly bogged down. The spontaneous uprising of the Cuban people failed to materialize. Trapped on the beaches and in the swamps, the invaders begged the United States for air support. At the very same moment, the Americans were denying, before the United Nations, any involvement in the fighting, and Kennedy refused the request for air cover. The attack collapsed and hundreds of exiles were captured and put into Cuban prisons.

As the extent of actual United States involvement became known, the Administration stood condemned both of foolhardiness in approving such a project and of indecisiveness in allowing it to fail. The misadventure lowered the American reputation abroad for efficiency, cast the CIA into the same mold as the Russian spy agencies, encouraged insurgents throughout Latin America, and consolidated Castro's power within the island and threw him even further into the open arms of Moscow.

In December, Castro declared his loyalty to Marxism-Leninism.

The Bay of Pigs debacle had a profound and immediate effect on Kennedy himself. It increased his determination to stop the Communist advance even at the possible cost of a direct atomic confrontation with the U.S.S.R., and probably led him further along the interventionist path elsewhere in the world. It also instilled in Kennedy a distrust of advice from the Pentagon and the CIA.

The Bay of Pigs provided part of the somber backdrop for the Vienna summit conference between Kennedy and Nikita Khrushchev in early June 1961. The Russian leader declared his support for "peaceful coexistence" between the two nations, but he also confidently predicted world Communist success through "wars of liberation" against the decaying capitalist countries. He further warned that Russia would not hesitate to intervene in such struggles if capitalist nations bolstered "rotting regimes" standing in the way of Communist triumph. Before the meeting was over, Khrushchev threatened to sign a separate peace treaty with East Germany, thus upsetting the status quo in Central Europe and imperiling Berlin. Kennedy reiterated that the United States would maintain the existing international balance of forces and would protect Berlin, which was considered crucial to American interests.

During the next twelve months, the two superpowers went on a spree of belligerent posturing. Congress acceded to Kennedy's request for more conventional arms by boosting the weapons budget by 15 percent. Russia began testing a new series of atomic bombs of increased destructiveness, and the United States resumed atmospheric nuclear tests on April 25, 1962, claiming that they were essential to maintaining a balance with the Soviets. Actually, American technology and nuclear weaponry were far superior to the Russians', but United States policymakers were determined not to relinquish their lead. And during the autumn and winter of 1961–62, President Kennedy inspired a domestic passion for building bomb shelters.

Before the end of the summer of 1962, the situation in Europe grew more ominous. The Russians saw Berlin as the symbol of the threat posed by a rearmed West Germany, allied with NATO against the Soviet bloc. Berlin was also an embarrassment, its growing prosperity was in stark contrast to the spartan existence in East Germany, and it attracted tens of thousands of East German refugees. Just after midnight on August 13, East German forces began tearing up streets and erecting barriers along the line dividing the East and West zones of the city. Four days later, work began on a high, solid wall. Russian intentions were unclear, the West Berliners were frantic, and the Americans reacted slowly at first. Kennedy responded strongly, reaffirming United States support for "free" Berlin, but the crisis began to fade as it became clear that the wall was defensive rather than offensive in intent.

In such a hostile atmosphere, the phrase "peaceful coexistence" as a description of international relations was rather farfetched. The United States became increasingly concerned over expanded Russian trade and arms supply to Cuba. On October 14, high-altitude U-2 flights revealed the construction in Cuba of sites for medium-range missiles, sites that would be completed within a short time. This information led to the most dramatic confrontation between the superpowers, when miscalculations on either side could have led to Armageddon.

In Khrushchev's thinking, the placement of such weapons a mere ninety miles from the American mainland would redress a military imbalance of long standing, in which American missiles were poised along the Soviet borders in Turkey and elsewhere. But in installing missiles outside Russia for the first time, especially in the Western Hemisphere, the Kremlin was also challenging the existing balance of power and perhaps also testing the American will to resist. After Vienna and the Bay of Pigs, Kennedy and his advisers were determined not to give in.

Distrustful of the intelligence agencies and the military, Kennedy turned to a special team consisting mostly of older, experienced public servants. The group—including Robert Kennedy, McNamara, General Maxwell Taylor, former Secretary of State Dean Acheson, Undersecretary of State George Ball, and McGeorge Bundy, who had been dean of the faculty at Harvard and was now on the White House staff—were divided in their thinking. Some, like Acheson, agreed with the Joint Chiefs of Staff that a preemptive air strike should be launched before the bases were completed, even though this would almost certainly result in

Cuban and Russian deaths. Some others argued that the missiles were not much of an additional threat to American security, since Soviet ICBM's could already reach every major target in the United States. Perhaps the Cuban missiles could be "traded" for outmoded American missile installations in Italy and Turkey?

Kennedy chose to meet the challenge head-on, and quickly. On October 22, he demanded that the Russians dismantle the missile sites and remove the weapons immediately, and declared that the United States would consider any missile attack from Cuba as coming directly from the Soviet Union and would respond accordingly. The President also heeded the advice of his brother and McNamara and declared a naval blockade (or "quarantine," to avoid an overt act of war) of Cuba to prohibit the delivery of additional missiles, then shrouded in ominous metal cases on the decks of Russian ships making their way across the Atlantic. He also indicated that he was willing to take every necessary step to get the missiles out, and he activated a huge military strike force, including 156 ICBM's, for an invasion of Cuba in the event all else failed. Kennedy had, in fact, already ordered the Jupiter missiles out of Turkey, but he believed that he could not now use such steps to bargain his way out of the crisis.

Since Russian naval strength in the western Atlantic was then microscopic, the blockade had the advantage of leading from American strength and of placing the onus of an overt breaking of the peace on the Russians. All attention centered on what would happen when the first Soviet vessels encountered American warships. The crisis palpably eased on October 24, when a dozen Russian ships halted at sea or turned back. But the construction of the sites in Cuba continued.

On October 26, Khrushchev sent a long letter to Kennedy, basically backing down from the confrontation and hinting that he would withdraw the missiles if the Americans would pledge not to invade Cuba. As Kennedy and his advisers discussed this proposal, a second letter arrived, proposing an exchange of the Russian missiles for the United States missiles in Turkey and Italy. As plans began again for a strike against Cuba, Robert Kennedy devised a brilliant scheme that ultimately resolved the crisis. The President responded positively to the first letter, and ignored the second communication entirely. On October 28, the Russians announced that the Cuban sites were being dismantled. The President insisted, however, on United Nations verification. Castro refused to allow UN observers into his country, and thus the United States never did make the noninvasion pledge.

The Cuban missile crisis demonstrated Kennedy's toughness, forced Khrushchev to back down completely and seriously weaken his position in the Kremlin, revealed how readily the American military was willing to resort to arms, and disclosed how difficult it was for either of the great powers to bend to their will even small, militarily and economically dependent satellite nations. It also literally brought the world to the edge of nuclear war. The leaders in Washington congratulated themselves on the successful management of the crisis, and the wisdom of the flexible-response doctrine, which gave them a whole range of military options. What worked well in this instance, however, would not necessarily work so well on other occasions.

Competition with the Soviets was nowhere better revealed than in the space race, triggered by the successful launching of Russia's Sputnik, the world's first man-made satellite, in 1957. The implications of this achievement were unclear, but the spirit of the cold war immediately suggested a gap to be closed as soon as possible. New legislation provided support for science education at all levels, and the National Aeronautics and Space Administration (NASA) was given a mandate to surpass the Soviets. The sub-orbital flight of Commander Alan B. Shepard, Jr., on May 6, 1961, was followed less than three weeks later by Kennedy's pledge to put an American on the moon before the end of the decade. In February 1962, John H. Glenn circled the earth three times in orbit, and a number of successive space triumphs—marred by the deaths of three astronauts in an Apollo rocket fire in January 1967—led ultimately to Neil Armstrong's famous first step on the moon on July 20, 1969. The United States did indeed far outdistance the Russians in such space feats, doubtless generating some new military advantages along the way, but the cost was extremely high. The Apollo program alone amounted to more than $40 billion.

Kennedy's Latin American policy was not directly caught up in the competition with the Russians, but it was ultimately obsessed with the specter of Castro and the threat of Communism in the Western Hemisphere. The policy was designed to strengthen governments against socialist revolution through increased economic growth and benefits for the masses of people, and to this end, the Alliance for Progress pumped more than $9 billion into Latin America. The projected economic growth rates were never achieved, however, as increases in gross national product were consumed by rising birth rates, siphoned off for the use of corrupt leaders, or stymied by the United States' insistence on private investments only. When no more Castros appeared in the Western Hemisphere, enthusiasm for the Alliance waned in Washington.

President Kennedy's relations with the Russians were not always tense, and his enunciation of cold-war rhetoric not always unrelieved. He noted the possibilities of detente with the U.S.S.R. and occasionally reiterated the theme of a speech he made in Seattle in November 1961, that "there cannot be an American solution to every world problem." In June 1963, in a speech at the American University, Kennedy called for a "world safe for diversity" and announced that discussions would soon begin on a treaty banning atmospheric nuclear tests. The Limited Test Ban Treaty was signed by the United States, Russia, and Britain on July 25, ratified by the United States Senate in September, and eventually initialed by more than one hundred nations. The treaty did little to abate the arms race, and underground nuclear tests continued, but it did help alleviate the serious problem of atmospheric radioactive fallout and stood as a symbol of the need to control the use and development of nuclear weapons.

In 1962, American policymakers regarded Vietnam as a peripheral problem. Cuba and Berlin occupied center stage. But Southeast Asia was not ignored, and fateful decisions were made about American involvement in a struggle that would cast long shadows across the nation's subsequent history.

After World War II, the United States opposed the reimposition of European dominance over former colonies in Southeast Asia, and American representatives even attended the first flag raising of the postwar government of what later became North Vietnam in September 1945. But after the French were militarily defeated in Vietnam, former French Indochina was divided into Cambodia, Laos, and Vietnam, and many leaders in the area developed strong ties with Russia and China. The Americans, with Eisenhower's blessing, in effect replaced the French as the principal sponsors of non-Communist forces in the region. The 1954 Geneva Accords provided for a cease-fire and a demilitarized zone with "temporary" partitioning of Vietnam along the seventeenth parallel.

The intractable difficulties in Laos should have provided a clue to the potential problems in Vietnam. Even with considerable American economic and military aid and the consistent presence of the CIA, the Laotian government was still not able to secure the country against the advances of the Communist insurgents, the Pathet Lao. In July 1962, an agreement in Geneva neutralized the country and provided for shared power among the contending parties in a new government. This arrangement was short-lived, however, and Laos was plunged once again into war. The only rational act of American policy was Kennedy's decision not to send American troops to the struggle, even though a number of Pentagon advisers actually recommended the use of nuclear weapons. But the lessons of Laos were lost as they might apply to Vietnam.

The leader who emerged in the South was Ngo Dinh Diem, a Roman Catholic mandarin from the North who was a strong nationalist and anti-Communist. Nonetheless, almost everyone agreed that the most popular national figure, with the best chance of winning the national elections also promised in the Geneva agreements, was Ho Chi Minh, the leader of the North Vietnamese and a Communist. For this reason, and because the United States had never signed the Geneva Accords in the first place, national elections never materialized. The North Vietnamese, however, were determined to pursue their goal of national unification under Communist leadership, and they began overt support of an indigenous insurgent movement in the South—the National Liberation Front (NLF), or Vietcong.

In 1961, Kennedy sent two trusted advisers, General Maxwell Taylor and MIT professor Walt W. Rostow, to Saigon to observe and make recommendations as to what American policies in that country should be. Reaffirming the doctrine of containment, their report called for a renewed commitment to South Vietnam to protect the country from Communist domination through various forms of aid, including more civilian and military advisers, military supplies, and a task force of American troops. Though Kennedy did not approve the report, the level of American support for Diem significantly increased. The CIA, which had long been involved in Southeast Asia, especially Laos, supported a program of "strategic hamlets," whereby rural villages would be fortified and protected from the Vietcong. Theoretically, the insurgents would then lose their greatest potential base of support.

The United States looked increasingly to Diem to win the loyalty of his people and blunt the insurgent drive, especially in the countryside. But Diem embarked on policies that ultimately caused the Americans to withdraw their support. Some Vietnamese Buddhists began protesting against the domination of a Roman Catholic regime. Encouraged by his brother, Ngo Dinh Nhu, and sister-in-law, Madame Nhu, Diem retaliated with violence, ordering police and soldiers to beat up monks and ransack pagodas. The monks responded with more demonstrations and some even set fire to themselves in protest against the government. These events not only gained worldwide attention but they eroded Diem's popular support at home. In a telegram of August 24, 1963, the United States withdrew its support from Diem, thus clearing the way for a group of South Vietnamese military leaders to overthrow the regime. In the process, Diem was assassinated.

The preference of Kennedy Administration military planners, including the President himself, for the tactics of counterinsurgency shaped much of the American activity in Vietnam prior to 1965. Special military units like the Green Berets, trained in guerrilla warfare, would supposedly defeat the Communists at their own game. Kennedy certainly did not envision a massive commitment of American ground forces to the struggle, and would almost certainly have vetoed such a notion at the time. But he increased the level of American support for South Vietnam significantly from about 600 advisers and aides in 1961 to more than 16,000 in late 1963. These increases were modest when compared with the degree of military commitment Kennedy was prepared to make in Berlin or Cuba, but they were immensely important as a commitment of American prestige and in establishing a policy direction that would be extremely difficult to reverse.

President Lyndon Johnson essentially followed in his predecessors' footsteps, except that America's role as the bastion of "freedom," the committed foe of Communism, the strong, reliable ally, was drawn even more sharply by the Administration of a man who thought of international challenge and conflict very much in the vivid personal terms of his native Texas. This President, who found his greatest satisfaction in helping disadvantaged groups to help themselves, was drawn increasingly into the maelstrom of foreign affairs.

Kennedy's Alliance for Progress, though well intentioned, did not go very far in bringing democracy or prosperity to Latin America. The emphasis shifted very early to battling Castroism and insuring the stability of United States allies in the hemisphere. Johnson approached these nations to the south in a less sophisticated, more condescending manner.

On April 24, 1965, a coup was launched against the military junta in the Dominican Republic in an effort to restore constitutional government in that country. In the chaos, the United States embassy requested assistance, and Johnson responded by sending in 14,000 American troops. The revolt had largely succeeded with a minimum of violence when the troops arrived; but their presence reversed the tide of events and maintained the military government in power. The President and the State Department went to great lengths to justify American intervention, even to the extent of propagating stories about impending massacres. The clear message to Latin America was that the Johnson Administration would not hesitate to interfere by force in the affairs of other countries in the hemisphere in order to defend United States prerogatives and interests. Even the spirit of the Alliance for Progress was now dead.

But what brought down the Administration, and brought the United States into one of the most troubling eras of its history, was the growing military involvement in Southeast Asia. Johnson took an equally hard-nosed attitude there, informing the American ambassador to Saigon, within days after Kennedy's death, "I am not going to lose South Vietnam." Neutralization of the conflict—

or accepting things as they were—was out of the question, since this would inevitably recognize the Communist insurgents and probably lead to their ultimate victory. Though intelligence reports indicated that most of the resistance to the South Vietnamese government was coming from within the country, American officials constantly emphasized North Vietnamese support for the resistance. From the very beginning, a civil war was portrayed as a foreign invasion which the United States was determined to stop.

The reasoning behind American policy in Southeast Asia was actually quite simple. If the United States backed down in Vietnam, it would lose its dependability as an ally; Communism and "wars of liberation" everywhere would be strengthened by a North Vietnamese "victory." If Vietnam were lost, there would almost certainly be a bloodbath in the South as the Communists took over, and Laos, Cambodia, and Thailand would—like dominoes—surely fall. If the United States lost its will in Southeast Asia, doubts would arise about its commitments everywhere—to Japan, to Western Europe, to Berlin. In this generation of American political leaders, for whom World War II was the most profound international experience, the analogy of Munich in 1939 came quickly to mind. "Appeasement" was to be avoided at all costs. As Presidential adviser Walt W. Rostow put it, "Vietnam is a clear testing ground for our policy in the world."

This was essentially the same containment strategy that underlay United States foreign policy throughout the postwar era. One American admiral always carried with him a graphic illustration of the greatest fear: a huge map of Asia with menacing red arrows sweeping from mainland China through Southeast Asia and toward India, South Korea, and Japan. The American mission was to blunt and contain this "aggression" emanating from Peking and concocted in Moscow.

The fallacies in these arguments were obvious to a few in the beginning. China and Russia were, as most experts were aware, seriously at odds over a number of issues, even to the extent of bloody fighting along their common border. Southeast Asia was composed of a variety of different cultures and groups, whose identity was expressed in a strong sense of nationalism. The fate of Laos was thus not necessarily the fate of Cambodia or Thailand. While Chinese cultural influence throughout the region was strong, almost equally powerful was a traditional resistance to the imposition of Chinese power. The National Liberation Front (NLF) in South Vietnam, or the Vietcong, was encouraged and aided by the North Vietnamese, but to a very large degree it represented a popular, indigenous resistance to an increasingly corrupt regime. In this swirl of nationalism and social change in a new post-colonial era, however, Washington saw only the spread of international Communism. Only a few days after Johnson came into office as President, National Security Action Memorandum 273 identified the major objective of the United States in South Vietnam: "to assist the people and Government of that country to win their contest against the externally directed and supported communist conspiracy."

The ideas that justified the prosecution of the war also drove the United States deeper and deeper into the conflict. Once American prestige had been committed, once American lives had been lost, once Vietnam was perceived as a "test" of American will and reliability (an issue actually created by the rhetoric of American policymakers), there was no turning back. It was genuinely unthinkable that a third-rate power like North Vietnam could successfully resist American determination to strike a blow for "freedom." No President, least of all Lyndon Johnson, wanted to be the first American Commander in Chief to "lose" a war. Furthermore, most American leaders failed to see the dangers and pitfalls ahead, the most serious of which was the fact that the insurgents had but to persist and survive in order to "win."

The military regime that replaced the Diem government in Saigon had no more success in defeating the NLF. The Pentagon continued to recommend the commitment of American ground troops to get the matter over with quickly. Perhaps this course was not followed sooner merely because most political leaders did not think it would be necessary against a country like North Vietnam. This assumption proved to be incorrect. American power—based on technological superiority and overwhelming firepower—was simply not so effective in a backward country against small, "invisible" guerrilla cadres. As the "strategic hamlet" program and

American counterinsurgency efforts failed, the United States stepped up its military and economic assistance. This escalation of the war was reciprocated by the other side, until the struggle grew to totally unanticipated proportions.

Johnson approved covert operations against North Vietnam shortly after coming into office, since he was convinced that the Vietcong would collapse without support from the North along the Ho Chi Minh Trail, a series of jungle-covered roads and paths winding down from North Vietnam through Laos and into the South. Some North Vietnamese villages were bombed in these early stages, by American planes flown by Thai pilots. Part of Operation 34A, as it was called, entailed cruises by United States destroyers off the North Vietnamese coast for intelligence gathering and backup for other operations. On August 2 and 4, 1964, two destroyers reported attacks by hostile torpedo boats in the Gulf of Tonkin. After launching an air strike against the small North Vietnamese navy, Johnson sought a congressional resolution endorsing retaliation and permitting any other steps to protect American lives. The Gulf of Tonkin Resolution was passed unanimously in the House and with but two dissenting votes in the Senate. Johnson now had the legal authority to proceed, even without a formal declaration of war.

The Gulf of Tonkin affair was indicative of troubles to come. There is no certainty even today that these American ships were actually attacked. The ships were not damaged, and no debris from the presumably destroyed torpedo boats was ever found. The North Vietnamese craft were never visually sighted; they were observed only on radar. These uncertainties were never fully shared with the Congress. Moreover, not only was American responsibility for planning and implementing Operation 34A concealed, but direct United States involvement was specifically denied.

Under the umbrella provided by the Gulf of Tonkin Resolution, the escalation of the war proceeded consistently and "logically" in response to apparent military needs. Ironically, the decision-making process within the United States government went on very much as it was supposed to. Decisions were made "at the highest level" (that is, in the White House) even on such specific items as bombing targets. Delicate military and political factors were weighed and discussed before each new commitment of forces and expansion of the struggle. Pentagon computers kept detailed information on logistics, supplies, and "body counts," and increasingly sophisticated electronic and other equipment were designed and placed in service. This was a classic application of the flexible-response doctrine, where a whole range of options was analyzed and implemented, from the various counterinsurgency and clandestine, small-scale operations in the beginning to the commitment of large conventional ground forces. The problem was that these carefully crafted escalations more and more resembled a disastrous spiral: American commanders demanded additional support to "win the war"; the support was, more often than not, provided and found insufficient; and commanders requested even more troops and equipment. The Pentagon claimed that all that was needed was the end of Communist infiltration into the South, while military and civilian leaders ignored the degree of independence of the NLF and the corruption in the South Vietnamese government and army. The "light at the end of the tunnel" seemed to grow dimmer each time a field commander or Washington policymaker mentioned it.

The United States devised a variety of tactics to deal with the guerrillas, who struck quickly and disappeared and managed to control most of the countryside, especially at night. "Search and destroy" missions—in which Vietcong forces were identified and then attacked with mobile troop units, artillery, and air power— became routine. The most difficult aspect of the fighting for American soldiers was distinguishing enemy forces from the general population. The NLF sought shelter and protection among the villagers and recruited women and even children into their ranks. The Americans became suspicious of nearly every Vietnamese. Inevitably, a number of noncombatants were killed and their villages destroyed. "Free fire" zones were designated, in which anyone who moved was presumed to be the enemy. Defoliants were sprayed by aircraft over large sections of jungle in an effort to search out enemy troop concentrations and movements.

Larger numbers of American soldiers were sent to Vietnam, increasingly after induction through the military draft. The 16,000 troops in Vietnam at the end of 1963 rose to more than 181,000 by the beginning of 1966. At the end of that year, the total—not including United States forces offshore or in Thailand—had risen to 375,000, and to 485,000 in 1967 and 535,000 in 1968. The peak of American troop strength in Vietnam was 543,000, reached in April 1969.

The United States began the conflict with variations of counterinsurgency tactics, but as more and more troops arrived, the emphasis shifted to conventional techniques, sophisticated technological gimmicks, and overwhelming air power. Mobile ground-to-air missiles supplied by the Chinese and the Soviets enabled the NLF cadres to down an American plane occasionally, but the real danger to American pilots came over the air defenses of North Vietnam. The United States persisted with thousands of air sorties over virtually every inch of South Vietnam, and this campaign was gradually extended to the southern portions of the North in February 1965. In June 1966, President Johnson authorized bombing in the area surrounding Hanoi, and in November he permitted attacks on Hanoi itself. By 1967, all of North Vietnam was subject to American air attacks.

Incredibly, the United States dropped more tons of bombs (three million) in Southeast Asia, even as early as 1968, than it had dropped in all of World War II. By the end of 1972, the Americans had dropped more than three and a half times the tonnage of bombs used between 1941 and 1945. Some American leaders thought, to paraphrase one commander, that the country had to be destroyed in order to be saved.

The impact of this massive American presence in Southeast Asia was registered not only in the physical destruction of villages and swaths of jungle but in the culture of a preindustrial people. A rural society organized into small villages for centuries was caught in the nationalist struggles for power after the fall of Western colonial rule and then was suddenly thrust into a highly technological and deadly modern war. Traditional social bonds were shattered and the economic base collapsed. The cities—especially Saigon—swelled with refugees from the countryside. The influx of American materials and troops created severe social problems—from a thriving black market to rampant prostitution—and changes in ancient habits and values. As they concentrated their attention on the destruction of the Vietcong, the Americans, by their very presence, helped to expand and fuel the political and economic corruption that ate away at the South Vietnamese government and eroded its popular support.

The impact of the American escalation at home was also dramatic. The military budgets skyrocketed from roughly $55 billion in 1965 to more than $80 billion in 1968. The Administration's antipoverty and urban-redevelopment programs were simply overwhelmed as a result: in eight years, OEO's Community Action Program received about the same amount of funds that was spent in one month in Vietnam. By 1968, the Great Society was over. But what many increasingly perceived as a waste of material resources was perhaps less troubling than the rising toll of American lives. As more troops were sent abroad, American units took over the brunt of the fighting. In 1964, 112 Americans were killed in action in Vietnam. The totals escalated to 1,130 in 1965; 4,179 in 1966; and 7,482 in 1967. The substantially higher totals of enemy casualties (doubtless, highly inflated in any case) were little comfort to American parents and to the millions of young men who were vulnerable to military conscription. The rise of the American death toll, to an average of almost 150 per week, was a major factor in increasing disenchantment with the war and spreading antiwar sentiment well beyond the campuses.

Most Americans initially supported the President and the military leaders, though the average citizen had little understanding of the global significance of the struggle in Vietnam or how it related to American national interests. In the public mind, dulled by decades of cold-war rhetoric, the necessity to resist Communism was considered explanation enough.

The first resistance to the war was fitful, but it grew steadily on college campuses, though students could usually avoid military service if they were enrolled in a college or university. As the intensity of American involvement increased, as more and more Americans were killed, as the Administration's promises of "victory" went unrealized time and time again, the antiwar movement strengthened. An antiwar rally in New York City sponsored by Students for a Democratic Society (SDS) in April 1964—even before the Presidential campaign got fully underway—drew some 20,000 people. That summer—the same summer when civil-rights volunteers poured into Mississippi—the National Committee to End the War in Vietnam was organized.

In the spring of 1965, on hundreds of college campuses, "teach-ins" were held in which professors and students discussed and condemned the waste and injustices of the war. As the level of American combat troops in Vietnam soared, the protests became larger and less restrained. The basic tactic was nonviolence, but some demonstrators destroyed their draft cards (a serious federal offense) and others raided selective-service offices to burn records. A New York City protest in April 1967, involving more than 125,000 people, was the largest antiwar demonstration in American history. In October, 75,000 demonstrators marched on the Pentagon in Washington to show their displeasure with American policy. Photographs of young soldiers standing in front of the Pentagon with their guns pointed at young demonstrators, who sometimes inserted flowers into gun barrels, appeared on front pages across the country. Some dismissed these efforts as simply unpatriotic, and others condemned them as Communist-inspired. But as the list of antiwar spokesmen grew (Martin Luther King joined them on April 4, 1967), such charges were more difficult to sustain. When it became obvious that United States efforts in Vietnam were not succeeding and that the war might drag on interminably, taking the lives of American boys, popular resistance swelled and even found a voice in the halls of Congress.

The turning point came in early 1968, when the NLF launched a major attack against thirty-six of forty-two provincial capitals in South Vietnam in January 31, during the annual Tet holiday. This Tet offensive penetrated even into the grounds of the United States embassy in Saigon. Communist troops captured the major city of Hue and managed to hold it for a month. Ultimately, the Vietcong were driven back, and General William Westmoreland declared an American "victory." But President Johnson was deeply disturbed. The Tet offensive demonstrated that the NLF, even after years of intensive American bombing, search-and-destroy missions, and massive military and economic aid to the Saigon regime, could mount a major coordinated attack throughout the country and inflict heavy damage. Clearly, no place in South Vietnam was secure. The Communist forces did sustain heavy casualties, which took more than a year to replace, but they had won a significant political victory. Westmoreland called for an additional 206,000 American troops to pursue this new "advantage." Johnson called together a blue-ribbon panel—including Dean Acheson, McGeorge Bundy, and George Ball—to assess Westmoreland's request. The panel advised the President to forget about military victory, wind down the war, and redouble his efforts for a negotiated settlement.

Johnson maintained all along that he only desired peace in Vietnam, but not at the price of a South Vietnamese surrender to the Communists. Negotiations, mostly behind the scenes, were extremely delicate. The North Vietnamese were adamant that they would not give up their part in the struggle, or the goal of victory in South Vietnam. They refused to admit publicly their role in supplying the NLF or agree to any terms prohibiting such assistance. The United States proposed a cease-fire, and evacuation of all "foreign" troops from the country, and the cessation of military aid from the "outside." This would have left Saigon with a distinct advantage, after years of American military and economic assistance. Johnson insisted that Hanoi respond with some "positive gesture" to his peace overtures. But the Americans and South Vietnamese were reluctant to deal directly with the NLF, which they officially regarded as the illegitimate puppet of the North; and Hanoi was equally reluctant to recognize what they regarded as the imposed regime in Saigon without reciprocal recognition of the Vietcong. As popular support for the South Vietnamese government wore thinner and thinner, the North Vietnamese were even less willing to agree to any such "peace plan." Yet Johnson was determined not to negotiate from weakness or to accept a Communist government in the South. He had an almost visceral sense of dishonor attendant to abandoning an ally.

The United States had vast military power in its favor, but there were limitations on the ultimate force—such as nuclear weapons —that could be brought to bear on the enemy. Hanoi and the NLF had guerrilla tactics and a good deal of popular support in their favor; but their principal advantage was their demonstrated willingness to endure and persist in the struggle indefinitely. In the United States, time was running out.

As the antiwar movement swelled at home, Johnson saw the national consensus for the war collapsing, if such a consensus had ever existed in the first place. Having exhausted what he considered the acceptable military alternatives, Johnson withdrew from the 1968 Presidential race and took a final stab at a peaceful settlement. He reduced the bombing of North Vietnam at the same time that he withdrew from the political contest, and he helped initiate the peace talks, which began in Paris on May 10. As a spur to continued negotiations, and to help the Democrats, who were in deep trouble in the campaign, Johnson halted all bombing of North Vietnam on October 31. On January 18, 1969, negotiations opened in Paris among the four parties involved, almost precisely one year after the Tet offensive.

As the decade ended, and despite the beginning of the peace talks, the Vietnam War continued. Nixon's "secret plan" to end the conflict was about the only prospect for peace that most Americans could hope for. But the struggle in Southeast Asia was not the only event that suggested momentous changes for the United States. Shifting attitudes about religion, family, sex, and politics, coupled with new patterns of behavior—especially among the nation's youth—promised to undermine many traditional features of American life and redefine what for generations had been unquestioningly accepted as the American Dream.

11

The Radical and Libertarian Sixties

DANIEL Bell's book, and its title, *The End of Ideology: On the Exhaustion of Political Ideas in the Fifties,* published in 1960, seemed perfectly plausible as the Eisenhower Presidency drew to a close. "In the Western world," Bell wrote, "there is today a rough consensus among intellectuals on political issues: the acceptance of the Welfare State; the desirability of decentralized power; a system of mixed economy and of political pluralism." Bell duly noted rising dissatisfaction among young intellectuals, and the power of new "instrumental" ideologies in Africa and Asia. But in the West, "the old passions are spent." Intellectuals, young and old, had rejected "the old apocalyptic and chiliastic visions."

At the beginning of the sixties, it did seem, as Bell suggested, that the sources of social discontent had been diminished, if they had not dried up altogether. By 1960, the United States had become in every sense an urban nation. Urban mass-consumption culture—entertainment, fashion, art—was no longer rooted in a place; it was omnipresent, a national norm that penetrated in one way or another into virtually every nook and cranny of the country, often through an information system designed to market the material goods of an affluent society. Regional peculiarities persisted, but like other aspects of American diversity (ethnic identification, for example), they were noted and prized partly because standardization of the national culture had proceeded so rapidly and completely.

These technological and economic changes provided fresh strength for the urbanization of American society and for the growth of a pervasive, nationwide consumer culture that churned up a seemingly endless demand for gadgets, personal products and services, and the whole array of material goods associated with modern society. Luxuries became necessities in a popular mind conditioned by mass advertising. Possessions determined as never before one's position in society, and television hawked products in such a way that ownership of them was perceived more as a right than an opportunity. This consumer culture—shaped by the new communications technologies and postwar consumer attitudes—seemed in the early sixties all-pervasive, universally accepted, and invincible.

But the 1960's was a decade of challenge, when America's social institutions, folkways, and ethical and moral values were held up to searching examination, often found wanting, and modified with radical surgery. As radical sociologist C. Wright Mills declared in a 1960 letter to the *New Left Review,* "The Age of Complacency is ending. Let the old women complain wisely about 'the end of ideology.' We are beginning to move again." The more venerated the institution—religion, science, higher education, marriage—the more extensive the criticism, the more radical the new formulations. What remained of the old fusion of Puritan, Protestant, and Northwest European capitalist ethic after the challenges of the twenties now rapidly eroded before the mass assault of the sixties. Portions of the Old South, sections of the rural Midwest, and isolated pockets in New England remained true, at least in voice, to the ways of their fathers, and there was individual resistance to the sweeping innovations, especially from members of conservative religions and the Republican Party. By the end of the sixties, however, the great majority of Americans had accepted by act if not by profession so many of the new ways that the country was simply no longer so clearly dedicated as it once had been to old virtues and values: mystical religion, hard work, thrift, sobriety, optimism, progress. By 1970, the country could be characterized as mostly secular, hedonistic, spendthrift, sensual, and perhaps even pessimistic.

The reagents of this momentous shift in national values were many, varied, and some of respectable age. Urbanization, industrialization, new technology, and the nation's swift rise to productive supremacy were among the most important forces involved, but the challenge to older values was also often issued from unexpected quarters—by the children of the advantaged middle and upper classes, by the old men of the staid and venerable Supreme Court of the United States, and by a group of older, black clergymen in the South. Some of the dissatisfactions with materialist culture ran deep in the utopian thinking of the American past, but the more immediate intellectual and cultural fields of force that turned the social dog days of the Eisenhower decade into the tumultuous sixties are still obscure.

Perhaps the major intellectual and religious influences underlying the change in the American temper came from Europe through the spread of the existential attitudes associated with the writings of two Frenchmen, Jean-Paul Sartre and Albert Camus. Sartre was often difficult reading, but the novels and essays of the younger Camus—a brilliant and appealing leader of the French Resistance against the German Occupation, and editor of *Combat,* which after peace arrived became for a time the most influential journal in France—had enormous appeal in younger educated circles around the world. Sensitive Americans also inhaled existential doctrines from the plays of Samuel Beckett and Eugene Ionesco. In religion, the work of numerous towering European theologians was translated into American terms on a popular level by such young radical Protestant leaders as Thomas J. J. Altizer and William Hamilton, who initiated the decade's hottest religious controversy by publishing *Radical Theology and the Death of God* (1966).

Existentialism suggested, among other things, that the position of ethically driven man in an amoral and uncaring universe was essentially an absurd one. Camus himself seemed to give mortal point to his doctrine by perishing at an early age in an appalling automobile accident in rural France. Since the great majority of men had to act, the question was how and by what code. Not, the existentialists argued, by state statute or by common law reaching back for hundreds of years or by the religious injunctions meant for pastoral tribes of antiquity, but rather by the internal human urges applied to the constantly changing and often irrational situations in which man found himself. This was, in their term, *situational ethics.*

The erosion of traditional Christian theology, long under attack from science and rationalism, was accompanied in the sixties by vigorous attacks on the traditional structure and government of the church. Like the leaders of the Social Gospel movement at the start of the century, many of the young radical clerics—Protestant and Catholic alike—began to insist that man's ethical sense and conscience superseded the authority of both clerical and lay officials, and even common and civil law. Hence, clerics were often found in the vanguard of the movements—for example, to ordain women and resist the draft. But if traditional theism was under attack, that did not mean the elevation of rationalism as the lodestar of the young. On the contrary, something similar to a romantic revival in religion was underway. Christ, with his doctrine of love and resistance to unjust institutions, became a hero figure of the young, as attested by the strange mixture of Christian ethics and countercultural styles in the popular musical "Jesus Christ Superstar." On a more subdued level in the sixties, and much more visibly in the seventies, young and old alike eschewed the complexities and uncertainties of theology and followed the enthusiasms of fundamentalist religion, enunciated by popular spokesmen like Billy Graham and Oral Roberts and hundreds of tub-thumping evangelists, mystics, and lay healers, and thirsted for such varying answers as those offered by Zen Buddhism, a hundred varieties of other Hindu-inspired creeds, and, on a much lower level, spiritualism and astrology.

Politically, the intense disappointment of many old leftists with Russia, the clear inapplicability of most varieties of radical conservatism, and the explosion of all the expectations built around John Kennedy and his Camelot by the crack of the assassin's rifle in Dallas left a great many people of all ages, and most of the young, with nowhere to go except to the dreary center that had produced nothing much domestically for ten years except peace and prosperity. And there the cautiousness of Eisenhower and even Kennedy in domestic affairs, the stubborn refusal of Congress to act on the most vital issues, and the inability or disinclination of the massive, bumbling regulatory bureaucracy to serve and protect the public, especially when action interfered with the annual bottom lines of industries they were supposed to regulate— all created a disenchantment with the federal government. The end products were political attitudes far different from those depicted in Bell's *End of Ideology*. Instead of merging toward the center into a consensus politics, important segments of the American population began to express by words and deeds a great variety of actions with one common denominator—an antipathy toward the fundamental institutions of the country and the people who were running them, the so-called establishment. Some were impelled toward an almost total anarchism, and some toward the formulation of intense revolt against existing social institutions through new techniques and mechanisms of political change. The spirit of revolt was especially prevalent among draft-age youth as the Vietnam War escalated into a major conflict.

Shapers of radical political thought in the 1960's consciously sought to avoid the doctrinal disputes and reliance on overseas Marxist influences—especially the Soviet Union—that had hurt earlier attempts to fashion and sustain a vital, "authentic" American left. Radical political thought was derived from a variety of sources, including C. Wright Mills, a member of the old left, who wrote *White Collar: The American Middle Class* (1952) and *The Power Elite* (1956). Mills increasingly came to see America as dominated by powerful, interconnected social and economic elites which crushed the potential for true liberation and democracy. Perhaps even more important was another member of the older generation —Herbert Marcuse. Returning to the dialectical reasoning of Hegel, Marcuse emphasized the inevitability of historical change, in *Reason and Revolution* (1940), and found a connection between the Freudian conception of society's repression of human instincts and the imperatives of capitalism. In *One Dimensional Man* (1965), Marcuse argued that modern America was a society in which basic human needs were repressed and sublimated in gadgets and material goods and meaningless hedonistic diversions, and "in which ideas, aspirations, and objectives that, by their content, transcend the established universe of discourse and action are either repelled or reduced to terms of this universe." In order for America to transcend its repressive society and achieve a truly free and just existence, radical changes would be required. Marcuse's ideas linking political and cultural repression struck a responsive chord in the youthful New Left, and his works became required reading in, and out, of the classroom on virtually every college campus.

A major demographic factor also underlay the inclination toward major social change—the increasingly youthful character of the population. Immediately after World War II, the nation's birth rate soared. This baby boom, the result of new marriages, reunited families, and high expectations in the postwar years, continued until 1955. The number of births per one thousand people reached 24.1 in 1950 and 25 in 1955, and then dropped to 17.5 by 1968. Throughout the 1960's, the increasing proportion of young people in the society added to the disposition to court the new and question the old.

Two talismanic events occurred in the early sixties that heralded the rise of youth as the most influential single group in changing American mores in the following decade. In February 1960, four freshmen from the all-black North Carolina State Agricultural and Technical College sat down at a segregated Woolworth's lunch counter in Greensboro and began the protest movement which spread rapidly across the South and provided fresh strength to the nonviolent civil-rights struggle guided by Southern churchmen and the National Association for the Advancement of Colored People. In June 1962, the Organization of Students for a Democratic Society gathered in Port Huron, Michigan, and issued a powerful statement against what they perceived as the shallow, hypocritical, and materialist society in America.

Neither of these movements was, of course, entirely new. The sit-ins were a rather logical extension of the long-standing struggle for black rights through adoption of the nonviolent tactics against segregation laws that began in the 1950's. The search for a suitable alternative to the established pattern of American values and aspirations was also deeply rooted in the nation's past and expressed in utopian ventures and based on religious or idealist goals. The youth revolt of the sixties was, however, especially influenced and informed by the examples of a few personalities and ideas from the generally somnolent fifties.

The beats, or beatniks, were completely out of step with the dominant tendencies of the Eisenhower years, and they were thus all the more visible to their compatriots of the next decade. Their small number included some compelling personalities who stood in high relief against the background of the time. In the mid-1950's, Jack Kerouac, a former athlete from Columbia University, turned to writing and published his so-called novel, *On the Road.* He had already coined the phrase the "beat generation." Essentially, Kerouac's message was to drop out of society and its mad rush for material objects and empty success, and to turn one's attention inward. "To find oneself is to find God," he wrote. In the quest, as he reported in *On the Road,* Kerouac went on the bum dressed in any rags he could find, sleeping in any pad at hand, and living off the land as he could.

Kerouac had a direct influence on a small group of poets who eventually came together in San Francisco, including Allen Ginsberg, Lawrence Ferlinghetti, and Gary Snyder. Ginsberg—the author of *Howl,* a book of sensitive and mystical poems—was attracted to Kerouac both mentally and physically, an attraction which he openly confessed. In the sixties, Ginsberg was an active influence on youth, reading his poetry on scores of college campuses and participating in demonstrations. Ferlinghetti also had a profound effect on at least the cultivated youthful mind of the late fifties and early sixties. A native New Yorker, Ferlinghetti graduated from the University of North Carolina and then ventured to San Francisco, where he opened the nation's first all-paperbound bookstore, City Lights, Inc. He published the poetry of the dean of modern American poets, William Carlos Williams, and also, despite many official obscenity charges, the work of Ginsberg, Gregory Corso, and himself. Ferlinghetti was, among the beats, perhaps the most interested in sexual themes, though he also fed Ginsberg's fascination with Zen Buddhism, an interest taken up in a more or less superficial fashion by hordes of youngsters during the next decade.

Emphasizing dope, undisciplined sex, four-letter words, long hair, unshaven faces, and unkempt clothing, the beats announced that they were ceasing to compete, becoming "outcasts." They gathered in often squalid quarters in Greenwich Village in New York, the North Beach region of San Francisco, and around Los Angeles, intent upon developing their "secret souls" and thus joining with "the soul of the world." Their unconventional philosophy and strange ways attracted enough public attention to turn their haunts into modest tourist attractions.

The beats provided some precedent for the much more significant and widespread counterculture movement of the sixties. With cries of "Trust no one over thirty" and "The establishment is always wrong," thousands of young people turned their backs on the past and set off in search of an entirely new social order, of "alternative life-styles" to the repressive, boring, meaningless existence of their largely middle-class parents. The counterculture was, certainly in the beginning, a phenomenon defined more by resistance to established social and economic patterns than by the proffering of clear cultural or political alternatives. As the very name implied, the counterculture opposed the dominant culture of modern America. It rejected rationalism and science, and what Theodore Roszak termed "the myth of objective consciousness." Instead, the emphasis was on intuition, self-realization, direct personal contacts, and a stripping away of the superficial materialism and manipulative structures of Western society. Roszak, in his book *The Making of a Counter Culture: Reflections on the Technocratic Society and Its Youthful Opposition* (1969), saw modern society as alienating and dehumanizing, with human relationships and purposes shaped entirely by machines and the imperatives of commerce and a false objectivity. He advocated a return to participatory democracy, small-scale community, and the powers of mystical insight and a reliance on nature and the "magical powers of the personality."

Adopting the habits of the beats and sharing the revived interest in primitivism and mysticism, the young during the sixties exhibited a strong tendency to shock and dismay established society. Disdaining the short-cropped hair of the successful bond salesmen of the fifties, young men grew their hair long and sported beards. The gray-flannel suit became passé as blue jeans were adopted as the universal uniform. Young women in turn affected the miniskirt and raised it by the end of the decade almost to the point of no further revelations. They also discarded lipstick and the usual mass-consumer beauty products, and adopted the masculine look of denim. This lack of attention to personal appearance was, for some at least, a studied statement of contempt for the conventional norm.

At a time when jobs were relatively plentiful, some among this startling generation disdained ordinary work, preferring to make their living on a hit or mostly miss basis. The "urban hippies" (a name conferred upon them by a San Francisco gossip columnist) often crowded together in cheap, cold-water flats or lofts where as many as ten or fourteen of both sexes slept in one room on pads on the floor. For food and other bare necessities, they depended on their more fortunate fellows, an occasional check from home, or what they could scrounge from the streets. A few with artistic pretensions fashioned leather belts and other craft items to sell to passersby. Quite simply, they deserted the world of materialism, wages, profits, and consumption. Underclothed, underfed, and often in need of medical care, they denied the acquisitive world of their parents.

In an even more formal indictment of the dominant culture, many hippies joined the commune movement that had a spectacular growth during the sixties. At its height, an estimated three to four thousand communes existed, some founded by idealists disillusioned with the urban, capitalist world, some by mystics, and some by political and social ideologues who professed anything from socialism to total anarchism and a variety of authoritarianisms. But basic to most of the rural communes—some of which lasted only for a summer—was the desire to flee from the city and to live off the land on natural products untainted by machinery and man-made chemicals and plastic packaging. Ironically, the communes that endured were often the ones that employed some type of farm machinery to increase production and were ordered by either a religious or a scholarly ethic.

The counterculture of the 1960's was a social rather than a genuinely political phenomenon, and expressed itself through music, language, customs—especially the relations between the sexes—and the shared and heightened experience of drugs. The overall effect was intentionally psychedelic—splashing colors, pure experience, a completely new dimension.

Instead of the romantic music of their elders, the youth of the sixties adopted rock as their own. It was a mixture of traditional country music, jazz, and the insistent beat and poignant chords of Afro-American rhythm and blues, epitomized in the rising popularity of performers like Buddy Holly, Elvis Presley, Bo Diddley, and later the Beatles, Jimi Hendrix, and a legion of acid-rock groups where electronics and sheer volume reigned supreme. Concurrently, a radical change in the dance produced patterns that were highly individualized, sensual, and freewheeling.

Language was also changed. Zealously discarding the circumlocutions and euphemisms of their elders, both sexes turned to the Elizabethan use of four-letter Anglo-Saxon words until the distinction between the masculine and feminine languages of the past was practically obliterated. A new vocabulary also appeared, drawn from the rock-music world and the street. The effect, as in dress, music, and manners, was to distinguish, identify, and shock.

Nothing, certainly, was more shocking to the older generations than the youthful penchant for narcotic drugs. Hashish, or "hash," the North American version of the Indian hemp plant, which produced a sense of euphoria, became a thriving commodity on college campuses, among the hippies, in sections of the inner city, and, in varying degrees, throughout the society, even though it was illegal. Marijuana, or "grass," drawn from the same source, was even more prevalent. While the precise physiological and psychological effects of the hemp derivatives are not known, most were not classified as "hard narcotics" and their impact was minimal unless they were used frequently. This was not the case with heroin and the derivatives of opium, which prevailed among "hard"-drug users. Unfortunately, many adolescents were also induced to try LSD, a derivative of lysergic acid and a very potent drug that produced temporary hallucinations and could induce a psychotic state with lasting damage to the body. Drug addiction was widespread among U.S. troops in Vietnam and returned with a new generation of veterans to middle-class America and to the white and black slums of the major cities.

The psychedelic culture romanticized the drug experience, and drug cultists like the former Harvard researcher Timothy Leary touted LSD and other substances as "liberating" and "mind expanding," helpful aids in the search for personal identity and inner peace. By the end of the decade, the country was faced with a major narcotic problem, accompanied by all manner of social evils, including a rising crime rate generated in part by growing drug habits. By the end of the seventies, the milder drugs, like marijuana, and in some instances the stronger ones, like heroin, were commonplace—among the poor, in junior and senior high schools, on the college campuses, and at middle-class cocktail parties. Deaths from drug overdoses and permanent damage from "bad trips" reduced the popularity of LSD and the hard narcotics among college youth and the middle class, but they continued to ravage the weak and the poor, especially in the inner city.

The politics and political thought of the sixties reflected the questioning of social institutions, challenges to cultural prescriptions, and the vitality and insistence (and sometimes the confusion and self-righteousness) of youth. The politics of the youth movement were radical, at least at first glance. The Port Huron Statement of the SDS, written in 1962 by Tom Hayden, was the most impressive manifesto of youth's discontent and its aspirations for the future, an "agenda for a generation" and the basic document of what became known as the New Left.

Based on a qualified Emersonian premise of faith in "the potential of man" and not on "his deification," the Port Huron Statement condemned existing society for its lack of vision, its racial bigotry, its complacent use of "superfluous abundance" while two-thirds of mankind, including millions of Americans, were undernourished, its reverence for science and especially technology, resulting in masses of useless gadgets, its unthinking "sapping of the earth's physical resources," its manipulation of the so-called democratic system, and in general its support of colonialism and imperialism. The positive goals of the statement called for the establishment of a "participatory democracy" in all realms of life, including the universities and colleges. Once established, the new politics should be directed toward a reestablishment of the sense of community among all colors and kinds of people by encouraging their sense of participation in the society.

The major objective of this activity should be to achieve a life of "quality" and not of quantity, in the sense of either goods or money. Especially in the economic sphere, work of whatever kind should "involve incentives worthier than money or survival. It should be educative, not stultifying, creative, not mechanical; self-directed, not manipulated, encouraging independence, a respect for others, a sense of dignity and a willingness to accept responsibility. . . ." To achieve this new heaven on earth, the manifesto deplored all types of violence. "It is imperative," its final statement on values read, "that the means of violence be abolished, and the institutions—local, national, international—that encourage nonviolence as a condition of conflict be developed."

Since most of the small group gathered at Port Huron—and most of the New Left generally—were students or former students, it was natural for them to turn a major part of their attention to the universities, which attracted more of their invective than possibly any other institution. They indicted the educational process as supportive of the social status quo, from which most of society's ills issued, for centering undergraduate activity on the real nonessentials of life, for stultifying any creative instincts they may have had, for preventing any real discussion and debate through dictatorial administrations and inept or completely boring experiences, and in their social life for attempting to keep them adolescents through exercising the power of *in loco parentis*. Particularly astonishing was the fact that such a statement of idealist and activist values should have come from the more fortunate children of the fifties, constantly criticized for their apathy toward almost any goal except material success, security, and conventional habits and deportment.

If the injustices and callousness of modern American life prompted the rise of the student left, its training ground was the civil-rights movement, in which thousands of students participated. After the bitter segregationist response to the efforts of Freedom Summer in 1964, the first of many major campus protest demonstrations erupted—not in the South but at the University of California at Berkeley. The immediate provocation was a university administration order to remove radical literature from Sproul Plaza, a site often used for political discussions and activities. When a student was arrested for violating the ban, more than a thousand protesting young people occupied the Plaza, and the "Free Speech Movement" was born. The leader of the movement, a veteran of the summer's civil-rights activity named Mario Savio, declared, "We have encountered the organized status quo in Mississippi, but it is the same in Berkeley." After thirty-two hours, the administration backed down. Later in the fall, however, several other students were threatened with disciplinary action, and enraged students occupied the administration building. They were forced out two days later by the police, and more than eight hundred were arrested. This led to a boycott of classes that virtually shut down the university.

The protest was not only on behalf of free political expression but against the arid, nondescript existence many students saw in front of them in the mid-sixties. "The chrome-plated consumers' paradise would have us grow up to be well-behaved children," Savio complained. "But an important minority of men and women coming to the front today have shown that they will die rather than be standardized, replaceable, and irrelevant."

Hundreds of colleges and universities experienced some form of student protest in 1964 and 1965, including student occupations of campus buildings and intervention by the local police. These demonstrations usually had a direct relationship to the Vietnam War. Fear of the draft doubtless kept a great many young men in schools and colleges long after they had any desire to be there for educational reasons. Some vented their general resentment against the nation's social and political system by attacking the universities, while others perhaps found in protest movements a way to compensate for their guilt at being the privileged few immune to military service. It is notable, in any event, that student protest dropped sharply with the end of the war and conscription.

The decline of the New Left and the overt radicalism of the counterculture can also be traced to a number of other factors. The New Left was highly disorganized, and even the major groups became fragmented toward the end of the sixties. These divisions compounded the lack of solid political theory and direction that had always characterized "the movement," and made it utterly impossible to identify a central idea, purpose, or group. Some New Left types moved so far toward the fringes of violence, drugs, or insanity that they disappeared from the scene altogether. The serious reform organizations—including civil-rights groups—were increasingly harassed and compromised by government officialdom, especially the Federal Bureau of Investigation and local police agencies, which engaged, secretly, in illegal break-ins, wiretapping, and intimidation. Finally, many aspects of the counterculture—especially fashions and greater sexual permissiveness—were adopted with astonishing rapidity by the majority culture, as many political causes—such as equal rights for women, minorities, and the poor—were taken up by the established political system and carried into the seventies. In this sense, the radicalism of the sixties appears quite similar to a number of earlier reform movements in American history, such as Populism.

The New Left spawned its share of crazies, whose threats of disruption were often theatrical and sometimes deadly serious. Abbie Hoffman, a founder with Jerry Rubin of the Youth International Party—called YIPPIE!—wrote a book entitled *Revolution for the Hell of It* (1968) and staged political theater to demonstrate the absurdity of established authority, including a plan to run a greased pig through the streets of Chicago during the 1968 Democratic national convention as an insult to Mayor Daley's police. The yippies called, among other things, for an end to the Vietnam War, the legalization of marijuana and psychedelic drugs, the total disarmament of all people including the police, the conservation of natural resources, full employment, and the abolition of money.

The SDS had grown slowly for the first few years of its existence after the declaration at Port Huron, but with its persistent opposition to the Vietnam War and its political efforts at the community level it flowered. It attracted supporters and sympathizers on practically every American campus, and generated the ideology and structure—such as it was—for the New Left. Some factions of SDS grew more and more radical, however, and eventually the organization sprouted the small Weatherman faction in 1968, devoted to violence both as a discipline and a means of securing outright revolution. After the debacle at the Democratic national convention in 1968—where yippies, Weathermen, and thousands of concerned, less radical students converged in an effort to stop the nomination of a pro-war candidate—the SDS broke apart. Hoffman, Tom Hayden, a Black Panther leader named Bobby Seale, and four others were indicted for conspiracy to disrupt the convention and immediately became popularly known as the Chicago

Seven. After a dramatic, and often theatrical trial, the jury acquitted the defendants of the conspiracy charges and held five guilty of the lesser charge of crossing state lines to incite riots. The Weatherman faction went underground, its violence to trickle over into the following decade.

After the passage of the Voting Rights Act in 1965, the main agenda of the struggle for black civil rights in the South had been cleared. Martin Luther King, Jr., and the Southern Christian Leadership Conference seemed uncertain about the next steps to take, and, ironically, their momentum and support began to decline as their reforms were enacted into law. Most everyone agreed, however, that eliminating the less obvious forms of discrimination—especially in Northern cities—and improving the dismal economic plights of blacks and other minorities were foremost on any list of items remaining to be accomplished. King organized the Poor People's Campaign to dramatize the continuing ravages of poverty, and the plodding wooden wagons winding up the highways from the rural South to camp out in the nation's capital were part of an effort to broaden the dimensions of the civil-rights movement, to focus on economic as well as political issues, as they affected people of all races. King's death removed the most charismatic figure of this wing of the movement, and while the campaign continued under King's successors, it did not meet with success.

At the same time, more radical leaders, such as Stokely Carmichael, came to the fore, brandishing Black Power slogans, declaring the superiority of African culture and customs, linking the liberation of blacks in America with struggles for oppressed peoples in the Third World, abandoning the tactics and rhetoric of nonviolence, and resisting the dominance of whites in the civil-rights movement. In a sense, the significant political victories of the civil-rights movement had called attention to the distance blacks yet had to go to achieve full equality in American society. The Black Panther Party was the most dramatic evidence of the new militancy. Founded in Oakland, California, in 1966 by Huey P. Newton and Bobby Seale, the Panthers had few active members, but their leaders were often forceful and articulate. Eldridge Cleaver, who wrote a best-seller polemic, *Soul on Ice* (1968), while he was in prison, was the organization's "minister of information."

The Panthers openly displayed weapons, denounced racial and class oppression in a vague Marxism-Leninism, and linked their spirits with other revolutionaries in developing African and Asian countries. The Panthers were, however, one of the few black militant groups in this period that sought alliances with radical whites. The Panthers also experienced factionalism, however, and some members went underground, some fled the country (including Newton and Cleaver), and others were gunned down in police raids.

As black militancy increased, the life and thoughts of one black leader became especially widely studied. Malcolm Little had joined the Nation of Islam, or Black Muslims (a strange concoction of Islam and home-grown black resentment against the "white devils"), changed his name to Malcolm X, and became a principal spokesman and major organizer for the group. As his popularity rose, he was expelled from the Muslims by their leader, Elijah Muhammad, in 1963, probably because Muhammad feared that Malcolm might surpass all others in the hearts of the faithful. In a search for the true sources of his faith, Malcolm journeyed to the Islamic holy city of Mecca and returned with a new allegiance and a conviction that racial hatred was evil in whatever guise. He formed the Organization of Afro-American Unity, and was especially appealing to Northern urban blacks with his stirring and uncompromising message. He was assassinated in 1965 while addressing a black congregation. Malcolm's *Autobiography* captured the essence of his life and message, however, and continued to influence various parts of the black movement well into the seventies.

The violence and radicalism of the sixties drifted into terrorism by a handful who went underground, and prompted a concerted —and sometimes illegal—resistance from the nation's law-enforcement agencies, especially the FBI. J. Edgar Hoover, Richard Nixon, and a number of other national leaders believed that these radical expressions were manifestations of a deeply rooted, coordinated (and Communist-inspired) effort to undermine the society and overthrow the government. Federal agents infiltrated radical organizations and burglarized their files and offices, encouraged local law-enforcement agencies to stop the Black Panthers at almost any cost (which most police forces were more than happy to do), and wiretapped the telephones and opened the mail of suspected individuals. The FBI even wiretapped Martin Luther King's telephone, put electronic bugs in his offices and hotel rooms, and sent the civil-rights leader threatening anonymous messages.

The New Left was, in reality, hardly structured at all. Radical factions began to turn their fire against one another: blacks against whites, men against women, theoreticians against romantics, non-violence against violence. The New Left was less a coherent movement than a phenomenon that grew more disparate in time.

One fundamental problem was the absence of a genuine radical tradition in American history and politics: the New Left could not depend very much on the old left for inspiration and example. A second major difficulty was the lack of theory in New Left thought, and a resulting absence of structure, precise goals, and clear priorities. Resistance against the Vietnam War became a crusade, consisting of many different types of people and many viewpoints concerning American society as a whole. Some resisted the war because it sullied the best traditions of American democracy; others saw the war as a vile, and perfectly logical and expected, extension of United States capitalist imperialism; and still others loathed the war because it was a struggle the United States could not win. Even when resistance to the war was tied in some fashion to larger problems in the society and economy, the connection was often vague and the implications unclear. Most New Left spokesmen, from Mario Savio to Tom Hayden and Abbie Hoffman, condemned impersonal bureaucracy and its inherent inertia against creativity and change. But they were simply not clear on the alternatives. "Power to the people" was a catchy slogan suitable for chanting in the streets. But it was no substitute for social analysis or theory, and provided no direction for action.

The least philosophical among the New Leftists were Hoffman and the yippies, who concentrated on bringing the social system down by political comedy. Their brand of revolution ("for the hell of it") was not especially compelling among those like Malcolm X who sought social change as a necessary step toward the genuine liberation of oppressed peoples and the lower classes. There was probably a fissure throughout the political radicalism of the sixties, separating the sons and daughters of affluence, determined to deny the vapidity of their middle-class heritage, and the offspring of desperation, poverty, and racism. The revolutionary sentiments of some during the sixties were deadly serious; for others, they were tools to shock satisfied parents and establish personal identity.

Some elements of the counterculture were perhaps too readily adopted by the dominant culture, but some did not stand the test of time and experience. In the desire to crack the encrusted values and habits of middle-class white America, almost any sort of errant behavior—even when self-destructive—tended to be embraced by many young people as an affirmation of "identity" and "freedom." History was a burden to be tossed aside, not plumbed for inspiration. But, once the initial rebellion was over, elementary principles of governance and social life were rediscovered in hundreds of communes throughout the country ("You can't eat if you don't work"), as if such questions had never been addressed before.

The counterculture was ill-defined, and its participants ranged from the political ideologues of the New Left and committed utopians to diet faddists and wandering moochers out for a good time. The heady spirit of youthful rebellion and the reverence for intuition and immediate experience often sheltered self-indulgence and an almost total abandonment of critical standards and self-discipline (even of the sort necessary to build new life-styles and communities). History, standards, and discipline were doubtless suspect in part because they were affirmed, at least verbally, by the dominant culture. Thus, for many young people, the good life was a mixture of hedonism and laziness; art was literally any product of expression no matter how dismal or banal; and formal learning was useless and oppressive. The counterculture also, of course, produced its own norms and consumer fads and petty hypocrisies. Though the creativity and insight of youth during the decade cannot be denied, Americans over thirty could perhaps be forgiven their suspicion that the youthful view of life as a "trip" was little more than a permutation of prolonged mass adolescence.

Like the twenties, the sixties was a decade that seemed conveniently set apart, a watershed or plateau from which one could see both a very distinct past and the future. This was, of course, only partly true. Historians may well discover many more bands of continuity running through the last half of the twentieth century than we now can see. Certainly, the changes registered in the sixties were dramatic, even when they were superficial, and endlessly probed and chronicled by communications media drawn to the flashy event and public "happening." The whole cultural atmosphere was ripe for a symbolic act of any sort. Even from the near perspective of 1980, the rhetoric of the New Left seems naïve, the threats of revolution ring hollow, the horror at changing social customs too exaggerated, and all a bit embarrassing in the sense of a popular fashion now very much out of style. But there was substance behind the raised fists and harsh slogans of the New Left and the campus demonstrations: a war, racism, and the failure of government to meet basic human needs. Even if the protesters were often silly, the culture was changed and the political focus of an era was redirected: in styles of dress and music, in attitudes toward sex and marriage, and in a general reassertion of individualism and self-discovery. The political agenda was altered, to include not only the usual concerns with national security and economic policy but compelling new emphases on racism, poverty, environmental pollution, the dangers of nuclear energy, and the corruption of public officials and some national institutions. In the seventies, these themes predominated in ways that perhaps even the members of the New Left did not anticipate.

Themes of equal rights were taken up by the Supreme Court, which reformers of an earlier generation had condemned as one of the most undemocratic and reactionary influences in the nation. Beginning with the unanimous *Brown* decision in 1954, which ordered the desegregation of all public schools, the court interpreted the Constitution with a particular view toward justice and equality. In a series of landmark decisions over the next decade or so, following the lead of Chief Justice Earl Warren, the court revolutionized judicial thinking in many other spheres of political and social life. The *Baker v. Carr* decision in 1962 enunciated the "one man–one vote" principle, and ordered representative schemes in the states to reflect the actual distribution of population. By *Gideon v. Wainwright* (1963) and *Miranda v. Arizona* (1966), the court widened due process to require legal counsel for prisoners faced with serious charges and the right to consult with a lawyer before making any statements to the police. In 1973, the court affirmed the right of women to obtain abortions and thus encouraged the campaign for women's rights. And in a series of cases that expanded its much earlier one permitting the importation into the United States of James Joyce's *Ulysses,* the Justices—in a not always straight progression—so broadened and blurred the legal distinction between pornography and art that the Supreme Court has been termed by some the true originator of the "permissive society."

Changes in sexual attitudes and the role of women in American society were among the most persistent and potentially significant of those initiated during the sixties. Of all the youthful vagaries, people over thirty found casual attitudes toward sex and marriage the most difficult to accept, at least in the beginning. Whatever the moral peccadillos of the older generation, and they were doubtless many, they had sought to shield their amatory excursions from public view and cloak them in the traditional arguments for chastity before marriage (especially for females) and fidelity afterward. Great numbers of young people, however, disdained these practices and indulged in cohabitation openly, talked about it, and spurned the conventional institution of matrimony. These tendencies were strengthened by the fact that prevailing American attitudes toward sexual practices were often hypocritical and oppressive. By the mid-seventies, college students had won the right to live in coeducational dormitories, obtain birth-control pills from the campus health services, and even get discounts on abortions. Where the collegians led, high-school students often followed, and in such an atmosphere the legal, religious, and ethical structures ordering sex, marriage, and childbearing and rearing were being vastly modified.

By 1975, the marriage rate in the United States had dropped precipitously, in part because of the number of couples living together outside of marriage. On the other hand, the divorce rate reached the staggering annual total of over a million for the first time, a figure representing almost exactly half of the total marriages that year. Even that figure did not represent the true condition of one of the oldest institutions of humankind, as hundreds of thousands of marriages were broken by the simple act of a spouse walking away from his or her mate and children.

These changes in the institutions of marriage and the family were hardly attributable to the counterculture alone. They had been building for decades, and were associated with the trials and pressures of a technological, urban, mass-consumption culture. They were also connected with the changing roles of women in the society and with patterns of sexual relations and practices that had existed, though less visible, for some years before the sixties. Between 1948 and 1953 an Indiana University scientist published a series of volumes on human sexuality that were best sellers and were to have a profound effect on future relationships between men and women. Alfred C. Kinsey's works, heavily statistical and based on the latest methods of survey research, sought to discover just what Americans were doing sexually. He found, to the expressed surprise of just about everybody, that gaps between the law, conventional morals, and actual practice were astonishingly wide, and that the older precepts of abstinence before marriage, monogamy afterwards, and the avoidance of sexual deviations as defined by most state codes were being dishonored at massive rates by the general population.

The old sexual codes were further undermined by the widespread introduction on the commercial market in 1963–64 of drugs capable of contraception. The Pill in effect gave women the chance to control birth and removed the fear of unwanted pregnancies that had served as a deterrent to illicit sex. Beyond that, it also provided one form of liberation that accompanied a broader women's struggle for a new place in American society.

A year before the Pill appeared, Betty Friedan's *The Feminine Mystique* was published, and became almost a bible for the new feminism. Women should no longer be satisfied with the goals set for them by men, Friedan argued; they should demand more than the prospect of being housewives and mothers—a fair shake in education and opportunities for careers, equal pay, and advancement. In short, what Friedan asked for was full economic and social equality for women in America. The book became a best seller, and especially appealed to so-called career women in the major cities.

The women's movement toward equality with men was highly influential in changing fundamental social institutions. Like most movements for substantial social change, it had its true believers, recent converts, loyal followers, fellow travelers, closet sympathizers, backsliders, and committed opponents. Some women burned their brassieres in public demonstrations, while others reaffirmed their traditional role as mothers and helpmates in the home. A few swore off company with the oppressive male sex altogether, while more sought better relationships with men through a stronger female identity. The front-line forces were filled with young college women who had enlisted in many of the progressive causes of the day, especially the black struggle for civil rights in the South, and found themselves quickly relegated to traditional women's work, housekeeping and clerical jobs, and regularly passed over for consideration as officers and leaders even in local organizations. Stokely Carmichael's remark that the correct position for white females in the civil-rights movement was "prone" was a call to arms for militant feminists.

Disillusioned, many women turned to the developing SDS as an arena in which to exercise their ambitions—with much the same results. A separate women's caucus was organized, helping to split SDS and to cement the idea that gave rise to the organized movement for feminine liberation and groups such as the National Organization for Women (NOW) in 1971 and the National Women's Political Caucus.

Until very late in its development, the women's liberation movement was not significantly aided by the normal processes of democratic government. President Kennedy did appoint a Commission on the Status of Women in 1962, which recommended a number of changes in existing laws. One change, equal pay for equal work irrespective of sex, passed the Congress; but its enforcement was lackadaisical until the 1970's. The revelation of the 1970 census that women's wage levels were still little more than half those of men gave further ammunition to the belief that women as well as blacks had constituted for American capitalism a convenient and peripheral labor force that could be used in boom times at low wages and then discharged almost at will in times of contraction—a factor that helped explain much of capitalism's maximization of profit and minimization of losses.

Equality of economic rewards was, however, only a small part of the rising demands of women's liberation forces. Among other goals they set for themselves were equality of opportunity for education, for entrance into the learned professions, for advancement and promotion in private as well as governmental enterprises. Perhaps more unsettling to the more conservative-minded and certainly to the great majority of men were women's demands for equality in sexual, marriage, and divorce matters. They deplored the masculine attitudes of machismo—which valued women only as sex objects—and they claimed the same rights to sexual freedom as had been traditionally accorded males. Last, they demanded that inexpensive and easy abortions be made legal, a cause furthered by some economy-minded legislatures viewing the huge payments made to thousands of deserted mothers with dependent children, and by the Supreme Court's 1973 decision legalizing abortions despite the fervent opposition of the Roman Catholic hierarchy and many assorted right-to-life groups.

In 1972, Congress accepted the so-called Equal Rights Amendment (ERA) outlawing all discrimination on the basis of sex. For the remainder of the decade, the political activists of the movement were engaged in the effort to get two-thirds of the states to accept. For a time, the friends of the proposed amendment to the United States Constitution, who included First Ladies Betty Ford and Rosalynn Carter and most national political leaders, were optimistic. But then the apparent conservative urge of the country slowed the process and by 1980 the measure still lacked the necessary votes to make it part of the Constitution, even though Congress had extended the time limit past the six years usually allotted for consideration for ratification. Meanwhile, however, the federal requirement for equality of treatment between the sexes in all federal grants and contracts had gone a long way toward achieving many of the rights guaranteed to women in the proposed amendment. Under the necessity of reporting to HEW the results of all hiring and promotion activities and justifying the actions as regards women and other minorities, the universities—for example —were slowly but obviously changing the complexion of their faculty and administrative staffs. The armed forces disbanded their female units entirely, as women were admitted presumably on the same basis as men. Women were even admitted to the military service academies and by the end of the seventies were serving aboard ships in the United States navy. On city streets, armed women police officers, often paired with male policemen on patrols, were a common sight.

The tides of radicalism and libertarianism which surged forward in the sixties washed into the subsequent decade, sometimes with considerable force. But even though the pace and drama of change, and the severe questions about the nation and its values raised by the Vietnam War, urban riots, and the civil-rights movement, disturbed the great majority of Americans, most clung to a faith in their country. Most citizens were neither radical nor terribly dissatisfied, but they were concerned about American institutions and wanted very much for those institutions to work. Most elements of the population held to the notion that the United States was superior, with an economic system second to none. "Love it or leave it," one slogan insisted. The 1970's would sorely try this confidence.

12

The Troubled Seventies

OF the four Presidents who held office between 1961 and 1976, none served two full elected terms. One was assassinated; one withdrew from the race because of massive opposition to his foreign policies; one resigned in the face of virtually certain impeachment and probable conviction for high crimes in office; and one was never elected in the first place and lost his bid for an elected term. The first President of the 1980's joined in the struggle to shore up sagging confidence in national leadership.

This was a bleak and sobering record for any democracy and is understandable only in the light of the social turbulence of the time and the will to violence. At the same time, the nation was undergoing a series of social and economic changes—ranging from new patterns of urbanization and a continuing decline of the inner cities to the new economic developments along the country's "southern rim"—that affected the lives and prospects of millions of Americans. Tragically, during this period when both peoples and institutions were in flux, the nation's formal political institutions were, for the most part, curiously unresponsive to the massive changes going on.

Certain basic political and social facts underlay these conditions. The Democratic Party dominated Congress throughout the sixties and seventies, but its majorities were often riddled with dissension. Old and generally conservative committee chairmen wielded the greatest legislative power, until a modest revolt by new House members in 1974 unseated a few of the old warhorses. The key to legislative success was compromise, but organized special-interest groups proliferated and made compromise, and meeting the needs of unorganized interests, more difficult to achieve. By 1980, the two major parties had become less effective as organizing forces in the nation's political life. Television, rather than party affiliation or support, was most important, and each election seemed to generate new coalitions and public responses.

The powers of the Presidency grew, while Presidential control over a sprawling bureaucracy declined. The "imperial" Presidency was, in fact, as much as anything else an outgrowth of the determined effort to achieve effective control over the operations of the federal government. The almost constant Presidential concern with foreign policy—brought about in part by the slowly developing but persistent Russian challenges to American dominance in Africa, the Near East, Asia, and even in the Western Hemisphere, and by the clamorous ambitions of the generally poverty-stricken Third World for independence and a fair share of the world's goods—not only shaped the modern Presidency but helped explain the lack of creative domestic policy and legislation for most of the period. At the same time, the fear of monolithic Communism became a dogma that drove one Administration after another to confusion and disaster.

The post-Eisenhower years witnessed the acceleration of long-standing forces and the initiation of new ones. The nation enjoyed the greatest economic prosperity in its history, yet millions languished in poverty and millions more struggled to earn a decent living. As political rhetoric touted the virtues of free enterprise in the struggle against godless Communism, the concentration of the American economy in fewer and fewer corporate hands proceeded: in 1971, only one percent of United States corporations controlled more than 85 percent of the assets and net profits from manufacturing. Mergers increased in number and size, and economic competition grew less significant. A handful of conglomerates controlled the resources and power of empires, and the line between private and public entities was blurred. In 1960, about one-tenth of the American labor force was directly or indirectly dependent on defense appropriations. This was the age of corporate liberalism, as big business and big labor cooperated under the eyes of big government.

Transportation and communications technology linked the destinies of American citizens as never before, while also fragmenting the urban landscape into discrete pockets of black and white, rich and poor. A nation where more than three-quarters of all households had a washing machine and at least one automobile, and all but about 15 percent had TV sets and refrigerators, in 1970 nevertheless stood on the verge of intense questioning about the meaning and quality of life. Mass-consumption economy and urbanization had created a new living environment and material culture for America, yet they had clearly not supplied answers for all of America's needs or wants. The nation, with abundant natural resources, ended the seventies struggling with an energy shortage.

The United States had become in every sense an urban nation. Urbanization and urban culture were so pervasive, so dominant, that the very existence of the city as a discrete congregation of people was called into question. More than three-quarters of the country's population lived in metropolitan areas in 1970, within a minuscule portion of the nation's total land area; yet by the same time more than two-thirds of this urban population, and a similar proportion of urban jobs, resided outside the more tightly clustered central cities. The metropolitan density curve, which once fell off sharply at the edge of the central districts, now sloped more gently toward the distant suburbs, reflecting a more even distribution of urban dwellers across a much vaster area than seemed possible, given the constraints of technology, in the nineteenth century. Most central cities, particularly in the older industrial belt, consistently lost population after 1950, while metropolitan areas everywhere grew in size or at least held their own. Some observers talked of a "suburban nation," and one urban geographer, Brian J. L. Berry, referred to a process of "urbanization without cities." These trends seemed still very much in evidence by 1980, with urban decentralization even beginning to spread beyond the boundaries of the largest metropolitan areas.

This metropolitanization of urban America, underway since the end of the nineteenth century, was accompanied after 1950 by a significant shift of national population and resources to the lower half of the nation, known popularly as the "southern rim" or Sun Belt. In the century following the Civil War, the South and West had provided a market hinterland for the urban-industrial core of the Northeast and Midwest, supplying raw materials and cheap labor to Northern factories and investment opportunities and new markets for Northern businessmen, corporations, and banks. In the 1930's, the South was identified as the nation's number-one economic problem, and a variety of public and private efforts concentrated on reducing the depth of the region's social and economic difficulties. But by 1970 it was increasingly the older industrial cities of the North that cried out for assistance as people and jobs moved south and west toward more open space, cheaper land, and a warmer climate.

This process of "regional succession" reflected economic trends and technological developments that changed the way of living and doing business across the country. For one thing, heavy industry accounted for less and less of the nation's overall economic activity. Services rather than manufacturing dominated, and the proportion of white-collar employees among the country's work force increased with each census. The national economy also became increasingly decentralized, with sales personnel, business affiliates, and branch offices strung across the country. A service-oriented economy did not require the large investment in physical plants and the restriction to a single place that characterized most heavy industry. And when large central headquarters were required, they were more and more often to be found outside the Northeast—in Atlanta, Dallas, Houston, or Los Angeles.

The transportation and communications revolutions of the century reshaped the American landscape, especially after 1950. Wide paved roads gave way to multilane highways and eventually to vast limited-access expressways crisscrossing the country. Early experiments with the electronic transmission of visual images in the 1920's burgeoned after World War II into a massive new industry, as television eclipsed radio and motion pictures as the principal mass-entertainment and advertising medium. The miniaturization of electronic components—partly an outgrowth of the space program—led to great leaps in the scale and capacity of the communications system, especially in satellite technology, computers, and information storage and retrieval. These changes rendered the centralization of many economic and administrative activities and functions more a matter of choice than necessity, and increasingly businesses chose to occupy cheap and ample land on the urban periphery. The electronics, computer, advertising, information-processing, and service industries were most conveniently located in large, single-story structures rather than in multistory factories, and this also fueled the suburban movement of businesses and jobs.

Richard Nixon's rise to the Presidency seemed to reflect this shift of power to the suburbs and to the South and West. A native of Southern California, he resided for years in Washington and then in private law practice in New York City; he was not rooted in or associated with any one place. Many of his friends and supporters, especially of his Presidential candidacy, had made their fortunes in the Sun Belt—in oil, electronics, light manufacturing, and banking. Nixon harbored a deep distrust of the established Eastern elite and New York intellectuals. His choice of "little White Houses" in Key Biscayne, Florida, and San Clemente, California, followed perfectly in the new demographic trends.

Nixon had made the most dramatic comeback in American history. A political fixture throughout the fifties, well known to the public since Eisenhower sent him on trips and missions that kept him very much in the news, Nixon was a complex man, little understood except possibly by his closest advisers. Shy in public, oddly embarrassed even when reviewing troops or receiving visiting dignitaries, Nixon had devoted his life to seeking office. He held a heroic conception of political leadership; his book, *Six Crises,* glorified bold initiative and courage under fire. Nixon, basically a conservative, was not the hostage of any political ideology; he was a political opportunist less interested in carrying out a specific political design than in overcoming challenges and making some impact on the course of history. He was determined to be a responsible, aggressive, and strong President, even at the risk of direct confrontation at home and abroad.

Nixon appointed as his national-security adviser a Harvard professor, Henry Kissinger, who had served as a close consultant to Nelson Rockefeller. A native of Germany, Kissinger was a student of *realpolitik* in nineteenth-century Europe, eager to practice in the highest councils of government the lessons he had learned from his studies of foreign policy and political power. Kissinger also had a knack for intense, persistent negotiation and a talent for publicity that eventually made him an international celebrity. William

Rogers, a member of Nixon's New York law firm, was appointed Secretary of State; but Richard Nixon made his own foreign policy, and Kissinger generally carried it out.

Nixon and Kissinger viewed the world as dominated by the two superpowers, where every move, every event, recalibrated a delicate balance of forces and possibilities. Every incident was weighed for its geopolitical significance. Kissinger, especially, held to the notion of linkage between distinct events and policies: a move by either of the big powers anywhere in the world was inherently related, or linked, to other elements of their relationship, including broad initiatives for a nuclear-arms pact or expanded trade and scientific cooperation. Isolated events, Kissinger thought, should be deliberately linked in negotiations, to provide the right combination of threats and incentives needed to achieve the maximum benefit for national interests. The corollary, however, was that a failure or stumble by the United States anywhere in the world would almost certainly weaken its strength and credibility elsewhere, on every major issue.

America could thus not afford to lose the Vietnam War. Nixon approached Vietnam as a challenge, and even more than Lyndon Johnson, he was determined neither to blink in the face of the enemy nor to give in. Kissinger offered a more sophisticated justification for involvement in Indochina: Vietnam was a test of American will and reliability and a barometer of strength between the United States and the Communist countries.

Expanded four-party peace talks began in Paris on January 18, 1969, involving both the South Vietnamese government and the National Liberation Front, as well as the Americans and the North Vietnamese. In November, Nixon announced his Vietnamization policy (the "secret plan" to end the war that he had mentioned during the campaign), which involved the buildup of South Vietnamese military strength through intensified training and an infusion of new arms and equipment, while United States military forces were gradually withdrawn. This plan recognized implicitly that opposition to the war at home stemmed from American casualties, and not so much from aversion to American support for the South Vietnamese regime. Not an entirely new idea, Vietnamization seemed to Nixon and Kissinger the only approach that could forestall defeat for the South Vietnamese—at least for a while—and also extricate United States military forces with honor, and without weakening the American international position. The strategy also required, in Nixon's view, a consistently firm hand and a willingness to punish the enemy for violating any understandings or seeking a military victory while American troops were being pulled out. Vietnamization, the Administration concluded, could only succeed if it were not mistaken for weakness.

American forces in South Vietnam had long been frustrated by the presence of North Vietnamese and NLF troops just across the border in Cambodia, outside the area authorized for American attack. Intelligence reports also indicated a key North Vietnamese military-headquarters unit located in the border sanctuaries. Less than a month after his inauguration, Nixon approved a request from the American commander, General Creighton Abrams, to bomb enemy targets in Cambodia, a neutral country.

On March 17, 1969, under cover of strict secrecy, the first B-52 raid was launched against Cambodia. Not only were the press and public not informed, but most military commanders did not know, and even secret military records were deliberately and carefully falsified to conceal the raids. Congress was not notified, though several sympathetic legislators were given a very general report of the situation. These operations were conducted under direct Presidential orders, and Nixon and Kissinger followed their progress with close attention. Kissinger kept such decisions under the tight control of the White House, and information was not shared completely even with the Secretaries of State and Defense.

Cambodia's position in the Indochinese conflict was very delicate indeed. The North Vietnamese had long made limited use of the Cambodian border areas as sanctuaries, and there was little that Cambodian Prince Norodom Sihanouk could do about it. But he attempted to follow a policy of neutrality, keep Cambodia out of the war, and limit the role in his country of both the North Vietnamese and the Cambodian leftist insurgent movement, the Khmer Rouge.

Cambodian neutrality had been respected by President Johnson, but Nixon and Kissinger were not sympathetic to Sihanouk's position. They believed that the bombing would test Sihanouk's willingness to cooperate with the United States; at the same time, by expelling the enemy from the border sanctuaries, it would assist in maintaining the security of South Vietnam. They took his public silence on the secret American bombing as a sign of his support.

Instead, the American bombing raids drove the Communist forces deeper into Cambodia, away from the border areas and toward the capital of Pnom Penh, and Sihanouk found it increasingly difficult to maintain a posture of neutrality. The Indochinese war was, as a result, widened and intensified. Sihanouk was overthrown in March 1970 by his cousin and a group of right-wing military men led by General Lon Nol, who became Prime Minister of the new government.

Nixon decided to support the new regime and supply it with arms. The Cambodians were encouraged to raise an army of more than 220,000 men and launch a full-fledged effort against the North Vietnamese and the Khmer Rouge, which Washington perceived as virtually identical. American bombing operations continued along the border, and on April 30, 1970, a combined force of American and South Vietnamese troops entered Cambodia in search of the elusive Communist headquarters. Lon Nol immediately protested this action, but to no avail. Nixon went on national television to announce and explain the Cambodian incursion. "If, when the chips are down," the President said, "the world's most powerful nation, the United States of America, acts like a pitiful, helpless giant, the forces of totalitarianism and anarchy will threaten free nations and free institutions throughout the world." Nixon pledged that American troops would go no farther than twenty-one miles into Cambodia and would be withdrawn by June 30.

The invasion of Cambodia further galvanized the peace movement. More than 250,000 people had participated in the largest antiwar demonstration in American history in Washington in November 1969, and immediately after the Cambodian action campuses across the country erupted again. On May 4, 1970, four students were killed by National Guard troops at Kent State University in Ohio during an antiwar demonstration.

The Cambodian invasion also aroused congressional critics of the war. On May 11, the Senate Foreign Relations Committee approved an amendment sponsored by Senators Frank Church and John Sherman Cooper restricting future military action in Cambodia. As finally passed, the Cooper-Church Amendment prohibited the presence of American troops and advisers in Cambodia after June 30, and also the use of American air power in support of Cambodian ground forces. This unprecedented amendment reflected deep and growing congressional concern over the Administration's unilateral use of the warmaking power, and over the course of affairs in Indochina.

These suspicions were further encouraged by the publication in *The New York Times* and *The Washington Post* of the Pentagon Papers, a top-secret review of American involvement in Southeast Asia prepared by specialists in the Defense Department. The documents recounted the major decisions that led the nation deeper and deeper into the conflict, and presented some intelligence information on which these decisions were based. The papers showed, in a number of instances, that the real bases for decisions often contrasted vividly with public statements and declarations to the electorate and the Congress. The secrecy of the war now became a major political issue. The Administration attempted to stop the printing of these documents, but the Supreme Court refused to permit the prior restraint of publication, and the first installment appeared on June 13, 1971. The papers had been delivered to the *Times* by a former Pentagon researcher, Daniel Ellsberg, and the government immediately brought criminal charges against him for the unauthorized release of classified information.

The war dragged on. In Cambodia, Pnom Penh was isolated by the Khmer Rouge soon after the American invasion, and Lon Nol's forces struggled with increasingly less success in the countryside. In Vietnam, Hanoi kept up the pressure in the South, compounding the low morale and corruption which had long plagued the South Vietnamese government and military. As American troops were withdrawn on a more or less regular schedule (only about 140,000 remained at the end of 1971), the South Vietnamese assumed more and more of the burden on the ground. But American power was unleashed in the air. Vietcong strong points in South Vietnam were subjected to a relentless bombardment and areas of Cambodia became free-fire zones for United States and South

Vietnamese aircraft. Interpreting the restrictions of the Cooper-Church Amendment broadly, the administration continued American air action in Cambodia, justifying it on the grounds that it protected American forces in South Vietnam. In actuality, many air operations directly supported Cambodian troops in their struggle with the Khmer Rouge.

On December 26, 1971, Nixon launched a massive bombing campaign against the North for violations of understandings with the United States in connection with the peace talks. In March 1972, the North Vietnamese struck across the demilitarized zone separating the two countries in a major new offensive, and on April 15 the United States resumed the bombing of Hanoi and the port of Haiphong, which had been suspended for four years. Even as American combat troops were being withdrawn, the United States demonstrated a willingness to escalate the war in order to protect South Vietnam and the policy of Vietnamization. In May, Nixon announced that North Vietnamese ports, including Haiphong, had been mined. That August, the last American combat troops left Vietnam.

Peace negotiations proceeded as each side jockeyed for position and advantage. North Vietnam insisted on nothing less than a settlement that insured their ultimate victory, and the United States desired a solution that would provide at least a reasonable period for President Thieu and his government to consolidate their position and fend off Communist advances with increased American military and economic aid.

In 1972, the outlines of a peace settlement were worked out, mainly in negotiations between Kissinger and Hanoi's representative to the talks, Le Duc Tho. There was to be a cease-fire. The North Vietnamese agreed to allow Thieu's government to remain in power while elections were planned in the South. For its part, the United States formally recognized in the agreement the presence in South Vietnam of North Vietnamese troops—about 145,-000 of them in mid-year. This concession shocked and appalled Thieu, who believed that it severely undermined his government's chances of survival, and he threatened to scuttle the peace talks. Washington finally persuaded the South Vietnamese leader that the United States would monitor the cease-fire and intervene if

North Vietnam took advantage of the situation. Tons of military hardware were shipped to Saigon, and Nixon wrote Thieu personal letters assuring him of American resolve. On December 18, Nixon ordered a massive B-52 bombing of Hanoi and Haiphong to show both Thieu and the North Vietnamese that the United States was committed to the peace settlement and the defense of South Vietnam.

The formal peace agreement was signed in Paris on January 27, 1973. North Vietnam released 590 American prisoners of war by April 1 and promised assistance in identifying and locating the missing-in-action. The last American personnel, serving mainly in support roles, left Vietnam on March 29.

The war in Cambodia continued. The Khmer Rouge were not bound by the Paris agreement—the Americans had always overestimated Hanoi's control over the Cambodian Communists—and they continued to attack government outposts and drive Lon Nol's forces, and millions of peasants, back into the crowded, collapsing city of Pnom Penh. The insistence of the Americans and South Vietnamese that an anti-Communist Cambodian government was essential to the survival of South Vietnam forced the struggle to a final conclusion. Just as hostilities ended in Vietnam, the United States launched an air offensive against enemy forces in Cambodia. In an effort to stop American participation in the fighting, the United States House of Representatives voted on May 10, 1973, to block the use of funds for bombing in Cambodia, and the Senate expanded and strengthened the measure. Nixon vetoed the bill on the grounds that it imperiled American credibility, endangered the Lon Nol government, and interfered with a peace settlement. The House failed to muster the two-thirds majority necessary to override the veto, but the President and congressional leaders later compromised and agreed that the bombing would stop after August 15.

By the time the bombing ended in August 1973, the entire eastern half of Cambodia had been subjected to intensified bombing in an effort to keep Lon Nol's government alive. More than 539,000 tons of American bombs were dropped on Cambodia—more than three times the amount dropped on Japan during World

War II. But the Khmer Rouge persisted, and on April 17, 1975, they entered Pnom Penh and soon thereafter began the evacuation of the city, and all other large towns, in a drastic and brutal effort to totally destroy the corrupt influences of the former government and build a pristine Communist state.

The Paris agreement was observed mostly in the breach. President Thieu ignored many of the political provisions of the pact. Hanoi consolidated its forces, chopped away at the South Vietnamese, and waited for a favorable moment to strike. Once American troops were removed from Vietnam and Nixon pursued the bombing in Cambodia, Congress was increasingly less inclined to provide military and economic aid to Saigon or Pnom Penh. On April 30, North Vietnamese forces captured Saigon as the last American civilians and some of their Vietnamese friends scrambled aboard military helicopters atop the United States embassy. An era in Southeastern Asian history had come to an end, though violence and suffering continued.

Vietnam was, for Nixon and Kissinger, but one piece of a larger puzzle dominated by the shapes of the big powers. Nixon saw an opportunity to reach some basic understandings with the Soviet Union on the world order he contemplated, and the Russians had encouraged movement away from cold-war tensions by expressing their interest in new forms of cooperation with the United States almost immediately after Nixon's election. Both nations were determined to maintain their military capabilities, but also desired to avoid the crushing expense of a full-fledged arms race. Military leaders on both sides decried any movement toward disarmament, but arms limitation seemed in the best interest of both nations as long as one did not gain a measurable advantage over the other. The Russians were increasingly anxious about the potential threat posed by China and interested in improving their own domestic consumer economy, and the Americans were worn down by the long, expensive travail in Southeast Asia.

Negotiations toward a Strategic Arms Limitation Treaty (SALT) began in 1969, with the purpose of slowing the arms buildup by placing a ceiling on certain types of weapons and even reducing the numbers of others, in a phased series of discussions and agreements that would lead eventually to a stabilization of the military balance and perhaps even a reduction in nuclear weapons. This was, in any case, the expressed hope of both parties.

Though Americans occasionally tried to use the talks to restrain Soviet aid to North Vietnam, the United States genuinely desired to make the SALT negotiations a success. A treaty was finally hammered out that curbed both land and sea missile forces in both countries, and limited the number of antiballistic missile (ABM) sites to no more than two cities in each country. The treaty also permitted the construction of many more weapons in some categories, however, and did not reduce the number of nuclear warheads in either nation's arsenal.

The treaty, known as SALT I, was signed by Leonid Brezhnev and Richard Nixon in Moscow in May 1972. This was the first visit ever by an American President to the Soviet Union, and the conviviality of the occasion inaugurated the spirit of detente, a thawing of United States-Soviet relations, and a movement toward scientific, cultural, and political cooperation, and toward continued negotiations on arms limitation. The United States Senate ratified SALT I on August 3.

In July, the Nixon Administration announced that large sales of American grain had been made to the Soviet Union, which would help further the spirit of detente, assist the Russians with their periodic agricultural shortages, and boost the income and security of American farmers. The price of grain and other basic foodstuffs rose immediately as a result, but in Nixon's view this was a small disadvantage compared with the emerging economic relationships between the superpowers and the geopolitical leverage this trade gave to the United States.

In addition to warming relations between America and Russia, the Nixon Administration began to take those between the United States and mainland China out of the deep freeze. Formal diplomatic relations had been severed for decades, and the United States persisted in its recognition of Chiang Kai-shek's regime on Formosa as the legitimate government of all China. Chinese and American troops had clashed bitterly in Korea. The leader of the People's Republic of China, Mao Zedong, followed a very strict revolutionary Communist line, emphasizing the need to strengthen the country's rural areas, break down the bourgeois spirit everywhere, prevent the rise of capitalist corruption in the cities and among the elite, and at every opportunity resist the United States and its imperialism and warmongering. The China lobby in the United States, composed of supporters of Chiang and his Republic of China, kept this image of godless, radical Communism ever before the American public. The Chinese and the Russians, in their view, were united in an effort to achieve Communist world domination.

By the 1970's, the mainland Chinese were no longer, however, a firm anchor of this "world Communist conspiracy" American conservatives kept referring to. Over the years, the People's Republic of China had a number of differences with the Soviets, and conflicts along their common border sometimes reached the level of armed struggle. The Chinese believed that Russia's brand of Communism had become repressive and elitist, and the Russians looked on the Chinese as primitives who threatened Soviet security in Asia. After years of cold-war rhetoric that warned of the unified international Communist conspiracy, American policymakers were slow to recognize the significance of the worsening Sino-Soviet split and the opportunity it presented to the United States to play one great Communist power off against the other. Liberal Democratic leaders who considered a rapprochement with mainland China were politically vulnerable: ultraconservatives still blamed Democratic liberals for the loss of China in 1949.

But Richard Nixon, a conservative Republican with a record of support for Taiwan, also recognized that the Sino-Soviet split presented a gigantic opportunity for the United States immediately perhaps to end the American dilemma in Southeast Asia and in the long run to score heavily in the geopolitical balance of forces. The Russians were already expressing their fear of China by easing their tensions with the United States, and improved Sino-American relations could be the ultimate deterrent to Russian international ambitions. This opportunity also appealed to Nixon because it constituted a bold and dramatic reversal of previous policy, a moment of historical significance. Nixon sent Kissinger on a secret mission to Peking in 1971, and Kissinger returned from his discussions with China's major statesman and diplomat,

Zhou Enlai, with an invitation for the American President to visit the People's Republic early the following year.

The announcement of this impending visit shocked politicians at home and military planners and diplomats in Moscow, and the Nixon trip to China captured world attention. Beginning on February 21, 1972, Nixon spent eight days in the People's Republic, walking along the Great Wall, visiting briefly with an aging Mao Zedong, attending formal banquets where friendly toasts were exchanged, and discussing with Zhou and other Chinese leaders the initial steps that would ultimately lead to the reestablishment of full diplomatic relations.

The move toward China was Nixon's most inspired diplomatic initiative, a stunning breakthrough that cast the American President even more into the center of world attention, and one that was perhaps possible only for someone with such obvious anti-Communist credentials. For the remainder of the decade, Sino-American relations improved, even after Mao's death, until President Jimmy Carter formally recognized the People's Republic and the nations exchanged ambassadors on January 1, 1979.

In other ways as well, Nixon's concern with the international balance of power and Kissinger's concept of linkages provided the structure for American foreign policy and, along with domestic political constraints, dictated American responses to world events. The Nixon Doctrine, which the President announced on a trip to Asia in July 1969, declared that the United States would assist its allies in the struggle against armed aggression and political subversion but would not commit American troops to foreign shores except as a last resort.

One result of the policy was significantly to increase arms sales to American allies, even of sophisticated warplanes and electronic gear. Nixon personally ordered that Iran, for example, the strongest American military ally in the Middle East, be permitted to purchase virtually anything except nuclear weapons from the American arsenal. The Shah thus became the world's leading arms buyer, with money derived largely from boosting the price of Iran's oil to the West. In a more general sense, this international application of Vietnamization was the basis of American policy toward the Third World, and to some degree toward Western

Europe and Japan as well. Through linkage, every region and country of the world was brought into the balance-of-forces equation.

Some regions of the world were more volatile than others. The Middle East, especially, was a constant trouble spot. Conflict between Israel and her Arab neighbors threatened to flare up into major warfare at any moment. The Six-Day War of June 1967 resulted in the Israeli capture of the Sinai Peninsula, the Golan Heights, the Gaza Strip, and the east bank of the Suez Canal. Arab resentment at this quick, decisive defeat festered until 1973, when the fourth and largest Arab-Israeli war erupted during the Jewish holy day of Yom Kippur. This struggle was longer and bloodier, and the Arabs were able to secure a relatively more favorable military position.

The situation in the Middle East posed a serious problem for American foreign policy. The collapse of Israel would create a vacuum for the Soviets to fill, and continued fighting threatened the stability of the entire region. At the same time, any long-term solution to the crisis would have to deal with the question of the Palestinians, who after years of struggle had been uprooted from their homeland, much of which now lay in Israel. Solutions would be difficult not only because of the long-standing animosities of the contending forces but also because of the power of the pro-Israeli vote in the United States, which made conciliatory gestures toward the Arab states very difficult.

Kissinger attempted to fashion a peace agreement by first pressuring the Russians to stay out of the Middle East and, second, encouraging better relations between Israel and Egypt, the largest Arab state and Israel's major enemy in the recent wars. The Americans successfully negotiated a cease-fire agreement in November 1973 and arranged the assignment of a United Nations peacekeeping force in the Sinai. Kissinger attempted to build on this momentum through "shuttle diplomacy," flying back and forth across the desert, from Tel Aviv to Cairo to Damascus to Amman, carrying the latest peace offers from country to country.

The major stumbling block to the talks was always the Palestinian issue. The Arabs insisted on a homeland for this displaced people, while the Israelis saw this as a direct and continuing threat to their security. Kissinger's negotiations did not result in the comprehensive peace settlement he sought, but he was able to generate new confidence in the good offices of the United States, especially among the Arabs, and pave the way for the more dramatic breakthroughs later in the decade. One thing was certain: a new, compelling American imperative in the Middle East was an uninterrupted flow of oil to the United States and other Western nations. The Arab oil embargo in 1973, as a result of Washington's support of the Israelis in the Yom Kippur War, showed the vulnerability of the developed nations to this new weapon and the importance of the Middle East to the social and economic well-being of all Americans.

Nixon continued the North American condescension toward Latin America, even backing further away than Lyndon Johnson from John F. Kennedy's short-lived efforts to create a new sense of trust and cooperation in the hemisphere. The main emphases were on maintaining friendly governments in power, isolating Fidel Castro and his revolution, and protecting the interests of North American investors and corporations. The most dramatic instance of United States intervention in the region during Nixon's Administrations was the overthrow of Chile's freely elected Marxist president, Salvador Allende Gossens, in September 1973, by a group of right-wing military leaders—a coup that had the covert support of the American CIA. Allende presumably committed suicide during the coup, and the United States quickly recognized the new government.

Public opposition to the Vietnam War and increasing awareness of abuses by the executive branch and the CIA in the conduct of foreign affairs stimulated a rising sentiment in Congress to place greater controls on Presidential authority. The passage of the Cooper-Church Amendment in 1970 and the attempt by the House and Senate to cut off funds for the bombing of Cambodia in 1973 were among the first efforts directly to challenge Presidential conduct of the Indochinese war. In July 1973, the Senate Armed Services Committee began investigations into the secret B-52 raids in Cambodia in 1969 and 1970. Testimony revealed the elaborate precautions taken, including the falsification of military records, to keep knowledge of these clandestine operations against a neutral country from the Congress and the American people. Some legislators flatly accused Nixon of violating the Constitution by unilaterally making war without the required approval of Congress. As a result, Congress passed the War Powers Act, which mandated legislative approval before United States troops could be committed to armed conflict abroad, except under certain emergency conditions and for a limited time. Nixon considered this legislation an unconstitutional interference with the Commander in Chief's responsibility to act decisively in international affairs, and vetoed the measure. This time, on November 7, 1973, the Congress overrode the President's veto and the War Powers Act became law.

Like most recent American Presidents, Richard Nixon was drawn to the challenges of foreign affairs and frustrated by the domestic-policymaking process. The consistent American diplomatic position and delicate secret negotiations that could be so effective in dealing with foreign crises were lacking at home, where public opinion was usually divided on major issues and the political risks were far greater. But even on the domestic front, Nixon demonstrated his concern for planning and control, his penchant for drama and bold initiative, and his determination to adopt policies that would give him the best possible chance of reelection in 1972.

When Nixon came into the White House, many of Johnson's social and economic programs continued in a revised form, if they continued at all. Though they were often perceived as failures—because they did not solve the urban crisis or eliminate poverty—these efforts demonstrated that some problems could indeed be alleviated, if not eliminated, by throwing money at them. By the mid-seventies, the income levels of many poor people, and especially elderly people, had been significantly improved, even allowing for inflation. Hunger had been virtually eliminated, even if poverty had not. America's social and economic problems continued, however, especially those concentrated in the nation's cities, and these problems threatened to grow worse.

Nixon, who clearly relished the challenges of foreign affairs, was far less comfortable with the challenges at home—especially the plight of the older industrial cities that lost population and jobs and experienced rises in crime, poverty, and poor housing after 1960. Like many other Republicans and some conservative Democrats, Nixon believed that even national problems could best be attacked at the local and state level rather than through the massive, unwieldy—and traditionally Democratic—bureaucracy in Washington. The major initiative toward the end of the Johnson Administration, the Model Cities program, designed in the aftermath of the urban riots, attempted to bring substantial, coordinated federal social and economic assistance (but very little physical development) to the inner city areas most obviously in need of help. Nixon unceremoniously scuttled this woefully underfunded program and moved for legislation that would return money and, presumably, initiative to states and local areas.

One method was federal revenue sharing, which provided for the return of a certain portion of federal tax monies to states and localities, to be spent for a wide variety of projects and needs, generally to be determined at the state and local level. Another, even more significant pillar of what Nixon referred to as his New Federalism was the Community Development Act of 1974, which provided assistance to local communities in the form of one block grant rather than in a number of categorical grants earmarked for specific purposes. Local officials were given greater latitude in deciding how the funds were to be spent. The amount of the block grants was determined by a formula based on population, density, age of housing, and the degree of local poverty. In order to be eligible for community-development funds, communities had to complete a housing-assistance plan, indicating how the locality intended to insure an adequate supply of low-income housing.

The community-development block grant approach did encourage more initiative and creativity in city hall and made it easier for communities to address certain major problems. But some communities spent their allocation on noncontroversial physical improvements rather than new social programs, and most cities tended to scatter the resources for maximum political benefit rather than concentrating them where they could do the most good. The new approach did result in more attention to troubled communities with enough energy and local resources to succeed with some government help, but it implicitly recognized that the worst inner-city areas were beyond salvation, and in most cities these areas were written off and essentially abandoned.

The Nixon Administration also attempted to address the huge and complex problems of federal public-assistance programs, increasingly termed the "welfare mess" by liberals and conservatives alike. Some critics found the program demeaning and inadequate, permitting neither subsistence nor human dignity. Others believed the welfare system was racked with fraud and threatened the work ethic. Nixon had generally been critical of welfare because it undermined free enterprise and individual initiative, but he was also aware that public assistance could not be abandoned. He was especially impressed by an idea advanced by University of Chicago economist Milton Friedman, the "negative income tax." The notion was disarmingly simple: persons earning below a certain income would receive graduated payments from the government through the federal income-tax system. This had the advantage of keeping bureaucracy to a minimum, preserving the dignity of the recipients, and setting an income floor below which no American family should fall. Daniel Patrick Moynihan, a Harvard sociologist who served as Nixon's urban-affairs adviser, fashioned this idea into a proposal that was introduced in Congress and given the Presidential blessing. But as other concerns—especially Watergate—descended on the White House, and liberals and conservatives in Congress could not agree on the amounts those on welfare would receive or other details of the program, the measure slowly faded from the scene. A new, comprehensive federal welfare system was not enacted during the seventies.

A new domestic problem—and an international one, as well—was brought dramatically to the fore by the Arab-Israeli War of 1973: the dependence of the United States on foreign petroleum. The Arab oil embargo (from October 1973 until March 1974) boosted gasoline and home-heating oil prices, threatened supplies, produced lines at gasoline filling stations, and conjured up fears of rationing, black markets, rampant inflation, and a falling living standard.

The major oil-producing nations (other than the United States) formed the Organization of Petroleum Exporting Countries (OPEC) as a cartel to control the supply, distribution, and price of oil for economic and political advantage, and end the exploitation of nations producing raw materials by the developed world. The embargo was lifted, but the era of cheap energy was over. Oil, which cost only a few dollars a barrel in 1969, more than doubled in price in 1973 and doubled again in 1974. By the end of the decade, the price of light Arabian crude oil had soared to almost $25 a barrel, and the price of gasoline at the pump in the United States rose from roughly thirty-five or forty cents per gallon in 1970 to $1.25 in early 1980. Apart from threatening a way of life and standard of living premised on plentiful, cheap energy, the surge in oil prices was the major contributing factor to the double-digit inflation rates that plagued the country in the seventies. The 1973 price hike helped push the annual inflation rate to more than 12 percent in 1974 and to more than 13 percent in 1979.

The seventies witnessed, in fact, the joint occurrence of two economic phenomena previously considered mutually exclusive—stagnation and inflation. The growth rate of the economy declined and unemployment and consumer prices rose. The pundits dubbed it "stagflation." Climbing prices were perhaps the greatest political threat, as Americans watched their savings and pay checks shrink from year to year. The United States inflation rate had averaged about 2.4 percent annually between 1950 and 1970. But in the seventies it sometimes climbed to two-digit numbers and threatened to become virtually permanent at around 6 to 8 percent a year, at a minimum. The economic difficulties also included a growing balance-of-payments deficit, as Americans purchased more goods from abroad (especially Japan) than they produced and exported, and as the price of foreign oil skyrocketed, and this created a declining confidence in the dollar, which generally fell in value on world money markets after 1973.

President Nixon was well aware that Republican Administrations were especially vulnerable in times of economic difficulty, and the 1972 elections might well turn on the state of the economy. He announced, on August 15, 1971, a series of dramatic measures, including a ninety-day freeze of wages, prices, and rents; higher tariffs on imported goods; and freeing the dollar from the price of gold and permitting it to float in the international money markets. The wage and price freeze would at least temporarily ease public anxiety about inflation, and perhaps take the momentum away from the rapid rise in prices, and higher import charges and a more realistically valued dollar (that would be more competitive with other world currencies) would help the balance-of-payments problem, stimulate American exports, and respond to the complaints of many industries—textiles, electronics, and automobiles, for example—about unfair foreign competition in the United States domestic market.

The Administration also sensed the public's concern for stability following the doubt, turmoil, and unnerving social change of the sixties, and a major emphasis—especially as the election approached—was on "law and order," safety in the streets, and a return to basic and comfortable American values. The President held White House prayer breakfasts featuring noted clergymen such as the Reverend Billy Graham. Vice-President Agnew, appearing in towns and cities across the country to raise money, attacked the major newspapers, television networks, and Eastern intellectuals as "effete intellectual snobs" out to ruin the President, appealed to the instincts and sentiments of "middle America," and underlined the importance of law and order.

Nixon also realized the political importance of the South, a traditionally conservative region that might be weaned away from the Democrats and offset the strong Democratic tendencies of the industrial cities of the Northeast and Midwest. Some Nixon advisers pointed to the strong Southern support for Barry Goldwater in 1964 and mapped out a new Southern strategy for political success. Besides carefully cultivating Southern politicians like South Carolina's Senator Strom Thurmond, Nixon—after successfully nominating Warren E. Burger of Minnesota to replace the retiring Earl Warren as Chief Justice—attempted to secure at least one seat on the United States Supreme Court for a "strict constructionist" (read "conservative") Southerner. When Johnson appointee Abe Fortas resigned from the court, Nixon nominated, first, Clement Haynsworth of South Carolina and, when he was not confirmed by the Senate, G. Harrold Carswell of Florida. Both nominations ran into serious difficulty: the nominees had, at best, mediocre judicial backgrounds, and they both had a record of prejudice toward blacks. Neither nomination was approved by the Senate, and Nixon lashed out at Capitol Hill for its prejudice against the South. Eventually, Judge Harry Blackmun of Illinois was nominated by the President and confirmed.

The 1972 Republican national convention in Miami was choreographed in detail by the White House. The timing was precise, and the script prepared for maximum national television and media exposure. The predictable result was the overwhelming vote in favor of the renomination of Nixon and Spiro Agnew.

The Democrats were not so well organized. After showing surprising strength in the primaries, North Dakota Senator George McGovern—a former supporter of Robert Kennedy—emerged as the Democratic nominee. McGovern tapped Senator Thomas Eagleton of Missouri as his running mate, and though his acceptance speech went out over the airwaves in the wee hours of the morning, in contrast to Nixon's precise prime-time delivery, the Democratic Presidential candidate looked forward to a close campaign.

McGovern's run for the White House was ill-fated from the beginning. Press reports that Eagleton had at one time received electroshock therapy for a psychological illness led to his withdrawal from the ticket only two weeks after his nomination. McGovern quickly replaced him with Kennedy family member, and former director of the Peace Corps, Sargent Shriver, but the damage had been done. Nixon's Committee to Re-elect the President, headed by Attorney General John Mitchell, appeared professional, effective, and superbly well-heeled. With the biggest campaign chest in the nation's history, the Nixon forces rolled forward while the Democrats stumbled.

The final result was not surprising. Nixon won in the most lopsided landslide in American history, with 61 percent of the popular vote and all but seventeen electoral votes. McGovern managed to carry only the state of Massachusetts, and Nixon ran especially well in the South, thus suggesting the wisdom of the Southern strategy. Commentators who had mused about the possible collapse of the Republican Party after the Goldwater debacle of 1964 now touted the inroads the party had made in areas of traditional Democratic strength and predicted possible erosion of the Democrats' power in Congress in future elections.

Nixon seemed strangely anxious in his moment of greatest victory. On the eve of his inauguration, he asked for the resignation of all his Cabinet members, a request normally indicating displeasure with their service or the desire to make sweeping changes. No such changes occurred, but the morale within the Cabinet sank at the very beginning of the long-awaited second term. In more important ways, Nixon's electoral triumph was the beginning of what appears in retrospect as the inexorable unraveling of his Presidency.

A minor criminal trial which began on January 8, 1973, continued as Nixon was inaugurated. Seven men who had been arrested on June 17, 1972, for breaking into the Democratic national-committee headquarters in the Watergate residential and office complex in Washington pleaded not guilty; but they were convicted. The circumstances in the case were routine enough until three of the seven—E. Howard Hunt, G. Gordon Liddy, and James McCord—were linked to the White House, Nixon's reelection committee, and the CIA.

The Senate voted in February, without dissent, to establish a select committee to investigate the incident, but the first real break in the case came the following month, when James McCord informed John J. Sirica, the trial judge, that the defendants were under intense political pressure to remain silent, that perjury had been committed at the trial, and that other high-ranking government officials were involved in the break-in. McCord also offered to cooperate.

The White House at first attempted to ignore the investigation, belittle the crime as a "third-rate burglary," and divert public attention to other domestic issues and world events. But the troublesome inconvenience of what became simply known as Watergate grew into a crisis, as revelation followed revelation and the scandal was traced to the Oval Office of the President of the United States.

In May 1973, the Senate select committee began its nationally televised hearings under chairman Sam Ervin of North Carolina. Archibald Cox of the Harvard Law School was appointed special prosecutor to pursue the investigation for the Justice Department. Several days later, Nixon issued a statement denying any knowledge of the burglary or of personal pay-offs to the burglars for covering up the involvement of higher-ups in the crime. The President also admitted, however, that he had restricted the initial investigation by the FBI into the burglary, but only because of possible national-security implications.

As investigation of the cover-up was directed more and more toward the White House, the President announced on April 30 the resignations of his two chief assistants—H. R. Haldeman and John D. Ehrlichman—and Attorney General Richard Kleindienst, though he praised their record of public service and lamented the irrational political pressures that forced him to take such a drastic step. He also announced the dismissal of White House Counsel John Dean, who Nixon claimed was unable to prepare a requested "special report" to him on the burglary and cover-up. Elliot Richardson was appointed Attorney General, and Nixon later named General Alexander M. Haig, Jr., as interim White House Chief of Staff to replace Haldeman.

In June, Dean testified before the Ervin committee that President Nixon had participated in the cover-up even after Dean had warned him about the possible ramifications. Dean alluded to several conversations in the Oval Office in which Nixon discussed with various staff members how the Watergate investigation could be stymied or directed away from the White House, mostly on the grounds of protecting national-security information. Dean also alleged campaign abuses: secret funds and contributions "laundered" by passage through Mexican and other foreign banks to conceal their origin.

The White House moved quickly to undermine Dean's testimony, but the seeds of doubt had been planted in the public mind. The committee moved deliberately in its investigation, but the role of Nixon remained the major question. In the words of the ranking Republican member, Howard Baker of Tennessee, the critical question was: "What did the President know and when did he know it?" Further revelations only served to heighten the controversy.

The revelation that Nixon had approved in July 1970 a plan proposed by Tom Charles Huston, a Presidential aide, for illegal break-ins, wiretaps, and mail-opening in the name of national security dealt a serious blow to the President's protestations of innocence. Nixon withdrew his support of the Huston plan within five days, but only after FBI director J. Edgar Hoover opposed the scheme out of distrust for White House staffers. It was also revealed that Hunt and Liddy had supervised a previous burglary of Daniel Ellsberg's psychiatrist, in September 1971, in an effort to find damaging information on the man who released the Pentagon Papers to the press and was under government prosecution. Among other things, this revelation resulted in the dismissal of all charges against Ellsberg. That a group called the "plumbers" had operated from the White House, using questionable and illegal tactics to plug information leaks in the bureaucracy, added further to a sense that Nixon had a very twisted notion of Presidential prerogative, reacting to events with a siege mentality and with illegal methods. Subsequent justification by Nixon and others stressed the "higher" responsibilities of the Presidency and the use of questionable or illegal practices by predecessors.

The most dramatic revelation came on July 16, when a White House aide testified before the Ervin committee that Presidential conversations in the Oval Office were recorded on tape. The opportunity now existed to refer to a true record of various conversations mentioned by Dean and others, and to discover what the President knew and when he knew it. Nixon had, in fact, begun to review the tapes as early as June 3, without either destroying them or revealing their existence. Upon their public discovery, the President immediately prohibited his staff from listening to any of the tapes. Cox subpoenaed the recordings of nine conversations as evidence. Nixon refused to turn over the tapes on the grounds of "executive privilege," a claim with ambiguous constitutional foundation intended to preserve the integrity of Presidential communications and preserve the separation of powers. Judge Sirica ruled that such a doctrine could not interfere with a criminal investigation and that the tapes must be presented to the special prosecutor. This decision set off a chain of White House appeals to higher courts. On October 12, the United States Court of Appeals upheld Sirica's ruling.

Matters went from bad to worse for the Administration. In October, Vice-President Agnew resigned, pleading "no contest" to charges that he failed to report income received in 1967 while he was governor of Maryland, in computing his federal taxes. He was sentenced to three years on probation and fined $10,000. The investigation of Agnew had also revealed his receipt of bribes while he was Vice-President. Nixon nominated Representative Gerald R. Ford of Michigan as Vice-President. Ford was confirmed by the Senate and became Vice-President on December 6, the first not elected Vice-President (appointed under the terms of the new Twenty-fifth Amendment) in American history.

Nixon realized that defending himself and his Administration against the special prosecutor, the Senate committee, the news media—led by reporters Carl Bernstein and Bob Woodward of *The Washington Post*—and a rising tide of public opinion placed him at a severe disadvantage, and he acted to exert his authority and blunt the momentum of the investigations. On the evening of October 20, he fired Archibald Cox. Attorney General Richardson and Deputy Attorney General William Ruckelhaus immediately resigned in protest. Dubbed the "Saturday night massacre" in the press, Nixon's move shocked the public, enraged Capitol Hill, and, instead of derailing the Watergate investigations, gave them added force. More than forty Watergate-related bills were introduced in Congress the next week, about half proposing investigations leading to the possible impeachment of the President. The White House announced that the nine tapes would be turned over to Judge Sirica, and Leon Jaworski of Texas, a former president of the American Bar Association, was named special prosecutor.

Nixon's attorneys reported to Judge Sirica on November 21 that an 18½-minute gap existed in the tape of a conversation between the President and Haldeman on the arrests of the Watergate burglars. Nixon claimed that his secretary had erred while making a transcription, but a subsequent court investigation concluded that the erasure was deliberate.

The entire Administration was by this time deeply embroiled in Watergate. Certain basic activities continued, of course, but new policy initiatives or sustained diplomatic negotiations were impossible. The executive branch was increasingly distracted and paralyzed, to the point that the President and his staff were virtually consumed with Watergate. On March 1, 1974, a federal grand jury indicted Haldeman, Ehrlichman, Mitchell, Presidential assistant

Charles W. Colson, and three others in the Watergate cover-up. Nixon was named as an unindicted co-conspirator, though this information was kept secret. In April, the House Judiciary Committee, in its impeachment investigation, requested scores of additional White House tapes, as did the special prosecutor. The President again went on television and announced that he would turn over transcripts of the tapes requested by the Judiciary Committee and also make them public; the next day, however, the request by the special prosecutor was denied. On May 9, the Judiciary Committee opened formal impeachment hearings.

The White House tapes were often confusing and inconclusive: the recorded conversations were generally curt or rambling, with few complete sentences, and often filled with slang and scattered obscenities. Some portions were omitted from the transcripts as inaudible. The transcripts contained nothing to indicate that the President knew in advance of the Watergate break-in, but they clearly showed that Nixon was deeply concerned about the direction of the Watergate inquiry and that he attempted to slow down and divert the investigation, especially when it began to point toward the White House. If the tapes were not sufficient to convict the President of any crimes, they were nevertheless a political disaster. The public was shocked at the crude language used in the Oval Office, the occasional anti-Semitism that crept into the discussions, and the calculating manner in which the President and his aides approached the Watergate "problem." All this contrasted vividly with Nixon's public defense of his Administration, with his public invocation of basic American values, and with his much publicized support of law and order.

The Supreme Court ruled in July that the President must turn over to the special prosecutor the sixty-four additional tapes he had requested in April. Three days later, on July 27, the House Judiciary Committee passed the first article of impeachment by a vote of 27–11, charging Nixon with obstruction of justice in aiding the Watergate cover-up. Altogether, three impeachment articles were approved by the committee, to be presented to the full House for consideration.

On August 5, the White House released the transcripts of three recorded conversations of June 23, 1972, which appeared to implicate the President even more deeply in the cover-up. Nixon admitted that for political as well as national security reasons he had encouraged the FBI to stop the Watergate investigation. Finally, on August 8, in a televised address to the nation, Richard M. Nixon announced that he was resigning from office, an act unprecedented in American history. The next day, after a tearful farewell to the White House staff and assembled friends, Nixon left for his home in California and Gerald R. Ford was sworn in as the thirty-seventh President of the United States.

Ford's Administration was dominated by the aftermath of Watergate. After the political trauma of the previous two years, and the increasing isolation of an aloof Chief Executive in the White House, the public seemed fascinated by the "average" American family that was to occupy the executive mansion. Television cameras captured the new President preparing his own breakfast in his suburban Washington house, and commentators spoke almost reassuringly of Ford's rather nondescript and conventional political background.

The honeymoon of the new Administration ended, however, on September 8, when Ford issued an executive pardon for Richard Nixon, covering all the crimes the former President committed or might have committed while in office. The public outcry swamped the White House with telegrams, letters, and phone calls: if Nixon was guilty, many people reasoned, then he should be made to suffer the legal penalties. Even Presidents should not be "above the law": that, in fact, had been what Watergate was all about. The outcry was softened by the general public perception that Ford acted out of compassion and a desire to avoid the possible trauma of bringing a former President to trial and sending him to jail. No pardons were issued, however, for others convicted of Watergate offenses, and Dean, Haldeman, Ehrlichman, Mitchell, and others served prison sentences.

In one sense, the outcome of Watergate was a cause for celebration: the constitutional system worked. Even the most powerful office in the world could not stand above the law, and the Congress, the courts, and elements of the federal bureaucracy had proceeded responsibly, if haltingly, in dealing with a major political crisis that would have torn the political systems of many other

countries into shreds. But in another sense Watergate was a shocking and continuing wound.

After the travail and controversy of Vietnam and the despair
over the assassinations of the sixties, the American public was
confronted with the resignation of a President under the cloud of
almost certain impeachment for high crimes in office, and the
criminal conviction of a Vice-President, a former Attorney General—the chief law-enforcement officer in the land—the two top
assistants in the White House, and the President's legal counsel
and others close to the nation's highest elected official. The investigations of Watergate also revealed a disquieting contempt in the
White House for the constitutional rights of American citizens and
a willingness to condone and even promote questionable and illegal activities—including improper use of the Internal Revenue
Service to harass political "enemies"—for political and "national
security" reasons. It was the greatest instance of Presidential abuse
of power in American history, and it severely shook public confidence in the Presidency and in the effectiveness and integrity of
government at virtually all levels.

Suspicion of politicians, and especially of Presidential power,
shaped and limited Ford's Administration. Congress continued to
assert a new authority gained in the Watergate struggles with the
executive branch, especially in efforts to prevent future abuses of
power and revise the election laws. The Federal Election Campaign
Act of 1976 limited individual campaign contributions, established spending limits for federal elections, and created a matching
federal fund (financed through income-tax checkoffs) for Presidential campaigns. The law did not limit campaign committee
gifts, however; thus, it permitted labor unions and other organized
interest groups to retain their influence. Congress generally
reacted against what many perceived as a far too powerful and not
sufficiently accountable executive—termed the "imperial Presidency"—that had exceeded the limits of wisdom and propriety
and had contributed to adventurism in Vietnam and the illegalities
of Watergate. Congress looked with particular suspicion on
United States military involvements abroad, undertaken without
adequate consultation and legislative approval. Ford and Henry
Kissinger, who had stayed on as Secretary of State, recommended

support of friendly factions in the Angolan civil war, especially since the Soviets were heavily supporting the Marxist elements in that African country. Congress opposed all covert American aid, however, and specifically prohibited assistance to Angola in December 1975.

Public attention also focused on the clandestine branches of the intelligence services, which some suspected of involvement in Watergate and other abuses. A blue-ribbon commission headed by Vice-President Nelson Rockefeller—who had been appointed by Ford and confirmed by Congress—reported on June 10, 1975, that its investigation of the CIA discovered questionable and illegal practices, particularly secret operations within the borders of the United States, which were specifically prohibited by the CIA charter. CIA agents had infiltrated black and antiwar groups, opened mail destined for overseas, kept files on some 300,000 American citizens and political groups, wiretapped international telephone calls, and even experimented with the effects of various drugs and chemicals on United States citizens without their knowledge. Evidence was also uncovered documenting CIA efforts to assassinate foreign leaders, including President Diem of South Vietnam, Cuba's Fidel Castro, and Chile's Salvador Allende. These revelations caused a public uproar and led Congress to insist on greater oversight of CIA activities and to emphasize the prohibitions against certain types of covert activity.

The most dramatic foreign-policy incident during Ford's Administration began on May 12, 1975, when Cambodian forces captured a United States commercial vessel, the *Mayaguez*, and its thirty-nine crew members, in the Gulf of Siam. Ford sent United States naval and air power, and a force of United States marines, to recapture the ship. The *Mayaguez* and her crew were surrendered unharmed by the Cambodians, but not until fifteen marines were killed in combat and even more died in a helicopter accident.

Ford's domestic policies followed very closely the moderate-to-conservative Republican positions that he had long advocated in Congress. Complaints against the bureaucracy continued, and the President's main economic goal was a balanced budget to check rising inflation. Ford's belt-tightening led to an unemployment rate of 9.2 percent in June 1975 and put economic issues at the center of the upcoming Presidential election. The Ford White House also declared that the "urban crisis" was over, clearly indicating that this term was more a barometer of urban violence and disorder than a description of complex, deep-seated, and persistent social and economic problems, which were, in some ways, even more serious than before.

War, defeat, Watergate, economic recession and inflation were all major issues of the time, but there were also other, less dramatic, but no less significant, trends that shaped American life in the seventies. Opinion polls traced a definite drop in Americans' confidence in the future and in the ability of established institutions to deal with major national problems, especially economic problems. The "crisis of confidence," as commentators dubbed it, peaked after Nixon's resignation and in some cases devolved thereafter into a fatalistic cynicism. At the same time, there was a new stress on personal indulgence. Individual self-discovery and improvement grew into national movements, as books, magazines, and television contained any number of schemes reputedly leading to better health, greater peace of mind, deeper self-awareness, and enhanced personal capacity for love, work, satisfaction. The emphasis seemed clearly to have shifted from the political dimension to the personal, from the protests of the sixties and early seventies to the liberation of the individual. As essayist Tom Wolfe put it, the seventies was the "Me Decade."

In popular fashion, much of the counterculture had simply been subsumed, though very much within an urban, mass-consumption context. Long hair styles, rock music, and casual dress were the rule rather than the exception, though the traditional look began to reassert itself toward the end of the decade. Cultural standards were markedly fragmented, depending on one's age group or life-style. But the relaxed, "laid-back" look of the seventies was not simply spontaneous but rather quite calculated, and driven by advertising and the fashion industry; it reflected a new stress on famous clothing labels, faddish Western cowboy garb for the best-dressed in downtown Manhattan or Chicago, and designer blue jeans.

Part of the basis for the "Me Decade" was doubtless a desire for personal identity in a time of social and political uncertainty and frustration. A rising interest in ethnicity favored the hyphenated Americans, and found perhaps its ultimate expression in *Roots,* a book and subsequent television movie by Alex Haley that recounted the history of his family from Africa to the rural South. Causes flourished and found their expression in groups ranging from special-interest organizations (to preserve the environment or stop abortion, for example) to loose aggregations of people in pursuit of self-improvement—to lose weight, stop smoking, or cope with parenthood, middle age, or growing old.

There was a revival of interest in religion, especially among so-called born-again Christians, who found new purpose in a personal relationship with God and shared that purpose with millions of others through television and mass solicitation. The organized churches benefited from these trends, but the religious spirit of the time was not narrowly denominational and not necessarily supportive of established religious institutions. From a secular perspective, these new interests seemed clearly a product of the same cultural tendencies—doubt, frustration, reduced confidence in government and the economic system—that led to other forms of mysticism and self-discovery.

The United States Supreme Court continued to wrestle with the balances between individual and collective rights during the decade, and in general dealt with the implications of the landmark decisions rendered by the Warren Court. In April 1971, the court decided that busing could be used to achieve racial balance and end desegregation in the nation's schools. In June 1972, the death penalty, as then written into state statutes, was declared unconstitutional, though in a 1976 decision the court determined that death was not an inherently cruel or unusual punishment and was permissible if statutes were not arbitrary and discriminatory. Also in 1976, the court gave a significant boost to affirmative action to redress past racial injustices by declaring that blacks and other minorities could gain retroactive job seniority. In 1977, the court loosened the strictures of its earlier *Miranda* decision (1966) concerning police behavior toward suspects. The Supreme Court's most controversial decision was rendered in January 1973, when it ruled in favor of elective abortions by women during the first three months of pregnancy, on the grounds that this was a personal right. Abortion was, in fact, the most volatile moral issue of the time and the least easily solved through political compromise. Politics also showed the effects of the "Me Too" generation. The identification of citizens with political parties reached an all-time low in the seventies: a third to a half of Americans questioned in various opinion polls identified themselves as "independents," who voted on the basis of candidates and issues rather than party loyalty. Able to reach the voters directly through mass-media advertising, candidates were less dependent on political parties for generating popular support. New congressmen were not content to sit quietly on the benches for several terms before taking a full-fledged role. The large group of new Democratic faces in the House of Representatives in 1974, the "Watergate babies," asserted itself very early, and even engineered the toppling of several established committee chairmen. Political parties, and the broad and diverse voter coalitions that they encouraged, were less effective than before in stabilizing and organizing the political process.

The broker politics of the New Deal era had depended on strong, organized interests and the negotiations and compromises among them. In the seventies, organized, well-financed interest groups were perhaps the most dominant single factor in the federal policymaking process. These interest groups became increasingly specialized and less willing to accept compromise as a legitimate outcome of their efforts. The American Medical Association, the National Rifle Association, the National Association of Manufacturers, and the oil companies were among the most successful lobbies in Washington, and their ranks were joined by a plethora of other groups representing specific occupational interests and issues.

The new issues of the seventies, which quickly spawned scores of various organizations, were energy and the environment. The environmental movement grew in part out of the counterculture emphasis on nature and resistance against materialistic, artificial culture. A nationwide call to protect the environment was issued on Earth Day—April 22, 1970—when groups, mostly young people, gathered across the country for discussions and demonstrations reminiscent of the beginnings of antiwar protest. These groups expanded and eventually joined established conservation groups and developed effective lobbies and exerted considerable pressure for the passage of antipollution laws, ranging from strip-mining controls to new air- and water-quality standards and prohibitions against dangerous chemicals used in factories and on farms.

The energy crisis was first perceived by the general public in 1973, when the Arab oil embargo demonstrated United States dependence on foreign energy, even though some experts had been warning for years of the rapid exhaustion of the world's supply of fossil fuels and the necessity to develop alternatives. Many Americans—perhaps a majority—persisted in believing that the crisis was manufactured by the giant multinational oil companies in order to hike prices; and the behavior of these corporations, and their bulging profits, certainly gave credence to this view. But the crisis was real enough. The series of price increases later in the decade led to various federal efforts to curtail consumption and increase domestic energy production, and helped to convince most people that the problem was indeed serious and long-range.

The need for energy and the concern for the environment were sometimes contradictory. Proposed energy laws reduced environmental-quality standards and emphasized energy production. Factories that had been converted from coal to natural gas to lessen air pollution now were advised to reconvert to coal because it was much cheaper and the United States contained about one-third of all the world's known coal reserves. Environmentalists and energy proponents could agree on the long-range virtues of solar power, which was nonpolluting and inexhaustible; but almost all agreed that solar power could meet only a small percentage of the nation's energy needs in the foreseeable future. A number of experts recommended nuclear power as the ultimate alternative: the technology was available and the source was virtually endless. Environmentalists resisted, however, arguing that nuclear-energy production involved intolerable risks to the environment and to human beings; and their position seemed to be supported by the near-disaster at the Three Mile Island nuclear plant in Pennsylvania in 1979, where an accident almost resulted in the release of deadly radiation over the surrounding countryside.

Opposition to government bureaucracy was almost as widespread as concern for environment and energy. Ever since the New Deal, bureaus and agencies had proliferated, in response to growing needs and public demands for services. The federal budget more than doubled during the seventies. "Big government" had long been anathema to conservatives, but by the end of the decade, leaders of both political parties were touting the virtues of a balanced federal budget, and some even advocated a constitutional amendment prohibiting deficit financing. In an era of inflation and limited economic growth, the popularity of Keynesian economics faded. In 1978, California voters approved a measure that placed a lid on property taxes and cut state revenues substantially. Known as Proposition 13, the idea spread to other states, especially those with high property taxes. Bureaucracy and taxes became major political issues, and almost every politician found it obligatory to condemn bloated government agencies and red tape, waste, and inefficiency.

The disillusionment with established political authority took away many of the advantages of incumbency and political notoriety, and helped pave the way for the rise of a virtual political unknown to the first rank of Presidential contenders in 1976. Jimmy Carter (James Earl Carter, Jr.), a peanut farmer and businessman from a small town in south Georgia, announced more than a year before the election that he was a candidate for the nation's highest office. A graduate of the United States Naval Academy, submarine officer, state legislator, and "progressive" governor of Georgia, Carter was no political neophyte; but observers scoffed at his chances. Actually, Carter had decided to run for President as early as 1972, and as chairman of the Democratic national-campaign committee in 1974 he traveled over the fifty states meeting party people and supporting local Democrats in their campaigns. His careful work at the grass-roots, and particularly in the early caucus and primary states, paid off. "Jimmy who?" was on his way to election as thirty-eighth President of the United States.

Carter ran openly as a Washington outsider, untainted by scandal and the inefficiency of big government. He pledged repeatedly that he would never lie to the American people, and his rural Georgia background obviously appealed to many voters. His momentum was blunted in the late primaries by a fast-charging Governor Jerry Brown of California, but Carter was nominated on the first ballot at the Democratic convention in New York City in July. He selected Senator Walter Mondale—a well-known liberal and protégé of Hubert Humphrey—as his running mate. Among the Republicans, President Ford fought off a strong bid for the nomination by former California governor and movie actor Ronald Reagan. In order to appeal to the more conservative, Reagan-oriented ranks of the party, Ford unceremoniously dumped Rockefeller from the ticket and chose instead Senator Robert Dole of Kansas.

The campaign skirted around and ignored many major issues. Ford appealed for election to the office he had held since Nixon's resignation, and Carter did his best to hold together the traditional elements of the Democratic coalition and ride the tide of public reaction against the Republicans into the White House. Carter's most evident weakness—he was a white Southerner—was turned into an asset when Southern blacks gave him their support, because of his courageous resistance to white racism during the civil-rights struggles and because of his obvious cultural rapport with blacks in the South. Economic troubles, especially unemployment, seemed of most concern to the voters, and Ford's Administration had not had spectacular success in addressing these problems. Carter also won an edge over the President in a series of televised debates between them. Nevertheless, as the campaign drew to a close, Carter's lead narrowed and almost vanished. The Georgian won just over half the total popular votes cast and outpaced Ford in electoral votes, 297 to 240. Carter swept his native South, restoring that region decisively to the Democratic Presidential column, and much of the industrial Northeast and Midwest, while Ford took virtually every state in the West and challenged Carter in the border states.

Carter's inauguration in January 1977 put the first President from the Deep South (with the exception of Lyndon Johnson, who was generally regarded as from the Southwest) into the White House since Andrew Jackson. He entered office with a long list of promises: to reduce unemployment, which he regarded as more serious for the country than inflation; cut the military budget;

curtail the proliferation of nuclear weapons and negotiate a second strategic-arms limitation agreement with the Soviet Union; balance the federal budget; and reduce the number of federal agencies from 1,900 to 200 and end the maze of red tape in Washington. His inaugural address called for eventual nuclear disarmament.

The new President's foreign policy got off to a shaky start when he dispatched Secretary of State Cyrus Vance to Moscow to renew the arms-control discussions Ford had been forced, because of conservative pressures within his own party, to delay—and Vance went in a flurry of public Administration proposals and pronouncements for major slashes in the nuclear forces of both sides. The Russians did not like to conduct business in this fashion, however, and Vance was rebuffed. The Administration altered its approach thereafter, and discussions proceeded on the details of specific, and considerably more limited, arms reductions. The President decided in June 1977 to drop plans to build the controversial B-1 bomber, the proposed replacement for the aging B-52, and he opted instead for the cruise missile—an unmanned, lightweight, relatively inexpensive rocket that could carry a nuclear warhead, be launched from land, sea, or air, and fly so close to the ground that it defied even sophisticated radar defenses. Later, Carter also refused to approve production of the neutron bomb.

The lengthy discussions finally resulted in the SALT II agreement, which the American and Soviet leaders signed in Vienna in June 1979. In September, a nuclear nonproliferation pact was signed by the United States, the U.S.S.R., and many other nations in an effort to prevent the spread of nuclear-weapons technology, especially to the volatile Third World.

One of Carter's greatest foreign-policy achievements was the negotiation and Senate approval of the Panama Canal Treaty, which he signed into law on September 7, 1977. The treaty, which provided for eventual Panamanian control of the facility, with a pledge that it could not be denied to the United States, overcame the fierce resistance of American conservatives and a determined move in the Senate to kill it.

The problems of the Middle East proved to be even more challenging and significant for the maintenance of world peace. The tensions in the area were dramatically broken in November 1977, when Egyptian President Anwar Sadat accepted, amid a storm of protest in the rest of the Arab world, Israeli Prime Minister Menachem Begin's invitation to address the Israeli parliament in Jerusalem. But peace talks between the two leaders failed to produce results. The Egyptians were determined to exact some Israeli concessions on the Palestinian issue, and the Israelis insisted on blocking any arrangement for a Palestinian state or protectorate right on their borders, which they believed would constitute a constant threat to their security.

In 1978, as Israel continued to battle Palestinian terrorists, Begin and Sadat met separately with Carter to present their peace proposals. The momentum of Sadat's dramatic visit to his enemy of more than thirty years had diminished considerably, to the point where a peace agreement seemed less and less likely. Finally, in September, Carter invited Begin and Sadat to the Presidential retreat at Camp David in the Maryland mountains for continued, private discussions. After almost two weeks of intense, secret talks, the three leaders emerged to announce agreement on the dimensions and basic outlines of a peace settlement. Israel agreed to a phased withdrawal from the lands taken during the 1967 war, and both countries agreed to work for a peace treaty within three months and a resumption of normal diplomatic relations within one year. The Camp David agreements did not, however, resolve some of the more crucial and controversial issues, including the presence of Israeli settlements in the Sinai and provisions for a Palestinian homeland.

The decade ended without a definitive resolution of all these problems. The Israelis did pull back from the Sinai on schedule, and Begin eventually ordered the dismantling of the Israeli settlements in formerly Arab territory. Relations between Israel and Egypt continued to improve, and the dangers of a Middle East war shifted from Israel and her immediate neighbors to Iran and Afghanistan.

Carter's domestic policies also quickly ran into trouble. Administrative initiatives on welfare reform, energy, and a national health-insurance system suffered because of congressional resistance, public confusion and controversy, and Carter's movement on too many fronts at one time. A major difficulty was the Administration's awkward handling of Congress. The new President's veto of a major water-projects bill alienated many congressmen, and White House staffers did a poor job of coordinating legislation with the Democratic leadership and soothing ruffled feathers on Capitol Hill. The Administration finally settled on a few major initiatives.

One of these was a comprehensive energy policy and program, to reduce United States dependence on foreign oil without economic catastrophe. No legislation was, however, so susceptible to the pressures of powerful special interests or so difficult to sell to a public that still doubted the reality of the crisis and resisted any reductions in the standard of living. Carter called for support of his program as necessary for the long-term national security of the nation, and he termed the struggle for energy independence as "the moral equivalent of war." The war was not very effective. After lengthy debate, intense lobbying, and considerable revision and weakening of the President's original proposals, Congress did approve on October 15, 1978, an energy package that included the gradual deregulation of newly discovered natural gas, increased taxes on gas-guzzling automobiles, tax credits for energy-saving devices in homes and businesses, and encouragement for conversions of power plants from oil and gas to coal.

A new round of OPEC price increases in 1979 sent gasoline prices sharply upward in the spring and summer and produced long lines at gasoline filling stations as supplies of gas dwindled. These developments provided new momentum for the Administration's energy efforts, and Congress finally approved a standby system of gasoline rationing in the event of a national emergency fuel shortage. Other Carter proposals, pending in Congress as the decade ended, were a windfall-profits tax on the oil companies (which stood to reap huge profits from the deregulation of domestic fuel prices) and the establishment of an Energy Mobilization Board.

Reaching workable and acceptable compromises among competing energy interests (the oil companies, utilities, consumer groups, urban and rural constituencies, among others) seemed an almost impossible task, especially since Congress searched for solutions that were as nearly equitable—from region to region and from group to group—as possible. Two major approaches contended for acceptance: a reliance on the market and rising prices to curtail consumption, or the regulation and management of consumption (as through rationing) to insure equity and minimize the impact on lower-income groups. The first was criticized as inequitable, the second as overly bureaucratic and inefficient. Administration policy reflected a mixture of these approaches.

The problems of American dependence on foreign oil were compounded by new crises in the Middle East. Carter's good offices in bringing about the real possibility of peace between Israel and Egypt, coupled with new and promising initiatives toward black Africa conveyed by United Nations Ambassador Andrew Young, a veteran of the Southern civil-rights struggle and a friend of the President, were hopeful signs for world peace. And the signing of the SALT II agreement suggested the continuation of detente, even though it faced difficulties with ratification by the Senate. But other forces intervened to at least temporarily shatter the delicate balance in the Middle East and threaten a renewal of the cold war between the superpowers.

Iran's role as policeman of the Persian Gulf region, assisted with large amounts of American military aid, was suddenly, drastically changed. The collapse of the Shah's regime in Iran in early 1979, after months of popular protest, led to the establishment of a radical Islamic state in that country under the leadership of Ayatollah Ruhollah Khomeini, who preached an anti-Western doctrine aimed at the Americans and Soviets alike. Despite warnings of Iranian retaliation, the United States government admitted the exiled Shah into the country for the purpose of receiving medical treatment for the condition that eventually led to his death. In November, a group of young militants stormed the American embassy in Teheran and took fifty-two American diplomatic personnel hostage, demanding an American apology for past actions in the country and the return of the Shah to Iran, with all his wealth, as the conditions for their release. As Iranian crowds chanted "Death to America" and "Death to Carter" in the streets of Teheran, American public opinion rallied behind the President and there was talk of war.

As Iranian-American relations deteriorated, the Soviet Union sent an invading army into the neighboring state of Afghanistan in December, in an effort to prop up a sagging pro-Soviet regime in Kabul. This was the first movement of Soviet troops into a country outside the Eastern bloc (generally considered within the Russian sphere of influence) since World War II, and Soviet intentions were unclear.

These events and the Administration's firm but restrained reaction prompted a major shift in the public-opinion polls, which now swung sharply upward in Carter's favor. The White House also reevaluated its policies toward the Soviet Union and initiated what appeared by early 1980 to be major shifts away from detente and the principal directions of United States foreign policy. Carter withdrew the SALT II treaty, which was already in some trouble in the Senate, imposed an embargo on shipments of American grain and advanced technology to the Russians, and called for a postponement or boycott of the summer Olympic games, scheduled for 1980 in Moscow. In his state-of-the-union address in January 1980, Carter proposed a reimposition of selective-service registration, increased military spending, and greater flexibility for United States intelligence agencies, and declared that the Persian Gulf region was critical to the national security of the United States. This Carter Doctrine was offered as a warning to the Russians that any further aggression in this region could well result in war.

The decade thus ended on a somber note, with continuing inflation at home, the instability of the dollar in international money markets, skyrocketing prices of gold and silver, and the prospect of an end to detente and the renewal of cold-war tensions between East and West. Social and economic conditions at home were especially troubling, as the nation seemed poised on the brink of yet another recession and productivity was falling.

Of all the domestic problems, inflation seemed the most difficult. No one knew how to deal with it. President Nixon's imposition of wage and price controls in 1971 had been singularly unsuccessful, serving not to stop long-term inflation but merely to restrain it artificially for a short period. By the end of the decade, the problem was even more severe. An inflation rate of about 5 percent in 1977 jumped to 13.3 percent in 1979, driven by rising oil prices. As the Carter Administration shifted its attention from unemployment (which had dropped in the same period from 8 to just under 6 percent) to inflation, the President repeated his firm opposition to wage and price controls in any form, as being fundamentally unworkable and a cure that was in some ways worse than the disease. He counted, instead, on reduced federal spending, opposition to a tax cut, and high interest rates to cool down the economy. It was unclear whether these measures would work. The prime interest rate was the highest it had been in American history by the end of 1979, yet the prices of gold and silver shot upward. Gold, which had cost about $100 an ounce in 1973 rose over $600 and then $700 an ounce in late 1979 in a series of quick, sharp fluctuations reflecting investor uncertainties about the future. The average citizen suffered from inflation in more substantial ways: Americans spent on the average 36 percent of their disposable income on housing in 1979, which was almost twice what they had had to spend ten years earlier. The average single-family home that sold for $37,800 in 1974 was priced at $69,000 in 1979, an increase of more than 82 percent in just five years.

Social problems associated with race and the dilemmas of American cities persisted. Though the campaign against racial segregation continued throughout the seventies, and affirmative-action legislation mandated the active redress of past discrimination against blacks and other minorities, the civil-rights movement had lost direction and purpose. The Student Non-Violent Coordinating Committee (SNCC) was gone, and the Southern Christian Leadership Conference was afflicted by squabbling among Martin Luther King, Jr.'s family and supporters. The National Association for the Advancement of Colored People and the Urban League reasserted themselves and to some degree regained their dominant position among civil-rights organizations. Legally, the rights of blacks were more secure than ever, but black progress toward political, social, and economic equality was uncertain. The number of black elected officials increased dramatically after passage of the Voting Rights Act in 1965, and more than doubled in the seventies. Atlanta, Birmingham, Detroit, Los Angeles, Newark, and a number of other cities had black mayors as the decade ended. The access of minorities to educational and other opportunities definitely improved during the decade, and black incomes rose. But the seventies did not provide much relative economic improvement for blacks. The number of black families classified as poor remained roughly the same in 1979 as in 1969, and the gap between per capita income between whites and blacks did not narrow substantially.

The percentage of minorities and women in the work force increased during the seventies, and the number of families with two breadwinners rose significantly, in part because this was one way in which families could maintain their standard of living in the face of rampant inflation. In 1979, less than 16 percent of all American families fit the "typical" American model of a male breadwinner with a wife and kids at home.

American cities were still fragmented. Three-quarters of all black families lived in metropolitan areas in 1980, and more than half of all blacks lived in the inner cities. Of these, more than half could be found in the most dilapidated and impoverished neighborhoods. The unemployment rate among black teenagers in the inner cities, approaching 60 percent in some urban areas, suggested the emergence of a permanently unemployed or underemployed "underclass" of citizens unable to survive in the legitimate American economy and forced to rely on illegal enterprises for their livelihood. At the same time, government at all levels preached a doctrine of lowered expectations and the need for efficiency and economy, on the premise that even the United States could not afford the massive social programs of the sixties and the costs entailed in "saving" the worst inner-city neighborhoods and their populations. New York City flirted with bankruptcy through much of the decade, and tax-slicing amendments and referendums cropped up throughout the country.

As the United States entered the 1980's, energy and the economy were expected to head the list of challenges in the future, with preservation of the environment not far behind. There was concern, too, about the state of the world and the prospect of nuclear holocaust, though everyone forty or younger in 1980 had been reared in the shadow of the bomb. At the threshold of the eighties the urban nation, with its mass-consumption society, was remarkable in its technology and in many respects more prosperous and promising than ever. But the expectations of its citizens, their confidence in their institutions and their faith in the future, were perhaps more guarded and tenuous than at any time since the Great Depression. Most Americans looked forward reluctantly to 1984 and beyond.

Bibliographical Essay

T HIS bibliographical essay does not pretend to be comprehensive or complete. While few historians have attempted an interpretation of the years from 1920 to the present, except for textbook writers, scores of works have appeared which examine many aspects of the period, especially the culture of the twenties, the politics and economic policies of the thirties, the shaping of the postwar world during the Truman Administrations, and the social and political changes—and overseas involvements— of the sixties. Our understanding of the past naturally becomes less definitive as we approach the present. The historian of very recent times must often depend on a host of magazine, journal, and newspaper articles, and on polemics and exhortative works, many of which are highly biased and most of which are incomplete. Because of the uncertain quality of many of the sources—especially those covering the years since 1950—and because of space limitations, this bibliography, confined entirely to books, is highly selective and tilted toward the particular subjects emphasized in the volume.

1 RISE OF THE URBAN MASS MIND

Although Henry May, *The End of American Innocence* (1959), covers only the period from 1912 to 1917, it is very important to an understanding of some of the mass social movements of the twenties. Robert and Helen Lynd, *Middletown* (1929), a comprehensive sociological study of Muncie, Indiana, is also a prime historical source, as is the President's Research Committee on Social Trends, *Recent Social Trends in the United States* (1933). Although W. E. Leuchtenberg's *The Perils of Prosperity* (1958) is a general account of the decade, the chapters on morals and on the second industrial revolution are especially helpful. For two different views of the twenties by the same author, see P. A. Carter, *The Twenties in America* (1968) and *Another Part of the Twenties* (1977). Christopher Lasch, *The New Radicalism in America* (1965), provides insights into some of the major figures of the time.

Mass Culture. Although directed toward post-World War II society, Max Lerner's *America as a Civilization* (1957) contains much relevant information on the rise of mass society in the twenties. Equally oriented toward the present but as informative on the twenties is Philip Olson, ed., *America as a Mass Society* (1963). A must for all students of recent social movements is Dwight Macdonald's "Masscult and Midcult," which constitutes the first chapter of *Against the American Grain* (1962), a book largely devoted to social analysis by way of literary criticism. The role of technology in forging the consumer culture is emphasized in J. L. Meikle, *Twentieth Century Limited: Industrial Design in America, 1925–1939* (1979). G. E. Mowry, ed., *The Twenties* (1963), contains a selection of sources relevant to the mass social phenomena of the decade.

The City. The most comprehensive survey of cities in American history is D. R. Goldfield and B. A. Brownell, *Urban America: From Downtown to No Town* (1979). Other useful surveys, with an emphasis on the late nineteenth and twentieth centuries, include H. P. Chudacoff, *The Evolution of American Urban Society* (1975); C. N. Glaab and A. T. Brown, *A History of Urban America* (rev. ed., 1976); and Zane Miller, *The Urbanization of Modern America* (1973). Also see Blake McKelvey, *The Emergence of Metropolitan America, 1915–1966* (1968), an earlier but still interesting work. S. B. Warner, Jr., *The Urban Wilderness* (1972), is especially eloquent on the social and economic problems of twentieth-century American cities. Some of the basic outlines of suburban development were recognized in H. P. Douglass, *The Suburban Trend* (1925), but the best brief survey, especially on earlier suburban patterns, is K. T. Jackson, "The Crabgrass Frontier: 150 Years of Suburban Growth in America" in R. A. Mohl and J. F. Richardson, eds., *The Urban Experience* (1973).

Economic Institutions. The best introduction to the role of American business is T. C. Cochran, *American Business in the Twentieth Century* (1972), though George Soule, *Prosperity Decade* (1947), remains an important economic history of the twenties. For a blistering contemporary evaluation of the social impact of the new business, see J. T. Adams, *Our Business Civilization* (1929). J. W. Prothro, *The Dollar Decade: Business Ideals in the 1920's* (1954), illuminates the newer thinking of corporate management; and James Weinstein's *The Corporate Ideal in the Liberal State, 1900–1918* (1968) provides some essential background to understanding the role of capitalist institutions in shaping the thought and policy of the twenties and later decades. Along this line, see D. F. Noble, *America by Design: Science, Technol-*

ogy, and the Rise of Corporate Capitalism (1977). Although focusing on ongoing policy, the U.S. National Resources Committee, *Technological Trends and National Policy* (1937), is a basic source for the first postwar decade. For perceptive discussions of the growing scale of American business, see Robert Sobel, *The Age of the Giant Corporations* (1972), and Mira Wilkins, *The Maturing of Multinational Enterprise: American Business Abroad from 1914 to 1970* (1974). Otis Pease, *The Responsibilities of American Advertising* (1958), was the first intelligent excursion into an institution that still needs much more investigation. A more recent study, though hardly the last word on the subject, is Stuart Ewen, *Captains of Consciousness: Advertising and the Social Roots of the Consumer Culture* (1976).

Mass Transportation and Communication. Fortunately, historians have recently shown considerable interest in the impact of the automobile. The best overall survey is J. J. Flink, *The Car Culture* (1975), but J. B. Rae, *The American Automobile* (1965) and *The Road and the Car in American Life* (1971), are also solid works. Allan Nevins and F. E. Hill, *Ford: Expansion and Challenge, 1915–1933* (1957), is the second volume of an impressive three-volume work; and R. M. Wik's *Henry Ford and Grass-roots America* (1972) is a perceptive look at the rural impact of the Model T. C. G. Dettelbach, *In the Driver's Seat* (1976), examines the automobile in literature and popular culture. H. L. Preston's *Automobile Age Atlanta* (1979) is the first detailed investigation of the motor vehicle's impact on a single city. Ithiel de Sola Pool, ed., *The Social Impact of the Telephone* (1977), is uneven but quite interesting. Gilbert Seldes, *The Great Audience* (1950) and *The Public Arts* (1956), are still credible general works on the influence of the mass media on culture. For the particular institutions, see the standard works: on the tabloids, F. L. Mott, *American Journalism* (1950); on the movies, Lewis Jacobs, *The Rise of the American Film* (1939), and Robert Sklar, *Movie-Made America* (1975); and on broadcasting, Erik Barnouw, *A Tour in Babel* (1966), covering the years to 1933, and *The Golden Web* (1968), on the period 1933–1958.

Social Questions. Freda Kirchwey, ed., *Our Changing Morality* (1924), is a collection of pertinent essays by contemporaries. John Higham, *Strangers in the Land* (1955), is excellent on the subject of nativism. On the Ku Klux Klan, K. T. Jackson, *The Ku Klux Klan in the City 1915–1930* (1967), is the best available work. See also A. S. Rice, *The Ku Klux Klan in American Politics* (1962). On the more important developments in Protestantism as they affected social issues, see D. B. Meyer, *The Protestant Search for Political Realism*

(1960), and R. M. Miller, *American Protestantism and Social Issues, 1919–1939* (1958). Andrew Sinclair, *Prohibition, the Era of Excess* (1962), is scholarly and interesting.

2 THE POLITICS OF NOSTALGIA

The most comprehensive treatment of the politics of the twenties is J. D. Hicks, *Republican Ascendency, 1921–1933* (1960). Other skillful interpretations are A. M. Schlesinger, Jr., *The Age of Roosevelt: The Crisis of the Old Order: 1919–1933* (1957), and the works by W. Leuchtenberg and P. A. Carter already cited. Generally, Schlesinger depicts the decade's mistakes as a background for New Deal heroics, whereas Leuchtenberg and Carter are more impartial. One of the few good state studies is J. J. Huthmacher, *Massachusetts People and Politics, 1919–1933* (1959).

Harding, Coolidge, and Hoover. For the election of 1920 and its background, W. M. Bagby, *The Road to Normalcy* (1962), and R. K. Murray, *Red Scare* (1955), are quite good. On Harding, R. K. Murray, *The Harding Era* (1969), and Francis Russell, *The Shadow of Blooming Grove: Warren G. Harding in His Times* (1968), are recommended. Randolph Downes, *The Rise of Warren Gamaliel Harding* (1970), is an effort to correct some of the less favorable assessments of this particular President. W. A. White, *A Puritan in Babylon* (1938), is a brilliant and devastating interpretive study of Calvin Coolidge; C. M. Fuess, *Calvin Coolidge* (1940), is more comprehensive and sober.

E. A. Moore, *A Catholic Runs for President* (1956), should be supplemented with Oscar Handlin, *Al Smith and His America* (1958). A very good local study which casts light on the 1928 campaign is J. M. Allswang, *A House for All Peoples: Ethnic Politics in Chicago 1890–1936* (1971). Herbert Hoover has not fared well with either journalists or historians. H. G. Warren, *Herbert Hoover and the Great Depression* (1959), was an early attempt at fairness to the harassed President, and two later studies carried the effort further: David Bruner, *Herbert Hoover: The Public Life* (1979), which is perhaps the best one-volume biography available; and Joan Wilson, *Herbert Hoover: Forgotten Progressive* (1975). To maintain the luster of his own career, Hoover probably should not have written his often splenetic *Memoirs,* in particular *The Great Depression* (vol. 2, 1952). It is interesting to compare the political philosophy expressed in the *Memoirs,* in his *American Individualism* (1922), and in *The New Day* (1928) campaign speeches.

Farm and Labor Politics. Theodore Saloutos and J. D. Hicks, *Agricultural Discontent in the Middle West, 1900–1939* (1951), remains the most complete survey of the relationship between the farmer and politics; J. H. Shideler, *Farm Crisis, 1919–1923* (1957), the most exclusively devoted to the immediate postwar years. G. C. Fite, *George N. Peek and the Fight for Farm Parity* (1954), is good for the McNary-Haugen and export debenture schemes. On labor, see Irving Bernstein, *The Lean Years* (1960).

Social and Cultural Patterns. In addition to the volumes already mentioned, see Nathan Huggins, *The Harlem Renaissance* (1971), for a useful examination of this important cultural phenomenon; and W. M. Tuttle, Jr., *Race Riot: Chicago in the Red Summer of 1919* (1970), for essential background information on urban violence and the racial problems of the postwar years.

Liberals and Conservatives. Other aspects of the political struggles of the decade are examined in C. A. Chambers, *Seedtime of Reform* (1963), and in biographies of some of the leading liberal and conservative figures. Among the former are Howard Zinn, *La Guardia in Congress* (1959); Arthur Mann, *La Guardia: A Fighter against His Times 1882–1933* (1959) and *La Guardia Comes to Power 1933* (1965); and Richard Lowitt, *George W. Norris: The Persistence of a Progressive, 1913–1933* (1971). Among the better works on conservative figures are W. T. Hutchinson, *Lowden of Illinois* (2 vols., 1957), and Morton Keller, *In Defense of Yesterday: James Beck and the Politics of Conservatism* (1958).

Diplomacy. An unusually good collection of biographies of the Secretaries of State provides much useful information. M. J. Pusey, *Charles Evans Hughes* (2 vols., 1951), is an admiring work that may be balanced with the shorter but more critical Dexter Perkins, *Charles Evans Hughes and American Diplomatic Statesmanship* (1956). L. E. Ellis, *Frank B. Kellogg and American Foreign Relations, 1925–1929* (1961), does ample justice to his subject. Also see R. H. Ferrell, *Frank B. Kellogg and Henry L. Stimson* (1963), and the sympathetic study of Stimson by Elting Morison, *Turmoil and Tradition* (1960). On some of the specific diplomatic problems of the decade, see Merze Tate, *The United States and Armaments* (1948); Selig Adler, *The Isolationist Impulse* (1957); A. W. Griswold, *The Far Eastern Policy of the United States* (1938); J. K. Fairbank, *The United States and China* (1956); and Bryce Wood, *The Making of the Good Neighbor Policy* (1961).

3 THE END OF NORMALCY

The Hoover Administration. In addition to studies of Mr. Hoover and his policies, listed earlier, Albert Romasco, *The Poverty of Abundance: Hoover, the Nation, the Depression* (1965), should be consulted. Generally friendly to the Administration are W. S. Myers and W. H. Newton, *The Hoover Administration* (1936), and E. E. Robinson and P. C. Edwards, eds., *The Memoirs of Ray Lyman Wilbur, 1875–1949* (1960). Far more critical are R. G. Tugwell, *Mr. Hoover's Economic Policy* (1932), and G. V. Seldes, *The Years of the Locust* (1933).

Stock Crash and Depression. Broadus Mitchell, *Depression Decade* (1947), is a broad survey of the Depression years, with a heavy economic emphasis. F. L. Allen, *Since Yesterday* (1940), and Dixon Wecter, *The Age of the Great Depression* (1948), are more socially oriented. The best single account of the stock-market crash is the perceptive and witty work by J. K. Galbraith, *The Great Crash* (1955). Raymond Wolters, *Negroes and the Great Depression* (1970), and Donald Worster, *Dust Bowl: The Southern Plains in the 1930s* (1979), contain information on how particular groups and regions coped with economic disaster. A thought-provoking study of the impact of economic crisis on broader cultural and ideological currents is R. H. Pells, *Radical Visions and American Dreams: Culture and Social Thought in the Depression Years* (1973).

Roosevelt and the Election of 1932. The most complete picture of Franklin D. Roosevelt is to be found in the two multivolume works of A. M. Schlesinger, Jr., and Frank Freidel. Schlesinger's *The Crisis of the Old Order* contains a brilliant partisan account of Roosevelt and his activities through the Presidential election of 1932. The second and third volumes by Freidel, *The Ordeal* (1954) and *The Triumph* (1956), are more impartial and give an excellent picture of the Democratic Party during the twenties, as well as a splendid account of the 1932 election. J. M. Burns, *Roosevelt: The Lion and the Fox* (1956), is another well-written, full-length scholarly portrait; shorter studies are Richard Hofstadter, *The Age of Reform* (1955) and *The American Political Tradition and the Men Who Made It* (1948). The first volume of J. P. Lash's superb biography of Eleanor Roosevelt, *Eleanor and Franklin* (1971), treats the relationship between these two remarkable people, while the second volume, *Eleanor: The Years Alone* (1972), covers the years after F.D.R.'s death.

Among the innumerable portraits of the President by his close political friends, perhaps the best are R. G. Tugwell, *The Democratic Roosevelt* (1937); R. E. Sherwood, *Roosevelt and Hopkins* (1948); Frances Perkins, *The Roosevelt I Knew* (1946); and John Gunther, *Roosevelt in Retrospect* (1950). For anti-Roosevelt material, more or less on the personal side, see T. J. Flynn, *The Roosevelt Myth* (1948), which went through twelve printings, and E. E. Robinson, *The Roosevelt Leadership, 1933–1945* (1955).

4 THE NEW DEAL

Society and Political Thought in the Thirties. For the more important social changes during the thirties, see Dixon Wecter, *The Age of the Great Depression;* R. H. Pells, *Radical Visions and American Dreams;* and especially Robert and Helen Lynd, *Middletown in Transition* (1937). One of the first serious efforts to assess the importance of the nation's cities was prepared during the thirties and remains a basic source: the Urbanism Committee to the National Resources Committee, *Our Cities: Their Role in the National Economy* (1937). For varying ideological bases of the New Deal, as expressed at the time by some of the more philosophical New Dealers, see R. G. Tugwell, *The Battle for Democracy* (1935); Henry Wallace, *New Frontiers* (1934); and Thurman Arnold, *The Folklore of Capitalism* (1937). The first volume contains the speculations of a left-leaning intellectual; the second, of an agriculturally minded mystic and humanist; and the third, of a pragmatic, reforming legal scholar devoted to maintaining the competitive system.

Political Surveys. The best one-volume survey covering both the domestic and the foreign politics of the period is still the sparkling W. E. Leuchtenberg, *Franklin D. Roosevelt and the New Deal, 1932–1940* (1963). Both Schlesinger, *The Politics of Upheaval,* dealing with internal affairs to 1936, and the latest two volumes in Freidel's biography of Roosevelt, *The Triumph* and *Launching the New Deal* (1973), should be consulted. Among the hundreds of other books on New Deal politics, two of the best are Dexter Perkins, *The New Age of Franklin Roosevelt* (1957), and O. L. Graham, Jr., *An Encore for Reform: The Old Progressives and the New Deal* (1967). Carl Degler, *Out of Our Past* (1959), and Mario Einaudi, *The Roosevelt Revolution* (1959), are of interest because of their viewpoints; and D. R. Fusfeld, *The Economic Thought of Franklin D. Roosevelt and the Origins of the New Deal* (1956), and Thomas Greer, *What Roosevelt Thought* (1958), because of their special approaches. On the relationship between the New Deal and urban politics, B. M. Stave, *The New Deal and the Last Hurrah: Pittsburgh Machine Politics* (1970), and L. W. Dorsett, *Franklin D. Roosevelt and the City Bosses* (1977), are recommended. One of the best local studies is C. H. Trout, *Boston, the Great Depression, and the New Deal* (1977). Among the general histories of the era, R. S. Kirkendall, *The United States, 1929–1945* (1974), is especially good.

The New Dealers. Interesting group pictures of the principal New Dealers are presented in Joseph Alsop and Robert Kintner, *Men around the President* (1939), and in the Unofficial Observer, *The New Dealers* (1934). New Deal activities and accomplishments in the states are covered in Robert Burke, *Olson's New Deal for California* (1953), and Allan Nevins, *Herbert H. Lehman and His Era* (1963), for New York. On congressional supporters of New Deal policies, see J. J. Huthmacher, *Senator Robert F. Wagner and the Rise of Urban Liberalism* (1968). R. A. Lawson, *The Failure of Independent Liberalism, 1930–1941* (1971), examines a group of thinkers—including John Dewey, Thorstein Veblen, and Lewis Mumford—who leaned to the left of the New Deal.

The Court Fight and the Second Administration. J. Alsop and T. Catledge, *The 168 Days* (1938), is a colorful contemporary account of this heated controversy. D. Pearson and R. S. Allen, *The Nine Old Men* (1936), and Merlo Pusey, *The Supreme Court Crisis* (1937), are others of the same vintage. For a more recent treatment of the subject, see Leonard Baker, *Back to Back: The Duel between FDR and the Supreme Court* (1967).

The Opposition. Solid studies have recently been completed of the major opponents of the New Deal. See, especially, J. T. Patterson, *Congressional Conservatism and the New Deal: The Growth of the Conservative Coalition in Congress, 1933–1939* (1967), as well as works by New Deal opponents themselves, such as Herbert Hoover, *The Challenge to Liberty* (1934) and *Addresses upon the American Road, 1933–1938* (1938). George Wolfskill has written several volumes on the subject, including *The Revolt of the Conservatives* (1962), *A History of the American Liberty League, 1934–1940* (1962), and, with J. A. Hudson, *All but the People: Franklin D. Roosevelt and His Critics* (1969). The definitive biography of Louisiana's Kingfish is T. Harry Williams, *Huey Long* (1969), but Allan Sindler, *Huey Long's Louisiana* (1956), is still useful. C. J. Tull, *Father Coughlin and the New Deal* (1965), and Sheldon Marcus, *Father Coughlin* (1973), are concerned with the Michigan priest; and Leo Lowenthal and Norbert Guterman, *Prophets of Deceit* (1949), covers the rising Fascist activity in the country. Abraham Holtzman, *The Townsend Movement* (1963), gives the essential facts. The activities of the socialists are dealt with in David Shannon, *The Socialist Party of America* (1953).

Relief, Recovery, and Reform. Various strains of New Deal economic thought are to be found in Seymour Harris, ed., *The New Economics* (1947);

Alvin Hansen, *Full Recovery or Stagnation* (1938); and A. Burns and D. Watson, *Government Spending and Economic Expansion* (1940). Directed at the problem of recovery from depression are the Brookings Institution's *The Recovery Problem in the United States* (1936) and Theodore Rosenof's *Dogma, Depression, and the New Deal* (1975).

Unemployment and Relief. E. W. Bakke, *Citizens without Work* (1940); Donald Howard, *The WPA and Federal Relief Policy* (1943); Grace Adams, *Workers on Relief* (1939); and J. C. Brown, *Public Relief, 1929–1939* (1940), are the best contemporary works on unemployment and relief policies. The Social Security Act and its subsequent administration may be followed in Paul Douglas, *Social Security in the United States* (1936); E. E. Witte, *Development of the Social Security Act* (1962); and Charles McKinley and R. W. Frase, *Launching Social Security* (1970). A good local study of the effects of unemployment and the New Deal response is Barbara Blumberg, *The New Deal and the Unemployed: The View from New York City* (1979). The New Deal's experiments with building entirely new agricultural communities are covered in Paul Conkin, *Tomorrow a New World* (1959). J. L. Arnold, *The New Deal in the Suburbs: A History of the Greenbelt Town Program, 1935–1954* (1971), is the best book on the subject.

Labor. Irving Bernstein, *The New Deal Collective Bargaining Policy* (1950), and M. Derber and E. Young, eds., *Labor and the New Deal* (1957), contain perceptive interpretive studies of a complicated subject. Walter Galenson, *The CIO Challenge to the A.F.of L.* (1960), is best on labor's intramural struggle.

Agriculture, Conservation, TVA. Gilbert Fite, *George N. Peek and the Fight for Farm Parity* (1954), and Edwin Nourse et al., *Three Years of the Agricultural Adjustment Act* (1937), cover the early period of agricultural reform; Dean Albertson, *Roosevelt's Farmer* (1961), covers the later New Deal and war years. David Lilienthal, *TVA: Democracy on the March* (1944), is the classic, written by the man who contributed most to the giant project, but may be supplemented by T. K. McCraw, *TVA and the Power Fight, 1933–1939* (1971).

NRA and Other Business Policies. See R. F. Himmelberg, *The Origins of the National Recovery Administration: Business, Government, and the Trade Association Issue, 1921–1933* (1976), for the background and beginnings of the agency; and Sidney Fine, *The Automobile under the Blue Eagle* (1964), for a good detailed study of a particular industry. Hugh Johnson, *The Blue Eagle from Egg to Earth* (1935), and Donald Richberg, *The Rainbow* (1936), are the works of two chief administrators of the agency. A. Bernheim and M. G. Schneider, eds., *The Security Markets* (1935); R. M. Fisher, *20 Years of Public Housing* (1959); and C. L. Harriss, *History and Policies of the Home Owner's Loan Corporation* (1951), are all valuable on particular New Deal agencies. The best single volume dealing with the policies and impact of the New Deal on urban America is Mark Gelfand, *A Nation of Cities: The Federal Government and Urban America, 1933–1965* (1975).

5 THE TOTALITARIAN CHALLENGE

The best surveys of the complicated American foreign policy of the decade are R. H. Farrell, *American Diplomacy in the Great Depression* (1957), and Robert Dallek, *Franklin D. Roosevelt and American Foreign Policy, 1932–1945* (1979). See also the impressive W. Langer and S. E. Gleason, *The Challenge to Isolation, 1937–1940* (1952), and *The Undeclared War, 1940–1941* (1953), for the later years. Two volumes highly critical of American foreign policy are C. Tansill, *Back Door to War* (1952), and C. A. Beard, *American Foreign Policy in the Making* (1946).

The Far East. Excellent background is available in Griswold, *The Far Eastern Policy of the United States.* Directed at Depression diplomacy are Armin Rappaport, *Henry L. Stimson and Japan, 1931–33* (1963), and T. A. Bisson, *American Foreign Policy in the Far East, 1931–1944* (1944). For the crises preceding World War II, see Herbert Feis, *The Road to Pearl Harbor* (1950); F. C. Jones, *Japan's New Order in East Asia* (1954); and Paul Schroeder, *The Axis Alliance and Japanese-American Relations, 1941* (1958).

The Hoover Administration. William Meyers, *The Foreign Policies of Herbert Hoover* (1940), is a friendly general survey. For Manchurian and Chinese affairs, see S. R. Smith, *The Far Eastern Crisis* (1936), and R. Langer, *Seizure of Territory* (1947). Other important works are two biographies of Henry Stimson—Elting Morison, *Turmoil and Tradition* (1960), and Richard Current, *Secretary Stimson* (1954)—and the Secretary's own work, in collaboration with McGeorge Bundy, *On Active Service in Peace and War* (1948).

Isolation and Neutrality. The ten-year struggle between the isolationists and the interventionists is treated in Manfred Jonas, *Isolationism in America, 1935–1941* (1966); Selig Adler, *The Isolationist Impulse* (1957); Wayne Cole,

America First (1953); Walter Johnson, *The Battle against Isolation* (1944); and Dorothy Detzer, *Appointment on the Hill* (1948). On the lend-lease program, see W. F. Kimball, *The Most Unsordid Act: Lend-Lease, 1939–1941* (1969).

1940 Campaign and Pearl Harbor. M. E. Dillon, *Wendell Willkie* (1952), covers the early career of this Presidential contender. Joseph Barnes, *Willkie* (1952), and D. B. Johnson, *The Republican Party and Wendell Willkie* (1960), are more detailed on the election of 1940. The official explanation of events leading to Pearl Harbor is given in *Peace and War: United States Foreign Policy, 1931–1941.* A friendly but scholarly gloss on the official statements is H. Feis, *The Road to Pearl Harbor.* Two highly critical revisionist works are C. A. Beard, *President Roosevelt and the Coming of the War, 1941* (1948), and R. A. Theobald, *The Final Secret of Pearl Harbor* (1954).

6 THE DIVIDED WORLD

War Diplomacy. The best survey is Gaddis Smith, *American Diplomacy during the Second World War, 1941–1945* (1967). Also important are Herbert Feis, *Churchill—Roosevelt—Stalin* (1957); W. H. McNeill, *America, Britain, and Russia* (1953); R. Beitzell, *The Uneasy Alliance: America, Britain, and Russia, 1941–1943* (1972); and two books by R. A. Divine, *Roosevelt and World War II* (1969) and *Second Chance: The Triumph of Internationalism during World War II* (1967). As the most important conference in determining postwar relations, Yalta has drawn considerable scholarly attention, including J. L. Snell, ed., *The Meaning of Yalta* (1956), and R. F. Fenno, Jr., ed., *The Yalta Conference* (1955). Also see W. L. Neumann, *After Victory: Churchill, Roosevelt, Stalin and the Making of the Peace* (1969).

The Cold War. The origins of the cold war have been among the most controversial subjects in American history in recent years. General summaries of cold-war diplomacy include N. A. Graebner, *Cold War Diplomacy, 1945–1960* (1962), and J. W. Spanier, *American Foreign Policy since World War II* (1960). More recent revisionist studies, which find the United States as at least equally responsible as Russia for the rise of worldwide big-power confrontation, include Gabriel Kolko, *The Politics of War* (1968), covering the years 1943–1945; Joyce and Gabriel Kolko, *The Limits of Power* (1972), covering the years 1945–1954; Walter LaFeber, *America, Russia, and the Cold War, 1945–1966* (1967); and Lloyd Gardner, *Architects of Illusion: Men and Ideas in American Foreign Policy, 1941–1949* (1970). A leading critique of the revisionist argument is R. J. Maddox, *The New Left and the Origins of the Cold*

War (1973). More balanced accounts are J. L. Gaddis, *The United States and the Origins of the Cold War, 1941–1947* (1972) and *Russia, the Soviet Union, and the United States* (1978); T. G. Patterson, *Soviet-American Confrontation: Postwar Reconstruction and the Origins of the Cold War* (1973) and *On Every Front: The Making of the Cold War* (1979); and Daniel Yergin, *Shattered Peace: The Origins of the Cold War and the National Security State* (1977).

On foreign policy during the Truman Administrations, the former President's *Memoirs* (2 vols., 1955–56) are invaluable. For a highly critical look at Truman's policies, see D. F. Fleming, *The Cold War and Its Origins, 1917–1960* (2 vols., 1961); R. M. Freeland, *The Truman Doctrine and the Origins of McCarthyism* (1972); and Athan Theoharis, *Seeds of Repression: Harry S. Truman and the Origins of McCarthyism* (1971). On more specialized topics, see Akira Iriye, *The Cold War in Asia* (1974); M. S. Sherry, *Preparing for the Next War: America Plans for Postwar Defense, 1941–48* (1977); and M. B. Stoff, *Oil, War, and American Security: The Search for a National Policy on Foreign Oil, 1941–1947* (1980).

Asia. On United States influence in and relations with China, see M. Schaller, *The U.S. Crusade in China, 1938–1945* (1979); Barbara Tuchman, *Stilwell and the American Experience in China, 1911–45* (1971); and W. I. Cohen, *America's Response to China* (1971). Among older studies, M. Zinkin, *Asia and the West* (1953), and H. M. Vinacke, *The United States and the Far East, 1945–1951* (1952), are good general accounts. Herbert Feis, *The China Tangle* (1953), and A. J. Kubeck, *How the Far East Was Lost* (1963), reflect main currents of contemporary opinion. E. M. Martin, *The Allied Occupation of Japan* (1948), should be consulted on the beginnings of a significant postwar alliance. On the role of Asia in postwar relations among the big powers, see Yonosuke Nagai and Akira Iriye, eds., *The Origins of the Cold War in Asia* (1977).

The Korean War. McGeorge Bundy, ed., *The Pattern of Responsibility* (1952), is a friendly account of American policies leading to, and during, the war. For MacArthur's version of his dismissal, see his *Reminiscences* (1964). The Administration's case is given in R. Rovere and A. M. Schlesinger, Jr., *The General and the President* (1951). J. W. Spanier, *The Truman-MacArthur Controversy* (1959), is a scholarly account.

Eisenhower. For a general view of both foreign and domestic policy during the first Administration, Dwight D. Eisenhower's *Mandate for Change* (1963) is very important. This may be supplemented by—among other accounts—R. E. Rovere, *Affairs of State* (1956); H. S. Parmet, *Eisenhower and the American Crusades* (1972); D. B. Capitanchik, *The Eisenhower Presidency and American Foreign Policy* (1969); and Douglas Kinnard, *President Eisenhower and Strategy Management* (1977). Studies of other major figures of the same period include M. A. Guhlin, *John Foster Dulles* (1972), and J. T. Patterson, *Mr. Republican: A Biography of Robert A. Taft* (1972).

7 PROSPERITY AND PESSIMISM

War Society. The social changes made by the war are discussed in Richard Polenberg, *War and Society: The United States, 1941–1945* (1972); J. M. Blum, *V Was for Victory: Politics and American Culture during World War II* (1976); W. F. Ogburn, *American Society in Wartime* (1947); and in the relevant chapters of A. R. Buchanan, *The United States and World War II* (2 vols., 1964), which is mainly devoted to military events.

Economic Institutions. For postwar developments in economic institutions, among the best studies are J. K. Galbraith, *American Capitalism* (1952) and *The New Industrial State* (1967).

On businessmen and the business system, see T. C. Cochran, *The American Business System* (1957); F. X. Sutton, *The American Business Creed* (1956); James Burnham, *The Managerial Revolution* (1941); and C. W. Mills, *The Power Elite* (1965), the last a radical critique of postwar American society and economy.

The move to suburbia and the results for the people involved as well as for the city are covered in K. T. Jackson, "The Crabgrass Frontier: 150 Years of Suburban Growth in America," in R. A. Mohl and J. F. Richardson, eds., *The Urban Experience: Themes in American History* (1973); and in L. H. Masotti and J. K. Hadden, eds., *The Urbanization of the Suburbs* (1973), and Herbert Gans, *The Levittowners* (1967).

Other valuable works on the growing problems of the modern city are K. B. Clark, *Dark Ghetto: Dilemmas of Social Power* (1965); Lee Rainwater, *Behind Ghetto Walls: Black Families in a Federal Slum* (1970); K. E. Tauber and A. F. Tauber, *Negroes in American Cities: Residential Segregation and Neighborhood Change* (1969); Scott Greer, *Urban Renewal and American Cities* (1965); Frances Piven and R. A. Cloward, *Regulating the Poor: The Functions of Public Welfare* (1971); Jane Jacobs, *The Death and Life of Great American Cities* (1963); Jean Gottmann, *Megalopolis: The Urbanized Northeastern Seaboard of the United States* (1961); and A. H. Hawley, *The Changing Shape of Metropolitan America: Deconcentration since 1920* (1956). A superb biography of an individual who did more than any other to shape the modern development of New York City is R. A. Caro, *The Power Broker: Robert Moses and the Fall of New York* (1974).

Mass Culture and Pessimism. For the further development of mass culture, see B. Rosenberg and D. M. White, eds., *Mass Culture* (1957), a collection of essays mostly by sociologists. For the growing pessimism in American society, see the works of Walter Lippmann and Reinhold Niebuhr, but especially *The Phantom Public* (1925), *Preface to Morals* (1929), and *The Public Philosophy* (1955), by Lippmann, and *Does Civilization Need Religion?* (1928), *The Nature and Destiny of Man* (1941), and *The Self and the Dramas of History* (1955), by Niebuhr. Christopher Lasch's *The New Radicalism in America* (1965) contains information and opinions about both men. The best biography of Lippmann is Ronald Steel, *Walter Lippmann and the American Century* (1980). On the moods of modern literature, see Malcolm Cowley, *The Literary Situation* (1954), and Edmund Wilson, *The Shock of Recognition* (1955).

8 THE POLITICS OF STATICS

The Truman Period. In addition to the works cited earlier, a number of other worthwhile studies treat the major domestic issues and incidents of the Truman Presidency, which has been the subject of increasing historical attention. The best general works on the Truman Administration are A. L. Hamby, *Beyond the New Deal: Harry S. Truman and American Liberalism* (1973); R. J. Donovan, *Conflict and Crisis: The Presidency of Harry S. Truman, 1945–1948* (1977); and B. J. Bernstein, ed., *Politics and Policies of the Truman Administration* (1970). Also interesting is Susan Hartmann, *Truman and the 80th Congress* (1971). On the issue of loyalty, the congressional investigations, and Joseph McCarthy, see A. D. Harper, *The Politics of Loyalty: The White House and the Communist Issue, 1946–1952* (1969); Robert Griffith, *The Politics of Fear* (1970); R. M. Freeland, *The Truman Doctrine and the Origins of McCarthyism;* and Athan Theoharis, *Seeds of Repression.* For a contemporary defense of McCarthy, see W. F. Buckley, Jr., and L. B. Bozell, *McCarthy and His Enemies* (1954). An excellent study of the sources and context of McCarthyism is M. P. Rogin, *The Intellectuals and McCarthy: The Radical Specter* (1967).

Elections and Politics. For the elections of 1948, see C. D. MacDougall's *Gideon's Army* (1965), the first of three projected volumes on the Progressive Party of 1948; and for background, R. A. Garson, *The Democratic Party and the Politics of Sectionalism, 1941–1948* (1974). Also interesting is H. S. Parmet, *The Democrats: The Years after F.D.R.* (1976).

The Eisenhower Administration. There are far fewer general histories of the Eisenhower Presidency than of the Truman years. C. C. Alexander, *Holding the Line: The Eisenhower Era, 1952–1961* (1975), provides basic information. Also see G. W. Reichard, *The Reaffirmation of Republicanism: Eisenhower and the Eighty-third Congress* (1975), and Capitanchik, *The Eisenhower Presidency and American Foreign Policy.* On politics in general, see S. Lubell, *The Revolt of the Moderates* (1956); Arthur Larson, *A Republican Looks at His Party* (1956); and Dean Acheson, *A Democrat Looks at His Party* (1955). On Adlai Stevenson, see K. S. Davis, *The Politics of Humor: A Biography of Adlai E. Stevenson* (1967), and J. B. Martin, *Adlai Stevenson of Illinois* (1976). For Eisenhower Administration policies on urban America, see Gelfand, *A Nation of Cities.* On the nuclear-test ban debate, see R. A. Divine, *Blowing on the Wind* (1978), which covers the years 1954–1960. For background on the emerging and extremely important civil-rights issue, see Gunnar Myrdal, *An American Dilemma* (2 vols., 1944); August Meier and Elliott Rudwick, *From Plantation to Ghetto* (3rd ed., 1976); and J. H. Franklin, *From Slavery to Freedom* (4th ed., 1974).

9 THE POLITICS OF TURMOIL AT HOME

The Kennedy Administration. The Kennedy Administration and the Kennedy family have been the subjects of numerous studies that reflect both the continued national fascination with the personalities involved and the importance of the early sixties in shaping the subsequent history of that decade and the next. Among the first and most favorable works on the Kennedy Administration are A. M. Schlesinger, Jr., *A Thousand Days* (1965), and Theodore Sorensen, *Kennedy* (1965). An excellent collection of essays, prepared shortly after the President's death, is Aida Donald, ed., *John F. Kennedy and the New Frontier* (1966). More recent works include Harris Wofford, *Of Kennedys and Kings* (1980), which focuses on both John and Robert Kennedy as well as Martin Luther King, Jr.; and H. S. Parmet, *Jack: The Struggles of John F. Kennedy* (1980), which traces JFK's life to 1960 and includes material on Joseph F. Kennedy, Sr. Also of interest is J. F. Heath, *John F. Kennedy and the Business Community* (1969). Bruce Miroff, *Pragmatic Illusions* (1976), is a harsh critique of the Kennedy Presidency by a political scientist. An excellent and highly favorable biography of Robert Kennedy is A. M. Schlesinger, Jr.'s *Robert Kennedy and His Times* (1978).

Civil Rights. C. M. Brauer, *John F. Kennedy and the Second Reconstruction* (1977), is the best single study of the Kennedy Administration and the civil-rights movement, though it should be supplemented with Schlesinger's *Robert Kennedy and His Times.* D. G. Garrow, *Protest at Selma: Martin*

Luther King, Jr., and the Voting Rights Act of 1965 (1979), is an excellent account of one of the most dramatic moments of the civil-rights struggle. Also recommended are A. Meier and E. Rudwick, eds., *Black Protest in the Sixties* (1970); J. W. Button, *Black Violence: Political Impact of the 1960s Riots* (1978); Leon Friedman, ed., *The Civil Rights Reader* (1968); M. L. King, Jr., *Why We Can't Wait* (1964); F. B. Barbour, ed., *The Black Power Revolt* (1968) and *Report of the National Advisory Commission on Civil Disorders* (1968). Two good studies of major black protest organizations of the period are A. Meier and E. Rudwick, *CORE: A Study in the Civil Rights Movement, 1942–1968* (1973), and Howard Zinn, *SNCC—The New Abolitionists* (1964). Some insight into the prevailing racial opinion of the country can be had from W. J. Brink and Louis Harris, *Black and White: A Study of U.S. Racial Attitudes Today* (1967). The best study on Southern resistance to the civil-rights movement is N. V. Bartley's *The Rise of Massive Resistance: Race and Politics in the South during the 1950's* (1969). N. R. McMillen's *The Citizens' Council: Organized Resistance to the Second Reconstruction, 1954–64* (1971) should also be consulted.

The Johnson Administration. The most interesting biographical treatments to date are Doris Kearns, *Lyndon Johnson and the American Dream* (1976), and Merle Miller, *Lyndon: An Oral Biography* (1980), both largely based on interviews and other oral sources. Johnson's memoirs, *The Vantage Point* (1971), should also be consulted. Other relevant works include R. Evans and R. Novak, *Lyndon B. Johnson: The Exercise of Power* (1966), a journalistic account of the early Johnson Administration; and E. F. Goldman, *The Tragedy of Lyndon Johnson* (1969), and H. Y. Schandler, *The Unmaking of a President: Lyndon Johnson and Vietnam* (1977), which focus on the later Johnson Presidency.

Federal Policies. J. C. Teaford, *City and Suburb: The Political Fragmentation of Metropolitan America, 1850–1970* (1979), contains excellent background material on the rising political difficulties of American metropolitan areas in the fifties, sixties, and seventies. O. L. Graham, Jr., covers the idea and reality of planning at the national level in *Toward a Planned Society: From Roosevelt to Nixon* (1976). E. J. Yanarella, *The Missile Defense Controversy* (1977), is a good survey of the subject, covering the years 1955–1972. The Johnson Administration's War on Poverty has had a vast amount of attention from policy analysts and social scientists generally. Some of the best works are S. A. Levitan, *The Great Society's Poor Law* (1969); P. Marris and M. Rein, *Dilemmas of Social Reform* (1969); J. D. Greenstone and P. E. Peterson, *Race and Authority in Urban Politics: Community Participation and the War on Poverty* (1973); and Marc and Phyllis Pilisuk, eds., *How We Lost the War on*

Poverty (1976). D. P. Moynihan's *Maximum Feasible Misunderstanding: Community Action in the War on Poverty* (1969) is an interesting, and controversial, study by a Presidential adviser who later became United States senator from New York.

10 THE POLITICS OF TURMOIL ABROAD

General treatments of foreign policy in the sixties are greatly concerned with the Vietnam War and its implications for the nation and the world. Two works that are highly critical of the main directions of American policy, both foreign and domestic, are L. S. Wittnew, *Cold War America: From Hiroshima to Watergate* (1974), and Howard Zinn, *Postwar America, 1945–1971* (1973).

The Kennedy Administration. For an overview of Kennedy's foreign policy, from one perspective, see R. J. Walton, *Cold War and Counter-Revolution: The Foreign Policy of John F. Kennedy* (1972). On the Berlin crisis, see R. M. Slusser, *The Berlin Crisis of 1961* (1973), which portrays Khrushchev and the Soviets as the aggressors; and J. M. Schick, *The Berlin Crisis, 1958–1962* (1971). On the most dramatic foreign-policy incident during the Kennedy years, see Abram Chayes, *The Cuban Missile Crisis: International Crises and the Role of Law* (1974); H. S. Dinerstein, *The Making of a Missile Crisis: October 1962* (1976); and Robert Kennedy's interesting memoir of the event, *Thirteen Days* (1969). For background on Soviet concerns and directions, see H. S. Dinerstein, *Fifty Years of Soviet Foreign Policy* (1968).

The Johnson Administration. Among the better studies on foreign-policy matters other than the Vietnam conflict are A. F. Lowenthal, *The Dominican Intervention* (1972), and H. B. Moulton, *From Superiority to Parity: The United States and the Strategic Arms Race, 1961–1971* (1973). Johnson's views are well summarized in his *The Vantage Point.*

The Vietnam Conflict. The crucial American involvement in Southeast Asia has been treated in scores of works, most of a journalistic and many of a highly partisan nature. Michael Charlton and Anthony Moncrieff, *Many Reasons Why: The American Involvement in Vietnam* (1978), provides an excellent treatment of the prevailing American views, through interviews with many of the decision-makers concerned. Also of interest is A. M. Schlesinger, Jr., *The Bitter Heritage: Vietnam and America, 1941–1968* (1968). Frances FitzGerald's *Fire in the Lake: The Vietnamese and the Americans in Vietnam*

(1972) remains the most sensitive and vital account of the impact of the Vietnam conflict on the Vietnamese and shows the fundamental flaws in American assumptions about that country and about the war in general. L. H. Gelb and Richard Betts, in *The Irony of Vietnam* (1979), attempts to show that the decision-making process in the United States operated very much as it was supposed to throughout the Vietnam crisis, though this did not prevent increasingly deeper American involvement in a protracted struggle. Guenter Lewy's *America in Vietnam* (1978) is the first full-scale scholarly effort to provide a more favorable assessment of the American role in Vietnam.

11 THE RADICAL AND LIBERTARIAN SIXTIES

The best overview of the sixties published thus far is W. L. O'Neill, *Coming Apart: An Informal History of America in the 1960s* (1971), though it should be supplemented with Morris Dickstein, *Gates of Eden: American Culture in the Sixties* (1977). Morris Janowitz, a sociologist, offers a number of penetrating and stimulating observations about developments in recent American society in *The Last Half-Century: Societal Change and Politics in America* (1978).

The Supreme Court and Social Change. Among the most important institutions to participate in the social changes of the fifties and sixties was the United States Supreme Court, especially under Chief Justice Earl Warren. Archibald Cox, *The Warren Court: Constitutional Decisions as an Instrument of Reform* (1968), covers the major judgments of the court. Charles Rembar, *The End of Obscenity* (1968), covers the crucial decisions that opened the way for vastly greater freedom of expression, especially in the fine and the popular arts.

The Counterculture and the New Left. For background on the counterculture of the sixties, see Richard Miller, *Bohemia: The Proto Culture Then and Now* (1977), and T. Parkinson, ed., *A Casebook on the Beat* (1961), which includes major selections from the writings of the beats in the fifties. On the sociology of the counterculture, especially the concerns and attitudes of the nation's disaffected youth, see two books by Kenneth Keniston, *The Uncommitted: Alienated Youth in American Society* (1960) and *Young Radicals: Notes on Committed Youth* (1968). Theodore Roszak's *The Making of a Counter Culture* (1968) reflects much of the enthusiasm and the rationale for both the counterculture and the New Left; and Herbert Marcuse's *One Dimensional Man* (1964) was among the most influential ideological sources of the movement. Tom Wolfe provides an entertaining account of the radical culture in *The Electric Kool-Aid Acid Test* (1968).

The New Left should be examined, in part, within the context of the dilemmas of the left in twentieth-century American life and politics generally, and this is illuminated in Peter Clecak, *Radical Paradoxes: Dilemmas of the American Left, 1945–1970* (1973); Christopher Lasch, *The Agony of the American Left* (1969); and Loren Baritz, ed., *The American Left* (1971). On the New Left, see Paul Jacobs and Saul Landau, *The New Radicals: A History with Documents* (1966), which includes the basic information and primary sources; Kirkpatrick Sale, *SDS* (1973); and the writings of the New Left activists themselves, particularly Abbie Hoffman, *Revolution for the Hell of It* (1970).

Black radicalism and the Black Power movement are well covered in Barbour, ed., *The Black Power Revolt,* and A. Meier and E. Rudwick, *Black Protest in the Sixties,* as well as in a number of writings by black radicals themselves, including *The Autobiography of Malcolm X* (1964), prepared with the assistance of Alex Haley; Bobby Seale, *Seize the Time: The Story of the Black Panther Party and Huey Newton* (1973); H. P. Newton, *Revolutionary Suicide* (1973); H. Rap Brown, *Die Nigger Die* (1969); Eldridge Cleaver, *Soul on Ice* (1968); Angela Davis, *An Autobiography* (1974); and George Jackson, *Soledad Brother* (1970). A very good collection of primary source material is P. S. Foner, ed., *The Black Panthers Speak* (1970).

The Women's Movement. The rise of feminism in the sixties and seventies has led to an outpouring of books that examine the role of women in American history as well as the realities of the recent years. Among the best of these books are W. L. O'Neill, *Everyone Was Brave: The Rise of Feminism in America* (1969), and two books by William Chafe, *The American Woman: Her Changing Social, Economic, and Political Roles, 1920–1970* (1972) and *Women and Equality* (1977). In *The Modernization of Sex* (1976), Paul Robinson examines the work and influence of Havelock Ellis, Alfred Kinsey, and other authorities on sex and sex roles in America. Also recommended is Peter Filene, *Him/Her/Self: Sex Roles in Modern America* (1975). On the most recent women's movement, see G. G. Yates, *What Women Want: The Ideas of the Movement* (1975), and Sara Evans, *Personal Politics: The Roots of Women's Liberation in the Civil Rights Movement and the New Left* (1979).

12 THE TROUBLED SEVENTIES

Two works that give some insight into the concerns and aspirations of the decade are Irving Howe and Michael Harrington, eds., *The Seventies:*

Problems and Proposals (1972), and Henry Owen and Charles Schultze, *Setting National Priorities: The Next Ten Years* (1976).

The Nixon Administration. The Nixon Presidency is perhaps the most controversial since World War II, though many of the works about it are superficial polemics. One should perhaps begin with Nixon's own *RN: The Memoirs of Richard Nixon* (1978). Probably the most perceptive account of Nixon yet published is William Safire, *Before the Fall* (1975). Less satisfactory is Bruce Mazlish, *In Search of Nixon: A Psychoanalytic Inquiry* (1973). R. Evans, Jr., and R. D. Novak, *Nixon in the White House: The Frustration of Power* (1971), is a journalistic account focusing on the first Administration. Theodore White, *Breach of Faith: The Fall of Richard Nixon* (1975), concentrates on the later Nixon years. On the Nixon Administration and specific social and political issues, see V. J. and V. Burke, *Nixon's Good Deed: Welfare Reform* (1974), and L. Panetta and P. Gall, *Bring Us Together: The Nixon Team and the Civil Rights Retreat* (1971). Nixon's efforts, especially in the 1972 campaign, to gather the votes of conservative Southerners is covered in Reg Murphy and Hal Gulliver, *The Southern Strategy* (1971).

Vietnam and Southeast Asia. In addition to the works cited earlier, see Tad Szulc, *The Illusion of Peace: Foreign Policy in the Nixon Years* (1978). The most effective and compelling critique of the Nixon-Kissinger policies in Southeast Asia is William Shawcross, *Sideshow: Kissinger, Nixon and the Destruction of Cambodia* (1979). Kissinger's side of the story can be found in his memoirs, *White House Years* (1979).

Watergate. The most celebrated book on the Watergate scandals, Carl Bernstein and Bob Woodward, *All the President's Men* (1974), has also been made into a motion picture. The sequel, *The Final Days* (1976), recounts the end of the Nixon Administration as a result of the Watergate revelations. For the basic facts and chronology, see Congressional Quarterly, Inc., *Watergate: Chronology of a Crisis* (1974). In addition to Nixon's memoirs and the various accounts by John Dean, H. R. Haldeman, and others involved in the scandals, see the recollections of the principal Watergate trial judge, John Sirica, *To Set the Record Straight* (1979). Athan Theoharis provides historical background for a number of Watergate-related issues, in *Spying on Americans: Political Surveillance from Hoover to Nixon* (1978).

Political Issues and Problems. Major subjects of political concern include the shifting balance of power between the Chief Executive and the Congress, the decline of the major political parties in significance and authority, and the increasing importance of special interest groups in the political process. On these various subjects, see A. M. Schlesinger, Jr., *The Imperial Presidency* (1973); C. E. Ladd, Jr., and J. D. Hadley, *Transformations of the American Party System: Political Coalitions from the New Deal to the 1970s* (1975); and James Deakin, *The Lobbyists* (1966). D. S. Broder's *Changing of the Guard: Power and Leadership in America* (1980), based almost entirely on interviews, presents a fascinating picture of the activities and concerns of a new generation of political leadership in the country. R. W. Stookey, *America and the Arab States: An Uneasy Encounter* (1975), treats a subject that grew consistently in importance and interest through the decade.

The Ford Administration. John Casserly, a former speechwriter for Gerald Ford, presents a great deal of basic information on the Ford Presidency, including the major staff members, in *The Ford White House* (1977). John Osborne, *White House Watch: The Ford Years* (1977), should also be consulted.

The Carter Administration. Jimmy Carter's campaign autobiography, *Why Not the Best?* (1977), reflects many of the themes that proved so effective in winning public support for the former Georgia governor's trek to the White House. For partial records of the Carter Administration, see Robert Shogan, *Promises to Keep: Carter's First Hundred Days* (1977), and *The Carter Presidency: The White House at Mid-Term* (1978), a selection of articles. Also see J. T. Baker, *A Southern Baptist in the White House* (1977).

Index

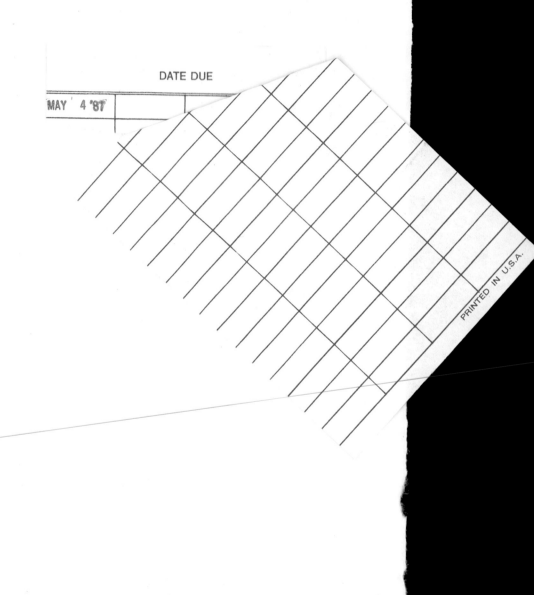

DATE DUE

MAY 4 '81

PRINTED IN U.S.A.